THE ARAB LEFTS

THE ARAB LEFTS

Histories and Legacies, 1950s–1970s

Edited by Laure Guirguis

EDINBURGH
University Press

Edinburgh University Press is one of the leading university presses in the UK. We publish academic books and journals in our selected subject areas across the humanities and social sciences, combining cutting-edge scholarship with high editorial and production values to produce academic works of lasting importance. For more information visit our website: edinburghuniversitypress.com

Edinburgh University Press Ltd
The Tun – Holyrood Road
12(2f) Jackson's Entry
Edinburgh EH8 8PJ

First published in hardback by Edinburgh University Press 2020

Typeset in 11/15 Adobe Garamond by
IDSUK (DataConnection) Ltd, and

A CIP record for this book is available from the British Library

ISBN 978 1 4744 5423 0 (hardback)
ISBN 978 1 4744 5424 7 (paperback)
ISBN 978 1 4744 5426 1 (webready PDF)
ISBN 978 1 4744 5425 4 (epub)

Published with the support of the University of Edinburgh Scholarly Publishing Initiatives Fund.

CONTENTS

CHAPTER ABSTRACTS

Chapter 1, by Orit Bashkin

My chapter traces the development of anti-Zionist thought among Iraqi Jewish communists. I begin in the second half of the 1940s, when middle-class and poor Iraqi Jews join the ranks of the illegal Iraqi Communist Party. I pay special heed to the League for Combating Zionism, which, albeit active for a brief period of time, played a seminal role in the conceptualisation of a radical Jewish-Arab identity. I then follow these Iraqi Jewish communists to Israel where, in the early 1950s, more than 80,000 Iraqi Jews rotted in Israeli transit camps, living in tents and wooden shacks. In response to these conditions, many of the former Iraqi Jewish communists joined the Israeli Communist Party, MAKI (*miflaga kumunistit israelit*; *al-hizb al-shuyu'i al-isra'ili*). During the 1950s, the members of the party, Jews, Muslims and Christians, consistently challenged the state's decisions relating to the Palestinian and migrant Jewish populations, especially the military regime under which Palestinians lived, Palestinian land confiscations, and Israel's decision to embark on war with Britain and France against Egypt in 1956. In the 1950s, MAKI won some 20 per cent of the vote in slums, poor cities and, especially, the transit camps.

I argue that looking at the neglected activities of Iraqi Jewish communists suggests a different periodisation of the region's history, in which leftist trends and commitment to leftist, communist and Arab Jewish ideas persist even after these radicals have left their Arab nation states. I likewise suggest that transregional and transnational networks are essential to understanding communist activities; we need to look regionally and, indeed, globally to understand how these radicals framed their identities.

Chapter 2, by Hana Morgenstern

After 1948, Arab and Jewish Marxists from various backgrounds met under the auspices of the Communist Party, where they co-founded its Arabic cultural and political journal, *al-Jadid*. In the aftermath of the destruction wrought by the Palestinian *nakba*, members of the group articulated the importance of a literary initiative that could address both the near-total destruction of Palestinian society and culture and the colonial repression and cultural erasure within Arab Jewish communities. This chapter examines this activity, discussing the ways in which they utilised the journal, as well as popular communist organising strategies such as intellectual clubs and festivals, to plant the seeds for the formation of a movement that aggressively opposed Zionist ideology, culture and policies. Simultaneously it strove to form a Palestinian-Jewish culture that supported the goal of democratic coexistence. The tension between these goals and the de facto segregation of Palestinians and Jews in 1950s Israel was dynamic in the journal, as was the struggle to define the precarious position of Arab Jews in relation to the Israeli mainstream, on the one hand, and the Palestinian minority on the other. Nonetheless, in the years to follow, a shared Palestinian-Jewish Arabic-language literature – which was simultaneously engaged with the reconstruction of Arabic cultural life and with shaping a Palestinian-Jewish aesthetics – was fostered by these collaborations.

Harnessing socialist realist and anti-colonial aesthetics in the service of this popular literary project, writers produced the first local corpus of oppositional, minor literature in Hebrew and Arabic, struggling to articulate the intersections between the working classes, Palestinians under military rule, refugees, Arab Jewish communities and other outliers of the Israeli state. The group's cultural and political work provided the only democratic cultural alternative to Zionist nationalism within Israel during the 1950s, formed part of the root system for the emergence of the movement for Palestinian national liberation in the 1960s, and bolstered Mizrahi (Arab Jewish) radical politics, literature and culture.

Chapter 3, by Matthieu Rey

This chapter aims to identify the main values shared by the Baathist founders, and how they affected their political practices. Lucien Febvre's concept of 'hierarchy of value' will help us to understand how these intellectuals intended to meet the main challenges of post-independence Syria. They were calling for an Arab renaissance that involved a moral revolution, based on socialism. In 1947, when legislative elections were set up, they turned their club into a political party. They were advocating liberal ideas and identified a constitution, free elections and a parliamentary system as key tools required to implement their programme. They nevertheless progressively adopted new stances, accepting military actions and ultimately supporting Nasserist ideas. Exploring this reversal of policy requires a thorough analysis of ideas, practices, political positions and context. From 1946 to 1955, liberal Baathist ideas vanished and a new revolutionary ethos emerged from the struggle.

Chapter 4, by Sune Haugbolle

The existing literature on Khalid Bakdash, long-time leader of the Syrian-Lebanese Communist Party, often sees him as the embodiment of the way in which the Soviet world communist movement ostensibly dominated Arab communism, leading to the uncritical acceptance of the canons of Soviet Marxism and the concomitant failure to formulate independent social analyses of the specific conditions of Arab societies. The evaluation of Bakdash as 'implanted' is symptomatic of a broader tendency to place non-Western communists on the fringe of local knowledge production, if not completely dismiss them. This chapter argues that such sweeping conclusions rest on methodological dominance of top-down history, in which party doctrine is made equivalent with (the lack of) party–society relations. If we instead pay attention to the micro-biographies of Arab communists, and to their internal disagreement and debates, a different picture emerges, namely that of everyday ideology. Inside the Syrian-Lebanese Communist Party, a rich contestation of the Moscow line took place. The chapter focuses on the deep disagreements surrounding the Syrian-Lebanese Communist Party's fatal decision to support the international partition plan of Palestine in 1947, despite previous resistance to partition within the party. By reading biographical literature on Bakdash in Arabic and contemporary debates in sources such as *al-Sakha* and *al-Tariq*, the chapter attempts to reconstruct the full extent of disagreement that was terminated when Farajallah al-Helou was forced to toe the party line in his infamous *mea culpa*, *risalat salim*, and ensuing doctrine under Bakdash's dominance. How did Bakdash deal with this discord? Which personal experiences and contacts with Palestine and Palestinians within the party influenced the debate? What was the role of everyday ideology in determining the party in line on such a crucial question as Palestine?

Chapter 5, by Daniela Melfa

At its onset, internationalism has been the horizon of struggle of communism and the spearhead of its strategy. In the Third World, however, it has been remoulded due to the spread of the nationalist wave and the challenge of underdevelopment. By focusing on the Tunisian Communist Party (PCT), this chapter examines key features of its commitment to the external front, notably in the 'tricontinental' arena, subsequent to the nationalist turn of the mid-1950s. After analysing the PCT's stance towards the Arab movement of national liberation, special attention will be devoted to the Palestinian and Sahrawi causes. The different stance adopted by the PCT – activism in the first case and taciturnity in the second one – sheds light on the party's priorities and networks, where pride of place was given to the Soviet Union and the Maghrebi communist parties.

Chapter 6, by Jakob Krais

Algerian delegations participated in World Youth Festivals from the first event in Prague. Their members represented communist, nationalist and even Islamist youth groups, but all used the festivals to publicise the cause of national self-determination. At the same time, they came into contact with representatives from other (former) colonies and from socialist countries, as well as with delegates of left-wing organisations from Western-oriented countries. The assertion of Algeria as a nation among others thus went hand in hand with the formation of international solidarity in an emerging network of leftist, anti-imperialist movements. In my contribution I present, on the one hand, the evolution of this kind of internationalist nationalism in the Algerian press (e.g. the communist *al-Jaza'ir al-jadida* or the Islamic scouts' paper *al-Hayat*) and, on the other, the development of views about the Algerian struggle (which was becoming a symbol of anti-imperialism) in the host countries, exemplified by the press in the GDR and Austria in 1951 and 1959, respectively.

Chapter 7, by Nate George

This chapter recovers the key contribution of the Moroccan revolutionary Mehdi Ben Barka – while touching upon other Arab militants, movements and states – in building the tricontinental coalition and framework for action. By emphasising the transformative role of political practice upon the development of Ben Barka's thought over several distinct conjunctures, it uses his political evolution to illustrate the historical trajectory of global anti-colonialism from national independence movements that drew upon liberal political traditions into national liberation revolutions operating in a dense internationalist and socialist framework, the framework of tricontinentalism. Central to both of these themes is Ben Barka's role in defining the concept of neocolonialism, institutionalising it within tricontinentalist milieux, and organising revolutionary action to overcome it. Finally, it also recovers the dialectical relationship between revolution and counterrevolution, absent in many accounts of the radical left, and how the relationships between these antithetical forces shaped one another. In sum, it argues that Ben Barka was pivotal in building a workable tricontinentalism that – for a brief yet crucial period – co-ordinated many of the anti-colonial forces of Africa, Asia and Latin America.

Chapter 8, by Gennaro Gervasio

The trajectory of the New Left in Egypt is peculiar within the history of Arab radical Marxist politics. In 1965, Egyptian communist parties decided to officially dissolve themselves and be absorbed into Nasser's (pseudo-)revolutionary platform. While both Nasser and these co-opted communists of the 'Official Left' somehow survived the June Defeat of 1967, a new wave of younger and more radical Marxists made its appearance on campuses and, later, in the factories, challenging the established 'revolutionary credentials' of the regime and their older comrades.

On the basis, mostly, of unpublished archive material and personal interviews, this chapter aims to shed light on the theory and political praxis of the Egyptian Radical Left in the 1970s. In particular, this chapter focuses on the experience of the 'far left', embodied by the *al-tanzim al-shuyu'i al-misri* (TshM), formed in 1969, which became the Egyptian Communist Workers' Party (ECWP, *hizb al-'ummal al-shuyu'i al-misri*) in 1975.

While this group attracted many radical intellectuals, and helped to spread the ideas of the new radical Third World Left (Vietnam, Cuba, Mao's China, etc.), this chapter argues that both TshM and ECWP remained trapped within a nationalist and pan-Arabist discourse, by de facto focusing on the national question at the expense of the social question.

Chapter 9, by Maha Nassar

Today, there is much debate about the extent to which Palestinians should engage with the Israeli Left. However, these debates elide a deeper history of strategic and discursive engagements that Palestinians have undertaken with Palestinian, Mizrahi and Ashkenazi leftists inside the Green Line. In this chapter, I recover the ways in which Palestinian nationalists circulated these leftist discourses throughout the Arab world through a close reading of the PLO Research Center's publications, including *al-Yawmiyyat al-Filastiniyya* (Palestinian Diary) and *Shu'un Filastiniyya* (Palestinian Affairs). I argue that by including the activities of an array of leftist and progressive groups inside Israel, from Rakah to Matzpen to the Red Front, these publications played a key role in writing Israeli leftists into the Palestinian cause, albeit with widely differing results. Examining these dynamics highlights the important historical cross-fertilisation of leftist and nationalist discourses and shows how Palestinians critiqued the relationship between Zionism and colonialism within a global leftist context.

Chapter 10, by Laure Guirguis

'Action Committees' and 'Militant Enquiry': these two words summarise the framework set up in 1969 by militants of the Organisation of Communist Action in Lebanon (OCAL, 1971) in-the-making in order to co-ordinate different fields of struggle and to anchor the Palestinian resistance in Lebanese social struggles at a time of intense mobilisation throughout the country.

A few years later, the chief initiator of this endeavour, the sociologist Waddah Charara (b. Lebanon 1942), settled with a few comrades in the Beirut 'poverty belt' to carry out militant enquiries in the area. By turning my gaze towards these two experiments, with a special focus on Charara's militant and intellectual trajectory, I trace the reframing of the Maoist notion of 'militant enquiry' as it is displaced and transformed between Europe, the Arab world and Afro-Asian geographies of resistance. I would like to show how militant circulations and processes of the re-signification of representations and know-how have shaped all the elements under study, beginning with the milieux of action up to the militants themselves, and their way of framing problems, defining actions to be taken, and locating themselves in this breadth of local/global interconnectedness. I combine three approaches: mapping the main channels of transmission of the notion; tracing the redefinition of the notion; and studying the intertwining of theorisation processes and bodily involvement in various milieux. The chapter draws on face-to-face and online interviews with former militants carried out between 2016 and 2019. It brings into conversation militant theoretical writings and memoirs, as well as the publications released by the organisations under consideration.

Chapter 11, by Philipp Winkler

This chapter examines the case of the Iraqi revolutionary Khalid Ahmad Zaki, who went to study in London and came into contact with radical left-wing groups active there in the 1960s, eventually joining Bertrand Russell's entourage. Inspired by their fascination with revolutionary movements in the Third World, Zaki returned to Iraq and attempted to launch his own revolutionary war in the southern marshes, only to be defeated by the Iraqi army after a few weeks. However insignificant his actions may have turned out to be within the greater picture of history, Zaki's memory lived on as the 'Che Guevara of the Middle East' far beyond the borders of Iraq, as he turned into a symbol of resistance against the prevalent trends among Arab communists for collaborating with existing regimes in their countries. Drawing on Enzo Traverso's reflection on left-wing melancholia, the chapter shows that, while remembering Zaki initially served the purpose of inciting further actions in his spirit, later commemorations portray him as a symbol of a bygone hope that never materialised.

Chapter 12, by Jens Hanssen

This chapter revisits two moments of crisis and critique in twentieth-century Arab intellectual history: a public debate between Arab leftists and nationalists in Cairo in 1961, and the appearance of Arab Marxists' scholarship on Materialism and Arabic-Islamic philosophy in 1971. Both moments are embedded in their global and regional contexts but are articulated by two sets of intellectuals. The first pits Muhammad Hasanayn Haykal against Clovis Maksoud over the relationship between the organic intellectual and the state. The second moment focuses on the Arab Left's historical-philosophical turn launched by the late Tayyib Tizini and culminating in Husayn Muruwwa's work *Materialist Tendencies in Arabic-Islamic Philosophy* of 1978. I am interested in the twin concepts of 'crisis' and 'critique' and what it tells us about the intellectual struggles within the Arab Left during the age of decolonisation and the global Cold War.

Chapter 13, by Samer Frangie

Surveying the past from an 'authoritarian' and 'sectarian' present, the episode of leftist militancy of the 1960s and 1970s appears as an anomaly in the history of the Levant. From the perspective of such a present, it seems that the afterlives of the Left can be apprehended solely through the register of melancholia. By tracing the various and often contradictory afterlives of the assassinated communist intellectual Husayn Murruwah, this chapter attempts to contextualise this present perspective and to historicise the current melancholia towards this past. The chapter is not about Muruwwa's autobiography per se, but about the travel of texts across changing political conjunctures and their interpretations against the shifting contours of the present. More specifically, the afterlives of Muruwwa's text provide one of the ways through which we can understand what is at stake in the manifold ways we inhabit the 'futures past' that haunt our present.

ACKNOWLEDGEMENTS

This volume results from ongoing discussions in various venues, from the conference Left-wing Trends in the Arab World to the workshop on the Archives of the New Left, which I organised at, respectively, the German Orient Institute in Beirut (OIB) in December 2016 and the International Institute of Social History (IISH) in September 2017, up to Hana Morgenstern and Mezna Qato's project of an Arab Left Reader, which was discussed at the University of Cambridge in April 2018.

I thank, for their financial support, the Orient Institute in Beirut (OIB), the International Institute of Social History (IISH), the Leibniz-Zentrum Moderner Orient (ZMO), the Thyssen Foundation and the Institute for Advanced Studies at the Central European University in Budapest, as well as Aarhus Institute of Advanced Studies, the European Union's Horizon 2020 Research and Innovation Programme under the Marie Skłodowska-Curie grant agreement no. 754513, and Aarhus University Research Foundation.

NOTES ON CONTRIBUTORS

Orit Bashkin is a historian who works on the intellectual, social and cultural history of the modern Middle East. She got her PhD from Princeton University (2004), writing a thesis on Iraqi intellectual history under the supervision of Professors Robert Tignor and Samah Selim. Since her graduation, she has been working as a professor of modern Middle Eastern history in the Department of Near Eastern Languages and Civilizations at the University of Chicago. Her publications deal with Iraqi history, the history of Iraqi Jews, the Arab cultural revival movement (the *nahda*) in the late nineteenth century, and the connections between modern Arab history and Arabic literature. Her current research project explores the lives of Iraqi Jews in Israel.

Samer Frangie is an Associate Professor in the Department of Political Studies and Public Administration and the director of the Center for Arab and Middle East Studies at the American University of Beirut. His research is at the intersection of the intellectual history of the Arab world and political theory, and examines the history of the Arab Left. He has published a number of articles dealing with various aspects of the history of the Arab Left, in journals such as *the International Journal of Middle East Studies*, *Modern Intellectual History*, *Third Quarterly* and *Thesis Eleven* among others.

Nate George is the Ibrahim Abu-Lughod Postdoctoral Fellow at Columbia University's Center for Palestine Studies. He holds a PhD in History from Rice University, an MA in Middle East Studies from the American University of Beirut and a BA in Cinema from the University of Iowa. His book project, *A Third World War: Revolution, Counterrevolution, and Empire in Lebanon, 1967–1982*, understands Lebanon as an important setting in an international civil war over the direction of decolonisation and the shape of political representation in the Eastern Mediterranean.

Gennaro Gervasio, a graduate of Naples 'L'Orientale', is currently an Associate Professor in *History and Politics of the Middle East and North Africa* at *Università Roma Tre* in Italy, having previously worked at the British University in Egypt (BUE) and in Sydney's Macquarie University. His research interests include: secularism and Marxism in the Arab world, the political role of Arab intellectuals, and civic activism and social movements in the Arab World (especially Egypt). His latest monograph is *al-haraka al-markisiyya fi misr 1967–1981* (The Marxist movement in Egypt 1967–81; Cairo: The National Centre for Translation, 2010), and more recently he has co-edited the volume *Informal Power in the Middle East: Hidden Geographies* (London: Routledge, 2014 and 2016).

Laure Guirguis is a historian who works on the political, social and cultural history of the Arab world, with a special focus on the Arab East. She is Associate Professor and fellow (October 2019–22) at Aarhus Institute of Advanced Studies (AIAS), Aarhus University. Her major publications include 'Vietnam and the Rise of a Radical Left in Lebanon, 1962–1976', *Monde(s). Histoire, Espaces, Relations* 1 (2018); *Copts and the Security State: Violence, Coercion and Sectarianism in Contemporary Egypt* (Stanford University Press 2016), and *Égypte: Révolution et Contre-révolution* (Presses de l'Université de Laval, 2014).

Jens Hanssen is Associate Professor of Arab Civilisation, Middle Eastern and Mediterranean History at the University of Toronto. He has held a SSHRC Insight Grant (2014–18) on 'German-Jewish Echoes in 20th-Century Arab Thought'. His overall research explores the intellectual entanglements between Europe, North Africa and the Middle East since the nineteenth century. He is author of *Fin de Siècle Beirut* (2005) and co-editor of *Arabic Thought Beyond the Liberal Age* and *Arabic Thought Against the Authoritarian Age* (Cambridge University Press, 2016 and 2018).

Sune Haugbolle is Professor of Global Studies at Roskilde University, Denmark, and editor of the *Middle East Journal of Culture and Communication*. He has published widely on social memory, media and political history in the Middle East, including *War and Memory in Lebanon* (Cambridge University Press, 2010) and *Visual Culture in the Modern Middle East* (ed.; Indiana University Press, 2013). His current research examines global histories of the Left.

Jakob Krais obtained his PhD in Islamic Studies from Freie Universität Berlin with a dissertation on historiography and nation building in Gaddafi's Libya. He is currently writing a book on sports and modernity in colonial Algeria, research for which has been funded by the special programme 'Islam, the Modern Nation State, and Transnational Movements' at the Gerda Henkel Foundation. His publications include: 'Muscular Muslims: Scouting in Late Colonial Algeria between Nationalism and Religion', *International Journal of Middle East Studies* 51, 4 (2019); 'Girl Guides, Athletes, and Educators: Women and the National Body in Late Colonial Algeria', *Journal of Middle East Women's Studies* 15, 2 (2019); and 'Youth and Sports in Algeria's Diplomatic Struggle for International Recognition (1957–1962)', *The Maghreb Review* 42, 3 (2017).

Daniela Melfa is Associate Professor of African History at the Department of Political and Social Sciences, University of Catania. She specialised in North African history, and in 2008 published her PhD dissertation on Italian wine growers in the Tunisian protectorate. Her further research enlarged upon European settlement in Tunisia, with a focus on missionary activities, gender roles and indigenous forms of agency. Her work-in-progress on the trajectory of the Tunisian Left led to the publication of *Rivoluzionari responsabili. Militanti comunisti in Tunisia (1956–93)* (Carocci, 2019). In 2012 she spent a trimester as visiting scholar at the Center for Middle Eastern Studies, University of California, Berkeley, and in 2017 was visiting professor at the

EHESS (Paris). She has been President of the Italian Society for Middle Eastern Studies (SeSaMO) (2017–19).

Hana Morgenstern is a scholar, writer and translator. She is a university lecturer in Postcolonial and Middle East Literature at Cambridge University and a senior fellow at Newnham College. Hana Morgenstern is co-director of the Documents of the Arab Left Project. She is currently at work on a book manuscript entitled *A Literature for All Its Citizens: Aesthetics of Coexistence in Israel/Palestine*.

Maha Nassar is an Associate Professor in the School of Middle Eastern and North African Studies at the University of Arizona, where she specialises in the cultural and intellectual history of the modern Arab world. She holds a PhD in Near Eastern languages and civilizations from the University of Chicago. Her first book, which received a 2018 Palestine Book Award, is entitled *Brothers Apart: Palestinian Citizens of Israel and the Arab World* (Stanford University Press, 2017). In it she examines how Palestinian intellectuals in Israel connected with global decolonisation movements through literary and journalistic writings during the 1950s and 1960s. Her scholarly articles have appeared in the *Journal of Palestine Studies*, *Arab Studies Journal* and the *Middle East Journal of Culture and Communication*. She is currently working on a social, transnational history of the Palestinian people.

Matthieu Rey is a senior researcher at IREMAM and a CNRS researcher specialising in contemporary Middle Eastern history, with a special focus on Syria's and Iraq's political systems. He is also an associate researcher at the Collège de France, Wits History Workshop and IFAS-Recherche. After carrying out a thesis about Syrian and Iraqi parliamentary systems in the 1950s, and after conducting extensive fieldwork in Syria and the Middle East from 2009 to 2013, he extended his research to other topics, mostly on state-building and policymaking in the contemporary Middle East. His focus ranged from the Cold War in the Arab world to the Syrian crisis, including various transverse subjects such as development policies. In 2018, he published a monograph on contemporary Syria (nineteenth to twenty-first century).

Abdel Razzaq Takriti is an Associate Professor, inaugural holder of the Arab-American Educational Foundation Chair in Modern Arab History, and Founding Director of the Center for Arab Studies at the University of Houston. A scholar of anti-colonialism, revolutions and transnational movements, he is the author of *Monsoon Revolution: Republicans, Sultans, and Empires in Oman, 1965–1976* (Oxford University Press, 2013; paperback edition 2016) and co-author and co-editor, with Karma Nabulsi, of *The Palestinian Revolution Website*, learnpalestine.politics.ox.ac.uk (Department of Politics and International Relations, University of Oxford, 2016).

Philipp Winkler obtained an MA in History from Friedrich-Alexander-University Erlangen-Nuremberg, Germany (FAU) in 2015, and spent April–July 2016 as an intern at the Iraq Institute for Strategic Studies, Beirut. Currently he is teaching, and writing his dissertation, entitled *The Arab Left and Its Reception of the Vietnamese and Cuban Experiences after 1967*, at FAU.

INTRODUCTION
THE ARAB LEFTS FROM THE 1950s TO THE 1970s: TRANSNATIONAL ENTANGLEMENTS AND SHIFTING LEGACIES

Laure Guirguis

Scholarship's long neglect of Arab left-wing trends in the 1950s–1970s is in keeping with the near-complete erasure of Arab radical and democratic traditions in public culture.[1] In 1989, the reassessment of Marxism that followed the collapse of the USSR and of a world perceived as bipolar epitomised the disorientation of the Left on a global scale.[2] Even ten years before the 1989 systemic collapse, the revolution in Iran, the Egypt–Israel peace treaty and the Soviet intervention in Afghanistan marked a watershed in the history of the Middle East and the demise of the Left as a leading force and a dominant imaginary. These structural changes disrupted the rules of knowledge production and the definition of the fields of knowledge,[3] while intensive media and political focus on the short term, and the apparently more threatening face of Middle Eastern societies, enhanced scholars' interest in political Islam. The defeat and 'left-wing melancholia'[4] henceforth appeared

[1] In this introduction, the names in parentheses in the text refer to authors of chapters included in this volume; other references are placed in footnotes.

[2] Jabar (ed.), *Post-Marxism*.

[3] Bozarslan and Guirguis, 'Presentation', *Alain Roussillon*.

[4] Traverso, *Left-wing Melancholia*; Brown, 'Resisting Left Melancholy'.

as the main appropriate ways in which to address the history of the Left, as evidenced by the sometimes contradictory afterlives of the assassinated communist intellectual Hussein Muruwwa (Frangie) and of Khaked Ahmed Zaki, the 'Che Guevara of the Middle East', whose rebellion in Iraq's southern marches is first remembered as having 'instigate[d] further action . . . whereas later commemorations have a rather resigned, mournful and depressed tone' (Winkler). Militants themselves were often the first to slip into auto-criticism, if not self-flagellation. These defeated leftists, though, have not been completely eradicated, nor have they remained silent. As Takriti observes in this volume, they made noticeable contributions to the history of the region, and militant experiments have shaped the sensibility as well as the intellectual and analytical skills of leading figures who fostered the development of social sciences and the renewal of literature and cinema in the Arab world.

Yet, the Arab Lefts of the 1950s to the 1970s recently surfaced in scholarship and revived in militant memories and multi-faceted archival practices, from the flourishing of novels, memoirs or fictional biographies to the digitisation and dissemination of militant documents through various channels, up to the writing of histories on these revolutionary times.[5] More strikingly, academics as well as former militants started raising new questions, adopting innovative approaches and searching for uncharted narrative spaces. For instance, the histories covering the period from the 1950s to the 1970s henceforth focused on the state and, from this perspective, addressed the histories of the Left through the prism of state and communist parties' power plays in the dynamics of global and Arab Cold Wars. Now, historians start painting a more complex picture of Arab communist parties' relationships with the state

[5] To mention but a few texts and initiatives carried out by former militants over the past years: Sawah, 'Hikayat'; al-Ulaymi, 'Memoirs of an Egyptian Communist' (al-Ulaymi also disseminated online numerous documents of the Egyptian Communist Workers Party); al-Bizri, *Sanawat*; Manna, *Les Parias de Damas*; al-Ikri, *Dhakirat*; Ben Haji Yahia and Abdessamad (eds), *Georges Adda. Militant Tunisien*; and Beydoun, 'Liban Socialiste'. Having preserved the entire collection of the clandestine journal *Socialist Lebanon*, published between 1966 and 1971 by the eponymous Marxist-Leninist group, Beydoun recently digitised it and made it available online at adrajarriyah.home.blog. For his part, the historian and former militant Habib Kazdaghli started digitising the archives of the Tunisian Communist Party in co-operation with Dijon Fondation Maison des Sciences de l'Homme.

and the USSR (Haugbolle, Melfa), deciphering leftist anti-state movements, and following individual trajectories. Further, new relationships with these past stories and histories are being forged, which involve re-imagining the temporal configuration or 'the manifold ways we inhabit "the future past" that haunts our present' (Frangie). In the *Archeology of Knowledge*, Foucault acutely pointed out the constitutive interactions between the institution of the archive, the definition of what is sayable and valuable, and the meaning of the present:

> L'archive, c'est d'abord la loi de ce qui peut être dit, le système qui régit l'apparition des énoncés comme événements singuliers. Mais l'archive, c'est aussi ce qui fait que toutes ces choses dites . . . se groupent en figures distinctes, se composent les unes avec les autres selon des rapports multiples . . .; c'est ce qui, à la racine même de l'énoncé-événement, et dans le corps où il se donne, définit d'entrée de jeu le *système de son énonçabilité* . . . c'est ce qui définit le mode d'actualité de l'énoncé-chose.[6]

Why have the long-eclipsed histories of the Left become enunciable and valuable, and why now? How does the re-engagement with this past relate to today's political landscape and conception of history and temporality? For whom?

To leftist militants as well as to academics, the 2011 momentum obviously marked a turning point, insofar as we consider it an apogee in a decade of dissent and deep social and economic change; in a regional, manifold, revolutionary process, still ongoing. Since the early 2000s, various kinds of protests have regularly erupted throughout the region, eventually leading to the collapse of long-lasting but nonetheless internally divided regimes. Revolutionary dynamics would sometimes reactivate structuring tendencies, such as identity politics. Sometimes, they would allow an overcoming, be it momentarily, of the multifarious cleavages and allegiances within societies, first and foremost the borders of class, gender, religion and sect. Whereas the mottoes 'The end of history' and 'There is no alternative' embody a stalled temporality that keeps people 'between an "intolerable present" and an

[6] Foucault, *L'Archéologie du Savoir*, 170–1.

"impossible future"',[7] Cairo in January 2011 and Lebanon in October 2019 offered a glimpse of hope for envisaging the possibility of a future and defining the present, whatever actually happened next. By epitomising the revival of revolutionary hopes, and the sense of urgency, the urgency of long-awaited social and political change, 2011 unexpectedly connected the nascent and fragile possibility of a future to past revolutionary desires.

The connections between our present political landscape and the heyday of revolutionary hopes in the 1950s–1970s took various shapes. To restrict myself to the Egyptian case, extensive research could be carried out on the multi-layered impact of the Egyptian uprisings on the complex interactions between younger and older militant generations, as well as on the remobilisation of activists of the 1960s–1970s or on their changing stances towards their past. The year 2011 led militants of both generations to reconsider this long-despised period and its leading figures. Arwa Salih is a case in point. A leader of the Egyptian Communist Workers Party, she was considered, in leftist milieux, a controversial figure for her role in the internal struggles that split the party and for her harsh critique of leftist militants' dogmatic stances and attitudes towards women.[8] She committed suicide in 1997, leaving behind her a series of essays, and recently captured the attention of newborn militants who have developed numerous narratives revolving around this fascinating and tragic figure.[9]

The same year, 2011, also highlighted scientists' dependence on obsolete analytical tools and triggered a renewal of methods, categories, questions and approaches. This is especially true in political sciences; scholars in the field of SMT, transitology and regime types expressed the need to forge new analytical tools and models allowing them to provide relevant explanations of Arab societies and politics at a time of multi-layered disruption.[10] This spurred historians to further examine the dynamics of rupture and continuities in militant and intellectual trajectories, as well as in the framing of

[7] Wright, 'Mutant City'.

[8] Salih, *The Stillborn*; Hammad, 'Arwa Salih's The Premature'.

[9] Ramzy, *Renegotiating Politics on Campus*, Chs 3 and 6.

[10] POMEPS, *Arab Uprisings*; Beinin and Vairel (eds), *Social Movements*; Della Porta, *Social Movements in Times of Austerity*.

revolutionary hopes on the long term. Whereas the Left had, since the late 1970s, been analysed mainly through the lens of its relationships with political Islam,[11] 2011 fostered the desire to shed light on the resilience of Arab radical and democratic traditions that took shape in spite of local and global wars, state coercion, neoliberal globalisation and repeated failures,[12] and to further rethink the Left beyond the secular and religious divide.[13]

The critical stance of this collection of essays lies in the authors' commitment to interrogating commonly accepted categories. First and foremost, how to capture the category of 'Left'? In a narrow sense, one could flatly define the Left by relying on individuals' and organisations' claims to belong to the Left, considered as a diverse field consisting of various trends in Marxism, socialism and anarchism that have emerged in the Arab World since the late nineteenth century.[14] Although these claims might in some cases appear contestable, this definition would not allow for deciphering what the Left actually meant at that time. Rather, I propose conceiving of the Left as a matrix of meaning and values, and opt for a dynamic process of definition. From this perspective, studying the Left in the 1950s–1970s requires locating it in the discursive and normative field of the time, which was structured by a series of debates between competing or convergent political forces and ideologies, in the interplay between local, regional and global challenges.

Let me sketch out a brief overview of the evolving power play in the 1950s–1970s. Discredited for having accepted the 1947 UN partition plan for Palestine, the Arab communist parties nevertheless remained powerful organisations in Iraq, Soudan, Tunisia, Syria, Algeria, Syria and Lebanon.[15] However,

[11] Dot-Pouillard, 'De Pékin à Téhéran' and 'Les Relations entre Islamismes, Nationalismes et Mouvements de Gauche au Moyen-Orient Arabe'; Sing, 'Brothers in Arms'; Abisaab, 'Sayyid Musa al-Sadr'; Ayari, 'Le Prix de l'Engagement'.

[12] Bardawil, 'Dreams'; Hanssen and Weiss, *Arabic Thought against the Authoritarian Age.*

[13] And before 2011, see Roussillon, 'Égyptianité, Arabité, Islamité'.

[14] Khuri-Makdisi, *The Eastern Mediterranean.*

[15] On the Arab communist parties see: Batatu, *The Old Social Classes*; Beinin, *Was the Red Flag Flying There?*; Botman, *The Rise of Communism in Egypt*; Budeiri, *The Palestine Communist Party 1919–1948*; Feliu et al., *The Communist Parties in the Middle East*; Franzén, *Red Star Over Iraq*; Halliday, *Arabia without Sultans*; Hamza, *Communisme et Nationalisme en Tunisie*; Ismael, *The Communist Movement*; Warburg, *Islam, Nationalism and Communism.*

they did not represent the sole, or even the major, leaders of the Left in the new world order that took shape under American hegemony in the aftermaths of the Second World War. In the 1950s, pan-Arabism in its Baathist and Nasserist veins had become the driving ideology in the Arab world and, at a time when the hero of Bandung and Suez was still embodying both opposition to imperialism and the establishment of a new political order, the creation of the United Arab Republic (UAR) momentarily raised most people's hopes for a pan-Arab anti-Western front. Nasser had actually monopolised the discourse of liberation. The failure of the Egyptian–Syrian Union in 1961 therefore created a deep sense of loss. It fostered a turn to the Left in pan-Arab movements: socialist claims shaped the Egyptian National Charter of 21 May 1962 (Hanssen) and the final document of the Baath Party's sixth National Congress (1963).[16] Further, it led to splits and withdrawals and, for instance, increased tensions within the Arab Nationalist Movement (ANM), resulting in the creation of radical left-wing groups in the whole region.[17] As for the Arab communist parties, they similarly went through political and organisational crises that triggered the formation of dissenting groups. Yet, the processes of decolonisation and the emergence of the Third World had brought to the forefront the Algerian, the Chinese, the Cuban and the Vietnamese revolutionary examples;[18] and the Sino-Soviet struggle for supremacy furthered the search for new models along Marxist lines in a critical move against Stalinism and the communist parties, but also against pan-Arab movements. Fuelled by hopes and scarred by successive defeats, the Arab New Left was born in the 1960s from the loss of faith in the ability of Arab regimes to achieve the long-awaited social, political

[16] On Nasser's socialism, see Rami Ginat, *Egypt's Incomplete Revolution*. On the ambivalent relationships between Communists and Free Officers/the Nasserian State, see Botman, 'Egyptian Communists and the Free Officers' and Tewfik Aclimandos, 'Officiers Libres et Officiers Communistes'. Before establishing the Arab Revolutionary Workers Party with Ilyas Morqos, the Marxist Syrian thinker Yasin al-Hafiz, who had affiliated with the Syrian Communist Party and thereafter with the Syrian Baath Party, contributed the writing of the documents of the 6th Congress and the socialist turn in the Party. On al-Hafiz, see Frangie, 'Historicism', and 'Exiled from History'.

[17] On the ANM, see Barut, *Haraka*; Kazziha, *Revolutionary Transformation*; Ibrahim, *Limadha*; Sayigh, 'Reconstructing the Paradox'; Takriti, 'Political Practices in the Gulf'.

[18] Mokhtefi, *Algiers, Third World Capital*; Guirguis, 'Vietnam'.

and national emancipation and the liberation of Palestine.[19] It is worth noticing that the numerous left-wing groups that grew out of pan-Arab movements and the Arab communist parties in the 1960s–1970s remain under-studied, although numerous documents and testimonies are available or easily accessible (Gervasio, Guirguis, Nassar, Winkler).[20]

What is the Left among these political and ideological trends spread between numerous organisations, which, certainly, often competed for political power or ideological hegemony, but also typically shared a set of overlapping or convergent values, goals and assumptions? 'Left' does not merely name one of these groups and trends according to a fixed definition. Rather, 'the Left' characterises a stance adopted in a specific situation, as well as the principles and values considered socialist or Marxist, to which the involved protagonists referred at that time.

One may state that Nasser, the Baath or dissenting groups inside the ANM have adopted leftist stances, but is that to say that they were leftist? The question is not aimed at listing groups and individuals in categories, but at opening up the discussion on these categories, and especially on the categories that name the major ideological trends existing within that period: Third-Worldism, Marxism, communism, Baathism, Nasserism, socialism, and nationalism in its *qawmi* and *watani* guises. What is the Left, then, if not a transregional and even transnational, though diversified, universe of meaning and values, a dynamically constructed universe of shared references? In the 1960s, the leftist matrix of meaning became prevalent in the discursive and normative field structured by debates on the best ways to lead the Arab/Palestinian revolution and achieve economic, social and political emancipation. Beyond the 'isms' and beyond academic turf battles, the study of the Left in the 1950s–1970s therefore implies a re-engagement not solely with

[19] For further discussion on the Arab versus the European and North American New Left, see Guirguis, 'Vietnam' and 'May '68'.

[20] On the New Left in the Arab world, recent scholarship includes: Bardawil, *When All This Revolution Melts into Air*, *'Dreams'* and *Revolution and Disenchantment*; Fiedler, 'Israel in Revolution'; Guirguis, 'Vietnam' and 'May '68'; Gervasio, *Al-haraka al-markisiyya fi misr*; Hammad, 'Arwa Salih's The Premature'; Hendrickson, 'March 1968'; Sadeghi-Boroujerdi, 'The Origins of Communist Unity'; Haugbolle, 'The New Arab Left'.

the history of the Arab communist parties (Haugbolle) but also with the political and intellectual history of Nasserism and the Baath, which have long been analysed through the narrow lens of nationalism.[21] Taking seriously the debates on moral and political values that stirred the Baath Party between the late 1940s and the early 1950s, Rey in this volume deciphers the framing of the Baathist founders' evolving political stances and practices. For his part, Hanssen revisits 'two moments of crisis and critique' (Hanssen), the first being the debate on the relationships between the intellectual and the state, which confronted Clovis Maksoud and Muhammad Hasanayn Haykal in 1961, and eventually contributed to the so-called socialist turn in Nasserian policy as evidenced in the Egyptian National Charter (1962).

All the authors in the book had to face the question of the relationships between nationalism and internationalism/socialism, be it at the core of their argument or more at the margins. The interplay of tensions and convergences between nationalism and internationalism/socialism did not consist in a problem that could be solved. Rather, it formed an aporia that arose from a double bind: from the changing stance of the USSR on this issue in theory and practice, and from the original sin, so to say, of post-Second World War internationalism that ultimately relied on nationalist claims since it took shape in the decolonisation processes. This aporia structured the debates and the political stances at local, regional and international scales, in various and complex ways. Krais traces the FLN's successful use of World Youth Festivals to construct Algerian nationhood in an international setting. Similarly, Melfa argues that the Tunisian Communist Party's nationalist turn in the mid-1950s 'did not erase its international commitment to socio-political changes, but rather channelled it into the defence of liberation struggles worldwide', albeit sometimes reluctantly as evidenced in the use of a double standard with regard to the Sahrawi cause.

The authors relocate the Arab Lefts in transnational dynamics and revolutionary networks, by paying thorough attention to the circulation of people, symbols, ideas and know-how in the region, as well as in the interplay between Europe, the Middle East and Afro-Asian geographies of resistance.

[21] Weiss, 'Left Out', and 'Genealogies of Baathism'.

In line with recent efforts in Middle Eastern Studies, this is a salutary move. Attempts to better understand the historical processes that made the 1960s a critical juncture, a 'transnational moment of change',[22] had given birth in the late 1990s to a new epistemological framework that addressed, from the periphery, the issues of the Cold War, national emancipation struggles and the transformation of political subjectivities.[23] The Arab Lefts, however, have long been set apart from emerging scholarship on transnational communism and the Global Sixties. This is now changing. Historians of the Arab world began considering the Arab Left from a transnational perspective.[24] Several authors have pointed out the formation of a transnational, though diversified, revolutionary culture; they described it by referring either to the sense of belonging to a 'global community of revolution' or to the production of an 'international language of dissent'.[25] So far, we still know very little about the formation of this transnational universe of meaning, as symbols, notions and know-how are displaced, translated and transformed through ever more complex itineraries.

In what follows, the authors typically share the assumption that the transnational, the local and the global do not consist in pre-existing scales of reference,[26] and interrogate their dialectical formation and local/global cross-fertilisation processes. Adopting a constructivist and dynamic approach towards transnational entanglements, most focus attention on the interplay between the main channels of transmission/translation, shifting theorisations, and militant experiments in context. This implies combining the study of transregional/transnational networks and venues of meetings with analyses of militant journals and theoretical or literary texts as well as of militant

[22] Horn and Kenney, *Transnational Moments of Change.*

[23] Westad, *The Global Cold War*; Alinder et al. (eds), *The Long 1968*; Christiansen and Scarlett (eds), *The Third World in the Global 1960s*; Jian et al. (eds), *The Routledge Handbook of the Global Sixties*; Suri, *Power*; Ross, *May '68 and its Afterlives*; AHR, 'The International 1968'.

[24] On the late nineteenth to early twentieth century, see Khuri-Makdisi, *The Eastern Mediterranean.* On the 1960s–1970s, see Bardawil, 'Dreams'; Guirguis, 'Vietnam' and 'May '68'; Pennock, *The Rise of the Arab American Left*; Takriti, *Monsoon Revolution.*

[25] Borrowing from, respectively, Takriti, *Monsoon Revolution*, 6 and Suri, *Power and Protest*, 23.

[26] Werner and Zimmermann, 'Penser l'Histoire Croisée'.

actions. Indeed, numerous militants were committed both to theoretical analysis or literary writing and to action on the ground. Deciphering the processes of re-signification and de-/re-identification in this breadth of local/ global interconnectedness therefore also leads us to place emphasis on the constitutive interactions between theorisation processes and bodily involvement in various milieux (George, Guirguis, Haugbolle). Three chapters focus on the framing of leftist anti-Zionist stances between Europe and the Arab world. Drawing on a thorough analysis of the PLO Research Centre's publications, Nassar deciphers how Palestinians engaged in common action with Palestinian and Jewish leftists inside the Green Line, circulated leftist ideas throughout the whole region, and elaborated their critique of the relationship between Zionism and colonialism within a transnational frame of reference. For her part, Morgenstern turns attention towards the Arabic cultural and political journal *al-Jadid*, the mouthpiece of the Palestine Communist Party, in which Arab and Jewish Marxists from various backgrounds struggled to address 'both the near total destruction of Palestinian society and culture and the colonial repression and cultural erasure within Arab Jewish communities' (Morgenstern). Following the trajectories of Iraqi Jewish Communists between the late 1940s and the 1960s, Bashkin shows how 'leftist trends and commitment to leftist, communist and Arab Jewish ideas persist even after these radicals left their Arab nation states' to settle in Israel (Bashkin).

To conclude, I would like to draw attention to little-explored paths of research that the study of the Arab Lefts can offer.

First, the literature on the 1960s has addressed an array of social, political and cultural issues, but has often neglected the economy.[27] In the aftermath of the 2008 crisis and the subsequent uprisings throughout the world, the question of capitalism and its discontents was put back on the agenda of social scientists.[28] Yet, socio-economic change in capitalist societies played a key role in the rise of new militant generations in the 1950s–1970s, and economic claims and critique lay at the core of militant writings. To mention but one significant text, the publication of *Class Struggles in Egypt* under the pen name of Mahmoud Hussein in 1969 impacted both Arab and France militant networks and contributed to raising the political awareness and analytical skills

[27] Nolan, 'Where Was the Economy in the Global Sixties?'.

[28] For example Hanieh, *Lineages of Revolt* and *Capitalism and Class in the Gulf Arab States*.

of a militant generation in the making.[29] Further, in some instances, leftist militants initiated more or less successful actions in factories, in informal neighbourhoods (Guirguis), in the impoverished countryside or in Palestinian camps, to the degree that the ruling regimes reluctantly tolerated this.[30]

Second, to what extent, and how, would the experiences of the Arab Lefts incite us to reframe the problem of revolutionary violence? For the Arab Lefts were embedded not only in transnational revolutionary networks but also in Cold War multi-centric dynamics of violence, and defined themselves as such against their enemy, and vice versa. The Cold War produced a matrix of war, which was also a matrix of meaning grounded in the exclusive distinction between friends and foes, that is, in an identitarian logic. For war, as an institution, puts to work a regime of truth, as Foucault would say, and this regime of truth has framed the formation of resistance discourses, symbols and strategies. From this perspective, shall we not consider the moving field of antagonistic discourses and strategies prevalent at that time, at global and local scales, and seek to identify the intricate dynamics of local and global processes within the formation of a global 'matrix of meaning'?[31] Did revolutionary struggles run the risk, from the outset, not only of being trapped in violence and identity politics, but also of contributing to the reproduction of this matrix of war? It would be worth deciphering the internal shifting frontiers in the Left considered as a diverse field, as well as its external frontiers – the 'imperial discourse' or religious-identitarian discourses which were also gaining momentum at that time – in order to assess whether, and if so how, the discourses on violence and the practices of violence – or violence as a transformative practice – might ultimately have held 'revolutionaries' and 'conservatives' 'locked in an uneasy embrace'.[32] How did militants make sense of revolutionary violence, and how did it structure or disrupt the consistency

[29] First released in French by Maspéro, the text was translated into Arabic by Waddah Charara and published by Dar al-Tali'a in 1970.

[30] In Lebanon, for instance, regarding solidarity actions in the Akkar see Chahal, 'La Tourmente et l'Oubli' and Seurat, 'Le Quartier de Bab Tebbane'; and concerning leftist involvement in factories see Traboulsi, *Sura*, Charara, *Hurub* and the movie *A Feeling Greater than Love* by Mary Jirmanous Saba, which interrogates the role of the Organisation of Communist Action in Lebanon during the strikes at the Ghandour factories in 1972–3.

[31] Jabri, 'Critical Thought'.

[32] Hanssen, *Critique of Violence*.

of the leftist universe of meaning? How have some militants attempted to disrupt the logic of violence or resisted resorting to violence?

Finally, in Europe as in the USA and in the Middle East, militants of the New Left were aiming at overthrowing interlocking systems of power and oppression, and have subsequently attempted to experiment with new forms of organisation, of leadership, of social life and of gender relationships. In this regard, it would be relevant to turn attention towards three cornerstones, the sectarian, the gender and the organisational issues, and to put into play once again the notion of transformative practices. For only the reiteration of practices, be they social, institutional or discursive practices, can ultimately transform structuring tendencies and social norms, as Butler would argue, and, before her, Kant. I would be tempted to argue that, in tackling these three issues, New Left militants have realised their most innovative experiments and experienced their greatest failure.

Bibliography

Abisaab, Rula Jurdi and Malek Abisaab, *The Shi'ites of Lebanon: Modernism, Communism, and Hizbullah's Islamists* (Syracuse: Syracuse University Press, 2017).

Abisaab, Rula Jurdi, 'Sayyid Musa al-Sadr, the Lebanese State, and the Left', *Journal of Shi'a Islamic Studies* 8, 2 (2015): 131–58.

Aclimandos, Tewfik, 'Officiers Libres et Officiers Communistes: Collaborations et Confrontations', *Cahiers d'Histoire. Revue d'Histoire Critique* 105–6 (2008): 175–202.

AHR, 'The International 1968', *American Historical Review* 114, 2 and 3 (2008).

Al-Bizri, Dalal, *Sanawat al-sa*^{c}*adat al-thawriyya* [The years of revolutionary happiness] (Beirut: Dar al-Tanwir, 2016).

Al-Ikri, Abdel Nabi, *Dhakirat al-Watan wa al-Manfa* [Memories of the homeland and exile] (Manama: Faradis li al-Nashr wa al-Tawzi', 2015).

Al-Ulaymi, Sa'id, 'Memoirs of an Egyptian Communist', *Al-Hiwar al-muttamaddin* 5,928, 5,932, 5,934, 5,940 (2018).

Alinder, Jasmine, A. Aneesh, Daniel J. Sherman and Ruud van Dijk (eds), *The Long 1968: Revisions and New Perspectives* (Bloomington: Indiana University Press, 2013).

Ayari, Michael, *Le Prix de l'Engagement Politique dans la Tunisie Autoritaire. Gauchistes et Islamistes sous Bourguiba et Ben Ali (1957–2011)* (Paris–Tunis: Éditions Karthala-IRMC, 2016).

Bardawil, Fadi A., *When All This Revolution Melts into Air: The Disenchantment of Levantine Marxist Intellectuals*, PhD dissertation (New York: Columbia University mimeo, 2010).

Bardawil, Fadi A., 'Dreams of a Dual Birth: Socialist Lebanon's World and Ours', *Boundary 2* 43, 3 (2016): 313–35.

Bardawil, Fadi A., *Revolution and Disenchantment: Arab Marxism and the Binds of Emancipation* (Durham, NC: Duke University Press, 2020).

Barut, Muhammad Jamal, *Harakat al-qawmiyyin al-'arab: al-nash'a, al-tatawwur, al-mas'air* [The movement of the Arab nationalists: inception, development and trajectories] (Damascus: al-Markaz al-'Arabi li al-Dirasat al-Istratijyya, 1997).

Bashkin, Orit, 'Arabic Thought in the Radical Age: Emile Habibi, the Israeli Communist Party and the Production of Arab Jewish Radicalism, 1946–1961', in Jens Hanssen and Max Weiss (eds), *Arabic Thought against the Authoritarian Age: Towards an Intellectual History of the Present* (Cambridge: Cambridge University Press, 2018): 62–86.

Batatu, Hanna, *The Old Social Classes and the Revolutionary Movements of Iraq. A Study of Iraq's Old Landed and Commercial Classes and of its Communists, Ba'thists, and Free Officers* (Princeton: Princeton University Press, 1978).

Beinin, Joel, *Was the Red Flag Flying There? Marxist Politics and the Arab–Israeli Conflict in Egypt and Israel, 1948–1965* (Berkeley: University of California Press, 1990).

Beydoun, Ahmad, 'Liban Socialiste. Conditions d'Émergence et Cheminement d'un Groupe de Jeunes Militants "Gauchistes" dans le Liban des Années 1960', unpublished paper presented at the conference *Arab Generations*, Collège de France, Paris, June 2012.

Ben Haji Yahia, Fethi and Hichem Abdessamad (eds), *Georges Adda. Militant Tunisien* (Tunis: Éditions Nirvana, 2016).

Botman, Selma, *The Rise of Communism in Egypt, 1939–1970* (New York: Syracuse University Press, 1988).

Botman, Selma, 'Egyptian Communists and the Free Officers: 1950–54', *Middle Eastern Studies* 22, 3 (1986): 350–66.

Bozarslan, Hamit and Laure Guirguis (eds), 'Presentation', *Alain Roussillon. Reform and Politics in the Arab World* (Paris: CNRS Éditions, 2018).

Brown, Wendy, 'Resisting Left Melancholy', *Boundary 2* 26, 3 (1999): 19–27.

Budeiri, Musa, *The Palestine Communist Party 1919–1948: Arab and Jew in the Struggle for Internationalism* (Chicago: Haymarket Books, 2010).

Charara, Waddah, *Hurub al-istitba'* [Wars of subjection] (Beirut: Dar al-Tali'a, 1979).
Chahal, Nahla, 'La Tourmente et l'Oubli', *Confluences Méditerranée* 17 (1996).
Christiansen, Samantha and Zachary A. Scarlett (eds), *The Third World in the Global 1960s* (New York: Berghahn, 2013).
Della Porta, Donatella, *Social Movements in Times of Austerity: Bringing Capitalism Back into Protest Analysis* (Cambridge: Polity Press, 2015).
Di-Capua, Yoav, *No Exit: Existentialism, Jean-Paul Sartre and Decolonization* (Chicago: University of Chicago Press, 2018).
Dot-Pouillard, Nicolas, 'Les Relations entre Islamismes, Nationalismes et Mouvements de Gauche au Moyen-Orient Arabe: Une Idéologie Implicite Nationalitaire à Caractère Tiers-Mondiste', in Bernard Duterme (ed.), *État du Monde Arabe* (Belgique: Syllepse CETRI, 2009).
Dot-Pouillard, Nicolas, 'De Pékin à Téhéran, en regardant vers Jérusalem. La Singulière Conversion à l'Islamisme des Maos du Fatah', *Cahier de l'Institut Religioscope* 2 (2008).
Feliu Martinez, Laura, Ferran Izquierdo and Francisco Veiga (eds), *The Communist Parties in the Middle East: A History of a Century* (London: Routledge, 2018).
Fiedler, Lutz, 'Israel in Revolution – Matzpen, the Palestine Conflict, and the Hebrew Nation', *Israel Studies* 22, 3 (2017): 153–76.
Foucault, Michel, *L'Archéologie du Savoir* (Paris: Gallimard, 1969).
Frangie, Samer, 'Exiled from History: Yasin al-Hafiz's Autobiographical Preface and the Transformation of Political Critique', *Thesis Eleven* 133, 1 (2016): 3–18.
Frangie, Samer, 'Historicism, Socialism and Liberalism after the Defeat: On the Political Thought of Yasin al-Hafiz', *Modern Intellectual History* 2 (2015): 325–52.
Frangie, Samer, 'Theorizing from the Periphery: The Intellectual Project of Mahdi 'Amil', *International Journal of Middle East Studies* 44 (2012).
Franzén, Johan, *Red Star over Iraq: Iraqi Communism before Saddam* (New York: Columbia University Press, 2011).
Gervasio, Gennaro, *Al-haraka al-markisiyya fi misr, 1967–81* [The Marxist movement in Egypt, 1967–81) (Cairo: al-Markaz al-qawmi li-l-tarjama, 2010).
Guirguis, Laure, 'Vietnam and the Rise of a Radical Left in Lebanon, 1962–1976', *Monde(s). Histoire, Espaces, Relations* 14, 2 (2018): 225–44.
Guirguis, Laure, 'May '68 and the Arab New Left: Transnational Entanglements at a Time of Disruption', *Critical Historical Studies* (under review).
Halliday, Fred, *Arabia Without Sultans* (London: Penguin, 1974).
Hammad, Hanan, 'Arwa Salih's The Premature: Gendering the History of the Egyptian Left', *Arab Studies Journal* 24, 1 (2016).
Hamza, Raouf H., *Communisme et Nationalisme en Tunisie de la 'Libération' à l'Indépendance (1943–1956)* (Tunis: Université de Tunis I, 1994).

Hanieh, Adam, *Lineages of Revolt: Issues of Contemporary Capitalism in the Middle East* (Chicago: Haymarket Books, 2013).

Hanieh, Adam, *Capitalism and Class in the Gulf Arab States* (New York: Palgrave Macmillan, 2011).

Hanssen, Beatrice, *Critique of Violence: Between Poststructuralism and Critical Theory* (London: Routledge, 2000).

Hanssen, Jens and Max Weiss (eds), *Arabic Thought against the Authoritarian Age: Towards an Intellectual History of the Present* (Cambridge: Cambridge University Press, 2018).

Haugbølle, Sune, 'The New Arab Left and 1967', *British Journal of Middle Eastern Studies* 44, 4 (2017): 497–512.

Hendrickson, Burleigh, 'March 1968: Practicing Transnational Activism from Tunis to Paris', *International Journal of Middle Eastern Studies* 44 (2012): 755–74.

Horn, Gerd-Rainer and Padraic Kenney (eds), *Transnational Moments of Change: Europe 1945, 1968, 1989* (Lanham, MD: Rowman & Littlefield, 2004).

Ibrahim, Mohsen, *Limadha? Munazzama al-ishtirakiyyin al-lubnaniyyin. Haraka al-qawmiyyin al-'arab min al-fashiyya ila al-nasiriyya. Naqd wa taḥlil* [The organisation of the Lebanese socialists, why? The Arab nationalist movement from fascism to Nasserism. Critique and analysis] (Beirut: Dar Al-Tali'a, 1970).

Ismael, Tareq Y., *The Communist Movement in the Arab World* (Abingdon: Routledge, 2005).

Jabar, Faleh A. (ed.), *Post-Marxism and the Middle East* (London: Saqi, 1997).

Jabri, Vivienne, 'Critical Thought and Political Agency in Time of War', *International Relations* 19, 1 (2005): 70–9.

Jian, Chen, Martin Klimke, Masha Kirasirova, Mary Nolan, Marilyn Young and Joanna Waley-Cohen (eds), *The Routledge Handbook of the Global Sixties Between Protest and Nation-Building* (Oxford: Routledge, 2018).

Kazziha, Walid, *Revolutionary Transformation in the Arab World: Habash and his Comrades from Nationalism to Marxism* (London: Charles Knight, 1975).

Khuri-Makdisi, Ilham, *The Eastern Mediterranean and the Making of Global Radicalism, 1860–1914* (Berkeley: University of California Press, 2010).

Le Foll-Luciani, Pierre-Jean, 'Algérianisation et Radicalisation. Les Étudiants Communistes de l'Université d'Alger (1946–1956)', *Cahiers d'Histoire. Revue d'Histoire Critique* 126 (2015): 97–117.

Le Foll-Luciani, Pierre-Jean, *Les Juifs Algériens dans la Lutte Anticoloniale. Trajectoires Dissidentes (1934–1965)* (Rennes: PUR, 2015).

Manna, Haytham, *Les Parias de Damas* (Paris: Decitre, 2017).

Mokhtefi, Elaine, *Algiers, Third World Capital: Freedom Fighters, Revolutionaries, Black Panthers* (London: Verso, 2018).

Mroué, Karim, *Un Demi-siècle d'Utopie: Mémoires d'un Dirigeant de la Gauche Libanaise* (Paris: L'Harmattan, 2011): 12–15.

Nassar, Maha Tawfiq, *Brothers Apart: Palestinian Citizens of Israel and the Arab World* (Stanford: Stanford University Press, 2017).

Mary Nolan, 'Where was the Economy in the Global Sixties?', in Chen Jian, Martin Klimke, Masha Kirasirova, Mary Nolan, Marilyn Young and Joanna Waley-Cohen (eds), *The Routledge Handbook of the Global Sixties Between Protest and Nation-Building* (Oxford: Routledge, 2018).

Olson, Robert W., *The Ba'th and Syria, 1947 to 1982: The Evolution of Ideology, Party, and State* (Princeton: The Kingston Press, 1982).

Pennock, Pamela, *The Rise of the Arab American Left: Activists, Allies, and Their Fight against Imperialism and Racism, 1960s–1980s* (Chapel Hill: University of North Carolina Press, 2017).

The Project on Middle East Political Science (POMEPS), *Arab Uprisings. New Opportunities for Political Science* (Washington: Institute for Middle East Studies, 2012), <https://pomeps.org/wp-content/uploads/2012/06/POMEPS_Conf12_Book_Web.pdf> (last accessed 30 October 2019).

Rabinovich, Itamar, *Syria under the Ba'th, 1963–66: The Army Party Symbiosis* (New Brunswick: IPST, 1972).

Ramzy, Farah, *Renegotiating Politics on Campus. Students in post-2011 Egypt*, PhD dissertation (Lausanne: University of Lausanne, 2019).

Ross, Kristina, *May '68 and Its Afterlives* (Chicago: University of Chicago Press, 2004).

Roussillon, Alain, 'Égyptianité, Arabité, Islamité: La Recomposition des Référents Identitaires', *Égypte/Monde Arabe* 1st series, 11 (1992): 77–136.

Sadeghi-Boroujerdi, Eskander, 'The Origins of Communist Unity: Anti-Colonialism and Revolution in Iran's Tri-Continental Moment', *British Journal of Middle Eastern Studies* 45 (2018): 796–822.

Salih, Arwa, *The Stillborn: Notebooks of a Woman from the Student-Movement Generation in Egypt*, trans. Samah Selim (London: Seagull Books, 2018).

Sawah, Wael, 'Hikayat bila bidayat [Stories without beginning]'. *Daraj*, 31 March 2018–date.

Sayigh, Yezid, 'Reconstructing the Paradox: The Arab Nationalist Movement, Armed Struggle, and Palestine, 1951–1966', *Middle East Journal* 45, 4 (1991): 609–29.

Seurat, Michel, 'Le Quartier de Bâb *Tebbâné* à Tripoli (Liban): Étude d'une Asabiyya Urbaine', *Mouvements Communautaires et Espaces Urbains au Machreq* (Beyrouth: Presses de l'Ifpo, 1985).

Sing, Manfred, 'Brothers in Arms: How Palestinian Maoists Turned Jihadists', *Die Welt des Islams* 1 (2011): 1–44.

Suri, Jeremi, *Power and Protest: Global Revolution and the Rise of Détente* (Cambridge, MA: Harvard University Press, 2003).

Takriti, Abdel Razzaq, *Monsoon Revolution: Republicans, Sultans, and Empires in Oman 1965–1976* (Oxford: Oxford University Press, 2013).

Takriti, Abdel Razzaq, 'Political Praxis in the Gulf: Ahmad al-Khatib and the Movement of Arab Nationalists, 1948–1969', in Jens Hanssen and Max Weiss (eds), *Arabic Thought against the Authoritarian Age: Towards an Intellectual History of the Present* (Cambridge: Cambridge University Press, 2018).

Traboulsi, Fawwaz, *Surat al-fata bi al-ahmar: ayyam fi al-silm wa al-harb* [Portrait of a young man in red: days in peace and war] (Beirut: Dar Riad el-Rayyes, 1997).

Traverso, Enzo, *Left-wing Melancholia: Marxism, History, and Memory* (Columbia: Columbia University Press, 2017).

Warburg, Gabriel, *Islam, Nationalism and Communism in a Traditional Society* (London: Frank Cass, 1978).

Weiss, Max, 'Left Out: Notes from the Struggle over Middle East Intellectual History', *International Journal of Middle East Studies* 51 (2019): 305–8.

Weiss, Max, 'Genealogies of Baathism: Michel Aflaq, between Personalism and Arabic Nationalism', *Modern Intellectual History* (2019): 1–32.

Michael Werner and Bénédicte Zimmermann, 'Penser l'Histoire Croisée: Entre Empirie et Réflexivité', *Annales. Histoire, Sciences Sociales* 1 (2003): 7–36.

Westad, Odd, *The Global Cold War: Third World Interventions and the Making of Our Times* (New York: Cambridge University, 2005).

Wright, Timothy, 'Mutant City: On Partial Transformations in Three Johannesburg Narratives', *Novel. A Forum on Fiction* 51, 3 (2018): 417–37.

Younes, Miriam, 'A Tale of Two Communists: The Revolutionary Projects of the Lebanese Communists Husayn Muruwa and Mahdi 'Amil', *Arab Studies Journal* 24, 1 (2016).

1

UNFORGETTABLE RADICALISM: *AL-ITTIHAD*'S WORDS IN HEBREW NOVELS

Orit Bashkin

Introduction

In August 2012, the novelist and former communist Sami Michael (born 1926) created a local storm when he delivered a speech on ethnic relations in Israel. The left-leaning Israeli blog 972+, which later published it, called the speech 'a "cri du coeur" that is full of love and grief'. In his speech, Michael, who was born and raised in Iraq and migrated to Israel in 1949, voiced important criticisms of the Israeli Left itself, as he reflected on the rift between Jews of Middle Eastern descent (known as 'Mizrahim' or 'Eastern Jews') and European Jews (known as 'Ashkenazim'):

> Until today, more than sixty years after the state of Israel was established, this rift has not been mended. Mentally, it takes the form of racism, and socially it expresses the gap in status . . .The salon leftists – and in Israel, it is worth noting, the leftists have never left the salon – repudiated Eastern Jewry as expendable 'raw material', or in the Communist jargon of that time: the 'lumpen-proletariat'. This was in spite of the fact that immigrants from Egypt, Lebanon and Bulgaria, and especially from Iraq, held an impressive Communist record from their countries of origin. The Communist establishment in Israel treated these immigrants with blatant arrogance. At the beginning of the 1950s there were immigrant camps in which 20 per cent of their

> dwellers voted for the Communist Party in the Knesset. Not one of them was promoted to a position of any value in the party. The Central Committee of the Communist Party was and still remains today more 'purified' of Mizrahi Jews than any other establishment in the state. The suspicion and arrogance towards the Mizrahi communities was a solid impenetrable barrier in the ranks of the Communist Party.[1]

Michael concluded that the country's discriminatory attitude towards Mizrahi Jews and Arabs qualified it for the title of 'most racist state'.[2] That a former communist and the head of the Association for Civil Rights in Israel should have such opinions is perhaps unsurprising. That the speech was delivered at the opening of an international conference of the Association for Israel Studies at Haifa University was unheard of. Some, in the minor scandal that ensued, complained that it was the most anti-Israeli speech they have ever heard.

Mizrahi activist and filmmaker Refael Balulu disparaged the many critics of this speech in an editorial he wrote for the newspaper *Haaretz*. Balulu rightly recognised the reasons for the duplicitous rage directed at Michael; here stood the Mizrahi critic, and he used the platform given to him not to thank his Ashkenazi patrons but rather to underscore the most uncomfortable truths in the Israeli public sphere. However, Balulu also missed an important point when he contextualised Michael's opinions within the Mizrahi cultural revival which typified the Israeli 2010s and of which Balulu was a part.[3] Michael's viewpoints were, in fact, also formulated in response to the historical context of the 1950s and 1960s, when Michael was a radical Arab Jewish activist in the Israeli state. Written in 2012, a time when a majority of Mizrahi Jews were voting for the right-wing Likud Party and other conservative, rightist and religious parties, Michael's speech faulted the Israeli Left for not keeping this radical spirit alive.

[1] <https://972mag.com/author-sami-michael-israel-is-the-most-racist-state-in-the-industrialized-world/52602/> (last accessed 2 March 2020).

[2] <https://www.haaretz.com/israel-news/author-israel-can-claim-the-title-of-the-most-racist-state-in-the-developed-world.premium-1.443908> (last accessed 2 March 2020).

[3] <https://www.haaretz.com/sami-michael-the-true-zionist-1.449051> (last accessed 2 March 2020).

This chapter reconstructs the Arab Jewish and leftist contexts Michael was once a part of, and the contexts he longed for in 2012. It argues that radical thought was prevalent in the Israel of the 1950s, 1960s and 1970s, although it was expressed in different genres. Moreover, the radicalism that was typical of the Arabic writings of Mizrahi Jews in the early 1950s also characterised their works even after they left the official communist circles and adopted Hebrew as their literary language, and it remained firm in their new literary works. In the late 1960s and early 1970s, Iraqi Jewish writings in Israel articulated a critique of ethnic nationalism, expressed much empathy with Palestinians, and conceptualised the relationships between different forms of racism in Israel. Thus, while other scholars consider the radical writings of Mizrahi Jews in Arabic as a 'phase' in their Israeli careers,[4] I see their writing in both Hebrew and Arabic as a continuum, which called for a humanistic and leftist vision.

A Painful Welcome

During the years 1950 and 1951, over 123,000 Jews left Iraq. Following a right-wing nationalist campaign that called for Iraqi Jewish citizens in Iraq to be treated as Israel had treated the Palestinians in Israel, and an intensive Israeli campaign aimed at the migration of Iraqi Jews, this community was forced to leave a motherland in which its members had resided for over a thousand years. The community in Israel was poverty-stricken due to 1951 Iraqi legislation that froze most of their assets in Iraq. Since the state of Israel lacked the financial resources to attend to the most minimal needs of the newcomers, these migrants were settled in transit camps, where Jews from Iraq, as well as other Middle Eastern countries and Europe, resided in tents and wooden shacks and suffered chronic unemployment. Prior to its migration to Israel, the Iraqi Jewish community was an affluent one; many of its members integrated into the Iraqi upper and middle classes and contributed to the country's Arab culture. In Israel, Iraqi Jews became part of the urban poor; in the transit camps, they had to endure poor food rations, horrendous sanitary conditions, an acute absence of educational and medical services and discrimination by the state establishment, especially in its labour and

[4] Berg, *Exile from Exile*; Berg, *More and More Equal.*

welfare bureaux, because of their Arab culture. The ruling Labour Zionist Party in Israel, MAPAI (*mifleget po'eley erez israel*, The Party of the Workers of the Land of Israel), used its power to ensure the political obedience of the migrants.[5]

MAKI (Hebrew, *miflaga komunistit israelit*; Arabic, *al-hizb al-shuyu'i al-isra'ili*), a party established in 1948, emerging from pre-state Jewish and Arab communist parties and led by Jewish and Palestinian communists, addressed the needs of these newcomers. MAKI was the only legal a-Zionist, and at times anti-Zionist, party in Israel, and it served as the political voice and cultural hub for many Palestinians, who became Israeli citizens after the Arab defeat in the 1948 war. The Palestinian community was severely traumatised, as most of its members were displaced and exiled during the war; in addition to this excruciating trauma, they now lived under a harsh military regime which severely limited their movement and labour rights.[6] While the state, on the basis of the models it inherited from the British, tried to cultivate docile Palestinian religious and conservative elites and silence any criticism articulated by the Palestinians, MAKI's Arab members articulated a different vision of Palestinian politics in Israel, a vision of equality and social justice.[7] The state's Labour Zionist leadership treated MAKI as a national pariah, greatly fearing its influence among the Palestinians and disenfranchised Jews. Despite the state's massive anti-communist campaign, Iraqi Jews joined the Communist Party. Some were communists already in Iraq, while others were motivated by the harsh living conditions in Israel.[8] MAKI, in fact, was very active in the transit camps, organising demonstrations and election campaigns. The fact that it was also a party with a rich platform for writing and publishing in Arabic very much appealed to the Arabised Iraqi Jews, and many wrote for Arabic publications in Israel. The most important platform was literary journals. As Maha Nassar has showed in a seminal study, Iraqi

[5] Bashkin, *New Babylonians*; Bashkin, *Impossible Exodus*; Bashkin, 'Unholy Pilgrims in a New Diaspora'; Bashkin, 'Arabic Thought in the Radical Age'; Rejwan, *The Jews of Iraq*.

[6] Robinson, *Citizen Strangers*; on the Palestinian citizens of Israel see also Nassar, *Brothers Apart*.

[7] Robinson, *Citizen Strangers*; Beinin, *Was the Red Flag Flying There*.

[8] Zilkha, *Al-sahayuniyya*; Bashkin, *New Babylonians*, 141–83.

Jews invigorated Arabic cultural and literary activities in the Communist Party's literary journal, *al-Jadid*.[9] Indeed, *al-Jadid* offered lengthy discussions of culture, politics, hegemony, self-criticism and literature, in addition to short stories and poems.

Another vital platform was *al-Ittihad*, which was founded in May 1944 by the Palestinian communists Emile Habiby, Emile Toma and Fu'ad Nassar. The paper was shut down during the British mandate in February 1948, but was revived four years later under the Israeli state. The newspaper was heavily censored and banned on many occasions (in fact, its successful appeal to the Israeli Supreme Court against its ban following an article critical of American politics in Korea is considered a landmark in the battle for free speech in Israel). Over the years, some of the most prominent Palestinian intellectuals of the time, such as Mahmoud Darwish, Samih al-Qasim, Tawfiq Tubi and Tawfiq Zayyad, wrote for it.[10]

Al-Ittihad reached out to Mizrahi Jews in general, and Iraqi Jews in particular, offering a useful platform for their demands. The paper featured stories and essays by Iraqi Jewish communists Sami Michael (under the pen name Samir al-Marid), Musa Huri (b. 1922) (under the pen name Abu al-Sharbat), Ishaq Kaflawi (b.1925), Menashe Khalifa (b.1927) and Shim'on Ballas (b.1930). All addressed the horrendous living conditions of Iraqi Jews; Khalifa and Kaflawi also wrote poetry in the Iraqi Jewish vernacular, while Ballas penned short stories about the impossible situation in the transit camps.[11] Sami Michael, a member of the newspaper's editorial board, reported on social conditions in the transit camps and the situation of Arab villages in which Palestinian residents suffered the military regime, and published literary works in Arabic. Emile Habiby was the first to discover Michael's talents; when Michael published an article challenging the assertion of David Ben Gurion (MAPAI's leader and Israel's first prime minister) that Israel was a socialist democracy, Habiby, the party's key intellectual, liked the article,

[9] Nassar, *Brothers Apart*.

[10] According to Mustafa Kabha, *al-Ittihad* sold 3,000 copies between 1948 and 1950 and 4,000–5,000 copies between 1952 and 1955, and it accompanied the culture of leaflets, performances in Arabic and popular Arabic poetry among the newcomers. See Kabha, 'Yehudim Mizrahim', 457.

[11] Kabha, 'Yehudim Mizrahim', 456–60.

contacted Michael and encouraged him to write more. He later reached out to Sasson Somekh, David Semah and Shim'on Ballas, who were active in the Party's literary venues.[12]

While Michael, Ballas and Sasson Somekh also wrote for the Hebrew newspaper of the Communist Party, *Kol ha-'am* (Voice of the People), *al-Ittihad* played a different role. First, it was written in Arabic, the mother-tongue of the Iraqi Jews, which, at least in the 1950s, they were unwilling to forsake. Second, since the newspaper protested most vigorously against the policies of the Israeli state towards both Palestinians and Arab Jews, it was the first to articulate a *linkage* between the two communities. Thus, for example, readers of *al-Ittihad* learned about Palestinians who had suffered severe limitation of movement to and from their villages under the military regime; and, concurrently, they read in the very same issues about the sufferings of Mizrahi Jews who were completely isolated in distant transit camps in the north and the south.

Communist writers, Jews and Arabs alike, invested their utmost efforts in cultivating politics of empathy. Their writings in Arabic indicated that Palestinians in Israel could share the pains of displaced Arab Jews and that Arab Jews could sympathise with the Arabs. Together, they would take part in a revolutionary struggle aimed at social justice and equality. As a young journalist, Sami Michael covered the entire country, from the northern transit camps in Afula to the poverty-stricken southern neighbourhoods of Beersheba. He described angrily and lovingly the sufferings of his Iraqi Jewish community, as in dozens of stories he relayed to an Arab readership the deaths of migrants due to the lack of health services in the transit camps, MAPAI's abuse of power given the complete dependence of the migrants on the state, and police brutality. The struggle against these horrendous conditions, as suggested by Eliyahu Zilkha, was to be fought with Arab partners. Thus, Zilkha argued that it was MAKI's role to have the newcomers 'transgress the iron wall' that the powers in Israel erected in order to isolate the newcomers from participating in the general struggle to better their lives.[13]

[12] Ibid., 457. For biographies and memoirs of activists and writers, see Ballas, *Be-guf rishon*; Somekh, *Life after Baghdad*; Somekh, 'Reconciling Two Great Loves'; Michael, *Gevulot ha-ruah*.

[13] *Al-Ittihad* 8, 7 (9 June 1951): 4; the story was entitled 'A Popular Gathering in Rehovot'.

Empathy was grounded in Arab Jewish commitment to an anti-sectarian position with respect to Muslims and Christians, and resistance to the state's attempts to divide the two communities on the basis of sectarianism (*ta'ifiyya*) and family ties (*'a'ailiyya*). Party leaders, most notably Emile Habiby, expressed their fear that Mizrahi Jews in general and Iraqi Jews in particular would be manipulated by right-wing parties, especially Herut, a party which showed great sympathy for the plight of Arab Jews (while denying their Arab culture). In several publications, Habiby pleaded with the Iraqi newcomers to abstain from supporting this party whose racism was no different from the anti-Semitism Iraqi Jews encountered in their homeland.[14]

Many writers stressed the importance of mutual understanding and joint trauma. They did not equate the *nakba* with the Jewish displacement from Iraq, but argued that these conditions created a basis for new affinities and coalitions. The Iraqi Jewish communist Yaqub Qujaman penned a column in response to these realities, contending that the struggle of the newcomers for their just cause was a part of a larger struggle for democracy, peace and true independence. Qujaman observed that the Iraqi migrants were settled in depopulated villages where Arabs used to reside, in order somehow to convince the newcomers that the displacement of the latter was in their best interests. He cautioned the Iraqi Jews against being cannon fodder in Labour Zionism's next war; similarly, their poverty should not be used as a way of asking for further American patronage through financial support which would supposedly rescue them from their misery. The solution, in his opinion, rested in a change of priorities; less funding for military causes and more for education, health and housing. And this solution would be achieved in a joint struggle.[15]

These opinions were also voiced in an exchange *al-Ittihad* held with two Iraqi Jewish readers. In July 1951, in a section dedicated to readers' questions, two Iraqi Jews acknowledged the fact that the Iraqi Communist Party played an active role in defending the rights of Iraqi Jews, and exposing the colonial conspiracy behind their forced migration. The readers then asked for the opinion of *al-Ittihad* concerning the ways in which Iraqi Jews were made to migrate (*tahjir*) to Israel and the relationships between this forced migration

[14] On Habiby's relation to Herut see Bashkin, 'The Barbarism from Within'.

[15] *Al-Ittihad* 8, 14 (28 July 1951): 3.

and the persecution of Muslims in Israel. *Al-Ittihad*'s response essay maintained that the forced migration of Iraqi Jews to Israel and the freezing of their assets should be viewed as a colonial conspiracy orchestrated by Iraq's most powerful politician, the pro-British Nuri al-Sa'id, the Americans and the British. The communists here, in Israel, the editorial added, took pride in the fact that their sister party in Iraq spearheaded the campaign against the persecution of Iraqi Jews. In Israel, continued the essay, the only way to sabotage colonialist ploys to divide Jews and Arabs was for the workers to form a joint struggle with all the democratic powers; this would protect Jews from becoming nothing more than cannon fodder in the service of the grand schemes of colonisers. For this reason, 'in the same manner that the Communist Party in Iraq led the struggle against the persecution of minorities, the Communist Party here is the chief defender of the Arab minority in Israel'.[16]

The essay advised readers that it was criminal to think that the oppression of the Arabs in Israel would yield any benefits for Iraqi Jews. This discrimination was harmful to the economic interests of Israel and caused Jews in neighbouring countries to be threatened and persecuted. While a true democratic state ought to be interested in peace, Zionist parties invested much effort in making Iraqi Jews turn against the Arabs in Israel. However, given that the newcomers from Iraq had seen what national persecution meant, they could see through these racist tactics. David Ben Gurion and his like, as well as their colonialist masters, had managed to displace the majority of the Arab citizens of the country, yet further displacement would never open a space for the absorption of Iraqi Jewish migration; such racism would make matters worse. The battle for democracy should thus be a shared one.[17] While the questions put by the two Iraqis might have been a rhetorical ploy by the newspaper's editors, the role of the piece was nonetheless important. It was meant to convey much empathy with Iraqi Jews, their anguish and their maltreatment, indicating that the editors took to heart their displacement and forced migration. At the same time, it included a cautionary message that displacing another people, the Palestinians, was hardly the solution to their economic hardships and sense of despair.

[16] *Al-Ittihad* 8, 11 (7 July 1951): 2.

[17] Ibid.

In conclusion, during the early 1950s, Iraqi Jewish and Palestinian writers emphasised a politics of empathy as a response to displacement, racism and systematic discrimination. Both Palestinians and Arab Jews lost a great deal when the state of Israel was created. *Al-Ittihad*, *al-Jadid*, and communist activism in general, provided these despairing communities with an anti-sectarian, revolutionary future, which offered some hope for the gloomy present. The simple prose style of the newspapers' articles and the effective message of dozens of social-realist short stories and poems conveyed a clear message, namely, that collaboration, coexistence and activism were the only responsible solutions for the tragedy and pain, and the seemingly unsolvable, ongoing predicament, of Arab Palestinians and Arab Jews in the new state.

Arabic Ideas in Hebrew Letters

The 1960s and 1970s seemed to have created important changes in the lives of Iraqi Jews. Many of the dwellers in the transit camps were resettled, some in slums built on the ruins of the old camps. Other Iraqi Jews bettered their conditions, using the social capital they acquired in Baghdad in order to find a place in Israel society. Their children embraced the ideology of the state. In the 1970s, many turned rightward, ultimately finding political representation in Zionist and right-wing politics. Tragically, as more and more newcomers became integrated into the state, especially after 1967, *al-Ittihad* chronicled the inability to create the joint Arab Jewish front so desired by the Arab Left in the 1950s.

These events seemed to have influenced the party itself. Musa Huri and Menashe Khalifa stayed in the party, leading its Iraqi Jewish branch, which remained active for years, especially in the city of Petah Tikva. However, two important leaders, the Qujaman brothers, left for Europe. In the early 1960s, many of MAKI's Arab Jewish intellectuals, Sasson Somekh, David Semah, Sami Michael and Shim'on Ballas, left the party. After the revelations of Stalin's crimes, the Soviet invasion of Hungary and the disdain shown by MAKI's Ashkenazi leadership towards Mizrahi Jews in the party, Somekh, Semah, Ballas and Michael felt that MAKI remained too rigid in its Stalinism and its automatic support for the Soviet Union. Nonetheless, they still maintained strong friendships with fellow Palestinian communist writers, especially Emile Habiby and Samih al-Qasim. Most importantly, these intellectuals remained loyal to the leftist and humanistic vision outlined by *al-Ittihad* in the 1950s. These politics of empathy, however, were now articulated in Hebrew and were veiled in the guise of literary works. These intellectuals, then, have never forsaken their belief that Arab–Jewish solidarity mattered; that Israeli treated its Arabs and Mizrahim in an appalling fashion; and that the left, in both Israel and Iraq, was the only hope for undoing these policies.

The ideals, nevertheless, were communicated in different modes. Somekh turned to translation, producing dozens of translations of Palestinian and Iraqi poems, now as a professor of Arabic literature at Tel Aviv University. Semah wrote studies of Arabic literature in *al-Karmil*, an Arabic journal he founded as a professor of Arabic literature at Haifa University. Most significantly, Ballas and Michael conveyed empathy with oppressed minorities, in Israel and outside, in the novels and short stories they published during the 1960s and 1970s (and they continued doing so in the coming decades). Michael revisited the transit camps in his novel *All Men Are Equal But Some Are More* (*shavim ve-shavim yoter*, 1974), which depicted the horrors of life in the transit camps. Many of the items he published in *al-Ittihad* as Samir al-Marid now fed his Hebrew text; in fact, many of the stories in the novel were based on actual cases he wrote about in *al-Jadid* and *al-Ittihad*. This was followed by two novels for young adults on the pogrom against Iraq's Jews in June 1941 known as the *Farhud* (*sufa ben ha-dekalim*, 1975) and on the transit camps (*pachonim ve-halomot*, 1979). Michael then returned to the themes of communism and Arab Jewish relations in a novel on the Israeli Communist Party and its Arab and Jewish members entitled *Refuge* (*hasut*, 1977), and in a novel on Arab–Jewish relations in the Iraqi Communist Party as Iraqi Jews were about to depart for Israel, called *A Handful of Fog* (*hofen shel 'arafel*, 1979). All of a sudden, spaces known only to communist activists and Iraqi Jews became familiar to Israeli readers. While none of these novels became a bestseller like Michael's novels from the 1990s, they presented to Israeli readers the realities they feared most, realities that *al-Ittihad* had covered so well in the 1950s: the pains of Palestinian leftists unable to identify with the state and remembering their past homeland (in *Refuge*), the stories of Jewish communists in Baghdad, their heroism and their solidarity with fellow Iraqis (in *A Handful of Fog*), the sufferings of Arab Jews in the transit camps, and the devastating effects of ethnic nationalism, manifested in the *Farhud*, which was the result, in part, of the importation of Nazi ideologies into the Middle East. Unsurprisingly, the novel about the transit camps angered many Ashkenazi readers; the novel on the *Farhud* became recommended reading by the Ministry of Education.[18] But the politics Michael outlined in the 1950s remained steadfast: only empathy and solidarity could be the basis for a shared life in the state of Israel.

Short stories and novels by Shim'on Ballas had much in common with those of Michael and with the writings of *al-Ittihad* in the 1950s. His 1964 novel *The Transit Camp* (*ha-ma'abara*) followed the tormented lives of those who dwelt in an anonymous transit camp. Many of the themes typical of his short stories in Arabic, which appeared in *al-Ittihad* and *al-Jadid*, in particular resistance to the state within the transit camps, appeared in the novel. During the late 1960s and 1970s he published beautiful short stories, many of them dealing with Iraqi Jews in Iraq, the transit camps and the Iraqi Communist Party. Motivated by the realities of the 1950s that still haunted him, he hoped his writings in Hebrew would make a difference. In this context, translation from Arabic into Hebrew became a subversive act:

> I wrote a lot on Arabic literature and culture. I also did the anthology of Palestinian stories that came out in 1969 . . . And the fact is that I began writing about Palestinian literature. No one had heard of Ghassan Kanafani before my translations of his short stories. Emile Habiby was also unknown as a writer when I began writing about him. Although I left the Communist Party in 1961, my political positions remained unchanged and I continued to write on social and cultural issues.[19]

Habiby, Ballas's mentor from the days of *al-Ittihad*, was now an author whose writings Ballas had to introduce to an ignorant Hebrew reading audience (Anton Shammas would eventually become *the* translator of Habiby into Hebrew). In the early 1970s, Ballas completed a PhD thesis at the Sorbonne, which became his book *Arabic Literature under the Shadow of War*, written in French and later translated into Hebrew and Arabic. His fictional works

[18] On the shift of Iraqi Jews to writing in Hebrew, see Berg, *Exile from Exile*, 43–150.

[19] <https://www.wordswithoutborders.org/article/at-home-in-exile-an-interview-with-shimon-ballas>.

in Hebrew were aimed at achieving the same goals he had as an Arab leftist. It was a writing 'without the Judeocentrism that has characterised Hebrew literature'.[20] Ballas did feel that he had to reconstruct himself and re-create a new subject through a borrowed language, and yet he believed that his narratives were utterly different from the state's ideology:

> Zionist ideology is essentially an Ashkenazi ideology that developed in a different culture, in different surroundings, in a different world and which came to claim its stake here in the Middle East through alienation and hostility towards the surroundings, with a rejection of the surroundings, with no acceptance of the environment. I don't accept any of this, this is all very different from what I am. I am not in conflict with the environment, I came from the Arab environment and I remain in constant colloquy with the Arab environment. I also didn't change my environment. I just moved from one place to another within it. The whole project of a nationalist conception, of Zionist ideology, of the Jewish point of view, the bonds between Jews in the diaspora and Israel, all of this is quite marginal for me and doesn't play a major role, it's not part of my cultural world. I am not in dialogue with the nationalistic or Zionist point of view, nor am I in dialogue with Hebrew literature. I am not conducting a dialogue with them. If anything, I am in dialogue with language itself.[21]

His literary works, then, endeavoured to fend off ideological connections within the language, and to make other contexts known to his readers.[22]

To illustrate how the literary works of Ballas captured the leftist ideology typical of the 1950s, his strong condemnation of ethnic nationalism and the plight of refugees, I want to consider two short stories he wrote in the late 1960s. The themes of these stories are typical of those of works published after 'the turn to Hebrew' of Iraqi leftists in the 1960s and 1970s. I have

[20] <https://www.wordswithoutborders.org/article/at-home-in-exile-an-interview-with-shimon-ballas> (last accessed 2 March 2020).

[21] <https://www.wordswithoutborders.org/article/at-home-in-exile-an-interview-with-shimon-ballas> (last accessed 2 March 2020).

[22] <https://www.wordswithoutborders.org/article/at-home-in-exile-an-interview-with-shimon-ballas> (last accessed 2 March 2020).

chosen to focus on two texts that seemingly shift to other themes; they deal with gender, with oppressed minorities who are neither Palestinians nor Arab Jews, and with genocide. And yet, carefully read, these stories mirror the same notions as those conveyed in *al-Ittihad*: they protest against displacement and forced migration; they focus on oppressed ethnic, social and religious groups at the margins of society; they cherish resistance to state politics; they speak of the pains of displaced people, the urban poor, and those discriminated against because of their racial identity; and they expose the violent meanings of migration and exile. These stories, then, pre-form the politics of empathy that Ballas preached during the 1960s.[23]

Ballas's short story *Farewell Road* (*derech preda*, May 1968) is narrated by a young Jewish communist, Ellie, who is about to report to an Iraqi police station after being summoned for investigation. Suspected materials in French are found in his apartment, and he is now to provide the state with an explanation. The plot takes place as Jews begin to leave Baghdad (around 1950). Fearful for his future, Ellie slowly loses all contact with reality, and the plot is peppered with his dreams and nightmares about his possible – unknown – future.

A respectable clerk who lives in the elite Jewish neighbourhood of Bustan al-Khass, Ellie is nonetheless a frequent visitor to a local brothel, which often serves as a safe house of sorts. His lover, a prostitute by the name of Salima, hides him there in times of trouble. The Madame, Umm Ahmad, is happy to see Ellie returning to her institution after he has avoided it for a while:

> I stood by the Madame, smiling foolishly; she turned her head to the house's inner court, shouting: Ya Salima, *the fugitive* returned! I looked into the court and did not see Salima, and yet here she was, running towards me with open arms. Upon seeing her, I was overtaken by a nervous laughter. She put her arms around my waist, clinging to my body. '*Traitor*, where have you been?'[24] [emphasis mine]

Salima, 'a mythological goddess', is Kurdish and Jewish; she is known as 'Salima the tall'.[25] The arrival at her brothel is represented in the text as a return to a

[23] Berg deals with the two stories I analyse in *Exile from Exile*, 140–3.

[24] Ballas, 'Derech preda', *Mul ha-homa*, 25.

[25] Ibid., 26.

beloved homeland. Salima, moreover, sees forsaking the brothel-turned-homeland as a sign of treason. Treason, in the story, has a double meaning: it is a concept with which the state defines a Jewish communist, and it signifies a man who deserts his beloved. Ellie has mixed feelings about Salima; he occasionally resents her, but most of the time he speaks of her in terms of endearment and gratitude: 'she protected me from my prosecutors'.[26] Now, harsh realities come between them, and she senses that he is about to bid farewell, just as his Jewish community slowly disappears from the Baghdadi landscape. She sadly notes that the other prostitutes 'say that the educated Jews come only to me . . . And now that the Jews are leaving . . . they make my life miserable.'[27] She then insists that Ellie spends his last night with her, despite the clients awaiting her, and the threats of the Madame. He leaves her, only to return a while later to spend the last hours of the night. They discuss his leaving once more:

> I will hide you, Salima said.
> Until when?
> Until you run away.
> And the books? I need them!
> You will get others. I will let your family know that you ran away.
> But I do not want to run away!
> You must. You are being persecuted here. This is not the place for you.
> Where is the place for me?
> This is no place for you. I know; don't laugh.
> I am not laughing.[28]

In the story, very few people know what awaits them in the future. Salima does not know what might happen to her beloved Jews and to her love, Ellie, who might be jailed by the state at any moment, die at the hands of the state, or migrate to Israel as other communists have done. As a communist, he has no place to go, no homeland to welcome him with open arms; only his Kurdish lover and her safe house. He finally leaves the brothel, to wander the streets of Baghdad. He knows that appearing at the police station means his

[26] Ibid., 29.
[27] Ibid., 30.
[28] Ibid., 37.

own vanishing, his parting farewell to Baghdad, its life and his own. He thus chooses to stay with Salima.

We know of prostitutes who hid Jews, especially after a major communist demonstration against Zionism and colonialism in 1946.[29] Here, however, Ballas uses the narrative about the prostitute, who is the only one willing to shelter a Jew, in order to construct the image of the leftist Arab Jew as a man who has no place to go. More broadly, the story captures the same excruciating predicament Iraqis Jews faced: either being persecuted at home or leaving for an unknown future in Israel. The text, moreover, uses the representation of the nation as a woman; it narrows the space of the homeland to that of the brothel, where the nation/goddess resides. The goddess, in this case, however, is a destitute yet proud Kurdish woman, who cares deeply for her communist lover. In the story, she epitomises the resistance and resilience of women in a society where the oppression of the urban poor reigns, and where poor women, especially those belonging to the persecuted Kurdish minority, have no means of making a living.

Ballas also represented the Iraqi nation as a poor woman in his story *Iya*. The story focuses on Zakiyya, a poor Shi'ite woman who works as a nanny for a Jewish family, whose members are about to leave Baghdad for Israel. Having no children of her own, Zakiyya feels that the Jewish family are her closest kin. Her favourite member of the family is a communist youngster who, upon leaving Baghdad, gives her a Qur'an to remember him by.[30] In both stories, leaving the woman-represented-as-nation is seen as a betrayal of a poor woman: Zakiyya the mother figure, and Salima the lover. Both, moreover, serve to underscore the idea that parting from Iraq meant bidding farewell not only to a hostile society but also to memories of childhood, warmth and love. And, just like Ballas's writings in Israel, the story shares the co-operation between the persecuted: those persecuted because of their religion (Jews and Shi'ites), those persecuted because of their ethnicities (Kurds), and those persecuted because of their beliefs (communists). The love, care and shared admiration of their homeland bond together the Jewish

[29] See the interviews with Ballas and Michael in the film *Forget Baghdad*, 2003 (director: Samir; produced by Dschoint Ventschr Filmproduktion).

[30] Ballas, *Keys to the Garden*, 78.

communist and his Iraqi Kurdish lovers, as the state invests its utmost efforts in severing these bonds.

Ballas's representation of the Kurdish prostitute as a symbol of a beloved yet highly dysfunctional Iraqi society relates to important currents in Iraqi Arabic literature, which were discussed in *al-Ittihad.* Iraqi nationalist elites looked upon prostitution as a 'social disease' and occasionally announced campaigns against brothels, seen as a threat to healthy family life and to the social order. Ballas clearly set his text in sharp contrast to these images. At the same time, a wide range of progressive and communist writers focused on the image of the prostitute as connoting love and sympathy, and as a symbol of a failing society. They had learned about the kind-hearted prostitute from the great masters in Europe, from Zola, Tolstoy and Dickens to Brecht. But they also localised these stories so that they fit the particular socio-economic conditions of Iraq. Most noted in this regard is Badr Shakir al-Sayyab's poetic representation of Iraq as a blind prostitute.[31] Ballas, however, has done something quite different. He evokes this image to remind Israeli readers of Baghdadi communism, of a much-needed empathy felt between Jews and Iraqis, and of common human decency. He also reminds Hebrew readers that Jews were not the only victims of the social norms in Iraqi society; others, such as Kurds, the urban poor and destitute women, were also brutalised by the state. In a society that oppressed the Palestinian Arabs, he thus evokes the memory of other persecuted minorities, women and Kurds, to call on different value systems, in Iraq, and in Israel.

Another of Ballas's short stories, *Aunt Ghauni* (*doda ghauni*, January 1967), centres on the relationship between an old Armenian woman and an Iraqi teenager, from when he is four years old up until he is about to finish high-school. The story is narrated in the voice of the teenager. As he child, he is mesmerised by his neighbours, an Armenian couple. While his mother does not welcome his frequent visits to the couple's home, the Armenian woman, Aunt Ghauni, who is childless, treats him with much affection and love. The child is curious about the Armenian house: the music, Aunt Ghauni's beautiful singing voice and the visitors who speak in a foreign language all capture his imagination. When his family leaves the alley where the two families live,

[31] Bahoora, 'The Figure of the Prostitute'.

his mother cries bitter tears. Aunt Ghauni still sees the narrator from time to time when she returns from church, and is happy to see him grow up. As he matures, the narrator witnesses how the Armenian woman ages, especially after bidding the final farewell to her husband. And yet the woman and her community attract him:

> I knew about her fate and the fate of her people; I knew some of them. I admired their industriousness, their silence; their cleanliness. They were strangers in the land, and did not mix much with the people. They barely learned the language of the country. Every Sunday, they wore their finest clothes to church. Their church was tiny and modest; its bells produced flat, swift, joyless sounds. On weekdays, they were busy at their daily work, sharing secrets with each other, reading their journals.[32]

At the end of the story, the Armenians are given the opportunity to leave their homes and return to Armenia. They sell their business happily and are eager to leave. Aunt Ghauni, sadly, cannot leave. She is too old, and she has no relatives in Armenia. She is left alone. The narrator offers to walk her home, where he sees a different Ghauni in an old photo; a cabaret singer, smiling to her orchestra and her admiring audience. Another photo she shows the narrator features a beautiful child, about six years old. It is her daughter. 'They took her . . . by force. "If you don't give her to us, we will kill you and your husband!" They beat me up with a belt made of nails; on my face, on my arms, on everything. I was so sick', she tells the narrator. 'I heard them shouting; she will be a prostitute for the Turks now! And she cried and shouted . . . I hear her cries to this very day.'[33] She then parts from the narrator. 'You are my son. You were a child when you first came to me, and now you are a man! A real man!'

Masterfully, Ballas takes the most horrific Jewish tragedies – genocide, pogroms, loss of loved ones and exile from a homeland – and tells them as the story of another oppressed minority, the Armenians, who dwelt in exile in Iraq after the genocide of the First World War. The exile from a historical homeland, Armenia, and the inability to return to it, are captured in the

[32] Ballas, 'Doda ghauni', *Mul ha-homa*, 57.

[33] Ibid., 58.

image of the old aunt longing for a lost daughter she can never see again. This agonising narrative, however, speaks to the pain of many groups in Israel: fellow Arab Jews, Holocaust survivors and the Palestinians. Ballas, then, situates a story about themes with which his Jewish and Palestinian readers are all too familiar in the context of modern Armenia and modern Iraq. Here, too, he focuses on a woman forced to stay in Iraq as her relatives and friends forsake her, in a way similar to Salima and Zakiyya. The aunt, however, also experiences the pains of migration and loss herself, having been expelled from Armenia.

Noticeably, the Armenians in Iraq have a lifestyle akin to that of Arab Jews in Israel in the 1950s, and to that of many newcomers to Israel in the first decade of its existence. They do not integrate into society; they do not know the local language well; and they remain loyal to a culture and a language destroyed by war and displacement. They are different from migrants to Israel, however, in that they are happy to return to their country of origin. At the same time, the Armenians in Iraq are also similar to Palestinians who, while living in Israel, refuse to integrate with the dominant Hebrew culture and remain faithful to their culture. As with the Armenians, the memories of the past, the longing to return to a desecrated homeland, shape their daily lives and their hopes and visions. And it is an Iraqi Jew who re-creates the histories and voices of these three communities in his writing. His own empathy, with Jews, Arabs, Palestinians, Armenians and Arab Jews, shapes his narrative and the pain and trauma it conveys. Ballas, then, insinuated to his readers that for the Jewish protagonist of his story maturity and growing up meant coming to terms with horrible historical truths. In doing so, he hoped, as his communist peers had hoped in the 1950s, that the pains of oppressed minorities from afar might inspire compassion for oppressed minorities in the present, much closer to home.

Conclusion

Until very recently, the historiography of Mizrahi Jews in Israel told a story of minority groups whose members rose against the state in the riots of Wadi Salib of 1956, when North African Jews paralysed the city of Haifa for a few days, continued into the Black Panthers of the early 1970s, and later exploded with the massive Mizrahi support for Likud, as retaliation against their former labour Zionist oppressors, in the Israeli elections of 1977, and with the sectarian religious and Sephardi parties of the 1980s and 1990s.[34] Revisionist studies, however, show that the resistance of newcomers from Arab lands to state politics began long before, and continued in interesting ways in the 1960s and 1970s; 1967 did not change much in this respect. Iraqi Jews took an active part in many forms of protests in all three decades, although in much greater numbers during the 1950s.[35]

The role of *al-Ittihad*'s writers in these historical dynamics was crucial. As early as the 1950s, Iraqi Jewish and Palestinian writers suggested that Israel was a racist country not just with respect to its Arabs, but also with respect to its Arab Jews, who were deemed second-class citizens and who lived under horrible conditions. Iraqi Jews fought to preserve the Arab culture of the newcomers and create a joint front between them and the Palestinians. In the 1970s, the specificities of the atrocious life in the transit camps had changed. But the leftist agenda, especially the calls for a humane approach to all members of society and the desire to underscore the pains of people discriminated against because of their religion and race, was reformulated by authors like Ballas and Michael, this time in Hebrew. Their Hebrew writing captured the same themes, focusing, sometimes, on transit camps and the abuse of Palestinian rights, and at other times on oppressed gendered, ethnic and social groups within Iraqi society who now represented new dilemmas typical of the Israeli/Palestinian locale. Their writing took a humanistic form, moving back and forth in relation to the realities of Israel-Palestine, whose fortunes, especially after 1967, seemed particularly bleak.

Bibliography

Bahoora, Haytham, 'The Figure of the Prostitute, *Tajdid*, and Masculinity in Anti-Colonial Literature of Iraq', *Journal of Middle East Women's Studies* 11, 1 (March 2015): 42–62.

Ballas, Shim'on, *Be-guf rishon* [In the first person] (Tel-Aviv: ha-Kibbutz ha-me'uhad, 2009).

Ballas, Shim'on, *Mul ha-homa* [Facing the wall] (Ramat-Gan: Agudat ha-sofrim ha-'Ivrim be-Yisrael le-Yad hotsa'at Masadah, 1969).

[34] Chetrit, *Intra Jewish Conflict in Israel.*

[35] Bashkin, 'Unholy Pilgrims in a New Diaspora', 609–22.

Ballas, Shim'on, 'Iya', trans. Susan Einbinder, in Ammiel Alcalay (ed.), *Keys to the Garden: New Israeli Writing* (San Francisco: City Lights, 1996).

Bashkin, Orit, *New Babylonians. A History of Jews in Modern Iraq* (Stanford: Stanford University Press, 2012).

Bashkin, Orit, *Impossible Exodus, Iraqi Jews in Israel* (Stanford: Stanford University Press, 2012).

Bashkin, Orit, 'Unholy Pilgrims in a New Diaspora: Iraqi Jewish Protest in Israel, 1950–1955', *The Middle East Journal* 70, 4 (Autumn 2016): 609–22.

Bashkin, Orit, 'Arabic Thought in the Radical Age: Emile Habibi, the Israeli Communist Party and the Production of Arab Jewish Radicalism, 1946–1961', in Jens Hanssen and Max Weiss (eds), *Arabic Thought against the Authoritarian Age: Towards an Intellectual History of the Present* (Cambridge: Cambridge University Press, 2018): 62–86.

Beinin, Joel, *Was the Red Flag Flying There? Marxist Politics and the Arab–Israeli Conflict in Egypt and Israel, 1948–1965* (Berkeley: University of California Press, 1990).

Berg, Nancy E., *Exile from Exile: Israeli Writers from Iraq* (Albany: State University of New York Press, 1996).

Berg, Nancy E., *More and More Equal: The Literary Works of Sami Michael* (Lanham, MD: Lexington Books, 2005).

Chetrit, Sami Shalom, *Intra Jewish Conflict in Israel: White Jews, Black Jews* (London: New York: Routledge, 2010).

Kabha, Mustafa, 'Yehudim mizrahim ba-'itonut ha-'aravit be-israel, 1948–1967' [Mizrahi Jews in the Arab media in Israel, 1948–1967] *'Iyunim bi-tekumat israel* 16 (2006): 445–561.

Michael, Sami, *Gevulot ha-ruah, sihot 'im ruvik rosenthal* [The bounds of the wind: conversations with Ruvik Rosenthal] (Tel Aviv: ha-Kibbutz ha-me'uhad, 2008).

Nassar, Maha Tawfiq, *Brothers Apart: Palestinian Citizens of Israel and the Arab World* (Stanford: Stanford University Press, 2017).

Rejwan, Nissim, *The Jews of Iraq: 3000 Years of History and Culture* (London: Littlehampton, 1985).

Robinson, Shira, *Citizen Strangers: Palestinians and the Birth of Israel's Liberal Settler State* (Stanford: Stanford University Press, 2013).

'Shenhav, Yehouda, 'The Jews of Iraq, Zionist Ideology, and the Property of the Palestinian Refugees of 1948: An Anomaly of National Accounting', *IJMES* 31, 4 (1999): 605–30.

Shiblak, Abbas, *The Lure of Zion: The Case of Iraqi Jews* (London: Saqi Books, 1986).

Shohat, Ella, *Taboo Memories, Diasporic Voices* (Durham, NC: Duke University Press, 2006).

Smooha, Sammy, *Israel: Pluralism and Conflict* (London: Routledge & Paul Kegan, 1978).

Somekh, Sasson, *Life after Baghdad: Memoirs of an Arab-Jew in Israel, 1950–2000*, trans. Tamar L. Cohen (Brighton: Sussex Academic Press, 2012).

Somekh, Sasson, 'Reconciling Two Great Loves: The First Jewish–Arab Literary Encounter in Israel', *Israel Studies* 4, 1 (1999): 1–21.

Zilkha, Yusuf Harun, *Al-sahayuniyya, 'aduwat al-'arab wa al-yahud* [Zionism: Enemy of the Arabs and the Jews] (Baghdad: Matba'at dar al-hikma, 1946).

2

BEATING HEARTS: ARAB MARXISM, ANTI-COLONIALISM AND LITERATURES OF COEXISTENCE IN PALESTINE/ ISRAEL, 1944–60

Hana Morgenstern

Introduction

In 1953, the Iraqi Jewish writer Sami Michael penned an editorial celebrating *al-Ittihad*, a Palestinian paper that had greatly influenced the Communist Party intellectuals in Baghdad. The newspaper was founded in 1944 by Palestinian communists Fu'ad Nassar, Emile Habiby and Emile Tuma, and sought to connect the struggle for Palestinian national independence with antifascism, communist internationalism and anti-colonialism.[1] Michael describes how the paper was smuggled into Iraq and the communist underground,[2] travelling 'with the youth through Baghdad's neighbourhoods and streets, tree-shaded park benches and busy cafes, its contents illuminated by the glow of an electric lamp inside a comrade's house'.[3] Communist newspapers, Michael notes, were characterised by readers as 'beating hearts' (*al-qulub*

[1] Nassar, *Brothers Apart*, 40; Bashkin, this volume.

[2] Communism was illegal in Iraq at the time. The article glorifies the risks taken by those who flouted the secret service and the police in order to transport and read the newspaper, despite the fact that a number of them were thrown into prison.

[3] Michael, 'Al-jarida al-atiya' min wara al-hudud. Unless otherwise noted, all translations are mine.

al-nabitha), organs that circulated ideas and news between movements in the region.[4] Like many of these newspapers, *al-Ittihad* circulated to various cities in the Arab world, featuring local news, essays, editorials, short stories and poems, educating readers through translation and publication of key Marxist texts, and reporting on global and regional political struggles. In the following passage Michael reflects upon *al-Ittihad*'s role in the political education of young communists in Baghdad:

> We used to rub our eyes and look at the real Baghdad, the barefoot Baghdad that suffers from trachoma and anaemia, the forgotten Baghdad whose geography has not been mapped and whose history is not discussed. The Baghdad that sleeps on the bridge walkways when night comes, where swarms of flies fight over dry breadcrumbs. We did not have to don new glasses to discover this truth. We merely had to destroy the old, fake glasses, the glasses of tradition, fear, selfishness and ignorance. *Al-Ittihad*, arriving from afar, helped us to destroy these glasses and rid ourselves of the short-sightedness that was imposed on us.[5]

This passage underscores the pedagogical and collective-making power of left newspapers in the heyday of communism and decolonisation, as well as the interconnected visions of Palestinian and Iraqi Jewish Communists as Arab Marxists. It was published on the ninth anniversary of *al-Ittihad* a few years after Sami Michael joined the newspaper's editorial board when he fled from Baghdad to Palestine/Israel.

Like Michael, other Arab Jewish intellectuals who had been involved in the Left in the Arab world joined the Israeli Communist Party (MAKI) and became involved with its Palestinian-led Arabic-language publications, actively collaborating with the Palestinian intelligentsia on work in *al-Ittihad* and on the MAKI-sponsored cultural journal *al-Jadid* (established by *al-Ittihad* in 1951 and published independently from 1953), whose mission was to form an anti-colonial literature and culture of resistance that would constitute the core of a popular political movement. Throughout the 1950s and early 1960s, major Palestinian and Mizrahi writers and intellectuals such as Jabra

[4] Ibid.

[5] Ibid.

Nicola, Sami Michael, Shim'on Ballas, Emile Habiby, Emile Tuma, Samih al-Qasim, David Semah, Mahmoud Darwish and Hana Ibrahim would draw on their common connection as internationalist Marxists of the Arab world and their common mission to combat the colonial erasure of committed Arabic culture and develop an anti-colonial Arabic alternative to the prevailing culture and literature of Zionism and ethnic separatism during the 1950s and 1960s. They utilised the journal, as well as popular Communist organising strategies such as intellectual clubs and festivals, to promote Arabic literacy, cultural education and the formation of a literary scene after the destruction of the Palestinian *nakba*. Simultaneously, they strove to form a Palestinian-Jewish literary oeuvre made up of short stories, poetry, criticism and educational writing on heritage, which supported the goals of combating cultural erasure, military occupation, poverty and racism, and supporting democratic coexistence. The tension between these goals and the de facto segregation of Palestinians and Jews is dynamic in the journal, as is the struggle to define the precarious position of Arab Jews in relation to the Israeli mainstream, on the one hand, and to the Palestinian minority on the other. Nonetheless, in the years to follow, a shared Palestinian-Jewish Arabic-language literature – which was simultaneously engaged with the reconstruction of Arabic cultural life and with shaping a Palestinian-Jewish aesthetics – was fostered by these collaborations.

Radical Networks and Affiliations

How are we to understand what led these intellectuals to share in a politico-cultural vision, given Zionism's hegemony among Israeli Jews after 1948 and the major difference between Arab Jewish and Palestinian communities in their relationship with Zionist rule? I propose to read this collaboration in light of a cluster of interconnected histories that provided alternative imaginaries for Palestinians and Arab Jews in their opposition to Zionist, colonial paradigms. Broadly, these alternatives are rooted in the regional and international networks of Marxism, communism, pan-Arabism and anti-colonialism, which were fundamental to political developments in the Middle East and Africa during the first six decades of the twentieth century. This milieu fundamentally shaped the political, social and cultural world views of the intellectuals involved in this movement, tied them to local and international progressive movements, enabled them to think about democracy and liberation across national and religious borders, and exposed them to an oeuvre of progressive Arabic and international literature. Drawing on the coexistence of historic Palestine, communists spent two decades in an internationalist Palestinian–Jewish struggle against partition and for a state for all its inhabitants within the Palestine Communist Party (PCP) and the National Liberation League (NLL). During the same period, the Iraqi Jews who later joined the party were part of a communist and leftist literary culture that celebrated the confluence of Arab and Jewish identities and vociferously opposed Zionism. The culture of Arab–Jewish coexistence resonated with their experience in the Iraqi Communist Party as well as with the national state of affairs that Jews had been accustomed to in Iraq before the 1940s.[6] As Bashkin notes, Iraqi Jews had long been integral participants in Iraqi nationalism and in the development of Arabic intellectual and literary life. Jewish intellectuals had begun defining themselves as 'Arab-Jews' during the monarchic period beginning in 1921, demonstrating that they 'not only considered themselves citizens of the new nation of Iraq but [had] also adopted a new Arab ethnicity'.[7] Ironically, communist Jews of the Arab world, who embodied the culture and life-world of progressive Arab–Jewish coexistence that the PCP struggled to form, only joined the local movement after 1948.

Beginning in 1947, the Palestinian *nakba*, the Arab–Israeli war and the establishment of the state of Israel brought about the near-destruction of Palestinian society and culture, while setting in motion events that would also lead to the demise of the Jewish community in the Arab world. Although these two communities suffered from different modes of colonial exploitation under the Zionist establishment, they were both subject to anti-Arab racism, Orientalism and cultural colonisation, including the forced erasure of Arabic language, literature and heritage.[8] Palestinian intellectuals bolstered Arab Jewish understanding of the importance, and the possibility, of an

[6] Bashkin, *New Babylonians*, Ch. 5.

[7] Ibid.

[8] For an analysis of the colonial position of Jews of the Arab world in Israel see Shohat, 'Sephardim in Israel', 1; Massad, 'Zionism's Internal Others'; Orit Bashkin, *Impossible Exodus*.

anti-colonial initiative that resisted the erasure of Arabic and the cleaving of the Arab Jewish identity; Iraqi Jewish writers and intellectuals likewise supplied Palestinians intellectuals with regional and cultural solidarity and with literary materials from the burgeoning Arabic literary scene in Baghdad.[9]

Tracing these complex lines draws our attention to the regional history of Arab Marxism, internationalism and the communist parties in the Arab world, and to various local and regional radicalisms, components that shaped this application of Marxism, anti-colonialism and internationalism in Palestine/Israel. An analysis of these intersections engages directly with the relationship between micro and macro histories of the Left raised by the editor of this volume, as well as concomitant calls to deprovincialise Marxism from its Western European orientation and identify its specific contours within histories of the Middle East and the Global South.[10] In this vein, this essay will attempt to provide a deeper understanding of how universal principles and international streams interacted with particular and locally grounded circumstances, resulting in new and distinct cultural legacies.

For Palestinian communist intellectuals who remained in Israel after 1948, the cultural imagination of coexistence in Palestine was fundamentally informed by internationalism and by the twenty-year struggle for a democratic state waged by the Palestine Communist Party (PCP) and the National Liberation League (NLL) between 1929 and 1947. During this period, Jewish and Palestinian Arab communists working in Palestine believed that by building solidarity between their communities, they could form a political front capable of ousting the British colonisers, while combating the Zionist and Arab reactionaries whom they saw as agents of imperialism. However, designating class as the central form of shared interest between them did not successfully unite the two communities, whose political affiliations and analyses varied significantly. Nationalist conflicts between Palestinians and parts of the Jewish membership, especially around the 1936 Arab revolts, gave rise to political pressures that led to a 1943 split in the Party. Despite these events, the factions that emerged from that split continued to adamantly oppose partition and demand the formation of a democratic, Arab-Jewish state. After

[9] See Assadi, *Short Fiction*, 19.

[10] See for example Harootunian, *Marx After Marx*; Liu, *East-Asian Marxisms*.

the establishment of Israel, the newly re-formed Israeli Communist Party (MAKI) became even more embroiled in the tug-of-war between nationalism and internationalism. On the one hand, it supported the establishment of Israel and capitulated to partition under the Soviet line that viewed Israel as an anti-imperial force in the region; and on the other, it continued to oppose Zionism, fighting for Palestinian national determination and civil equality.[11] The complex position of Arab communists at this moment is well-expressed by Budeiri, who argues that the twenty-odd years during which Palestinian and Jewish communists 'waged a fierce struggle against the establishment of a [Jewish] "national home" and the partitioning of Palestine' attested to the fact that the last-minute acceptance of the partition plan in 1947 was not due to 'any internal ideological revision' but rather was a capitulation to the pressures of Soviet foreign policy, as well as to overwhelming political circumstances.[12]

In addition to its political roots in the Communist movement, many aspects of *al-Jadid* and the surrounding literary scene were influenced by the earlier programme featured in publications such as the NLL's journal *al-Ghad* and inspired by leftist Palestinian culture in the country before 1948. *Al-Ghad* was a theoretical, cultural and literary Marxist journal engaged in the local Palestinian scene, publishing anti-colonial Palestinian poets of the period such as Ibrahim Tuqan and Abu Salma. It was modelled on other Arab communist party journals that were designed to broaden the local communist movement by rooting Marxism in local politics and culture in order to make it accessible to a larger audience. Like *al-Jadid*, *al-Ghad* sought to attract a young intelligentsia to the party by creating a bridge between Marxism and the radical political and intellectual milieu. The journal boasted a literary and cultural section that included local, regional and international poetry and prose in addition to cultural criticism and articles on socialist realism. It also published theoretical introductions to Marxism and Marxist analysis of Arabic-Islamic heritage. In addition, from 1944 onwards, *al-Ittihad* regularly published realist, popular prose, as well as poetry that documented political resistance and the conditions of local communities. Even after 1953, short literary works

[11] Beinin, *Was the Red Flag Flying There?*, 125.

[12] Budeiri, *The Palestine Communist Party*, 115.

continued to complement and enrich journalism in the newspaper, although *al-Jadid* became the central Arabic cultural organ of the movement.

A Culture from the Ashes: Literary-Political Reconstruction in the Formative Years of *al-Jadid*

Al-Ittihad was the only pre-1948 Arabic-language newspaper that was able to resume publishing after the 1948 war; after a shutdown that lasted a number of months, it reopened in October 1948. During the war Habiby briefly escaped Haifa, his native city and the seat of the headquarters for the Communist Party; upon his return he joined the party and the editorial committee of *al-Ittihad*, which was in the process of becoming MAKI's communist Arabic-language newspaper. The Palestinian society that Habiby had been active in organising before the war had virtually disappeared; in Haifa it had been reduced from 75,000 to 3,000 Palestinians, almost all of its political leadership had fled, and only a handful of intellectuals and writers remained inside Israeli territory.

Habiby continued to be a chief figure and driving force behind *al-Ittihad* and *al-Jadid*, where he was a prolific cultural critic, journalist and editor and, later, a celebrated fiction writer. Having joined the Communist Party at the age of fourteen he rose to a prominent leadership position within MAKI, serving as a member of the Israeli Knesset. Tuma, who had also fled during the war, joined Habiby on *al-Ittihad*'s editorial board in 1951. Another towering figure in the Palestinian communist movement, Tuma was a Cambridge-educated Marxist historian, political theorist and journalist. The two were joined by the Palestinian intellectual Jabra Nicola, a Trotskyite who had been active in the PCP as a writer, editor, Arabic–Hebrew translator and critic of Stalinist policy during the 1930s. The fourth member of *al-Ittihad*'s editorial committee was Sami Michael, a former member of the Iraqi Communist Party who arrived in Israel in 1949, on the run from the Iraqi government due to his activities in the communist underground in Baghdad.[13] Recounting this story, Michael noted that the first thing he did upon arrival at Haifa airport was to ask for the local Communist Party headquarters.[14] Like Habiby

[13] For an account of Michael's escape from Iraq see Michael, *Gevulot ha-ruah*, 133–7.

[14] Ibid., 125.

and Tuma, Michael had significant background organising in an Arab communist party and working as a writer and editor for its publications, and he began publishing in *al-Ittihad* the same year. Between 1949 and 1953 Sami Michael authored a programmatic essay forecasting the appearance of *al-Jadid* as well as eight stories. Alongside a handful of Palestinian writers publishing in that catastrophic period, he penned socialist realist prose about Palestinians, Jews from the Arab world and Palestinian–Jewish solidarity in Israel/Palestine, pioneering the popular aesthetic that would come to characterise the journal a few years later. His activities also anticipated the intellectual collaboration between Iraqi Jewish and Palestinian intellectuals that was to become part of the magazine's culture and intellectual milieu.

Michael's political background provides an example of the common ground that Palestinian and Iraqi Jewish communists shared as Arab Marxist intellectuals. He integrated quickly into the circle around *al-Ittihad*, reporting on the conditions of the Palestinian villages under military rule, the transit camps, and the difficulties faced by new immigrants who had just arrived in the country from the Arab world.[15] He also worked with Nicola, Habiby and Tuma on the formation of *al-Jadid* and its aesthetic programme, penning a key piece calling for a movement for popular, progressive Arab resistance literature in 1950, which was soon followed by the introduction of *al-Jadid* as a cultural and literary supplement in *al-Ittihad*. The first piece calls for littérateurs to harness popular socialist realist literature in the service of three different areas: internationalism, Arab–Jewish understanding and the mobilisation of a local communist political movement.[16] Michael's fiction undoubtedly drew on the materials of his reportage, which gave him access to Palestinian areas that were out of bounds for Jewish civilians. He was also able to access and write about transit camps, the impoverished immigration camps where many Jews from the Arab world began their life in Israel, which were generally isolated from the main population centres. Living and working among Palestinians in the Wadi Nisnas neighbourhood of Haifa also gave him an intimate knowledge of that community. His *al-Ittihad* stories depicted common issues that Palestinians faced under military governance – regular

[15] Ibid., 142.

[16] Marid, 'Nahwa insha'adab sha'bi taqaddumi 'arabi fi isra'il', 48–9.

identification round-ups, expulsions, land seizures, the plight of refugees and the attempts of the military to turn civilians into informants. Michael's collection was part of a genre of literary works focused on local struggles, and planted the early seeds of a post-'48, popular anti-Zionist style. This style of popular literature, and especially short stories – emphasising narrative documentation of the local communities in terms of culture, habit, language and environs – shaped the work of Palestinian and Iraqi Jewish writers of the journal.

In 1953, in the city of Haifa, *al-Ittihad* (MAKI) launched its first issue of *al-Jadid*, an Arabic literary magazine of society, culture and politics. Habiby's inaugural speech kicked off the event, announcing that the magazine's mission was 'not merely to establish an organisation, but to incite a movement, a literary movement for the people in our land, a movement that begins with *al-Jadid* but does not end with *al-Jadid*'.[17] He then defined the mission of literature in relation to the specificities of the political struggle:

> In order to carry out their nefarious goals in our country and in the Near East, the colonisers and their collaborators create division between the Jewish and the Arab masses, and the policy of national oppression serves them best in this regard. Therefore the mission of popular Arabic literature in our country is to wage a full-fledged battle on national oppression, and to carry to the masses, here and in the Arab world, the message of Arab–Jewish fraternity, expressing manifestations of the common Arab–Jewish struggle in Israel, which is the essence of this connection and of the future of Arab–Jewish relations in this part of the world.[18]

Here Habiby situates anti-colonialism at the centre of *al-Jadid*'s cultural programme, locating Palestinian national oppression and the division of Arabs and Jews as mutually reinforcing political phenomena that enabled colonial modes of rule. The struggle for coexistence was thus intersectionally linked to the national self-determination of Palestinians as an anti-colonial ethics to emulate within cultural production. While this discourse instrumentalised

[17] Habiby, 'Al-insan hadaf al-adab wa mawduʿhu'.

[18] Ibid.

literature in many ways, and produced some prescriptive work, it also provided a blueprint for a series of inspired and dynamic practices that positively shaped the cultural agenda. These included poetic and intellectual exchanges, literary translations, a popular anti-Zionist literary programme that took up the plight of oppressed Palestinian and Jewish communities, and regular features on progressive Arabic culture and heritage.

Literature as News and Public Record

In fiction, and often in poetry as well, writers drew on these tenets of socialist and popular realism from the Soviet Union, the Arab world and the anti-colonial Left to support the conceptualisation of literature as a form of history, news and social documentary. This aesthetic approach was a general feature of socialist realism, and was readily applied by *al-Jadid* to the social and historical documentation of Palestinian society and to the chronicles of Arab Jews living in the transit camp. Likewise, the preservation of language, culture and the historical record became a pressing necessity in light of the Zionist establishment's determination to exclude Arab culture, whether Jewish or Palestinian, from state life.

An emblematic aspect of this project of popular literature was carried out under the banner of a collection of short stories called '*qisas isra'iliyya*' (Israeli Stories), including over thirty pieces published between 1953 and 1956. Addressing a symposium on the realist short story, Jabra Nicola characterised MAKI's Palestinian and Jewish intellectuals as 'Israeli, realist, and revolutionary writers'.[19] While this application of the term 'Israeli' could be seen as potentially assimilationist, the context of the project, coupled with a closer look at the political content of the stories in themselves, demonstrates that this move can more plausibly be understood as entailing a radical, if futile, attempt at de-Zionising and democratising the 'Israeli' cultural space from within: these 'Israeli Stories' included tales such as *Security Breach* (*akhalla bi al-amn*) by Hana Ibrahim, in which a young Palestinian man violates the military curfew to go to work on Christmas Day because he is desperate to procure his marriage dowry; Michael's *The Great Shadow* (*al-zill al-kabir*), in which a group of imprisoned Arab communists encounter a Palestinian

[19] Nicola, 'Al-qissa allati nuriduha', 8.

peasant who is being threatened with torture and expulsion if he does not collaborate with the Israeli army; Jamal Musa's *Blood and Tears* (*dima' wa radhadh*), in which a Holocaust survivor is abused by an Israeli policeman at a demonstration against the Israeli–German Reparations Agreement and eventually begins to imagine the policeman as an SS officer; Michael's *Two Women* (*imra'atayn*), in which a woman being accused of infiltration seeks legal and organisational help from leftist Jewish supporters to advocate for her and her and two young children to stay in the country; and a number of stories by Shim'on Ballas that tell the story of young men struggling to get work in the immigrant transit camps. Thus, under the banner of a people's literature, the 'Israeli Stories' exposed stories of poverty, unemployment, murder and expulsion that took place on the borders and in the underbelly of the state.

Anti-Colonial Heritage

Another aspect of the programme for coexistence was the emphasis on Arabic culture and heritage, as part of which *al-Jadid* featured pieces that traced historical Arab Jewish heritage, for example an article about Maimonides, the Sephardic Jewish philosopher and doctor who lived in Andalusia, Morocco and Egypt during the Middle Ages, aiming to show the influence of Maimonides' writings on Arab philosophy, thereby establishing a historical legacy of Arab–Jewish co-operation.[20] Aiming to recover Maimonides as an Arab Jewish figure, the article highlights how he was a well-integrated member of Jewish society as well as deeply rooted in Arabic culture. Interestingly, the religious persecution that forced Maimonides to leave his native Andalusia is not downplayed in the article, but rather viewed as a result of the religious fanaticism associated with the conflict between Muslims and Christians in an era defined by the Crusades. With a clear eye towards political persuasion, this fanaticism is portrayed as a threat to cultural development and coexistence, and as the outcome of the struggles between foreign powers rather than any internal dynamics of the local society.

Such articles reflected the beginnings of a popular local intellectual and literary agenda, characterised by a comprehensive focus on the popularisation of culture and literature on the basis of Marxist and anti-colonial thought. In

[20] Nicola, 'Musa ibn maymun'.

the first six months of the journal's publication the reader encountered essays that applied these popular frameworks to Arabic literature, heritage and culture. A piece by the Iraqi Jewish intellectual Ibrahim Khayyat reviewed works of contemporary Iraqi poetry.[21] Others examined Islamic history and classical Arabic culture, as in a critical piece by Jabra Nicola analysing the Kharajite revolt as a proto-Marxist, revolutionary historical event.[22] Arabic literature, art, folklore and heritage were made available to the general public, in line with a detailed programme laid out by Emile Habiby.[23] In an article by Emile Tuma, *al-Jadid*'s programme is distinguished from the establishment's approach to Arabic culture. Tuma critiques the Orientalist and chauvinist colonialist discourse of the Israeli establishment's new Arabic publishing house, The Arabic Book Chest (*sunduq al-kitab al-ʿarabi*), insisting that the chauvinism of its founders could only deter true cultural exchange.[24]

Poetry as Missive and Resistance: The Festivals

Of all *al-Jadid*'s ventures, the poetry festivals it organised have been accorded the greatest role in popularising literature and fomenting political resistance among the Palestinian population in Israel. Festivals were held in cities like Haifa and Acre, but were also recurrently arranged illegally in Palestinian villages under military rule, nevertheless attracting hundreds and sometimes thousands of participants. According to multiple accounts, the village festivals were often held in the town square, around which a crowd of people would gather, some carrying kerosene lanterns, while others watched from their windows or rooftops.[25] Audience members would listen, often for hours, while local poets recited verses on topics such as the struggles of the villagers and peasants, working-class solidarity, the plight of the refugees, massacres and land dispossession, and revolutionary struggles in other parts of the world. Unlike some of the poetry in *al-Jadid*'s pages, where poets had

[21] Khayyat, 'Al-ukhuwwa'. See also Khayyat, 'Al-shiʿr'.

[22] Nicola, 'Awwal haraka thawriyya fi al-islam'.

[23] Habiby, 'Al-insan hadaf al-adab wa mawduʿhu'.

[24] Tuma, 'Nahwa taʿawun thaqafi'.

[25] Descriptions taken from Marqis, 'Hasd shiʿr aw lawhat shaʿb', 15–20; Hoffman, *My Happiness Bears No Relation to Happiness*, 258–63; and Furani, *Silencing the Sea*.

begun experimenting with free verse and poetic enjambement, the festival poetry was usually constructed according to the rhyming, two-hemistich poetic conventions of classical Arabic literature, a form that was closer to the traditional classical heritage and religious texts to which literate and illiterate people had been exposed. This form was also more conducive to oral presentation. The language was clear and direct, so as to be more easily received and absorbed by the listeners. As part of his discussion of the festivals in connection with the central role of local Arabic poetry in Palestinian political life before 1967, Furani attributes the poetry's unique political power to the ability to 'be recited, memorized and disseminated with the agility unavailable to other forms'.[26] *Al-Jadid* published accounts of the festivals, usually including a sampling of the poetry that had been recited at the reading. Scores of poets participated in the gathering, including Hanna Abu Hanna, Tawfiq Zayyad, Salim Jubran, Rashid Husayn, Mahmoud Darwish and Samih al-Qasim. During the 1950s Sasson Somekh, David Semah and other Arab Jewish writers also participated in a number of poetry festivals.

At a poetry festival organised by the popular culture club in Acre in July 1958, the poetry engaged with themes of Palestinian–Jewish solidarity in the context of anti-colonialism and global solidarity, including readings by David Semah, Mahmoud Darwish, Samih al-Qasim, Hanna Abu Hanna and other poets. Al-Qasim read poetry about the anti-colonial struggle in Algeria, while Darwish's poem 'The Martyr' (*al-shahid*) tied the universal struggle for freedom to Palestinian and communist political motifs.[27] Dedicating one of the first poems he ever read publicly to 'every martyr in every struggle of the movement for freedom',[28] the young Darwish took to the stage and recited:

> To you, killed on the paths of the sun, Oh flame of steadfastness and sacrifice
> Oh, fire's beloved, Oh hope of the dawn, Oh anger of iron and flame,
> Oh vulture's departure on the spacious horizon, Oh vigilance of blood and vow

[26] Furani, *Silencing the Sea*, 40.

[27] Some poem excerpts and accounts of festivals events can be found in al-Khass, 'Muʾtamar watani bi-lughat al-shiʿr'.

[28] Darwish, *Al-shahid*, 19–21.

To you, killed on the trails of glory, in the fields of battle and roaming
Oh martyr, Oh son of volcanoes, Oh firebrand of the stubborn struggle
Oh call of the morning coming after the thickness of night,
Pouring light into the bosom of being
Oh you who light up the shadows with your free blood.[29]

Darwish's dialogic poetic conceit, a conversation between the poet and the martyrs, was another device commonly employed in festival poems. This approach fit well with the call-and-response dynamic that characterised the festivals, creating the sense of a dialogue between the poet and the audience. Darwish's dialogic verse thus rouses the audience into identifying with the martyrs that the poet speaks to, and then extols and mythologises, the listeners as martyrs in themselves. In this way, these literary works aim to shift the political consciousness of the audience as a group. A similar structure is operative in many of Darwish's poems, most notably his renowned piece *Record, I Am an Arab* (*sajjal ana ʿarabi*) which adopts the conceit of a conversation between a Palestinian fellah and an Israeli soldier. This style, grounded in classical motifs and re-popularised in the genre of the festival poem, became one of the landmarks of Palestinian poetry.

After Darwish's reading, David Semah recited a poem dedicated to Tawfiq Zayyad, entitled 'My Brother Tawfiq' (*akhi tawfiq*). The poet and activist Zayyad was being held in Dimona prison at the time of the festival, and his poetry was read out loud to the audience by Hanna Abu Hanna and Semah. 'You are not alone in prison', Semah tells Zayyad and the audience, 'Because here a whole people is imprisoned.'[30] Semah's poem is written in the rhymed and metred, two-hemistich classical Arabic form. As noted above, this form was often employed in festival poems, most probably because it was widely recognisable by the Arabic speaking public. While the language of Semah's poem leans towards Classical Arabic, including the use of some Koranic diction and vocabulary, the poem's images and message remain uncomplicated and accessible:

My brother Tawfiq! We revere hope
And love dominates our feelings

[29] Ibid.

[30] Semah, 'Akhi tawfiq', 39–41.

Rhymes obey without question
And lines compose themselves

Poetry flows from the heads of spears
When the chest can no longer bear feeling

Both of us are poets and poetry is a spring
Overflowing with faith and conscience

The love of the East feeds our hearts
We continue to live by its dictates

Your struggle makes the river Dijla flow
Gently, or seethe and churn

How many times have I soaked my limbs in the Dijla
And been drunk on its water when I was a child

We have a homeland
Our two peoples have a sky, flowers, winds and land

If they sow skulls in its dirt
Our harvest will be hope and light[31]

In this passage, Semah extols the connection between himself and Zayyad as resistance poets of the Arab world, whose two people live in the same 'homeland'. As they flow towards the East, the common origins of the poets intertwine in the river Deejla. The force of Zayyad's political struggle drives the motion of the river at the core of Semah's formative childhood memories of his native Baghdad. Semah thus transforms the River Deejla from a symbol of libidinal and cultural origins into a space of joint political struggle for Arab–Jewish coexistence and Palestinian liberation. He draws the connection between the two people, utilising a similar set of natural tropes that bind their collective bodies and fates in interrelationship under a common sky and the

[31] Ibid.

wind that blows between them. The final stanza above is in direct dialogue with a poem written by Zayyad on the occasion of the Kufr Qasim massacre of 1956, when a group of Palestinian villagers was killed by the Israeli army:

> Have you heard talk of the battle
> The people slaughtered like sheep
> The story is called
> 'The harvest of skulls'
> The scene of the crime:
> 'Kufr al-Qasim'[32]

Thus begins Zayyad's poem, published in *al-Jadid* in 1957, a long epic that ties the Kufr Qasim massacre to other massacres of the *nakba*, as well as to the Marxist struggle for national liberation. In response, Semah writes: 'If they sow skulls in its dirt/Our harvest will be hope and light.' This messianic line raises the image of the poet as prophet who boldly determines that the political struggle and its victims will fertilise the ground of social transformation. Upon this new common ground, the poem seems to suggest, the two peoples might, finally, live peacefully together in a common homeland.

Conclusion

In much the same way as internationalist communism, Arab Marxism and anti-colonial, anti-Zionist politics provided prototypes that enabled the coherence of this extraordinary cultural scene, the damage to these collective models led to the gradual demise of its activities. The 1960s saw the widespread exposure of the crimes of Stalin and the disillusionment of many with communist internationalism; this set the scene for the intensification of conflicts in MAKI and its eventual split into Jewish Zionist and (largely) Palestinian, anti-Zionist factions in 1965. These events formed a political backdrop to the personal disillusionment of Sami Michael and Shim'on Ballas with Stalinism and their exit from the party, alongside the slow assimilation of the Arab Jewish members of the scene into the Hebrew literary milieu. On the one hand, this assimilation was the result of an argument

[32] Zayyad, 'Hisad al-jamajim'.

surrounding the importance of the production of progressive literature and Arab culture accessible to Hebrew-speaking audiences. Yet it was also indicative of the gradual colonial erasure of Arabic culture in Jewish communities, and the impossibility for Jewish writers in Arabic of finding a readership. In the Palestinian community inside Israeli, the fight for progressive Arabic literature continued and even flowered throughout the 1960s, with the work of Habiby, Darwish and Samih al-Qasim exploding onto the world stage in the 1970s. Yet, although this coterie of writers went their own separate ways, some continued to work together on discrete literary projects, and the cultural blueprints they set in motion continued to take various forms in the generations to come. In addition to popular democratic social realism as a local style, the group identified a number of key themes and styles as salient anti separatist models for a neo colonial era: Arab and Muslim–Jewish cultural exchange throughout the ages, anti-colonialism aesthetics, bilingualism in literature, and politicised translation between Arabic and Hebrew. These functioned as precursors to both the popular and the political styles of Mizrahi Jewish and Palestinian writers, as well as to bilingual magazines and presses and anti-occupation and anti-separatist translation projects, models that continue to evolve throughout the contemporary period.

Bibliography

Assadi, Jamal and Saif Abu Saleh, *Short Fiction as a Mirror of Palestinian Life in Israel, 1944–1967: Critique and Anthology* (New York: Peter Lang, 2017).

Bashkin, Orit, *New Babylonians: A History of Jews in Modern Iraq* (Stanford: Stanford University Press, 2012).

Bashkin, Orit, *Impossible Exodus: Iraqi Jews in Israel* (Stanford: Stanford University Press, 2017. KOBO Books).

Beinin, Joel, *Was the Red Flag Flying There? Marxist Politics and the Arab–Israeli Conflict in Egypt and Israel* (Berkeley: University of California Press, 1990).

Budeiri, Musa, *The Palestine Communist Party 1919–1948: Arab and Jew in the Struggle for Internationalism* (Chicago: Haymarket Books, 2010).

Darwish, Mahmoud, *al-shahid* (The martyr), *al-Jadid* 5, 7 (1958).

Furani, Khaled, *Silencing the Sea: Secular Rhythms in Palestinian Poetry* (Stanford: Stanford University Press, 2012).

Habiby, Emile, 'Al-insan hadaf al-adab wa mawdu'hu' [Humanity is the goal and subject of literature), *al-Jadid* 1, 3 (1954).

Harootunian, Harry, *Marx After Marx: History and Time in the Expansion of Capitalism* (New York: Columbia University Press, 2017).

Hoffman, Adina, *My Happiness Bears No Relation to Happiness: A Poet's Life in the Palestinian Century* (New Haven: Yale University Press, 2010).

Khass, Muhammad, 'Mu'tamar watani bi-lughat al-shi'r' [A national festival in the language of poetry], *al-Jadid* 5, 7 (1958).

Khayyat, Ibrahim, 'Al-shi'r al-'iraqi al-hadith' [Modern Iraqi poetry], *al-Ittihad* (1951).

Khayyat, Ibrahim, 'Al-ukhuwwa fi al-shi'r al-'iraqi' [Fraternity in Iraqi poetry], *al-Jadid* 2, 10 (1955).

Liu, Jihui and Viren Murthy (eds), *East-Asian Marxisms and Their Trajectories* (London: Routledge, 2017).

Marid, Samir [Sami Michael], 'Al-jarida al-atiya min wara al-hudud' [The newspaper from across the borders], *al-Ittihad* (1 October 1953).

Marid, Samir [Sami Michael], 'Nahwa insha' adab sha'bi taqaddumi 'arabi fi isra'il' [Towards a popular progressive Arab literature in Israel], *al-Ittihad* 6 (1950): 48–9.

Marqis, Nimr, 'Hasd shi'r aw lawhat sha'b' [A harvest of poems or a portrait of a people]', *al-Jadid* 4, 7 (1957).

Massad, Joseph, 'Zionism's Internal Others: Israel and the Oriental Jews', *Journal of Palestine Studies* 25, 4 (Summer 1996): 53–68.

Michael, Sami, *Gevulot ha-ruah: sihot 'im rubik rozental* [The bounds of the wind: conversations with Ruvik Rosenthal] (Tel Aviv: ha-Kibuts ha-me'uhad, 2000).

Nassar, Maha, *Brothers Apart: Palestinian Citizens of Israel and the Arab World* (Stanford: Stanford University Press, 2017).

Nicola, Jabra, 'Al-qissa illati nuriduha' [The short story we want], *al-Jadid* 2, 5 (1955).

Nicola, Jabra, 'Musa ibn maymun wa-ta'aththuruh bi al-fikr al-'arabi' [Maimonides and his influence on Arabic thought], *al-Jadid* 1, 3 (1954).

Nicola, Jabra, 'Awwal haraka thawriyya fi al-islam: al-khawarij' [The first revolutionary movement in Islam: the Kharajites], *al-Jadid* 2, 4 (1955).

Semah, David, 'Akhi tawfiq' [My brother Tawfiq], *al-Jadid* 5, 7 (1958).

Shohat, Ella, 'Sephardim in Israel: Zionism from the Standpoint of Its Jewish Victims', *Social Text* 19/20 (Autumn 1988): 1–35.

Tuma, Emile, 'Nahwa ta'awun thaqafi' [Towards cultural co-operation], *al-Jadid* 1, 1 (1953).

Zayyad, Tawfiq, 'Hisad al-jamajim' [The harvest of skulls], *al-Jadid* 4, 1 (1957).

3

FREE ELECTIONS VERSUS AUTHORITARIAN PRACTICES: WHAT BAATHISTS FOUGHT FOR

Matthieu Rey

Introduction

The Baath Party has become the very symbol of the authoritarian regime in the Middle East. Hafez al-Asad in Syria and Saddam Hussein in Iraq exemplified the harsh dictatorship that dominated the two countries under Baathist rule. However, the premise of the Baathist ideology and the ideals put forward by its founders, such as Michel 'Aflaq and Salah al-Din Bitar, differed in many ways from this reality. On the contrary, with a strong commitment to nationalism, 'Aflaq and Bitar ascribed a high value to freedom and committed themselves to defending a true constitutional system in order to restore the Arab Nation. The present chapter aims to understand how and why the Baathist leaders shifted from this liberal background to take a more authoritarian approach to power.

In this chapter, while considering political evolutions in Syria between 1946 and 1955, I will argue that representations, values and political involvement are deeply linked. Politicians as ordinary people frame the reality that defines their actions. They nevertheless face a dilemma when what they believe to be right and good is in conflict either with other interests or, more often, with another point to which they ascribe a high value. Staging a revolution, defending the nation, placing the economy under state control, creating foreign alliances, promoting free elections are all examples of these 'values'. The present chapter aims to demonstrate that politicians prioritise their actions according to certain values, and consequently, each value is assigned a certain position in a hierarchy. This hierarchy changes depending on the context.

This approach addresses Lucien Febvre's concept, refined by Olivier Wieviorka, of 'the hierarchy of values'.[1] Febvre's original concept provided insight into the mental universe of François Rabelais. In this way, he was able to formulate the true meaning of the French author's atheism with reference to the cultural context of the sixteenth century. Wieviorka expanded the scope of the concept, pointing out the division created among French deputies in 1940 by the two key values of anti-Bolshevik and anti-German feeling. Studying Henri Becquart – a far-right representative during the 1930s, who violently slandered Roger Salengro, Minister of the Interior in Leon Blum's socialist government, and who founded one of the first resistance movements in France – and René Belin – leader of the leftist trade union General Confederation of Work in the late 1930s before becoming Minister of Work under Marshal Pétain – allows Olivier Wieviorka to highlight the relation between values, context and further political involvement. From this perspective, he demonstrates how the adherents of the former position, the anti-Bolsheviks, mainly became partisans of Marshal Petain while the adherents of the latter, the anti-Germans, built the resistance. This approach can be used to reframe our understanding of Middle Eastern activism. It above all helps us to clarify the elements that underpin a political shift in personal and party trajectories.

An examination of Syria between 1946 and 1955 furnishes a relevant case study in this respect. The parliamentary system that ruled the country allowed for multi-party politics, but, at the same time, a number of events shook the regime: military coups, regional unrest such as the war of 1948 and the rise of the rural question aroused new concerns in the political sphere. In the activist field, while often defined as a nationalist group, the Baath Party put forward 'socialism' as one of its key principles. Its members referred to themselves as progressive (*taqaddumiyyin*) and, consequently, claimed to

[1] Febvre, *Le Problème de l'Incroyance*; Wieviorka, *Les Orphelins de la République*.

belong to a leftist movement. By the same token, they adopted leftist vocabularies and examined in their newspapers and books the different socialist and communist experiments around the world. From this perspective, although often studied as a nationalist group, the Baath also belonged to the leftist realm. Studying their ideas and highlighting their ideological path allows us to understand how leftist groups can become defenders of authoritarian solutions. This perspective aims to question how cultural and political ideas interrelated at the end of the 1950s, undermining a certain view on liberalism.

Major research into the Baath Party and its involvement in Syria has provided insights into its rise, the core of its ideas – mostly as a pan-Arab movement – and its social background.[2] However, there has been little exploration of the cultural and social dynamics that affected the party, with focus instead on explaining postures and changes adopted during their rise to power. In this regard, previous researchers have often sought to identify the causes of the Baath's later success in their early period. Such analyses seem to somewhat deny value to the political ideas of the founders, placing them aside in order to scrutinise instead the opportunistic turn taken. Returning our attention to the founding ideas, however, may help us to understand how a liberal activist can become a partisan of dictatorship. As Jens Hanssen and Max Weiss have recently pointed out, historians need to further investigate the many paths taken by intellectuals and activists since the Second World War.[3] In this matter, a re-examination of the rise of the Baath, its ideological realignment and its dialogue with other leftist groups will help us to understand how these movements progressively adopted a non-liberal agenda while tackling the issues of freedom and constitutional rights. In the case of the Baath, I would argue that coming closer to alignment with Nasser on the defence of neutrality led the Baathists to forget their liberal ideas. Evidence of these trends can be found mainly in newspapers, autobiographies and the writings of leaders such as ʿAflaq.[4] The autobiographies of founders such as Jalal al-Sayyid, as well as those of newcomers such as Akram al-Hawrani,

[2] Abu Jaber, *Arab Baath Socialist Party*; Devlin, *The Baath Party*; Olson, *The Baath and Syria.*

[3] Jens Hanssen and Max Weiss, 'Introduction', in Hanssen and Weiss (eds), *Arabic Thought against the Authoritarian Age*, 22–3.

[4] ʿAflaq, *Fi sabil al-baʿath.*

further clarify our understanding.[5] This documentation helps to explain the Baathist hierarchy of values and its evolution.

The Baathist Hierarchy of Values and the Advent of Neutrality

In 1947, young scholars and professionals, recent university graduates, met together to promote a new message to the Syrian public. They called for the 'renaissance' (*ba'ath*) of the Arab nation. As primary legislative elections had to take place in June 1947, they set up a congress and turned a cultural club into a political party.[6] The Baath Party can be considered an autonomous voice as it did not adopt any of the ideologies exported from Europe, but rather combined different ideas to suggest a new way of thinking. Under the slogan of 'Unity, Liberty and Socialism', the Baathists advocated Arab unity in order to bring about the revival of the Arab world.[7] The Baathist leaders, particularly Michel 'Aflaq and Salah al-Din Bitar, were convinced that colonialism had divided the Arab nation and thus hindered its development. Liberty, which implied the free will of the nation, and socialism, sharing wealth among citizens, would be two important means of achieving this unity. As 'Aflaq explained several times, these words carried an emotional weight, providing a kind of moral code for political action. This proposition was enshrined in the party statutes, drawn up in 1947.[8]

Of the 48 articles in these statutes, fifteen were linked to general principles, four dealt with foreign policy, and six with internal policy. The four foreign policy clauses mentioned the need to act in order to defend historic Arab rights and to strengthen amicable relations between nations.[9] In 1947, like most other Syrian political groups, the Baath Party was not yet involved in the Cold War: it rejected the USA because it supported Turkey and Israel and was also afraid of Communist atheism.[10] Regarding internal policy, its programme reflected Syria's political battlefield. The first article defended

[5] Al-Hawrani, *Mudhakkirat*; al-Sayyid, *Hizb al-ba'ath al-'arabi*.

[6] Hizb al-ba'ath, *Nidal hizb al-ba'ath al-'arabi al-ishtiraki*, 18.

[7] Atrash, *The Political Philosophy of Michel 'Aflaq*, 77–82.

[8] 'Aflaq, *Fi sabil*, 154–5.

[9] Hizb al-ba'ath, *Nidal*, 27.

[10] 'Aflaq, *Fi sabil*, 322–5.

a parliamentary and liberal system; subsequent articles called for liberties, rights and direct elections. The Baath Party's hierarchy of values could be outlined as follows:

Arab Unity (goal)

Liberty = Parliamentary democracy	Unity = Majority in Parliament and defence of Arab interests	Socialism = National development

Baath values

1. Democratic institutions.
2. Revival of the Arab spirit.
3. National development.

Al-Ba'ath's editorial on 17 November 1947 showed the link between internal and international issues. The constitutional change that authorised a new mandate for incumbent president Shukri al-Quwatli was denounced as an act of treason on a par with the partition of Palestine.[11] Thus at this stage, democratic structures within the country seemed more important than any external issues.

The Baath statutes envisaged a comprehensive organisation of the party, which was divided into cells, branches and regions. However, at this early stage it probably had fewer than a thousand active members, the great majority of whom were teachers or students.[12] Their contribution to society and ability to answer a social need, through their work providing medical assistance in the villages or educational support to schoolchildren, goes some way to explaining the population's receptiveness to their programme.[13] Although it is difficult to evaluate their political commitment or the extent of their agreement on ideological principles, most of them seem to have been activists

[11] *Al-Ba'ath* (17 November 1947).

[12] Devlin, *The Baath Party*, 58.

[13] Batatu, *Syria's Peasantry*, 136.

working towards an ideal. However, most of their publications were only read by those who were interested in metaphysical or philosophical problems and had the intellectual capacity to understand them.

Nevertheless, thanks to their involvement in the student movement and in the national struggle, the Baath began to emerge as a new force to be reckoned with. They were active principally during demonstrations, denouncing the corrupt or fraudulent aspects of the system that prevented the people from having genuine political representation. However, Michel 'Aflaq and Salah al-Din Bitar had been taken unawares by the defeat in Palestine,[14] which suggests that the party had indeed been more concerned with internal movements than with international affairs until mid-1948. They protested against all imperialist attacks, but regarded them as part of a larger design. The advent of the *nakba* brought two major consequences. The moral shock of defeat made defence issues a priority for Arab nationalists. The demonstrations that followed, especially those at the end of December 1948, gave the party greater visibility. At student demonstrations the Baath Party became one of the voices denouncing corruption and the loss of Palestine.[15] Violence and repression created a new climate that impacted on the party's values.

One of the party's key values was *inqilab*, meaning 'turn' or 'change', although the meaning of the term was liable to shift. At the same time as calling for a parliamentary system and free elections, the Baath Party defined itself as an *inqilab* party. Michel 'Aflaq explained his thoughts on *inqilab* at some length,[16] understanding it as a psychological, social and moral way to restore the original strength of the Arab nation (before 1949). The vocabulary used is significant: according to 'Aflaq, *inqilab* can be considered revolution in its pre-modern sense.[17] The concept was mainly used to convey the opposite of decline, but at this stage it did not mean an appeal to political violence in order to overthrow the system. Instead *inqilab* envisaged the possibility that a new way of practising politics could emerge.

[14] As they recalled in 'Aflaq, *Fi sabil*, 238 and Bitar, 'Syria's Troubles', 22.

[15] Al-'Azmah, Private Papers (Damascus).

[16] 'Aflaq, *Fi sabil*, 153–93.

[17] On the meaning of the word 'revolution', see Rey *'Révolution', Histoire d'un Mot.*

This possibility presented itself when Husni al-Za'im staged a coup. On 31 March 1949, the army chief of staff ordered the arrest of the President of the Republic and the prime minister and immediately tried to change the entire political system. At the beginning, the Baath Party regarded the coup as a necessity because it considered that the political elite had obstructed the institutions and destroyed democracy by intervening in the elections. On 7 April, the party demonstrated in the streets in support of the new regime.[18] Husni al-Za'im kept the promises he had made before the coup: he instituted reform, expanded the army and implemented development programmes. However, as soon as he approved the Tapline project with the Americans – the pipeline crossing Iraq to the Mediterranean Sea – the Baath Party denounced his dictatorship. In the middle of May 1949, 'Aflaq wrote an article criticising al-Za'im's foreign policy and deploring his lack of attention to the Arab struggle. He was immediately arrested and, under threat of torture, asked the President to forgive him. The party could not accept that 'Aflaq had become a supporter of al-Za'im, but the crisis of confidence came to an end in August 1949 when al-Za'im was overthrown. Somewhat prematurely, the Baath Party hailed the coup by Sami al-Hinnawi as heralding the return of democracy.[19] An important shift took place inside the party when it agreed to take part in the new government: 'Aflaq was appointed minister of education, following an invitation from the Hama politician Akram al-Hawrani. The latter supported the formation of a national government that would include all the parties in order to counter the forces of imperialism.[20] Hence 'Aflaq entered the government and stayed there until the next elections.

Legislative elections were held in October 1949, soon after the second coup. Negotiations started between the parties to decide on the conditions under which they would set up a constitution. Baath activists were invested

[18] Devlin, *The Ba'th Party*, 53.

[19] Al-Sayyid, *Al-inqilabat*, 112–13.

[20] Akram al-Hawrani (1912–96) was born in the Hama area and became a defender of nationalist ideas and peasant rights during the 1930s. After the Second World War, he became close to young military officers such as Adib al-Shishakli. They were both volunteers in the Palestine War in 1948. In 1949, al-Hawrani supported military coups as a means of 'correcting' the Syrian political system. Akram al-Hawrani, *Mudhakkirat*, 1,003.

in the electoral fight, defending their ideas in public and holding numerous meetings and speeches.[21] Their main argument was that power should belong to the people and that they themselves represented the real Syrians. Their commitment to 'the people' was also addressed in the Baathist newspaper, which carried articles on the right to vote and how to vote, as well as discussing the most important issues of the day. [22] In spite of all their efforts, only Jalal al-Sayyid was elected to parliament. The clear winner of the elections was Hizb al-Sha'ab.

The new assembly had only just convened in November 1949 when Adib al-Shishakli staged a third coup.[23] The Baath Party did not seem unduly disappointed by this turn of events. It attributed its defeat in the elections to the corruption that was rampant in the country and believed the military might be able to restore the true voice of the people. Indeed, it appears that Michel 'Aflaq knew Adib al-Shishakli through his connections with Akram al-Hawrani.[24] Even though the government was overthrown, the 1949 parliament was not dissolved and the constitution remained to be written. While the Baath Party did not categorise the three coups as *inqilabat* in the sense of the 'true' political change they were looking for,[25] it seemed to support the military power as a possible way of establishing 'true democracy'. Eventually, power had to be returned to civilians and to parliament, as the latter was the only institution that could, however imperfectly, speak on behalf of the Syrian people.

In the first half of 1950, three trends emerged in the daily newspaper *al-Ba'ath*. Firstly, the main issues were the Syrian constitution and the establishment of real democracy. To this end, the 1950 Egyptian elections were widely covered to show the existence of greater democracy in Egypt.[26] The second trend was the discussion of social problems. Even though the first Baath Congress in 1947 had defended socialism, it did not mention how it might be applied in practice. During 1949 and 1950, many articles were published that

[21] *Al-Ba'ath* in October and November 1949.

[22] *Al-Ba'ath* (16 October 1949).

[23] Al-Sayyid, *Al-inqilabat*, 342.

[24] Al-Hawrani, *Mudhakkirat*, 1107.

[25] 'Aflaq, *Fi sabil*, 159–63.

[26] See for example *al-Ba'ath* (4 January 1950).

held up the People's Republic of China as a model. Slowly, economic and social questions became a major priority for the party: the teachers of Homs or the textile workers of Aleppo might be the avant-garde of the Arab revival. Thirdly, Arab issues were also frequently addressed. Reading through the articles on these issues, it is apparent that a major shift took place in 1950: the Baathists were not against the idea of an Iraqi–Syrian union, but they could not support the position of the Hashemite kings.[27] They were opposed to the fact that foreigners still continued to dominate the the country's economy and politics and supported the struggle for independence. Their main proof for this assumption regarding foreign control was the Tripartite declaration between Great Britain, France and the USA, which encroached on Syrian autonomy.[28]

The Korean War strengthened the Baath Party's conviction that neutrality was the better political option for Syria. The editorial on 8 July 1950 explained that this was the best position from which to defend the country.[29] Simultaneously, it was clear to the writer of the editorial that the Great Powers were less concerned with regional conflicts than with their own interests and that their main objective was to gain complete control of the region. On 25 November, a new editorial entitled 'Neutrality is the Arab position' put forward the idea that Arab unity could be equated with international neutrality.[30] As for the main Syrian political currents, the year 1950 was marked by a shift in the Baath Party's hierarchy of values. To defend and advance Arab unity, which had always been the main aim, two principles became increasingly important: neutrality as the best way of conducting foreign policy, and a focus on social issues to promote internal harmony. While military coups were not condemned, they were still regarded as inappropriate.

Criticisms of the Egyptian Free Officers

The Syrian press had been following events in Egypt since the Palestine War. The Syrian public was profoundly interested in the long-drawn-out fight between Great Britain and Egypt, which it saw as an important step towards

[27] *Al-Ba'ath*, 'Viewpoint of the Baath Party on the Issue of the Union with Iraq' (9 January 1950).

[28] *Al-Ba'ath* (9 April 1950).

[29] *Al-Ba'ath* (8 July 1950).

[30] *Al-Ba'ath* (25 November 1950).

the independence of the Arab Nation. From the moderate to the radical press, from *Alif Ba'* or *al-Balad* to *al-Ba'ath*, all shared the same point of view: Egypt wanted to gain its freedom and to control its own resources in order to be able to develop. On 20 October 1951, *al-Ba'ath* wrote that 'Arab people are rallying around Egypt', commenting on the abrogation of the treaty between Egypt and Great Britain and reminding its readers of the dangers of colonisation.[31] It was not a surprise to discover that the Egyptian monarchy had failed, but the military coup carried out by the Free Officers who seized power in July 1952 came as a complete shock.

On 23 July 1952, all Syrian newspapers described the events in Egypt as a coup. After a few days, the government and public opinion agreed with this interpretation: this was an internal political event which involved no external forces. The names of the new Egyptian officers filled the pages of the Syrian newspapers. For the first time, an Arab monarchy had been overthrown and Syrians, like other Arabs, were trying to understand the intentions of the new regime. Speeches and meetings proved that the military were in charge even if the commanders declared they wished to establish a civilian and non-corrupt system to which they would return power. Public opinion in Syria interpreted these events in the light of the country's recent past, as the Egyptian coup in many ways resembled those that had taken place in Syria. The question remained: what exactly were the military's objectives for Egypt? Syrians had experienced the rule of Sami al-Hinnawi, whose coup had intended to restore civilian power, and of Husni al-Za'im, who held on to power by widening his own personal influence. Since the end of April 1952, Adib al-Shishakli had been implementing a new policy, that of destroying the traditional parliamentary system.

Since independence, Syria had been governed by a parliamentary system, but in December 1951 Adib al-Shishakli acted against parliament in order to break the power of Hizb al-Sha'ab and to put an end to its policy of friendship with Iraq. After the coup, the parliamentary system collapsed as al-Shishakli and his followers did not believe that any kind of civilian power was capable of developing the country and ensuring its stability,[32] an attitude that alienated

[31] *Al-Ba'ath* (20 October 1951).

[32] Al-Sayyid, *Al-inqilabat*, 184–5.

many of his comrades. Al-Shishakli wanted to strengthen his control over Syria, and hence refused to consider returning to a parliamentary system. Most of the political parties chose to dissolve themselves, first the al-Hizb al-Watani and Hizb al-Sha'ab, then the Muslim Brotherhood and the Syrian Party of Cooperation.[33] In contrast, the Baath Party decided to continue its activities. It claimed to be the political teacher of the masses, helping the new system to build a new Syria. It perceived *taqaddumiyya* – progressivism – as the true line, although it still advocated a return to the parliamentary system, believing that the old-fashioned parties would gradually disappear. During a long meeting between al-Shishakli, the Baathist leaders and al-Hawrani, al-Shishakli reiterated his refusal to return to the parliamentary system.[34] This meeting led to a rift between al-Shishakli and al-Hawrani, and brought the Baath Party into opposition. On 26 April, a decree permitted and encouraged the Ministry of Interior to suppress all subversive activities of associations or political groups, and this was followed on 16 May by the dissolution of all political parties.

Michel 'Aflaq, Salah al-Din Bitar and Akram al-Hawrani fled from Syria together. This episode is very important in understanding the rise of the Baath Party and its internal changes. As has been described,[35] the merger of the Baath Party with the Syrian Socialist Party (al-Hawrani's party) was a key milestone on the road to power. Indeed, the latter, which lacked a proper ideological base, brought in a significant number of activists, perhaps as many as 2,500.[36] After a year of negotiations, a new party slowly emerged. Two factors helped to bring the two movements together. First, in late 1951 and 1952, the Baathist and Hawranist activists had fought side by side in a growing number of demonstrations against the adverse effects of the Korean War on the economy.[37] Consequently, the militants in the two movements had developed closer ties. Secondly, al-Shishakli's second coup forced al-Hawrani and the Baathist leaders to take a position on whether or not they wanted to change the regime. The merger of the two parties seemed to be the best and

[33] Al-Khayyir, *Adib al-shishakli*, 97.

[34] Al-Hawrani, *Mudhakkirat*, 1464.

[35] Devlin, *The Ba'th Party*, 63–5; Olson, *The Ba'th*, 30.

[36] Carré, *Le Nationalisme Arabe*, 45.

[37] Issawi, *An Economic History of the Middle East*, 26–7.

quickest way to counter al-Shishakli's dictatorial tendencies, and their leaders' exile strengthened this conviction. These attitudes showed that democracy had, in fact, been more important than a military coup, which was clearly not a genuine example of *inqilab*.

The first steps taken by the Free Officers in Egypt towards fulfilling their ideals were ambiguous in many ways. Did they defend democracy? They asked the parties to engage in auto-criticism. Did they promote civilian power? They gave swiftly-transferred power to General Neguib and dissolved Mahir's government. When Adib al-Shishakli visited Egypt on 11 December 1952, Muhammad Neguib recognised that the Free Officers had followed his path, declaring: 'I thank you because you are the first to visit us, and you were the first to attempt an *inqilab* as we have done, and to succeed in it.'[38] The two regimes seemed to be close in two ways. First of all, between June 1952 and February 1954, the Egyptian Revolutionary Command Council abolished the Constitution, destroyed the monarchy, founded a Republic, suppressed political parties and, finally, established a movement which had the same name as al-Shishakli's.[39] Secondly, the foreign policies of Egypt and Syria became increasingly aligned. Their approach to John Foster Dulles' mission and his meetings in Cairo and Damascus seemed to exemplify this common foreign policy. The two regimes first of all defended their own interests, rather than Arab ones.[40] They were not opposed to allying with Western powers, but refused any agreement that might imply a new colonial occupation or any limitations on their sovereignty. Adib al-Shishakli, in fact, quickly changed his view on the new regime and by the end of 1952 had initiated a profitable collaboration with Egypt.

Contemporary perceptions of Arab journalists and intellectuals also suggested a high degree of identification between the Free Officers and al-Shishakli's regime. For the Baathists and other Syrian politicians, the two movements presented a common threat to liberalism. The Free Officers called for 'free elections in order to compose a Constitutional Assembly

[38] Vigneau, 'L'Idéologie de la Révolution Égyptienne', 449.

[39] Vatikiotis, *The Modern History of Egypt*, 379–83.

[40] United States Department of State, *Foreign Relations of the United States, 1952–1954, Near and Middle East*, Vol. 5, 56–64.

and a referendum to obtain public agreement on all constitutional texts'.[41] In this sense, both Nasser and al-Shishakli represented a common evil to most subsequent Arab politicians: they proved that Arab armies tended to monopolise power. Two predominant features of these regimes drew the loudest criticism from the Baath Party, and most other progressive movements, such as the Communist Party. First of all, al-Shishakli and Nasser neglected the democratic basis of their regimes and prevented political parties from participating in elections. Secondly, during Dulles' mission in May 1953,[42] even though al-Shishakli denounced America's pro-Israel policy in public rumours circulated that negotiations and agreements to exchange economic, military and technical assistance were taking place and that the settlement of the Palestinian refugees was discussed.[43] The Baath Party spread these rumours and became increasingly critical of al-Shishakli's policy. At the end of 1953, the Baathist hierarchy of values had not changed much: elections and democracy were still a priority to be defended, while neutrality was to become a tool, or perhaps a weapon, in both Arab and Syrian internal struggles.

Neutrality First

When the Jebel Druze rebelled against al-Shishakli's dictatorship in January 1954, none of the political leaders believed that the uprising would prevail.[44] After a month, thanks to the secession of Aleppo, Adib al-Shishakli was forced into exile and the parliamentary system entered a new period. The Homs Pact, whereby most Syrian leaders – including Baathists – had promised to restore the liberal constitution of 1949 and to defend the rights and liberties of the people,[45] provided the basis for a 'return to democracy'.[46] But although parliament resumed its sessions, the politicians became more and more divided. In March 1954, Akram al-Hawrani, as one of the leading voices of the Baath

[41] For the Arabic text, see Al-Hakim, n. 1, file 119.

[42] United States Department of State, *Foreign Relations of the United States, 1952–1954, Near and Middle East*, Vol. 5, 1 ss.

[43] Lesch, *Syria*, 34.

[44] Al-Hakim, document 1, file 119.

[45] Ibid.

[46] According to Haddad, *Awraq shamiyya*, 67–77.

Party, refused to enter the government, and on 30 March he launched a sharp attack on the declaration introducing the new government. Syrian forces had seen all governments after the overthrow as provisional. An important issue, the upcoming elections, had to be organised by the government. A major radicalisation of the Baathist position took place during these months. The party denounced social oppression more vehemently and appealed for greater participation in strikes and workers' demonstrations. This was linked with the merger and with al-Hawrani's long history of involvement in struggles for peasant rights.

Struggles inside the party also reshaped its main objectives. Even though the merger had been agreed upon by ʿAflaq, Bitar and al-Hawrani while in exile in 1953, it had not been ratified at a Party Congress. The new Baath Party, which had now become the Arab Baath *Socialist* Party, was deeply divided into factions, all of which fought for dominance. This competition was clearly articulated in the editorials of the party's daily newspaper, *al-Baʿath*. The fight for neutrality, Arab unity and socialism led to the strengthening of each position and pushed the party towards greater radicalisation. Thus, in September, Akram al-Hawrani promoted the pursuit of neutrality in the legislative campaign.[47] As a consequence, the Baath Party became the leader of the progressive camp and its main driving force.[48] This could lead to the assumption that internal struggles prevented Baathist leaders from taking moderate positions in parliament or in public statements, but political alliances, including the Baath Party, systematically defended a neutral foreign policy and called for the government not to interfere in the elections, which had still not been called.

Although internal party struggles became more intense, foreign policy also played an important role in the public debate. The first Syrian cabinet after al-Shishakli's overthrow was headed by Shaʿabist forces who began negotiations with Iraq, but they were soon denounced by Egypt and the progressivists. When the Iraqi Prime Minister Fadil al-Jamali declared that Iraq wanted a new Arab pact in April 1954, it seemed clear to its opponents

[47] Al-Hawrani, *Mudhakkirat*, 1,668.

[48] It would eventually form an electoral alliance with the Communist Party, *Al-Hadara* (2 August 1954).

that a conspiracy was afoot. Did this help the progressivists and Nasser's government to draw closer to each other? The Baathists did not agree with the al-Jamali plan, so, using army officer Malki as their spokesperson, they asked other Arab countries to join forces against Israel.[49] The Baath recognised that the Egyptian or even the Saudi government would protect Syrian independence more efficiently. But the party could still not support Nasser's regime.

In Egypt, at the end of February 1954, President Neguib resigned but was reinstated in the face of pressure from the street. Since the July coup, the Revolutionary Command Council (RCC) had governed Egypt under martial law. But on 5 April, the RCC made an about-turn and decided on a series of measures to return Nasser to power.[50] According to *al-Ba'ath* and *al-Hadara*, the crisis in Egypt demonstrated the gulf between the Baath Party and Nasser. *Al-Hadara* strongly supported the demonstrations: the protests against Nasser represented the true will of the people.[51] Nasser, as the *Ba'ath* editorial wrote on 16 April, had built a personal dictatorship,[52] which was evidence of his treason, or at least his perfidy, and recalled the dictatorship established by al-Shishakli.

The Baathists not only fought against the early stages of Nasser's rise to power, they also condemned his foreign policy. The main issue was the Anglo–Egyptian treaty. The last Wafd government in November 1951 had abolished the treaty and forced the British government to negotiate a new one. Negotiations for a new treaty had been ongoing since the overthrow of the monarchy. On 27 July 1954, Nasser and Eden came to an agreement that provided for the complete evacuation of British troops within twenty months, but allowed Britain to return in the event of war against any Arab country or Turkey. These new terms met with harsh criticism in Syria, especially from the Baath Party, which condemned Nasser's alliance with a colonial power and the 'great return' of British forces to the canal.[53] In light of these actions, Nasser did not believe in neutrality and had no intention of promoting Arab

[49] *Al-Ba'ath* (13 April 1954).

[50] Vatikiotis, *History of Modern Egypt*, 384–5.

[51] See for example 'Student Demonstration against the Dictatorship', *Al-Hadara* (3 April 1954).

[52] *Al-Ba'ath*, 16 April; in the same issue, journalists are described as a political tribunal.

[53] *Al-Ba'ath* (3 August 1954).

neutralism and unification. At the same time, Pakistan and Turkey had signed a military pact, sparking demonstrations in Syria. As far as the Baathists were concerned, Nasser had allowed the British to intervene to help Turkey, when Turkish leaders had shown their enmity towards Syria. Nasser's attitude in this regard showed that he did not believe in the two main values of the Baath Party: democracy and neutrality.

On 14 October 1954, the second polling day arrived in Syria. A new parliament was elected in what were generally regarded as free elections.[54] Of the 135 members elected, twenty-two were Baathists. Their victory seemed complete as this number meant that half the party's candidates had won. Although other political forces gained more seats, such as Khalid al-'Azm's Democratic Coalition, the Baath Party was the most organised force in parliament. Soon its members were elected to the Foreign Affairs committee where they could shape foreign policy and attack the party's enemies.[55] When Faris al-Khuri declared that he was in favour of a 'useful collaboration with the West'[56] in his inaugural speech, the Baath Party followed al-'Azm's coalition in opposing al-Khuri's policy. In fact, although these two groups could have been considered as having won the election, they could not take power.[57] The fragmentation of parliament prevented the emergence of a stable majority, which strengthened the Baath's radical positions. Under these circumstances, these elections also resulted in a shift away from the party's 'traditional' values: since it had in a sense won the election, it could not call for a new one, even if the assembly was made up of a number of parties and coalitions. The elections showed that electoral freedom could hand power to the Baath Party, which in some senses affirmed one of its primary values. The party could now focus on foreign policy and its principal aim, Arab unity. Moreover, it became extremely sensitive towards Iraqi positions and the Arab struggle.

54 Matthieu Rey, 'Le Moment Electoral en Syrie et en Irak en 1954', 100.

55 Lesch, *Syria*, 55.

56 'Situation Politique', from M. Jacques-Émile to the Minister for Foreign Affairs, 9 November 1954, Damascus, file 521, Syria 1953–1958, Africa–Levant, La Courneuve.

57 That is, since Khalid al-'Azm did not become President of the Republic and the Baath Party remained a minority in Parliament; see al-'Azm, *Mudhakkirat*.

In August 1954, following negotiations with the Iraqi regent Abdullilah, Nuri al-Sa'id, the strong man of Iraq, returned to power. He froze all political liberties and political organisations, dissolved parliament and exercised sole power. He wanted a Western alliance in which Iraq would play an important role. He negotiated with the American, British, Turkish and Pakistani governments to obtain modern arms and to sign a military pact. His return to power and the election of a new parliament that was entirely under his control were deeply criticised in the Baath newspaper. Al-Sa'id's actions proved, according to *al-Ba'ath*, that he was plotting with the colonial powers against progressive countries such as Syria.[58] The paper's criticisms were repeated in parliament, and on 11 January 1955 the new Syrian government decided that foreign policy had to be guided by the principle of neutrality.

A 'drift towards neutrality'[59] took place in Egyptian foreign policy as well. Nasser defended an increasingly ambiguous position: the RCC refused any agreement which did not ensure Egyptian control and in which Great Britain and the USA participated, even if it still recognised communism as the main danger.[60] Thus in September 1954 Nasser promptly voiced his opposition to the speeches of the Egyptian Minister of National Guidance, Salah Salim, that recognised a common path for Iraq and Egypt; Nasser and Nuri al-Sa'id became enemies. In November 1954, Nasser called for a conference of Arab prime ministers in order to reject the Iraqi position. The Arab League resolution recalled that Arab foreign policy was based on the Arab Political Committee. This process demonstrated Nasser's gradual shift towards an attitude that was close to neutralism, or more precisely favoured non-intervention by the West in Arab politics.

On 24 February 1955 Iraq and Turkey signed the agreement that would become the Baghdad Pact. Two days later, Salah Salim arrived in Damascus to launch a counterattack. Since the beginning of 1955, *al-Ba'ath* had been strengthening its criticism of the Iraqi position. Editorials railed against 'Nuri's treason', as well as against the 'conspiracy' between Turkish Prime Minister Adnan Menderes and Nuri al-Sa'id.[61] In consequence, the Baath

58 'Nuri Declares War on Iraqi Liberties', *al-Ba'ath* (4 September 1954).

59 Podeh, 'The Drift toward Neutrality'.

60 Ibid., 164.

61 *Al-Ba'ath* (29 January 1955).

Party became extremely hostile towards any form of alliance with Iraq. On 11 February, some two weeks before the official announcement of the Baghdad Pact, a Baathist journalist said that Great Britain and Iraq together were trying to break up the alliance between Saudi Arabia, Egypt and Syria. The Syrian newspaper criticised the country's delegation in Cairo for being too weak. In fact, the Baath Party wanted to agree upon a new alliance with Egypt. Both were fighting for the true independence of the Arabs, or positive neutrality. The party called for the adoption of all possible means to destroy the agreement between Iraq and Turkey. Thus the Baath Party and Nasser were increasingly aligned on the issue of neutrality. This was the beginning of a Nasserite current in the Baath Party that would develop further until 1958. Even if the party did not entirely agree with Nasser, it began to defend Nasserite ways. In April 1955, the Syrian parliament had to ratify a new treaty between Egypt, Syria and Saudi Arabia. The Baath Party was one of the main actors in support of this new agreement, which seemed to indicate a Baathist conversion to Nasserism. Within a few months, the Baathists had moved from refusing to endorse the defence of an authoritarian regime to fighting against imperialist encroachment. As Akram al-Hawrani stated in his memoirs regarding the events of 1955, while the constitutional freedom of the Iraqi regime more closely resembled that of Syria than Egypt, it was no longer possible to follow the same path.

Three closely connected factors explained the Baathist shift towards the endorsement of Nasser's regime and, thereby, the Baathists' justification of authoritarian practices. First of all, struggles within the party promoted a new radicalisation of attitudes to social and international issues. This allowed the Baath Party and its leaders to gain an element of control over the fragmented parliament while simultaneously disqualifying their enemies and rivals. Since the Korean War, the concept of neutrality had become synonymous with self-defence, a principle that came to be championed by the Baath Party. The defence of neutrality also changed Baathist ideology. Under the pressure of regional concerns and internal political struggle, the Baath Party focused on the defence of neutrality as a way of defining Arab identity rather than supporting democracy. Thirdly, Nasser slowly became the Baathists' choice as the leader of neutrality in the region. Cold War culture was synonymous, within the Syrian political field, with a change in values. The only policies acceptable to a majority of politicians, with which few could openly disagree, was non-intervention by Western countries in Arab affairs and the initiation of a dialogue with the Eastern Bloc. These policies also contributed to the dynamics of political radicalisation. This is why neutrality might be considered a major factor in the Baath Party's defence of Gamal Abd al-Nasser, although the relationship between the party and the Egyptian leader always contained the seeds of mutual misunderstanding.

Bibliography

Abu Jaber, Kamal, *Arab Ba'th Socialist Party: History, Ideology and Organisation* (Syracuse: Syracuse University Press, 1966).

'Aflaq, Michel *Fi sabil al-ba'ath* (Damascus: s.n., 1959).

'Al-Sayyid, 'Abd, *Al-inqilabat al-'askariyya fi suriyya, 1949–1954* [The military coups in Syria, 1949–1954) (Cairo: Maktaba Madbuli, 2007).

Atrash, Mohammad, *The Political Philosophy of Michel Aflaq and the Baath Party in Syria* (PhD dissertation, Oklahoma, 1973).

Al-'Azm, Khalid, *Mudhakkirat khalid al-'azm* [Memoirs of Khalid al-'Azm], 3 vols (Beirut: Dar al-Nashr, 2003).

Al-Hawrani, Akram, *Mudhakkirat akram al-hawrani* [Memoirs of Akram al-Hawrani] (Cairo: Dar al-Madbuli, 2000).

Al-Khayyir, Hani, *Adib al-shishakli, sahib al-inqilab al-thalith fi suriyya, al-bidayya wa-al-nihayya* [Adib al-Shishakli, the author of the third coup in Syria, the beginning and the end] (Damascus: Maktaba al-Sharq al-jadid, 1995).

Al-Sayyid, Jalal, *Hizb al-ba'ath al-'arabi* [The Arab Baath Party] (Beirut: Dar al-Nahar li al-Nashr, 1973).

Batatu, Hanna, *Syria's Peasantry, the Descendants, its Lesser Rural Notables, and their Politics* (Princeton: Princeton University Press, 1999).

Bitar, Salah al-Din, 'Syria's troubles', *MERIP Reports* (1982): 21–3.

Carré, Olivier, *Le Nationalisme Arabe* (Paris: Fayard, 1993).

Devlin, John, *The Baath Party: a History from its Origins to 1966* (Stanford: Hoover Institution Press, 1966).

Febvre, Lucien, *Le Problème de l'Incroyance au XVIe Siècle, la Religion de Rabelais* (Paris: Albin Michel, 2003).

Haddad, Ghasan Muhammad Rishad, *Awraq shamiyya min tarikh suriyya al-mu'asir, 1946–1966* [Levantine documents on the history of Modern Syria, 1946–1966] (Cairo: Maktaba Madbuli, 2006).

Hanssen, Jens and Max Weiss (eds), *Arabic Thought against the Authoritarian Age: Towards an Intellectual History of the Present* (Cambridge: Cambridge University Press, 2018).

Hizb al-ba'ath, *Nidal hizb al-ba'ath al-'arabi al-ishtiraki 'abra mu'atamaratihi al-qawmiyya (1947–1962)* [The struggle of the Arab Socialist Baath Party through its national conferences] (Beirut: Dar al-Ṭali'a, 1971).

Hopwood, Derek, *Syria 1945–1986. Politics and Society* (London: Unwin Hyman, 1988).

Issawi, Charles, *An Economic History of the Middle East and North Africa* (New York: Columbia University Press, 1982).

Kaylani, Nabil, 'The Rise of the Syrian Ba'th, 1940–1958: Political Success, Party Failure', *International Journal of Middle East Studies* 3, 1 (1972): 3–23.

Lesch, David, *Syria and the United States: Eisenhower's Cold War in the Middle East* (Boulder: Westview Press, 1992).

Olson, Robert William, *The Baath and Syria 1947 to 1982, the Evolution of Ideology, Party and State, from the French Mandate to the Era of Hafiz al-Asad* (Princeton: Kingston Press, 1982).

Podeh, Elie, 'The Drift toward Neutrality: Egyptian Foreign Policy during the Early Nasserist Era, 1952–1955', *Middle Eastern Studies* 32, 1 (1996): 159–78.

Rey, Alain, *'Révolution', Histoire d'un Mot* (Paris: Gallimard, 1989).

Rey, Matthieu, 'Le Moment Electoral en Syrie et en Irak en 1954', *Maghreb-Machreck* 213, 3 (2013): 99–116.

Seale, Patrick, *The Struggle for Syria: A Study of Post-War Arab Politics, 1945–1958* (Berkeley: University of California Press, 1965).

Vatikiotis, Pananayotis, *The Modern History of Egypt* (London: Weidenfeld & Nicolson, 1969).

Vigneau, Jean, 'L'Idéologie de la Révolution Égyptienne', *Politique Etrangère* 22, 4 (1957): 445–62.

United States Department of State, *Foreign Relations of the United States, 1952–1954, Near and Middle East*, Vol. 5.

Wieviorka, Olivier, *Les Orphelins de la République. Destinées des Députés et des Sénateurs Français (1940–1945)* (Paris: Seuil, 2001).

4

DEALING WITH DISSENT: KHALID BAKDASH AND THE SCHISMS OF ARAB COMMUNISM

Sune Haugbolle

Introduction

Khalid Bakdash (1921–85), as the long-time leader of the Syrian and Lebanese Communist Parties, was a towering figure in Arab communism. Most of the scant existing academic literature sees him as the embodiment of the way in which the Soviet global communist movement, in Tareq Ismael's words, 'dominated' and 'controlled'[1] Arab Communism.[2] This dominance, so the literature claims, often led to uncritical acceptance of the canons of Soviet Marxism and a concomitant failure to formulate independent social analysis of the specific conditions of Arab societies.[3] The assessment of Bakdash as 'implanted', inserted and coerced from the outside, is symptomatic of a broader tendency to place non-Western communists on the fringe of local knowledge production, if not completely dismiss them. While many Communist leaders certainly did respond directly to Moscow, it is a reductive reading, which allows theoretical, methodological and sometimes ideological leanings to skew the evaluation of Arab Communism and Arab Left histories.

[1] Ismael, *The Communist Movement in the Arab World*, x.

[2] Ismael, *The Arab Left*; Ter Minassian, *Colporteurs du Komintern*.

[3] Suleiman, 'The Lebanese Communist Party'.

More than anything, it forecloses inquiry into their role in intellectual and political developments in the region.

Recent work by intellectual historians has redressed this tendency somewhat, although primarily in relation to writers and thinkers of the Arab New Left of the 1960s and 1970s.[4] In this chapter, I attempt to surmise what the social history of Arab communism can tell us about the nuances of internal dissent and debate in the movement. In doing so, I rely on biographies of Bakdash, and particularly on the way he, and the Syrian Communist Party (until 1964 the Syrian–Lebanese Communist Party) that he directed, reacted to the partition of Palestine. I narrate the period leading up to 1948 and the reactions that followed his decision to support the Soviet line. By analysing this crucial question, I turn the gaze towards Khalid Bakdash in his local context rather than Bakdash as Moscow's man. I hope to suggest ways in which we can produce histories of Arab communism that concern themselves with more than political strategy, but also speak to the broad agenda of the intellectual and social history of the Arab Left in its *longue durée*, exemplified by the present book. As a 'doer' more than a 'thinker', a political leader and not an intellectual in the conventional understanding of the term, Bakdash is exactly the sort of figure who has not received much attention, as opposed to the poets, novelists, theoreticians and editorialists of the Marxist-Leninist Left.

Reassessing the 'Minority Complex' of Arab Communism

Striking a balance between the obvious influences from Moscow and the equally obvious fact that Arab communists developed their thoughts and ideals in communication with their local milieu is far from easy. Indeed, the problem extends to the global historiography of the Left. One of the main areas of contention in the historiography of the Comintern has been the relationship between the International in Moscow and the national sections, or Communist parties. Here, there are three main schools of thought.[5] The first argues that, while Communist parties around the world may have started out as semi-independent bodies with views of their own, they rapidly became

4 For example Frangie, 'Exiled from History'.

5 Thorpe, 'Comintern "Control"'.

subservient to Moscow. Political opponents of communism first developed this position in the 1920s and 1930s. During the Cold War, Western writers hostile to the Soviet Union, and Trotskyites and other far-left opponents of Stalinism who believed that Lenin's successors perverted and subverted the ideals that had originally driven the Bolshevik Revolution and the creation of the Comintern, continued in the same vein. Historians writing along these lines remained influential up to the 1970s, and their basic premises continue to inform some of the analysis of the international Communist movement, including in the Middle East.

As part of the 'new labour history' that E. P. Thompson helped launch in the 1960s, another, more revisionist, reading developed. These writers were less interested in the high politics of the Comintern or the national Communist parties around the world, but rather in the lived experience of communists in their various settings: what they read, who their colleagues were, and how their local and transnational social networks informed their communism. This school of social history had a limited impact on scholarship on Arab communism during the Cold War, which remained often very ideologically skewed and methodologically inclined towards International Relations.[6] From the late 1970s onwards, a third view, which Andrew Thorpe calls post-revisionist, emerged as a reaction to both these schools of thought.[7] This approach rejects the idea that communists were marionettes manipulated by a Kremlin puppet-master, but argues that it is equally unrealistic to see them as acting totally within the context of their own labour movements and utterly unaffected by the Comintern. Most recent histories of communism adopt this tempered position.[8]

Inevitably, the questions historians ask and the sources they choose to consult will determine their evaluation of Arab communism. In the context of the new historiography of the Arab Left, it is important that we do not assign different research agendas to different periods and ideological strands. The four great strands of Arab Left history – Arab communism, Arab socialism (Baathism and Nasserism), Arab New Left groups and recent

[6] In particular Laqueur, *The Struggle for the Middle East.*

[7] Thorpe, 'Comintern "Control"', 639.

[8] Priestland, *The Red Flag*; Beinin, *Workers and Peasants.*

revolutionary/protest groups – all deserve to be examined through the lenses of high politics as well as intellectual and social history. As it is, scholarship on the two former traditions still invites more standard political histories than explorative social histories. This is perhaps not surprising, given that Nasserism, Baathism and communism influenced the state apparatus of the Arab republics, while New Left and protest groups had a more grass-roots character and those belonging to them remained in opposition, prison, exile, or six feet under. Orit Bashkin's work on Iraq has led the way, but many aspects of Arab communist life beyond the level of formal politics remain unexplored. At the very least, we should question the biases, including the theoretical and methodological biases, to which we subject these histories, not least since much of the new historiography reflects on, and is partly written by, people with a stake in the Arab New Left.

Ideological biases have always marred scholarship of the Left. While Maxime Rodinson, who wore his Marxist sympathies on his sleeve, loomed large over the literature on Arab Marxism in the 1970s, often written by Marxists, many other scholars of Arab communism, such as Walter Laqueur, were outrightly dismissive.[9] In such a vein, common claims that Arab Marxism was largely alienated from its own environment found resonance. By the end of the Cold War, many disillusioned Marxists joined the chorus, by way of remembering and reassessing their involvement and 'what went wrong'. These self-critiques also engendered institutional changes. Some communist movements even changed their name during the wave of self-criticism. For example, the Palestinian Communist Party became The People's Party in 1991.[10] Embracing a nationalist, or even sometimes an Islamist, position allowed disillusioned Marxists to rediscover the connection to the broad population.

The assessment of non-Western Marxist groups as inauthentic sticks in theoretical and historical work on the global Left. For some, the Marxian Left in the Global South was primarily an avant-garde, 'elitist rather than popular', that 'embraced a vision of modernisation that had in common with capitalism and imperialism a conception of the Third World as inexorably backward and behind.[11] It is a line repeated also by some former Marxists,

[9] Rodinson, *Marxisme et Monde Musulman.*

[10] Najjar, 'After the Fall', 337–60.

[11] Buck-Morss, *Thinking Past Terror*, 7.

who in retrospect regret their alienation from workers and peasants.[12] In this vein, Arab communists were part of a global tribe of unfortunate intellectuals who because of Moscow's direct influence followed a line that led them to self-exclusion from their surroundings. If the Comintern played a key role in directing the action, that provides a perfect explanation for why Arab Marxists and communists remained, in the words of Ter-Menassian who has explored this angle, a minority. In fact, they were minorities in two related ways, per Menassian. First, most of their members were initially from minority groups: Kurds, Armenians, Jews and Christians. Second, they never managed to 'Arabise' and hence integrate into their social environment, despite the fact that Soviet leaders already in the early 1930s had noted the problem and encouraged 'Arabisation'.[13] In that way, the minority base of Arab communists relates to their general cultural marginalisation and the purported domination of Soviet communism.

The minority complex is certainly both real and undoubtedly troubling for those involved in the movements at the time and today. At the same time, sweeping conclusions about the relative importance of real or imagined minority status also rests on the methodological dominance of top-down history, in which party doctrine is made equivalent with (the lack of) party–society relations. As anyone who has spent time with a wider range of source material than policy reports knows, Marxists were, and are, very much part of the social fabric of Arab societies. The Iraqi Communist Party has been examined from this angle arguably more than any other Arab communist party. Orit Bashkin's books on Iraqi Jewish history examine the rootedness of Iraqi communists, as does Tareq Ismael in his history.[14] Johan Franzén's political history of the ICP shows how it gradually transformed itself into an 'Iraqist' nationalist party – not dissimilar from other political parties in the country at the time – rather than merely being a Soviet 'satellite' party, which Third World communist parties are usually said to have been. For Frantzén, this syncretisation of political ideologies is key to understanding the role of the ICP in the region after Stalin's death in 1953. The ICP went from being a Marxist-Leninist party with a dogmatic understanding of Iraqi society to

[12] Haugbolle, *War and Memory*.

[13] Ter Minassian, Taline, *Colporteurs du Komintern*, 153.

[14] Ismael, *The Rise and Fall of the Communist Party of Iraq*.

becoming an *Iraqi* party espousing an ideology of *watani* (nationalist/patriotic) socialism.

Franzén's approach is mainly institutional, whereas Bashkin's approach is one of cultural history, drawing on individual biographies.[15] In order to develop a biographical approach to Arab communism, which dominates other kinds of intellectual history from Albert Hourani to Weiss and Hanssen, we must explore how we can merge intellectual and political history.[16] An obvious place to start is by zooming in on the individuals who shaped parties and movements, but who were not necessarily the most influential knowledge producers. At the same time, we should seek to understand contention inside these movements, rather than just the party line that strong and dominant leaders such as Bakdash made count. They obviously did so because of their relation with Moscow. This is just not the whole story about Arab communism. If we dig deeper into cultural and intellectual production in and around Communist movements, we begin to detect individual doubts, personal disagreement, internal debates, shifts and contradictions. If we situate Communists in their local context, a more intimate history emerges.

Bakdash's Role in Developing Communist Culture in Syria and Lebanon

The communist parties in Lebanon and Syria developed a political structure for a wider radical public that existed from the late Ottoman period, when students, journalists and artists debated and translated Marxist, anarchist and socialist works and ideas.[17] As a young law student in Damascus, Bakdash entered these circles, and at just eighteen years old he joined the Syrian Communist Party in 1930, the year when it merged with the Lebanese Communist Party to become the Syrian–Lebanese Communist Party. His biographers describe Bakdash, coming as he did from a powerful Kurdish tribe, as having had natural inclinations towards leadership.[18] He acquired the admiration and help of a Russian communist, who sent him to Moscow to study Marxist

15 Bashkin, *The Other Iraq*; Franzén, *Red Star*.

16 Hanssen and Weiss (eds), *Arabic Thought*.

17 Makdisi, *The Eastern Mediterranean*.

18 Mukhaybir, 'Khalid Bakdash'.

ideology. In Tashkent, he learned to speak and read Russian, which was to serve him well in his future political life. Emboldened by his sojourn, he returned to the Levant in 1932, and led an opposition against the leader of the SLCP, Fu'ad Shimali, accusing him of being an agent of the French police. Over the next two years, Bakdash positioned himself as a leader of this group of newcomers in the party, but also had to dodge French police, going underground for several periods. He finally succeeded in ousting Shimali and taking over as first secretary in 1934.[19]

Under the new leadership, the party expanded beyond the smaller circle of original members from the 1920s. Bakdash worked closely with many of the people who were to become central figures in the Lebanese and Syrian communist movements in the following decades, including Niqula Shawi and Farajallah al-Helou, who was to become Bakdash's main rival for leadership of the party. He travelled to Moscow and Paris, where he established close contacts inside the French Communist Party. During this period the party grew, but still struggled to attract members other than students and intellectuals. Khalid Bakdash began to translate Russian and French Communist literature into Arabic and helped to launch the magazine *al-Tali'a*. In *al-Tali'a*, and other periodicals and newspapers such as *al-Tariq*, Arab communists debated their ideological and practical priorities. The main question at the time was whether to ally with the National Bloc and other nationalist parties in Syria in the struggle to liberate Syria and Lebanon from the French. Through this work, Bakdash become close friends with the other editorial board members. *Al-Tali'a* was like a family, and editorial meetings would often merge with social gatherings of friends and relatives.[20] This way of forging political culture and ideological unity through friendship and socialisation is a common feature in small, close-knit political communities. It intensifies and personalises identification, but also tends to make politics a very personal matter during times of crisis and disagreement. Such times were coming for the Syrian and Lebanese communists.

In 1939, with France entering the Second World War, the government banned the FCP and hence restricted the operations of the SLCP. In response

[19] Ibid., 314.

[20] Mroué, *Un Demi-siècle d'Utopie*, 12–15.

to the Vichy regime and the Soviets joining the Allies in the war effort against the Axis powers, Bakdash helped to form a League for the Struggle against Nazism and Fascism in Syria and Lebanon, which was really a Communist front organisation, but drew in many different people who had not previously been active in the communist sphere. In this way, the Second World War confirmed the direction Bakdash and others had chosen for the party, which mirrored similar developments in Iraq, away from a restricted Leninist vanguard organisation, and towards a broad popular movement attracting – in Syria – particularly students, Kurds and workers. Bakdash was also instrumental in a more overtly pro-Moscow line, both in the Syrian and the Lebanese branches of the party. During the Second World War, he became a key informant and go-between for the Soviets, passing messages to the Syrian government at a time when they had no other way of communicating directly.[21] Following the establishment of a Soviet embassy in Beirut in 1944, many Lebanese communists, who had previously been wary of Stalin, shifted their allegiance to the Kremlin. Bakdash helped engineer these 'conversions' through his leadership. He cemented the alliance by visiting Moscow continuously, and by representing the SLCP in international communist conferences in France, Russia and Great Britain.

The Other *Mithaq Watani*

The partition of Palestine happened right in the middle of a general ascent for the party and for Bakdash as the 'dean' (*'amid*) of Arab communism, as people often call him even today. What followed from 1948 severely undercut public support for the Syrian and Lebanese communist parties, carefully established in the preceding decade and particularly during the war. It also changed the nature of the movement and led to international debates and ideological shifts, not least between the Lebanese and Syrian branches of the party.

Looking back at the 1940s and 1950s, veteran members of the Lebanese Communist Party, whose testimonies appear in the 1998 NBC documentary *The Parties of Lebanon* (*Ahzab Lubnan*), all emphasise the vitalism of the party. As the former leader of the LCP, Karim Muruwa, stresses, that vitalism

[21] Zamir, *The Secret Anglo-French War*, 155.

cannot just be appreciated by looking at its core members. Many influential families from all parts of the country joined or supported the LCP in those years. Communism was rooted in popular and organisational life. Muruwa remembers:

> Individual social movements and labour unions were under the control of the Communist Party. The Lebanese Partisans of Peace, headed by Antun Thabet, was active since 1949 and at times attracted thousands of sympathizers. There were the Communist-dominated trade unions. Mustafa el-Ariss, a veteran Communist, headed the Federation of Trade Unions, which encompassed the carpenters, builders and printers unions.[22]

These broad coalitions were the result of careful work to include more sections of society and to build alliances from below. The new tactics expressed themselves most clearly in the events of 1943 and 1944. When the LCP ran for elections in 1943, its campaign centred on two slogans: national solidarity and moderate democratic reforms. It downplayed any designs for building a socialist system or even for nationalising companies and land, and instead put itself forward as a reformist party focused on modernisation. These non-revolutionary principles were later embodied in the party's 'national charter' – the Communist *mithaq watani,* not to be confused with the Lebanese *mithaq watani* from the same year – drafted at the first public National Congress of the Communist Party in Syria and Lebanon held in Beirut between 31 December 1943 and 2 January 1944. One hundred and eighty delegates met at this Congress and drew up a set of by-laws for the organisation. For a party that had endured many periods of harassment and forced existence underground, the congress represented a high point of communist power and inclusion in national politics. It also showed the internal strength and dynamism of the party. Living clandestine lives, Bakdash and his comrades had learned how to forge strong bonds, but also to be tactical. In his later life as a sometime-outlawed leader, sometime-member of parliament in Syria, Bakdash would use this experience of moving between clandestine and public roles to make the most of his alliances at home and abroad.

[21] Karim Muruwa in *Ahzab Lubnan – al-hizb al- shuyu'i al-lubanani,* 2004. DVD. Beirut: NBC. Episode 2, 9.33–10.54.

The fact that the party had come to emphasise its national, rather than its communist international, character in both Syria and Lebanon was the result of long and divisive debates inside the party as much as of recommendations from Moscow. It also reflected the mood at the time. The independence of Syria and Lebanon planted a hope in many people that thriving independent nations could have a political space for communism, where they could freely develop and, over time, move their countries towards economic and social reform. The Third International (the Comintern) had dissolved itself in May 1943, throwing the nature of Soviet support into question. In response to this nationalist mood, the *mithaq watani* decided to split the SLCP into a Syrian and a Lebanese branch but to retain a joint leadership and Central Committee with Bakdash at the helm. Later, on 23 July 1944, with 118 delegates claiming to represent 10,000 organised Communists, the joint Central Committee decided that the two parties should have separate central committees, but that they should co-operate in organisational, political and other common interests through regular meetings between the two leadership groups.[23]

This frenzied political activity and reorganisation in 1943–4 was to have a decisive impact on the way the party, or parties, eventually responded to the Palestine crisis. On ther one hand, Farajallah al-Helou emerged as president of the Lebanese Communist Party, with Khalid Bakdash president of the Syrian Communist Party. The two men had different visions for communist organisation in the Levant, which was to become clear in due course.

Bakdash and the Palestine question

If Bakdash's life and leadership in the SCP and the SLCP had been largely successful up to the end of the Second World War, the partition of Palestine presented the movement with a huge problem. As the leader, he had a difficult decision to make, in terms both of where he thought the party should position itself and of how he should deal with internal dissent. When Britain referred the Palestine issue to the UN in 1947, the Soviet Union supported Zionist demands for statehood and voted for the partition plan. It is Bakdash's 'original sin', and by association that of Arab communism (this is how fateful many think it was), to have gone along with this decision. Before

[23] *Ahzab Lubnan*, Episode 2, 2:11–3:27.

reviewing Bakdash's position and debates within the party, it is worth considering the Soviet line first.

Existing historiography mentions several reasons why the Soviets ended up favouring partition. Ideological sympathy for Zionism was not one of them. They had largely continued following the rejection of the Zionist idea that Lenin had already in 1903 formulated as 'utterly untenable scientifically . . . and entirely false and reactionary in its essence'.[24] Lenin was of course very wrong about the former, as Soviet leaders over time came to realise. In 1947, the Zionist movement was a useful ally from the Soviet point of view. The Zionists were anti-British and contained socialist elements. Moreover, some of the leaders in Moscow came to see the creation of the state of Israel as the introduction of a progressive state in the Middle East. Finally, although there is no historical support for this assumption, they may also have sought to put a spanner in the works between US and British approaches to the Palestine issue, as many members of the Truman administration were against partition.[25] Walter Laqueur has even suggested that the Palestine issue simply was not very important for the Soviet leadership at a time when so many other balls were in the air, and that the pro-partition line was proposed and accepted at a relatively junior level.[26]

Khalid Bakdash received the message from Moscow and, through a bitter and divisive internal struggle, cemented it as the official position of the party, based on the reasoning that a solution to the Palestinian–Israeli conflict had to come from 'international legitimacy', defined as respect for United Nations resolutions that recognised Israel but gave Palestinians the right of compensation or return. Even in the Palestinian political realm, the Communist Party was the only Palestinian party that accepted UN Resolution 181 of 29 November 1947, which partitioned Palestine into two states, Arab and Jewish. Other Palestinians at that time considered the partition an act of treason, as did a majority of Syrians and Lebanese.[27]

By adopting the Soviet line, Bakdash made a dangerous gamble not just with regard to popular opinion in the country and in the region, but also

[24] Quoted in Ismael, *Communist Movement in the Arab World*, 57.

[25] Krammer, *The Forgotten Friendship*.

[26] Laqueur, 'Soviet Policy and Jewish Fate'.

[27] Najjar, 'After the Fall: Palestinian Communist Journalism', 352.

in relation to the party's own previous line. From its inception and up May 1947, the SLCP had consistently rejected any partition scheme. Its arguments during this period, based on scientific socialism and following Lenin, were that Zionism was a reactionary imperialistic movement, that partition was an imperialistic plot against the Arabs, that Arabs and Jews could and should live peacefully together and, most importantly, that the Jews did not constitute a nation. Hence, the idea of a Jewish national home was not valid. Yet, it suddenly became valid when, on 14 May 1947, the Soviet representative at the United Nations, Andrei Gromyko, announced that there were two nations (Arab and Jewish) in Palestine, with – quoting from his speech – 'equal historic roots in the country'. The Soviet Union voted for the partition plan, recognising Israel within an hour of its inception as a state. Moscow had briefed Bakdash about the new position and he dutifully made sure that the Syrian and Lebanese branches of the Communist Party followed their comrades in Moscow and changed their previous stand.

One could view the re-interpretation of the Palestine question as partly informed by a minoritarian view of the Middle East. According to Moscow's new interpretation, the Jews in Palestine constituted a nation-in-the-making, perhaps supporting Tar-Minossian's thesis that Bakdash continued to view the communist struggle partly through the eyes of minority groups in the region. In Rodinson's (possibly hackneyed) reading of Bakdash's personality, his Kurdish identity continued to influence his disposition, and sometimes, after a few drinks, could even turn anti-Semitic:

> Beaucoup de Kurdes ou de demi-Kurdes arabisés entre autres ont joué un rôle politique important, même dans le cadre du nationalisme arabe, sans qu'on songeât à leur reprocher leur origine, mais il fallait au minimum mettre l'accent sur l'assimilation, non sur l'origine. Or, son orgueil inné et sa volonté de puissance poussaient Khaled, quand son contrôle de lui-même se relâchait sous l'effet de l'alcool, à mettre en avant son kurdisme, à se vanter de son 'aryanisme' par rapport aux 'Sémites' arabes qui l'entouraient. C'était une 'supériorité' de plus. Telle était l'influence diffuse des doctrines racistes, surtout sur les personnalités qui pouvaient s'en servir pour se rehausser.[28]

[28] Rodinson, *Marxisme et Monde Musulman*, 420.

There is nothing to suggest that Bakdash sympathised with the Zionist movement, but perhaps he understood the minoritarian logic better than others, if that was indeed how Moscow sold him their line. Moscow further denounced the Arab–Israeli war as an imperialistic plot conceived by the British and King Abdullah of Jordan to prevent the establishment of the independent Arab state in the Arab portion of Palestine and to engineer its annexation to the British colony of Transjordan. The central co-ordination committee of the SLCP led by Bakdash stressed the point that the Palestine issue in essence represented the struggle against British–American imperialism, and called for unity in the attempt to force the Arab armies to withdraw from Palestine.[29]

The most lucid and detailed statement of the SLCP's stance on the Palestine issue can be read in a top-secret letter forwarded to the members of the Central Committee in the regional committees in Syria and Lebanon. The letter is quoted and discussed in *Ahzab Lubnan.*[30] It states that 'later events proved the correctness of the Soviet stance on the partition of Palestine and the opposition to the Palestinian war which was being encouraged by the British and American imperialists, the Arab reactionaries and the reactionary Zionism', in order to divert the attention of the Arab and Jewish masses from the struggle against the ruling reactionary forces and the British and American imperialists. Contrary to the 'propaganda' spread by the Arab nationalists, so the letter says, the Communist Party asserted that the imperialist danger was far greater than the Zionist threat, which was merely part of the imperialist menace. Besides, to consider the Jewish state as a 'homogeneous unit' is essentially a 'nationalist, bourgeois, chauvinistic view'. One needs to recall Marx's famous statement, the letter said, that 'in every nation there are two nations'. So it was with the Jewish state, where there was on the one hand a group of Arab and Jewish workers and communists working for national liberation, democracy and socialism, and, on the other, the 'reactionary, bourgeois Zionists, the agents of imperialism'. In conclusion, the Central Committee called for peace and the establishment of two independent states, Arab and Jewish, so that closer understanding might prevail between the Arab and Jewish masses.

[29] Ismael, *Communist Movement in the Arab World*, 57–70.

[30] *Ahzab Lubnan*, Episode 2, 14:29–15:39.

Critique, Chasm and Stalinist Show Trials

These are the ideological and linguistic acrobatics by which Bakdash made the party come round to Moscow's line, but it did not happen without great resistance. Bakdash essentially had to hammer his line through, which changed both the coherence of the communist movement and its mode of handling internal opposition. Immediately after May 1947, the prominent Lebanese communists Hashim al-Amin and Farajallah al-Helou expressed concern and even dismay that Bakdash had allowed international considerations and loyalty to Moscow to override political feelings that were so deeply rooted in Arab populations: the quest for liberation and independence. They also accused him of having made a strategic blunder, which could jeopardise the advances made in previous years. Shortly after 14 May 1947, Helou said to Bakdash, according to Karim Mroue's recollection of the events: 'Let us be committed to our country – think of how we can serve it best in the long run.'[31] He pointed out that support for the partition plan was going to be seen as an ideological 180-degree turn, which was nothing more than stating the obvious.[32]

However, sometimes stating the obvious can be a costly thing to do. In fact, al-Helou did more than criticise: he also recommended an alternative course of action, that the party should distance itself from the USSR on this point, but remain faithfully committed on others.

Al-Helou was not inherently anti-Soviet. In 1934, as a very young man and before joining the Party, he had travelled to the USSR and made a tour of the Asian Soviet Socialist Republics, which he described in glowing terms in the book *A New Humanity Building a New World* (1935). Rather, he made his criticism out of concern for the role he knew the cause of Palestine played in the Arab population. Very soon, it led to a direct confrontation with Bakdash and the people close to him. Perhaps it was part of the explanation for Bakdash's long-term success as a leader: he was good at forging friendships but never afraid to break them out of strategic and ideological concerns. Eventually, Farajallah al-Helou was not excluded, but forced to write a letter of apology and self-criticism, which is known as *risalat salim*. The letter is

[31] *Ahzab Lubnan*, Episode 2, 16:49–18:03.

[32] Mroué, *Al-shuyu'iyyun.*

reminisccent of the show trials of Eastern Europe, in which Stalinist regimes forced prominent communists to perform public *mea culpas* for corruption or collaboration with the West, despite the fact that national and international audiences often did not believe half of the charges that the accused admitted. In a recent book about these trials, *Curtain of Lies: The Battle over Truth in Stalinist Eastern Europe*, Melissa Feinberg argues that the primary purpose of these trials was not to convince the public.[33] Rather, they served to describe a world where the peace-loving socialist East was continually menaced by the imperialist West, which sent spies and saboteurs to wreck its economic development and plotted to destroy it in a nuclear war. As a form of political play-acting, the show trials communicated to East Europeans how they should see the world and clarified the consequences of non-compliance.

Equally in Lebanon, when al-Helou accused himself in *risalat salim* of a having a petty bourgeois state of mind, and of deviation, nationalism and lack of bravery, the public knew that he did not necessarily disown his opinions, but that the party had closed ranks around Bakdash's decision. As the first real instance of Stalinism within the party, *risalat salim* marked a turning point for Bakdash, who now represented a line at odds with Lebanese and Syrian communists who wanted a more open and internally democratic party. In that respect, the year 1947–8 is very enlightening for understanding the diversity of opinion and ideological direction within Lebanese and Arab communism. On the one hand, we have a strong, Soviet-oriented leader, Bakdash, who faces opposition to his line from, on the other hand, a broad section of the party. He managed to beat it into submission, but the criticism lingered on and eventually led to the complete separation of the Syrian and Lebanese branches. Fouad Abdel Nour, a Syrian communist and member of the communist party from the late 1950s, draws a similar picture of a broad opposition to Bakdash, which he repressed.[34] Such institutionalised thought-policing heralded a measure of anti-intellectualism and a betrayal of the democratic ideals that the SSCP had spelled out so clearly in the *mithaq watani* and that one can read in communist publications from the 1920s to the 1950s.

[33] Feinberg, *Curtain of Lies*.

[34] Abdel Nour, *A'ishna*.

Conclusion

For some Arab communists, Khalid Bakdash eventually came to stand for anti-intellectualism and top-down Stalinist control. Others admired his leadership and ability to steer the Syrian Communist Party through the treacherous waters of the Cold War, all the way up to his death in 1995. Even if one adopts the critical view, I hope to have shown here that he was part of a rich and diverse intellectual and political environment, which just a few years before 1947 had produced a document testifying to its national democratic commitment. The decision to follow the Soviet line in the partition of Palestine proved to be a turning point, and in some respects a breaking point, for the kind of broad, democratic Syrian–Lebanese communism that had produced the *mithaq watani*. The internal struggles that ensued and eventually led to separation of the Syrian and Lebanese communist movements perhaps also foreshadowed the new currents that were to become the Arab New Left from the late 1950s onwards.[35]

Today, Lebanese communists still vividly remember *risalat salim*. In an article in the Communist newspaper *al-Akhbar* from 27 June 2012, Vice-General Secretary of the Lebanese Communist Party Saadallah Mazraani used the story of Farajallah al-Helou to illustrate the struggle between an essentially democratic and popularly rooted communism that he argues the LCP returned to in the second congress in 1968, opposed to the Stalinist communism of Khalid Bakdash – the very same Stalinism that the New Left of the 1960s rebelled against.[36] After 1968, the party embraced a full restoration of al-Helou on all levels. There are statues, songs and even a play about him. The propaganda for Bakdash has a rather staler feel to it, much like the propaganda of authoritarian Arab leaders.

From a historiographic point of view, however, we can do much more with Bakdash than read him through the possibilities he closed down and the critics he attempted to silence. There are many Arab Communist traditions. We should be interested in the way they have communicated, deliberated, clashed and debated with their surroundings, as well as with an international

[35] Haugbolle, '1967 and the New Arab Left'; Guirguis, 'Vietnam and the Rise of a Radical Left'.

[36] Mazraani, 'Idhran'.

leftist public. Bakdash's Arab communism represents more than the extended grasp of Stalinism in the Middle East: it represents part of a dialogue over positions that intersected with other nationalist, socialist agendas, forums and publics. When the Arab New Left emerged in the 1960s, it was partly in reaction to the Arab communism of Khalid Bakdash. To take one example, Socialist Lebanon, a small vanguardist group of intellectuals who published influential pamphlets in the 1960s, warned against relegating the working class to 'the waiting room of history'.[37] They thought Khalid Bakdash's call to temper the populist inclination and instead ally with the Soviet line was a way of repeating the colonisers' verdict that the Arab populations were not yet ready to rule themselves: a patronising, counterrevolutionary position backed by the USSR. The Arab New Left also thought that this 'not yet ready' was the result of a particular economic determinist reading of Marx that Moscow advocated, which led to the notion of stagism as an argument for supporting the national bourgeoisie. By taking the stance he did in 1948, Bakdash thus inadvertently helped infuse the counter-position of stagism in the ensuing decades.

Bibliography

Abdel Nour, Fouad, *A'ishna waharimna wa shufna akhiran* [We lived, and we aged, and we finally recovered] (Beirut: Dar al-Farabi, 2014).

Ahzab Lubnan – al-hizb al-shuyu'i al-lubnani, DVD (Beirut: NBC, 2004).

Bardawil, Fadi, 'Dreams of a Dual Birth: Socialist Lebanon's World and Ours', *Boundary 2* 43, 3 (2016): 313–35.

Bashkin, Orit, *The Other Iraq: Pluralism and Culture in Hashemite Iraq* (Stanford: Stanford University Press, 2010).

Beinin, Joel, *Workers and Peasants in the Modern Middle East* (Cambridge: Cambridge University Press, 2001).

Buck-Morss, Susan, *Thinking Past Terror: Islamism and Critical Theory on the Left* (London: Verso, 2003).

Brown, Archie, *The Rise and Fall of Communism* (London: Ecco, 2009).

Feinberg, Melissa, *Curtain of Lies: The Battle over Truth in Stalinist Eastern Europe* (Oxford: Oxford University Press, 2017).

[37] Bardawil, 'Dreams of a Dual Birth'.

Frangie, Samer, 'Exiled from History: Yasin al-Hafiz's Autobiographical Preface and the Transformation of Political Critique', *Thesis Eleven* 133, 1 (2016): 3–18.

Franzén, Johan, *Red Star over Iraq: Iraqi Communism before Saddam* (New York: Columbia University Press, 2011).

Guirguis, Laure, 'Vietnam and the Rise of a Radical Left in Lebanon, 1962–1976', *Monde(s). Histoire, Espaces, Relations* 14, 2 (2018): 225–44.

Hanssen, Jens and Weiss, Max (eds), *Arabic Thought beyond the Authoritarian Age* (Cambridge: Cambridge University Press, 2017).

Haugbolle, Sune, *War and Memory in Lebanon* (Cambridge: Cambridge University Press, 2010).

Haugbolle, Sune, '1967 and the New Arab Left', *British Journal of Middle Eastern Studies* 44, 4 (2017): 497–512.

Ismael, Tareq Y., *The Rise and Fall of the Communist Party of Iraq* (Cambridge: Cambridge University Press, 2012).

Ismael, Tareq Y., *The Communist Movement in the Arab World* (London: Routledge, 2004).

Ismael, Tareq Y., *The Arab Left* (New York: Syracuse University Press, 1976).

Krammer, Arnold, *The Forgotten Friendship: Israel and the Soviet Bloc, 1947–53* (Champaign, IL: University of Illinois Press, 1974).

Laqueur, Walter, *The Struggle for the Middle East: The Soviet Union and the Middle East, 1958–68* (London: Routledge, 1969).

Laqueur, Walter, 'Soviet Policy and Jewish Fate: In Russia and in Israel', *Commentary* (October 1956).

Makdisi, Ilham, *The Eastern Mediterranean and the Making of Global Radicalism, 1860–1914* (Berkeley: University of California Press, 2013).

Mazraani, Saadlallah, 'Idhran Farajallah al-Helou', *al-Akhbar*, 17 June 2012, <https://www.al-akhbar.com/Opinion/71621> (last accessed 30 April 2019).

Mroué, Karim, *Un Demi-siècle d'Utopie: Mémoires d'un Dirigeant de la Gauche Libanaise* (Paris: L'Harmattan, 2011): 12–15.

Mroué, Karim, *Al-shuyu'iyyun al-arba'a al-akbar fi tarikh lubnan al-hadith* [The four greatest communists in Lebanon's history] (Beirut: Dar al-Saqi, 2009).

Mukhaybir, Shima' Fadil, 'Khalid bakdash wa durihu fi al-hayat al-siyassiya al-suriya hata al-'am 1930' [Khalid Bakdash, his role in Syria's political life since 1930], *Majallat jami'at takrit lil-'ulum al-insaniya* 17, 7 (2010).

Najjar, Orayb Aref, 'After the Fall: Palestinian Communist Journalism in the Post-Cold War World', *Rethinking Marxism: A Journal of Economics, Culture & Society* 19, 3 (2007): 337–60.

Priestland, David, *The Red Flag: A History of Communism* (New York: Grove Press, 2009).

Rodinson, Maxime, *Marxisme et Monde Musulman* (Paris: Éditions du Seuil, 1972).

Suleiman, Michael, 'The Lebanese Communist Party', *Middle Eastern Studies* 3, 2 (1967): 134–59.

Ter Minassian, Taline, *Colporteurs du Komintern: l'Union Soviétique et Minorités au Moyen-Orient* (Paris: Presses de Sciences Po, 1997).

Thorpe, Andrew, 'Comintern "Control" of the Communist Party of Great Britain, 1920–43', *The English Historical Review* 113, 452 (June 1998): 637–62.

Zamir, Meir, *The Secret Anglo-French War in the Middle East: Intelligence and Decolonization, 1940–1948* (London: Routledge, 2015).

5

A PATRIOTIC INTERNATIONALISM: THE TUNISIAN COMMUNIST PARTY'S COMMITMENT TO THE LIBERATION OF PEOPLES

Daniela Melfa

Introduction

The Sixth Congress of the Tunisian Communist Party (Parti Communiste Tunisien, PCT) (29–31 December 1957) is considered by former militants just as memorable an event as the Twentieth Congress of the Communist Party of the Soviet Union, held some 21 months earlier (14–25 February 1956).[1] The Sixth Congress marked a breakthrough, since it decided on the Tunisification of the party cadres and a nation-centred programme. 'It was the congress of self-criticism', points out Habib Kazdaghli, a historian who had been a party cadre in the 1980s. 'Until then, the party had been focused on external factors which are important but it had limited itself to them.'[2] To highlight the break, the party name was changed from 'Communist Party of Tunisia' (Parti Communiste de Tunisie) to 'Tunisian Communist Party' (Parti Communiste Tunisien).[3]

[1] Toumi, *La Tunisie. Pouvoirs et Luttes*, 306.

[2] Interview with Habib Kazdaghli, L'Ariana, 12 June 2016.

[3] Toumi, *La Tunisie. Pouvoirs et Luttes*, 291. Raouf Hamza argues instead that this change occurred at the Second Congress (20–1 April 1946). See Hamza, *Communisme et Nationalisme*, 15.

Although, in its early days, Marxism rejected nationalism and the nation-state as instruments of power of the bourgeois class, in the 1950s the nationalist option, with its emancipatory value, was rehabilitated with regard to the oppressed countries.[4] The Communist and Workers' Parties of the Socialist Countries gathered in Moscow in 1957 agreed upon 'the spirit of combining internationalism with patriotism' and 'a determined effort to overcome the survivals of bourgeois nationalism and chauvinism'.[5]

The internal nationalist stance did not erase the PCT's international commitment to socio-political changes, but rather channelled it into the defence of liberation struggles worldwide. A sense of responsibility tempered the revolutionary impetus of the PCT, that rejected maximalism at home in favour of a democratic and social revolution, and spared no effort on the external front, not without caution. Despite the sense of belonging to a global community of meaning, the nationalist-oriented PCT campaigned mainly for the Vietnamese cause and the Arab movement of national liberation. In this essay, I shall focus on two specific cases, that is to say Palestine – 'the foremost all-Arab concern'[6] – and western Sahara. While the Palestinian cause caused much ink to flow, especially following the 1967 and 1973 Arab–Israeli wars, an eloquent silence enveloped the Sahrawis' struggle, which Moroccan communists had opposed since the 1960s.

Anti-imperialist Struggles and Arab Solidarities

In 1967, the Secretary-General Mohamed Ennafaa declared: 'Tunisia is not an island isolated from the rest of the world. On the contrary, it is immersed in this world that the October Revolution has shaken to its foundations, fifty years ago!'[7] The 1987 preparatory document of the Ninth Congress of

[4] Ismael, *The Communist Movement*, 25.

[5] *Declaration of Communist and Workers' Parties of the Socialist Countries, Meeting in Moscow, 1957*, New York: New Century, December 1957, <https://www.marxists.org/history/international/comintern/sino-soviet-split/other/1957declaration.htm> (last accessed 7 June 2018).

[6] Hudson, cited in Takriti, *Monsoon Revolution*, 234.

[7] *Article Paru dans la Pravda du 31 Octobre 1967 sous la Signature du Camarade M. Ennafaa, En l'an 50 de la Révolution d'Octobre: Des Perspectives Nouvelles sont Ouvertes pour les Pays du Tiers-Monde*, Archives Habib Kazdaghli (AHK), Parti Communiste Années 1963–81 (I).

the PCT reiterated that 'independence does not entail an inward-looking focus and we think that our country, despite its small dimension, can play a specific role'.[8] By clearly siding with the forces of socialism, liberation and peace in the post-Stalin era, the PCT not only aimed to contribute to the struggle against imperialist and war-like adversaries, but also praised openness to external influences as a source of enrichment and counted on international solidarity as a lever against French encroachment (as during the 1961 Bizerte Crisis) and Bourguiba's crackdown on political opponents and trade unionists.

In a world dichotomously divided into progressive and reactionary forces, Tunisian communists loudly defended the right of peoples to self-determination and non-interference, and (though to a lesser extent) individuals who all over the world were paying the price of their militancy. The PCT's combativeness on the international front was expressed mainly through a militant press. In the war against imperialism, words and ideas had replaced the armed struggle as primary weapons.[9] Newspapers, communiqués and leaflets were circulated in Tunis but also abroad, especially after the party was banned in early 1963 in the aftermath of a failed coup d'état. Tunisian communist students settled in Paris, who released public statements and published the bulletin *Espoir*, were particularly vociferous.

Transnational networks and practices maintained a worldwide horizon of struggle. The PCT's cadres – notably Mohamed Harmel, a member of the Political Bureau who spent his exile in Prague (1963–72) – attended international meetings of the Communist and Workers' Parties (held in the 1960s), the congresses of communist parties, first and foremost the Communist Party of the Soviet Union,[10] and festivals such as those organised by the French *l'Humanité* or the Italian *l'Unità*. An arena for exchange and discussion was also provided by *La Nouvelle Revue Internationale. Problèmes de la Paix et*

[8] *Projet de Document du 9° Congrès du Parti Communiste Tunisien* (n.d.), p. 32, Archives Départementales de la Seine-Saint-Denis (ADSSD), Sous-série 261 J 7, Dossier 26 Afrique du Nord.

[9] 'Révolution Nationale et Sociale', *La Nouvelle Revue Internationale* 103, 3 (Mars 1967): 183.

[10] Even if Mohamed Harmel pretended not to have been a habitué in Moscow. La Guérivière, 'Le Désarroi des Communistes', *Monde* (12 June 1990).

du Socialisme, a journal founded in Prague in 1958 in order to preserve a formal linkage after the dissolution of the COMINFORM (Communist Information Bureau) (1947–56). News about Tunisia appeared periodically in the chronicle section along with more detailed articles signed mainly by Mohamed Harmel. Arab communist leaders were also involved in international forums on issues such as national liberation, Arab unity and socio-economic development in the Third World organised under the auspices of *La Nouvelle Revue Internationale*.

During the 1961 Anticolonial Conference in Tunis, Italian communists reproached Tunisian comrades for their 'absolute apathy' at the news of Patrice Lumumba's assassination and noticed that only Dr Slimane Ben Slimane, a former Neo-Destour militant close to the PCT and editor-in-chief of *Tribune du Progrès*, took to the streets with a few students as a sign of protest.[11] The Vietnam war (1955–75), on the other hand, stirred up strong emotions and a communist representative, Abdelhamid Ben Mustapha, joined the Tunisian Committee of Solidarity with the Vietnamese People, founded by Slimane Ben Slimane in 1967. Tunisians felt a debt of gratitude to the Vietnamese people due to the 1954 French defeat at Dien Bien Phu that had started the process leading to Tunisian internal autonomy (1955) and independence (1956).[12] In January 1968, on the occasion of the visit to Tunisia of US Vice-President Hubert Humphrey and South Vietnamese Minister of Foreign Affairs Tran Van Do, the joint committee organised demonstrations that sparked off the Tunisian March 1968.[13] Progressive Tunisians were also attracted to North Vietnam, which, as a former French possession, offered an inspiring experience of cultural decolonisation. Linguistic policies, and notably the attempt to elaborate a scientific vocabulary in the national language, were particularly appreciated inasmuch as the Tunisian higher education system was still dominated by the French language.[14]

[11] (Viaggio effettuato in Tunisia dal comp. Sen. Maurizio Valenzi dal 28/9 al 5/10/1961), Note sulla situazione in Tunisia e sul P.C.T., Archivio Fondazione Gramsci Roma [AFGR], Archivio Partito Comunista [APC], Estero (Paesi) – Tunisia, fasc. 0484, ff. 1,019–31.

[12] 'Le Peuple Tunisien contre l'Agression Américaine au Vietnam', *Espoir* (April–May 1965): 2.

[13] Hendrickson, 'March 1968', 755–74.

[14] Thiem, Le Van, 'Vietnam: Langue Nationale et Enseignement Supérieur', *Tribune du Progrès* 18–19 (May–June 1962): 13–14.

Though their perspective was worldwide, Tunisian communists were particularly concerned by the destiny of Arab and Maghrebi peoples. The Algerian war of independence (1954–62) was at the top of the PCT's agenda for the bonds of solidarity with the neighbouring people and the dangers resulting from the right of pursuit across the border claimed by the French. The PCT counted on the United Nations to support the Algerian cause and rejected French pressure on the Tunisian government to execute Algerian political prisoners in Tunisia.[15] The PCT also followed with great attention the Algerian leadership's socialist experiment that enacted key measures of economic nationalism[16] such as agrarian reform, hydrocarbon nationalisation and industrialisation.[17]

According to the PCT, Tunisian nationalism was not at odds with pan-Arab solidarity, yet unification should comply with a set of conditions. The Arab communist leaders recognised the existence of cultural, linguistic and territorial affinities as well as the political and economic potential of a unified Arab bloc. Nevertheless, Egyptian hegemony within the United Arab Republic (1958–61) demonstrated the limits of so-called bourgeois pan-Arabism. The alternative was a democratic and revolutionary Arab nationalism leading to a federation progressively set up on a voluntary basis and granting broad powers to local governments.[18] All ideological differences should be settled beforehand, and the socialist and anti-imperialist option was considered a prerequisite to unification. Dealing with the project of unification between Libya and Tunisia launched in 1973–4, the PCT was suspicious of such an impromptu plan, which instead gained the support of Tunisian pan-Arab groups, such as Al-Amal Al-Tounsi.[19] Even if Tunisian communists admired the Libyan President, Muammar Gaddafi, for having overthrown a corrupt monarchy, closed

[15] 'À l'O.N.U. la Cause Algérienne est Sortie Victorieuse', *al-Tali'a* (17 February 1957); 'Sauvons de la Mort les Héros Algériens!' Parti Communiste Tunisien, *Bulletin Intérieur* 1 (20 February 1957), ADSSD, Sous-série 261 J 7, Dossier 50 Afrique du Nord.

[16] Gelvin, *The Modern Middle East*, 236.

[17] 'Algérie. Nationalisations Importantes', *Espoir* (April 1971): 6; 'Algérie', *Espoir* (November 1972): 3.

[18] 'Échange d'Opinions. Le Mouvement de Libération Nationale des Peuples Arabes', *La Nouvelle Revue Internationale. Problème de la Paix et du Socialisme* 7 (1964): 118–32.

[19] Ayari, *Le Prix de l'Engagement Politique*, 121.

British and American military bases and undertaken the nationalisation of oil resources,[20] they deemed that Maghrebi countries should pursue a federative association as agreed at the 1958 Tangiers Conference.[21]

The internationalist vocation of the PCT followed concentric circles insofar as the wider workers' and communist solidarity gave way to the Third World liberation struggles and then to the inner circles of Arab and Maghrebi causes. At the core of the PCT's activism remained the nation-state (*watan*) as a basic unit whose autonomy and identity should be staunchly preserved.

Longing for the Palestinian State

The Arab communist movement that upheld the establishment of a democratic state in Palestine had to come to terms with Soviet support for the 1947 UN Partition Plan and prompt *de jure* Soviet recognition of the state of Israel in May 1948. Pre-Second World War opposition to Zionism had faded for tactical and political reasons, provoking disarray and rifts among the Arab communists. Nevertheless, the Soviet Union did not guarantee unconditional support for Israel. In the mid-1950s, it adopted a policy of solidarity with Third World peoples and was fully aware of their revolutionary potential. The Soviet endorsement of a 'non-capitalist path of development' led it to back progressive Arab regimes and legitimate their socialist (though not Marxist-Leninist) policies. Subsequently, the Soviet Union approached Egypt and intervened against the tripartite aggression in the 1956 Suez Crisis.[22]

The PCT, whose members in the colonial period were mostly Europeans and Tunisian Jews, adhered to the Soviet position, recognising the state of Israel and condemning the 1948–9 Arab military reactions. Soviet openness towards the Arab front coincided with the emergence of a Tunisian communist leadership particularly sensitive to the Palestinians' rights and prone to use virulent language against Zionism – considered the outpost of imperialism – and the USA in the Middle East. During the 1956 War, the PCT heaped praise on Egypt and advocated effective solidarity towards the

[20] 'Une Politique Extérieure Équivoque', *Espoir* (April 1971): 1 and 4.

[21] 'À propos de la Fusion Tuniso-Libyenne. Position des Communistes Tunisiens', *Espoir* (January–February 1974): 1–2.

[22] Ismael, *The Communist Movement*, 57–70.

'sister' country. In the eyes of the PCT the Suez crisis proved the determinant role of the Soviet Union against Israeli, French and British aggression and its immense strength worldwide in the service of freedom, independence and peace.[23] At such an international conjuncture, the Tunisian regime should have revised its pro-Western foreign policy, engaged with the socialist bloc in the spirit of Bandung and set up friendly contacts with Egypt. However, Tuniso–Egyptian relationships grew acrimonious due to the protection granted by Nasser to Salah Ben Youssef, the former Secretary-General of the Neo-Destour, who had been condemned to death in absentia, and in 1958, shortly after Tunisia had joined the Arab League, Bourguiba severed diplomatic relations with the United Arab Republic.[24]

Bourguiba opposed the intransigent policy of Arab leaders, notably Nasser, in the Middle East and advocated a pragmatic and gradual approach – 'the policy of "stages" he pursued so successfully in the fight for Tunisia's independence'[25] – consistent with UN resolutions. In the famous visit to the Middle East in March 1965, Bourguiba fostered – in his own words – realism and common sense against a maximalist strategy, and declared openness to negotiation with Israel in order to reach a reasonable compromise and lay the foundations for fruitful co-operation. Even if the PCT shared a legalistic stance in line with UN pronouncements, it did not make any public statement on the occasion of the maverick speech of the President, supposedly in order not to endorse a regime that refused to align with the communist bloc.[26] The PCT approached the Middle Eastern conflict through the lens of national interest, which led the party to reiterate criticism towards Bourguiba's pro-American foreign policy and to call for the normalisation of Tunisian diplomatic relations with the United Arab Republic and Syria.[27]

23 *Déclaration du Comité Central du Parti Communiste Tunisien*, Tunis, 18 November 1956, AHK, Parti Communiste Années 1956–59.

24 *La Rupture des Relations Diplomatiques entre la République Tunisienne et la République Arabe Unie. Déclaration du Bureau Politique*, Tunis, 17 October 1956, AHK, Parti Communiste Années 1956–59.

25 Merlin, *The Search for Peace*, 31.

26 Ibid., 38–9.

27 'Les Peuples Arabes face à la Politique Agressive des Sionistes et des Impérialistes', *Espoir* (July 1967): 3.

The 1967 war triggered protest demonstrations in Tunis, and the PCT promptly expressed its solidarity in defence of the Palestinians and the progressive regimes of the United Arab Republic and Syria. The PCT called for the immediate evacuation of occupied territories and respect for UN resolutions with regard to the refugee problem and the territorial partition into two states along the 1949 frontiers:[28]

> Certain Arab nationalist milieus . . . do not want to see in the UN resolution of November 1967 a positive basis capable of forcing the Israeli leaders to evacuate their occupation troops . . . we consider that the application of this resolution can only be positive for Arab peoples, included the Arab people of Palestine.[29]

The PCT's realism complied with the stance of the Soviet Union, which brought all its weight to bear in passing UN resolution 242. Its adherence to the Soviet position was such that progressive Tunisian personalities, such as Slimane Ben Slimane,[30] raised criticisms. The disappearance of the state of Israel envisaged by the Tunisian Group of Study and Socialist Action (better known as Perspectives) and its replacement by the creation of a Jewish State of Palestine and an Arab State of Palestine, eventually merging into a federation, was not endorsed.[31]

Despite the lightning defeat and wide territorial losses, the PCT gave an optimistic assessment of the historical conjuncture: 'We are aware of the difficulties that lie ahead, but we are persuaded that the Arab movement of national liberation went one step further and today the situation is by far more favourable than two years ago.'[32] At the 1967 Khartoum summit Arab countries made common cause, overcoming their previous disagreements

[28] 'Pour Faire Échec aux Pretentions Colonialistes des Agresseurs, la Lutte Anti-Imperialiste Continue!' *Espoir* (July 1967): 1; 'Les Peuples Arabes face à la Politique Agressive', 3.

[29] *Réflexions sur les Caractéristiques Nouvelles du Mouvement de Libération Nationale*, Intervention de Mohamed Harmel à la conférence internationale des Partis communistes et ouvriers (Moscow, June 1969): 13, AHK, Parti Communiste Années 1963–81 (I).

[30] Kazdaghli, *Abdelhamid Ben Mustapha*, 241.

[31] Gruppo di studio e di azione socialista tunisino, 'La Questione Nazionale Palestinese', 356–64.

[32] *Réflexions sur les Caractéristiques Nouvelles*, 12.

(*in primis*, on the war in Yemen) to converge on the 'Three No's' policy.[33] This effort was praised along with the pursuit of armed struggle in the occupied territories and the development of Palestinian nationalism that demonstrated Arab political and military advances. Finally, the Soviet Union provided substantial support, and international public opinion, not duped by the self-pitying rhetoric of Israel as 'little David', turned out to be favourable to the Arabs. Even in Israel progressive forces made their voice heard.[34] The PCT pointed out that 'effective solidarity, reinforced alliance between socialist countries and struggling peoples . . . represents the best weapon in order to discourage aggression, and defeat imperialist plans'.[35] Developments in Palestine strengthened the Communist view on US collusion with Israel and the pivotal role of the Soviet Union in supporting national liberation movements. Consequently, the Middle Eastern conflict was reframed in the binary logic of Cold War blocs.

Subsequent events confirmed the PCT's previous appraisals of the international and regional situation. The 1970 Black September was condemned as an attempt by the reactionary Jordanian regime to crush the heroic Palestinian resistance, whose armed struggle the Arab communists finally endorsed.[36] The 1973 War provided a further opportunity to praise the unfailing alliance of the Soviet Union against the manoeuvres of the American enemy and to reaffirm the demarcation line between friends and fiends. The deterioration of Soviet–Egyptian relations since Sadat's takeover[37] did not make a difference. Arab solidarity was enhanced around the legitimacy of Egyptian and Syrian claims to recover their territories,[38] and international sympathy

[33] 'Après la Réunion de Khartoum l'Objectif reste tout pour la Liquidation des Séquelles de l'Agression', *Espoir* (September 1967): 1.

[34] *Réflexions sur les Caractéristiques Nouvelles*, 12.

[35] 'Les Peuples Arabes face à la Politique Agressive des Sionistes et des Impérialistes', 3.

[36] 'L'Enjeu de la Lutte Libératrice dans les Pays du Proche-Orient', *Espoir* (January 1971): 9–10; 'Faire Échec aux Tentatives Répétées de Liquidation de la Résistance Palestinienne', *Espoir* (April 1971) 4; Ismael, *The Communist Movement in the Arab World*, 37.

[37] Ismael, *The Communist Movement*, 71–5.

[38] 'Déclaration des Communistes Tunisiens. Pour le Triomphe de la Juste Cause des Peuples Arabes!' *Espoir* (October 1973); 'Faire Échec aux Tentatives Répétées de Liquidation de la Résistance Palestinienne', *Espoir* (April 1971): 4.

towards the Arabs deepened Israel's isolation. The 1973–4 Arab oil embargo proved the effectiveness of Arab unity and autonomous decision-making in the anti-imperialist struggle.[39] Consequently, the Yom Kippur War boosted the PCT's optimism as the balance of power had clearly changed and the myth of the invincibility of Israel had been shattered.

The Right to Self-Determination: A Double Standard?

'The struggle of the Palestinian people for the recognition of their legitimate, inalienable national rights . . . is a fair fight', the PCT constantly upheld.[40] Even if with a minor emphasis, Arab communists also overtly supported the rights of minority groups such as the Kurds. The 1958 provisional Iraqi constitution granted the Kurds the right to self-determination and the communists viewed with particular favour their autonomy within the Iraqi Republic.[41] This standpoint and the PCT's concern for international scenarios – as in the case of the American naval blockade during the Cuban Missile Crisis of October 1962[42] – contrasted with the PCT's eloquent silence over the Sahrawi issue despite its relevance for the Maghrebi unification process. This silence discloses embarrassment, since the PCT was torn between its loyalty to revolutionary regimes (Algeria and also Libya, backed by the Soviet Union, which championed the Sahrawi cause) and solidarity with the reactionary Moroccan monarchy and public opinion that prevailed in the Maghreb at an early stage.[43] The Sahrawi question blurred the lines of demarcation between the opposing factions.

The PCT's private archives do not bear evidence of any official statement, not even during such controversial moments as the 1970 Massacre of Zemla, the 1975 Green March, the 1976 proclamation of the Sahrawi

[39] Les Étudiants Communistes Tunisiens, *Contre l'Agresseur Sioniste et son Soutien: l'Impérialisme U.S. La Lutte des Peuples Arabes s'approfondit et se renforce*, AHK, Parti Communiste Années 1963 (IV).

[40] *Réflexions sur les Caractéristiques Nouvelles du Mouvement de Libération Nationale*, 13.

[41] 'L'Étape Actuelle du Mouvement de Libération Nationale des Peuples Arabes', *La Nouvelle Revue Internationale. Problèmes de la Paix et du Socialisme* 10 (October 1963): 116–17.

[42] Communiqué of the PCT Political Bureau, Tunis 24 October 1962, AHK, Parti Communiste Années 1960–2.

[43] Mahroug, 'Sahara occidental', 16.

Arab Democratic Republic or the 1979 Sahrawi–Mauritanian agreement. Though the PCT tirelessly opposed Tunisian foreign policy, Bourguiba's pro-Moroccan stance with regard to western Sahara did not raise any grievances. The PCT's discreet stance was possibly due to the principle of non-interference in Moroccan internal affairs, even though the issue was internationally debated and Sahrawi claims endorsed in the mid-1960s by the Organisation of African Unity and the United Nations (notably with resolution 2229 of 20 December 1966). The PCT's reticence to intervene is all the more striking in the light of Soviet approval of UN resolutions in favour of self-determination and independence. The PCT also distanced itself from the Italian Communist Party, whose newspaper *l'Unità* monitored with sympathy the Sahrawi struggle,[44] and its French counterpart that defended in *l'Humanité* the right of Sahrawi self-determination.[45]

Nonetheless, the PCT was quite informed about western Sahara, as news from the Moroccan weekly *al-Kifah al-Watani*, headed by the communist Ali Yata, and *al-Bayane*, the francophone newspaper of the Moroccan Party of Progress and Socialism (PPS), circulated among the party cadres. Arguably the PCT, which hesitated to take a public stand, was concerned about the issue the comrades discussed in private. Indeed, the fellow parties corresponded and entertained good relations. As an illustration, the Tunisian communist underground press welcomed the PPS's legal recognition in 1974,[46] just as the PPS called for the legalisation of the PCT, which was extolled for the self-sacrifice of its militants and its purported popularity among the Tunisian population.[47] The PPS had spoken out against Sahrawi independence since the 1966 UN meeting in Addis Ababa when this solution was envisaged and bluntly claimed Melilla, Ceuta, the Chafarinas Islands, Ifni, Saguia el-Hamra and Río de Oro as 'authentic Moroccan territories'.[48]

44 For an analysis of *l'Unità* with regard to western Sahara, see Cillepi, *Sahara Occidentale*.

45 Letter from the PPS to the Political Bureau of the French Communist Party, Casablanca (20 October 1975), AHK, Parti Communiste Années 1963–81 (II).

46 'Une Série d'Événements Importants dans les Partis Communistes et Ouvriers du Maghreb et du Machreq', *Espoir* (February 1975): 7.

47 'Résolution du CC du PPS sur le 15e Anniversaire de l'Interdiction du Parti Communiste Tunisien', *al-Bayane* (10 January 1978): 1.

48 Yata, Ali, 'Ce qui Appartient au Maroc doit Retourner au Maroc. Éditorial n° 70 du journal *al-Kifah al-Watani* du 17 juin 1966', AHK, Parti Communiste Années 1963–81 (I).

Ali Yata, who authored the two-volume book *Le Sahara Occidental Marocain*, laid emphasis on what he termed the fundamental contradiction in Third World countries between nation-state and imperialism. Liberation from the colonialism of the Spanish Franquist regime and Moroccan national integrity was assumed as a prerequisite for democracy and social progress. Western countries coveted western Sahara for the recently discovered mineral deposits (firstly phosphates) and the military bases to be established in place of the Mediterranean outposts that had been closed. A state of barely 80,000 inhabitants would inevitably have fallen prey to imperialist greed.[49] The PPS attacked Algeria's aim of hegemony and propaganda intended to spread panic among the Sahrawi population and discredit the Moroccan regime. Algeria was also deemed responsible for creating a compliant Sahrawi leadership and upholding the myth of the Sahrawi people, who instead, according to the PPS, formed a whole with Morocco. The PPS stressed the national consensus over the Sahrawi issue and justified the peaceful 1975 march of hundreds of thousands of Moroccan volunteers towards the southern territories.[50]

It can be assumed that the PCT hoped that an equitable solution to the conflict would remove any hindrance to rapprochement between the Maghrebi countries. The Moroccan–Sahrawi conflict proved that the unquestioned principle of national unity was actually a treacherous terrain that required Tunisian communists to proceed with caution. 'Fellow parties', the PPS pointed out, 'can have their own opinions, share them off the record in a brotherly way, but never publicly oppose the line of a fellow party with regard to the internal affairs of its country.'[51] Echoing the moderate and reasonable stance displayed in internal affairs, the militants of the PCT complied with the PPS's recommended strategy, thus appearing 'responsible revolutionaries' even in relation to external struggles.

In conclusion, the PCT's internationalism displayed an outward-looking gaze oriented towards the defence of nationalism and the nation-state in Third

[49] 'Le Conflit du Sahara Occidental et le Mythe du "Peuple Sahraoui"', *al-Bayane* (17 May 1978), AHK, Parti Communiste Années 1963–81 (I).

[50] Letter from the PPS General Secretariat to the PCT Central Committee, Casablanca, 23 October 1975, AHK, Parti Communiste Années 1963–81 (II).

[51] Letter from the PPS to the Political Bureau of the French Communist Party, Casablanca, 3 November 1975, AHK, Parti Communiste Années 1963–81 (II).

World countries. Special attention was paid to Arab peoples' national rights, although the Palestinian and Sahrawi struggles attest that not all nationalist claims were treated on the same footing. Unlike Albert Memmi, who wrote that for leftists of his generation 'the word "nationalist" still evokes a reaction of suspicion, if not hostility',[52] Tunisian communists were not at all uncomfortable with the idea of nationalism. The paradox of an internationalism devoted to nationalist causes is more apparent than real. Nationalism in colonised countries such as Tunisia was not understood as an instrument of class rule linked to the ascendant capitalism. In developing countries, the fundamental contradiction did not pertain to the bourgeois and proletarian classes, but rather the dominant imperialist powers (and foreign capitalist monopolies) that strove to hold the upper hand with former colonies. For that reason, oppressed peoples turned to nationalism as a weapon of resistance and liberation and counted on a sound nation-state to sever the links of neocolonial dependence and initiate a move towards socialism. In addition, under Stalin's leadership (1922–52) the Soviet Union endorsed the doctrine of Socialism in one country that prioritised the implementation of communism within the country (i.e. a national communism) rather than the project of a global communist society. This major turn paved the way for the development of patriotic communist parties which, attentive to socio-economic and cultural peculiarities, engaged primarily in the struggle for socialism in their own country. In the end it could be argued that proletarian internationalism had moved towards an internationalism of progressive nationalist forces.

Bibliography

Ayari, Michael, *Le Prix de l'Engagement Politique dans la Tunisie Autoritaire. Gauchistes et Islamistes sous Bourguiba et Ben Ali (1957–2011)* (Paris–Tunis: Éditions Karthala-IRMC, 2016).

Cillepi, Gabriele, *Sahara Occidentale: l'Ultima Colonia Africana. Attori, Arbitri e Osservatori di una Lotta Lunga Quarant'anni*, undergraduate dissertation, University of Catania, 2016–17.

Gelvin, James, *The Modern Middle East. A History* (New York and Oxford: Oxford University Press, 2011).

[52] Memmi, *The Colonizer*, 72.

Gruppo di studio e di azione socialista tunisino, 'La Questione Nazionale Palestinese e il Problema della Rivoluzione', in Anouar Abdel-Malek (ed.), *Il Pensiero Politico Arabo* (Rome: Editori Riuniti, 1973): 356–64.

Hamza, Raouf H., *Communisme et Nationalisme en Tunisie de la 'Libération' à l'Indépendance (1943–1956)* (Tunis: Université de Tunis I, 1994).

Hendrickson, Burleigh, 'March 1968: Practicing Transnational Activism from Tunis to Paris', *International Journal of Middle Eastern Studies* 44 (2012): 755–74.

Ismael, Tareq Y., *The Communist Movement in the Arab World* (London and New York: Routledge, 2005).

Kazdaghli, Habib (ed.), *Abdelhamid Ben Mustapha. Écrits, Hommages et Témoignages* (Tunis: Rosa Luxembourg Foundation, Fondation Hassan Saadaoui, 2017).

Mahroug, Moncel, 'Sahara Occidental. Vers une Formule d'Autonomie à l'Espagnole', *Le Maghreb* 107, 1 (July 1988).

Memmi, Albert, *The Colonizer and the Colonized* (London: Earthscan, 2003).

Merlin, Samuel, *The Search for Peace in the Middle East* (Cranbury, NJ: Thomas Yoseloff, 1968).

Takriti, Abdel Razzaq, *Monsoon Revolution: Republicans, Sultans, and Empires in Oman 1965–1976* (Oxford: Oxford University Press, 2013).

Toumi, Mohsen, *La Tunisie. Pouvoirs et Luttes* (Paris: Le Sycomore, 1978).

6

INTERNATIONALIST NATIONALISM: MAKING ALGERIA AT WORLD YOUTH FESTIVALS, 1947–62

Jakob Krais

Introduction

The Algerian war of independence between 1954 and 1962 was a global rallying point for internationalist solidarity and a symbol of the liberation of the Third World. The international dimension of the national revolutionary movement led by the Algerian National Liberation Front (FLN) in those years has recently been well-documented and -studied.[1] Significant research has also been dedicated to the development of Algerian nationalism and its relation to leftist parties in Algeria and metropolitan France before the war of independence.[2] Much less attention has been devoted to the international activities of nationalist and leftist movements before the start of the FLN's publicity campaigns in 1955.[3] But in fact, various political groups had been actively promoting their cause on the world stage at least since the end of the Second World War. It seems that the international struggle was almost as important as activities in Algeria and France for the making of Algeria as an independent nation.

[1] Byrne, *Mecca of Revolution*; Connelly, *A Diplomatic Revolution*.

[2] See in particular Stora, *Le Nationalisme Algérien avant 1954*; Drew, *We Are No Longer in France*; Le Foll-Luciani, *Les Juifs Algériens*.

[3] The only study with a completely transnational perspective is Goebel, *Anti-Imperial Metropolis*, albeit with a much wider focus.

This contribution will look at one set of events that allowed Algerian anti-colonial movements to present themselves in an international arena: the World Youth Festivals between 1947 and 1959. Algerian national delegations already participated in the Festivals before Algeria came into being as an independent state and, as such, can be seen as having contributed to the construction of Algerian nationhood. As the Festivals were gatherings for young people, participants did not represent political parties directly, but only their respective youth branches or more or less independent youth groups like the scouts. Youth movements had, however, been central to the development of Algerian nationalism in the last decades of French colonial rule.[4] These groups, with their different political persuasions, all contributed to the evolution of ideas about the nation. Although the FLN, which would finally incorporate the other currents, is often seen as the epitome of a socialist, Third-Worldist liberation movement, communists and nationalists as well as liberals and Islamists had played their part in Algerian youth organisations.

On the basis of coverage in the press, this chapter will look at the motivations and aims of the different Algerian youth groups at the Festivals and discuss the question of what made these gatherings, which were organised primarily by communist movements, attractive for them. Alongside this, it will ask how Algeria was perceived in the host countries and what effects the participation of Algerians could have had. Specifically, one section will analyse in more detail reactions in two host countries, namely East Germany and Austria.[5]

Representing a Nation in the Making: Algeria at World Youth Festivals

The World Festivals of Youth and Students – in short, World Youth Festivals – are events organised by the World Federation of Democratic Youth (WFDY)

[4] According to a major nationalist leader, some local youth branches of the Algerian People's Party (PPA) actually had more members than the regular (adult) sections and the party even had, for a time, a special 'Central Youth Committee'. Cf. Ben Khedda, *Les Origines du 1er Novembre 1954*, 129. See also Krais, 'Youth and Sports', 246–50.

[5] There exist some studies on the perceptions of foreign visitors from the West, but not from Middle Eastern countries: Koivunen, 'A Dream Come True'; Piccini, 'There Is No Solidarity'; Chiriu, 'Summer 1953, Bucharest'. On Soviet perceptions of foreign participants see Koivunen, 'Friends, "Potential Friends", and Enemies'; Peacock, 'The Perils of Building Cold War Consensus'.

and the International Union of Students (IUS). The WFDY emerged in late 1945 from a gathering of left-wing youth organisations in London, but soon evolved into a communist front organisation. The IUS, founded in Prague in 1946, followed a similar trajectory and ultimately developed into an instrument of Soviet cultural diplomacy.[6]

This chapter deals with the first seven World Youth Festivals, which were held every two years between 1947 and 1959, in Prague, Budapest, East Berlin, Bucharest, Warsaw, Moscow and Vienna.[7] During the period in question, between 10,000 and 34,000 foreign visitors attended each Festival, and the number of national delegations increased from 71 to 133.[8] Already, the number of 133 nations in 1959, that is, before the major wave of decolonisation in Africa, indicates that delegations represented not only sovereign states, but also dependent territories like French Algeria. For colonies aspiring to independence it was obviously of particular importance to be included as a regular national delegation in an international event, alongside the superpowers and the European countries, including the colonial metropoles. Delegations from what would become known as the Third World, from independent or from still-colonised countries, were often more mixed than the essentially communist ones from the Global North.[9]

In the Algerian case, participants at World Youth Festivals – regularly numbering more than a hundred people – represented the communist Union of Democratic Youth of Algeria (UJDA) or the Association of North African Muslim Students (AEMAN), in which communist and nationalist activists were competing for influence. But Algerian delegations also included the two indigenous scout organisations that were close to the radical nationalists and to the Islamic reformists, respectively: after the split of this youth movement in 1948, the Muslim Algerian Scouts (SMA) developed into a reservoir of activists for the major nationalist party, the Movement for the Triumph of Democratic Freedoms (MTLD) under the

[6] Kotek, *Students and the Cold War*, 62–106; Sutton, 'Britain, Empire', 224–8.

[7] The Eighth World Youth Festival in Helsinki lies beyond the purview of this chapter, as it took place only in summer 1962 and thus after Algerian independence.

[8] Kotek, *Students and the Cold War*, 212.

[9] See also Koivunen, 'Friends, "Potential Friends", and Enemies'; Sutton, 'Britain, Empire', 228–37.

leadership of Messali Hadj. Their rivals, the Muslim Algerian Boy Scouts (BSMA), for their part, remained strongly linked to the reformist *ulema* around Sheikh Bachir El Ibrahimi, in whose orbit the movement had been founded in the 1930s.[10] Apart from that, we encounter members of the youth wing of Ferhat Abbas's liberal, moderately nationalist Democratic Union of the Algerian Manifesto (UDMA). Until all political movements were eventually absorbed by the FLN during the war after 1954, Algerian delegations at World Youth Festivals thus represented a rather broad spectrum of political forces, ranging from liberal and Islamist to communist and radically nationalist. Only in 1957 and 1959 was the Algerian delegation essentially an FLN mission.[11]

Another question pertained to the idea of the Algerian nation which the delegations to such an international gathering were supposed to represent. Although northern Algeria, where the majority of the Algerian population lived, was not even in legal terms considered a colony, but an integral part of France, an Algerian national delegation, separate from the French one, was apparently accepted without much discussion from the first Festival on. That might have been unproblematic for the communist-dominated WFDY and IUS, because an Algerian Communist Party (PCA), separate from the French organisation, had existed already since 1936.[12] But as a settler colony Algeria presented further intricacies: indigenous Muslim Algerians made up around 90 per cent of the country's approximately 10 million inhabitants in the 1950s, but almost none of them was a French citizen. The settler population of European origin and the indigenous Jews, who for the most part had also been full French citizens for generations, had a political voice and an economic standing disproportionate to their numbers.[13]

[10] Cf. Watanabe, 'Organizational Changes in the Algerian National Movement'.

[11] Due to the war situation, and with most nationalist and communist organisations banned, there are practically no reports on the sixth Festival of 1957 in the Algerian press, although a delegation in fact went to Moscow. Cf. Nait-Challal, *Dribbleurs de l'Indépendence*, 77–8. On the developments and tendencies within Algerian nationalism see also Stora, *Le Nationalisme Algérien*, 133–49.

[12] Cf. Drew, *We Are No Longer in France*, 95–105; Marangé, 'André Ferrat et la Création du Parti communiste algérien', 208–18.

[13] Cf. Stora, *Histoire de l'Algérie Coloniale*, 29–43.

The PCA, with its affiliated organisations was, in fact, the only Algerian movement taking part in World Youth Festivals which included people from all ethno-religious groups, whereas the other associations were exclusively Muslim.[14] When Algerian politics became more and more polarised after 1945, the PCA was somewhat caught in the middle. General anti-imperialist commitments notwithstanding, Maurice Thorez, the secretary of the French Communist Party (PCF), had famously described Algeria as a nation still 'in formation', which hence should not secede from France.[15] Until after the Second World War, the PCA depended heavily on its French counterpart; its leadership, which was largely of European origin, generally followed the PCF's policies. When nationalist demonstrations on the occasion of Allied victory in Europe on 8 May 1945 degenerated into riots in the north-eastern Constantinois region, Algerian communists vilified the activists as fascists, despite the fact that the French army and settler militias killed many thousands of Muslim Algerians in a brutal campaign of repression.[16] The communist-nationalist unity of two decades earlier, when Messali Hadj had led the first Algerian political movement, the North African Star (ENA), as an affiliate of the PCF, now seemed a distant memory.[17] But, as the joint participation of Messali's young supporters and the communist youth in the Festivals suggests, relations improved again after 1945. This was also due to the fact that the PCA underwent a process of Algerianisation, with Muslim cadres replacing those with a European or Jewish background, over the decade between the May massacre and the beginning of the war of independence. Eventually, even former members of the nationalist MTLD joined the Communist Party before,

[14] The term 'Muslim' in the context of late colonial Algeria does not refer to an actual religious orientation, but rather denotes an ethnic group that was not 'European' or 'Jewish', i. e. indigenous Algerians whose mother-tongue was normally vernacular Arabic, Taqbaylit (Kabyle) or Tamazight ('Berber') and who came from traditionally Muslim families. As an ethnic designation the term 'Muslim' was not in contradiction with a secular stance; for example, the communists had played a leading role in the Algerian Muslim Congress of 1936.

[15] Drew, *We Are No Longer in France*, 110–12; Stora, *Le Nationalisme Algérien*, 44–8.

[16] Drew, *We Are No Longer in France*, 146–53; Stora, *Histoire de l'Algérie Coloniale*, 91–2.

[17] Drew, *We Are No Longer in France*, 43–6; Stora, *Le Nationalisme Algérien*, 21–41; Stora, *Histoire de l'Algérie Coloniale*, 76–7.

inversely, a large part of the PCA and its organisations was finally incorporated into the FLN from 1955 on.[18]

'Raise the Name Algeria High among the Other Peoples': Algerians' Aims

The complex relationship between nationalists and communists in the post-war years is also evident in the aims the different Algerian groups pursued at World Youth Festivals. Articles in the PCA's Arabic-language paper *al-Jaza'ir al-jadida* (New Algeria) – a product of the Algerianisation policy – often stressed the strictly internationalist side of the event. In 1949 and 1951 the Algerian delegation, more precisely the communist UJDA, was mentioned only very briefly, if at all.[19]

A slightly different tone can be found in an article on the first Festival in 1947. Here, the author Ahmed Akkache, a student activist and member of the PCA's Central Committee, described the Algerian delegation in more detail, with mentions of several individuals and also non-communist movements, such as the Muslim Algerian Scouts.[20] This stress on a sort of Algerian anti-colonial unity in diversity resurfaced again with the fourth Festival: an article explicitly talked about 'young people with different political and religious opinions' and praised 'the broad Algerian delegation that represents different national currents and parties opposed to colonialism as well as different youth and student organisations'.[21] By 1953, the radicalisation of younger indigenous Algerian communists had led to a prioritisation of the anti-colonial, 'national' struggle, which implied co-operation with the nationalist and Islamist movements.

18 Le Foll-Luciani, 'Algérianisation et Radicalisation'; Drew, *We Are No Longer in France*, 153–74; on the FLN see also Stora, *Histoire de la Guerre d'Algérie*, 33–45.

19 Cf. 'Risalat shabb min al-mahrajan al-'alami fi budabast', *al-Jaza'ir al-jadida* (September 1949); 'Al-shubban yuhibun bi-shu'ubihim li al-kifah wa al-'amal li-ajli al-istiqlal wa al-salm', *al-Jaza'ir al-jadida* (September 1951).

20 Cf. Ahmad 'Akkash, 'Sa'a ma'a wafd al-shabiba al-jaza'iriyya li al-mahrajan al-'alami fi prag', *al-Jaza'ir al-jadida* (August 1947).

21 'Al-shabiba al-jaza'iriyya fi al-mahrajan al-'alami al-rabi'', *al-Jaza'ir al-jadida* (August 1953). Translations from Arabic, French and German are by the author.

This impetus appeared even stronger two years later, when the adhesion of communist militants to the FLN was well under way.[22] In fact, an article on the Warsaw Festival stated the purpose of Algeria's participation: 'Algerian youth assumes the duty of participating in this Festival, even though our country is enduring the hardship of bloody colonialist repression and terror, to convey the message about the state of our desperate country and to raise the name Algeria high among the other peoples.'[23] The PCA paper's line had changed: instead of rather generic reports just reproducing official declarations, in 1955 it offered its readers articles about Algeria and its image in the international arena. World Youth Festivals had become an important stage on which to perform Algerian nationhood and win global opinion over to the cause of independence.[24]

While in the communist paper the issue of national independence was taking precedence from 1953, Algerian nationalist movements had from the beginning tried to use World Youth Festivals to publicise their agenda. The result of the Algerian presence was tangible. As one scout paper put it: 'Algeria is no longer a simple geographic entity; it has become, for many, a country of flesh and blood, with a dark present and a future that, everyone wished, will be bright.'[25] An article on the Bucharest Festival from the paper *La Voix des Jeunes* (*The Voice of the Young*), edited by the two SMA leaders Mahfoud Kaddache and Omar Lagha, summarised the actual event in one sentence, while dwelling at length on the reception the Algerians received and their opportunity to make contact.[26] Already in 1947, a participant had described, in an article for the scouts' bulletin, how he felt as a representative of his people: 'By remembering this old docker, who when we were embarking [in Algiers to travel to the Festival] started crying, as he saw our badge with the Islamic crescent, I got a strong sense of the responsibility I assumed by representing our youth, their struggle, their life, their hopes in Prague.'[27]

[22] See also Le Foll-Luciani, 'Algérianisation et Radicalisation', 101–7.

[23] 'Sa-tarfa' al-shabiba al-jaza'iriyya ism al-Jaza'ir 'aliyyan bayna shubban al-'alam fi al-mahrajan al-'alami al-khamis fi farsufiya', *al-Jaza'ir al-jadida* (July 1955).

[24] See also 'Farsufiya tastaqbil al-shubban al-jaza'iriyyin bi-adhra' maftuha', *al-Jaza'ir al-jadida* (August 1955).

[25] Benmahmoud, 'Le Festival de Pologne', *al-Hayat* (November–December 1955).

[26] Drareni, 'Trente S.M.A. ont Participé au Festival de Bucarest', *La Voix des Jeunes* (September 1953).

[27] El Kechaï, 'En Route pour Prague', 287.

It is no coincidence that the *al-Jaza'ir al-jadida* articles on the fifth Festival employed the metaphor of 'raising' (*raf'*) the name of Algeria. In fact, from 1947 on, the raising of the Algerian flag was a contentious issue at several Festivals. The most radical nationalists at World Youth Festivals came from the SMA, which tried to capitalise on the occasion to display the flag to a wide audience in a European city.[28] According to Kaddache, the 'SMA's vitality manifested itself in their activities and their truth to the nationalist position: Algerian homeland, Algerian flag. At the Budapest World Festival the SMA led the Algerian delegation, marched past the Algerian flag and gave a speech that echoed the nationalist position of the PPA [Algerian People's Party] . . .'[29] The flag issue was all the more important to nationalist scouts at the time, since it had been at the centre of the May riots a couple of years before. According to the established narrative, this had been the first time Algerians had marched behind their green and white flag with the red crescent and star and demonstrated *en masse* for independence. Scouts who marched at the front, with the flag in their hands, became Algeria's first national 'martyrs'.[30]

The subject of the flag continued at the World Youth Festival in Vienna in 1959: the Austrian authorities had given in to French pressure and forbidden its display at the opening ceremony. *El Moudjahid* (*The Fighter*), the clandestine organ of the FLN, reported on this incident and even managed to turn this apparent setback into a success. To protest against the decision, in the end none of the participating delegations from 133 nations presented their flag in the stadium. This massive show of solidarity for the Algerians was

[28] See also Gauthé, 'Le Scout est Loyal envers son Pays'.

[29] Kaddache, 'Historique des Scouts Musulmans Algériens', 73–4. The Algerian People's Party (PPA) was the major Algerian nationalist party of the late 1930s and 1940s. It had been founded by Messali Hadj after the dissolution of ENA. Itself banned by the French authorities in 1939, the PPA continued to operate clandestinely afterwards. In 1946, Messali legally reconstituted the PPA as the MTLD, but both names remained in use, sometimes as a combined abbreviation (PPA-MTLD).

[30] See e.g. El Kechaï, *60 Années de Lutte*, 28–35; al-Hasani, *Mudhakkirat*, 20; Kaddache, 'Historique des Scouts Musulmans Algériens', 72; cf. also 'Isani, 'Al-'alam al-jaza'iri'. In fact, the flag had apparently not acquired its standard shape by 1947. In pictures from the Prague World Youth Festival the crescent is horizontal, not vertical, and the flag is inscribed with the name of the SMA in Arabic (*al-kashshafa al-islamiyya al-jaza'iriyya*). See e.g. Kechaï, 'En Route pour Prague', 288.

further enhanced when their flag was ostentatiously hoisted during an anti-colonial rally within the Festival programme a couple of days later.[31]

An Algerian perspective that differed from most communist or nationalist reports is provided by an account on the 1955 Festival from *al-Hayat* (*Life*), the bilingual journal of the BSMA (the scout movement close to Islamic reformism). While even the communist paper always placed special emphasis on Arab solidarity as part of wider anti-imperialist internationalism, this was especially important to the Islamic BSMA movement.[32] In fact, the text gave a brief characterisation of all Arab delegations attending. The author was most impressed by the Syrians and the Iraqis, but he also judged some delegations quite severely. The Egyptians were, in his view, too obviously on their government's propaganda line 'to be efficient', while the Palestinians did not help their cause by adopting too radical a stance. As the BSMA was arguably the Algerian movement with the most ideological distance from the WFDY, the author did not employ the celebratory and uncritical language present in other texts, most notably in the PCA press. What he bemoaned most were the ideological divisions within the Algerian delegation and the organisers' tight grip.[33]

It seems that the BSMA saw the Festivals rather as a possibility, among other things, to get in touch with possible allies from the Middle East in the struggle against colonialism, whereas Algerian communists were more interested in the potentially global reach of internationalist solidarity, beyond the Arab world, but largely confined to leftist organisations and, in particular, the powerful Eastern Bloc. Finally, the SMA, which saw itself as the spearhead of radical nationalism, apparently tried to use every opportunity to raise awareness of the Algerian situation in front of an international audience; hence, a gathering of communist youth movements could serve the purpose just as well as a jamboree with Christian scouts.[34]

[31] 'L'Algérie au VII-ème Festival de la Jeunesse', *El Moudjahid* (31 August 1959). On the flag issue see also Krais, 'Youth and Sports', 236–7.

[32] Cf. (e.g.) 'Al-shabiba al-jaza'iriyya fi al-mahrajan al-'alami al-rabi''.

[33] Benmahmoud, 'Le Festival de Pologne'.

[34] In fact, Algerian scouts sometimes combined the trips to the jamboree and to the World Youth Festival. Cf. (e.g.) Kechaï, *60 Années de Lutte*, 40–2.

'Guests of Honour': Views of Algeria

The Third World Youth Festival of 1951 took place in a Cold War hotspot, the divided city of Berlin, the eastern part of which had been declared the German Democratic Republic (GDR) capital less than two years before.[35] Algeria was no major concern for the East German press at the time, and the visitors from France – a country with 5 million communist voters, as one journalist recalled – were received warmly.[36] With the Korean War being the international issue of the day, the most celebrated delegations, apart from the USSR, came from North Korea and the People's Republic of China. But *Neues Deutschland* (*New Germany*), the organ of the Socialist Unity Party of Germany (SED), also published a picture of the Algerian delegation 'demonstrating for the freedom and independence of their homeland' at the opening ceremony.[37] Another article, this time from *Junge Welt* (*Young World*), the paper of the Free German Youth (FDJ), the GDR's official youth organisation, gave Algeria a prominent place in its coverage of an exhibition on colonialism.[38] Finally, the Algerians even received one of the numerous Festival awards, which were given as a sort of honorary gift to different delegations: while the major ones went, not very surprisingly, to the Soviet Union and the GDR, Algeria was awarded the prize of the Democratic Women's League of Germany (DFD).[39]

Despite its ideological line, the SED paper reported primarily not about Algerian communists, but about the Muslim Scouts. It presented the SMA as the country's most important youth movement and summarised its aims in the following way: 'educating Algerian youth towards patriotism, supporting national culture and fighting Anglo-American cultural barbarism. Its main

35 On the East Berlin Festival see Ruhl, *Stalin-Kult*, 9–47; Lemke, 'Die "Gegenspiele"', 467–95; Kotek, 'Youth Organizations as a Battlefield in the Cold War'; Kotek, *Students and the Cold War*, 189–99; Rutter, 'The Western Wall'.

36 'Kleine Begegnung mit Lucien', *Junge Welt* (4 August 1951).

37 'Jugend der Kolonialvölker in brüderlicher Solidarität mit der Weltjugend', *Neues Deutschland* (17 August 1951).

38 Haase, 'Wir kämpfen für ein Neues Leben!'

39 'Beste Delegationen feierlich Ausgezeichnet. Preis des Friedens und der Demokratie für die Sowjetjugend/Preis der Arbeit für die deutsche Delegation', *Neues Deutschland* (17 August 1951).

aim in the struggle is the national liberation of the people from the yoke of the French imperialists.'[40] The SMA leader, Lagha, 'a guest of honour in the Third World Festival', was not only quoted in this article, but a statement of his was even published in its entirety, both in *Neues Deutschland* and *Junge Welt*. In it, he thanked East Germans for their warm welcome and went on to suggest that his scouts should 'leave behind some drops of sweat in this now universal capital' and help reconstruct Berlin.[41] After the event, the GDR press printed a number of letters from participants who expressed gratitude to their hosts, among them several from Algeria.[42]

Eight years later, the context in which the World Youth Festival was held had changed significantly. The seventh Festival in Vienna was the first since Prague in 1947 that did not take place in the Eastern Bloc.[43] The Austrian government, under conservative Chancellor Julius Raab, had allowed the WFDY and IUS to organise the event in its capital, but refused all official participation. Hence, the rather marginal Communist Party of Austria (KPÖ), left without any parliamentary representation after recent federal elections, was the only local party to support the event. Except for the communist *Volksstimme* (People's Voice), the Austrian press had even agreed to boycott the Festival and not publish a single line on it.[44]

In 1959, the Festival's setting differed markedly from earlier events, not only as a consequence of the special position of neutral Austria in the Cold

[40] 'Die Jugend Algeriens ist mit dabei. Lagha Omar: "Wir werden uns den Weg zum Weltbund der Demokratischen Jugend freikämpfen!"', *Neues Deutschland* (26 August 1951).

[41] Lagha, 'Junge Algerier helfen uns aufbauen. Ein Freundschaftsbekenntnis der algerischen Pfadfinder', *Neues Deutschland* (10 August 1951); Lagha, 'Lagha Omar an die deutsche Jugend', *Junge Welt* (12 August 1951).

[42] Cf. 'Freundschaft über Ländergrenzen. Weltfestspiele Ansporn im Friedenskampf/Briefe an deutsche Jugend', *Berliner Zeitung* (10 October 1951); '"Ihr habt dem deutschen Volk den schönsten Sieg errungen". Briefe ausländischer Teilnehmer der III. Weltfestspiele an ihre deutschen Freunde', *Neues Deutschland* (20 December 1951).

[43] Before the communist takeover of 1948, Czechoslovakia was a liberal democracy traditionally oriented towards the West.

[44] On the Vienna Festival see Hans Hautmann, 'Die Weltjugendfestspiele 1959 in Wien', *Mitteilungen der Alfred Klahr Gesellschaft* 3 (1999), <http://klahrgesellschaft.at/Mitteilungen/Hautmann_3_99.html> (last accessed 2 March 2020). On the problems surrounding World Youth Festivals in neutral countries cf. also Krekola and Mikkonen, 'Backlash of the Free World'.

War. At the time of the Vienna Festival, the Algerian war of independence had already been going on for four and a half years and decolonisation had become a major issue of international politics. The KPÖ organ on the occasion of the Festival reminded its readers of the importance of the global 'national revolutionary independence movement': 'The victory of the Cuban revolution, the revolution in Iraq, the democratic subversion in Venezuela, the independence of Ghana and New Guinea, all these are heavy blows to the imperialist world system . . .: its days are numbered.'[45]

Consequently, Algeria occupied a much more prominent place in the coverage than had been the case in the GDR. The *Volksstimme* reported at length on the flag issue, which *El Moudjahid* had also seen as the most noteworthy incident of the Festival. Beyond that, it brought reports on the Algerian war in almost every issue.[46] The communist paper further accused the French and Austrian Socialists of supporting colonialism. In particular, it chastised the Socialist Party of Austria (SPÖ), which formed part of Raab's coalition government, for preventing Algerian delegates exiled in Tunisia from attending and claimed that it wanted to divert attention from colonialist crimes by condemning communist repression.[47] The SPÖ organ *Arbeiter-Zeitung* (Workers' Journal) – which also followed the general press boycott regarding the Festival – had, in fact, published an article that supported the Algerian independence movement, but also the opponents of 'eastern colonialism' in Hungary and Tibet, thereby undermining the Communists' message of supposedly uncompromising anti-imperialism.[48]

[45] 'Solidarität mit der Jugend der Kolonialländer', *Volksstimme* (30 July 1959). The article here certainly refers not to Papua New Guinea, but to Guinea (Conakry), the first part of the French empire in sub-Saharan Africa to attain independence, in 1958.

[46] On the situation in Algeria cf. Stora, *Histoire de la guerre d'Algérie*, 51–4.

[47] See 'Algerischen Delegierten die Einreise verweigert', *Volksstimme* (30 July 1959); 'Die Reporter der "Volksstimme" berichten vom Festival: Am Ufer der Donau brannte die Flamme der Solidarität', *Volksstimme* (1 August 1959); 'Am Rande', *Volksstimme* (5 August 1959).

[48] 'Der Imperialismus auf der Anklagebank: Der Völkermord darf nicht weitergehen. Vertreter der Unterdrückten Ungarns, Tibets und Algeriens protestierten gegen den westlichen und den östlichen Kolonialismus', *Arbeiter-Zeitung* (4 August 1959). See also Deréky, 'Zoff bei den Wiener Weltfestspielen', <http://www.univie.ac.at/webfu/texte/derekyoe.pdf> (last accessed 2 March 2020).

Views of Algeria had changed considerably from East Berlin to Vienna. This was certainly a result of general political developments that had brought the war in Algeria to the forefront of news reports and placed it at the centre of the concerns of leftist solidarity networks throughout the world. But even in 1951, when it seemed still unthinkable to many that their country could become independent in the near future, Algerian nationalists, and not primarily communists, had received comparatively large amounts of attention at the World Youth Festival. Their constant presence on subsequent occasions arguably helped put Algeria on the map of global anti-imperialism.

Conclusion

Taking into account the changes in the perception of Algeria between 1951 and 1959, it seems fair to say that the nationalists' use of World Youth Festivals to construct Algerian nationhood in an international setting was quite successful. The Festivals were deemed important enough for the FLN regime to propose organising the ninth edition in Algiers in 1965 (though in the end it did not materialise).[49] Especially during the war, the FLN had managed to mobilise international public opinion in its favour. While it constantly played on the sympathies of the socialist world, this tactic ultimately strengthened the national aspect to the detriment of the Communist Party.[50] In the internationalism of nationalist and Islamist groups, the WFDY and IUS were theatres among others; there was no interest in the specific concerns of the global communist movement beyond anti-colonialism.[51] As their prominent part in the East Berlin Festival has shown, the Muslim Scouts, at the time practically the youth movement of the nationalist MTLD, had succeeded early on in presenting themselves as the prime representatives of Algerians' aspirations. The PCA itself became more and more concerned with national liberation, until it eventually dissolved into the FLN.

In analysing press reports from Algeria, East Germany and Austria, this chapter has given some preliminary insights into the reciprocal perceptions of Algerians at World Youth Festivals prior to independence. These events,

[49] Koivunen, 'Friends, "Potential Friends", and Enemies', 238.

[50] Cf. also Connelly, 'Rethinking the Cold War'.

[51] Cf. also Krais, 'Youth and Sports'.

despite being hosted largely by communist state organisations, also offered opportunities for unusual freedoms and contacts that were out of the ordinary.[52] In this context, it would be informative to look at personal accounts which could provide perceptions outside the ideological discourse of internationalism and nationalism in the press.

Bibliography

'Akkash, Ahmad, 'Sa'a ma'a wafd al-shabiba al-jaza'iriyya li al-mahrajan al-'alami fi prag' [An hour with the delegation of Algerian youth to the World Festival in Prague'], *al-Jaza'ir al-jadida* (August 1947).

Al-Hasani, 'Abd al-Hafiz Amuqran, *Mudhakkirat min masirat al-nidal wal-jihad* [Memoirs from a trajectory of fight and struggle] (Algiers: Dar El Oumma, 1997).

Ben Khedda, Benyoucef, *Les Origines du 1er Novembre 1954* (Algiers: Dahlab, 1989).

Benmahmoud, Mahmoud, 'Le Festival de Pologne', *al-Hayat* (November–December 1955).

Byrne, Jeffrey James, *Mecca of Revolution: Algeria, Decolonization, and the Third World Order* (New York: Oxford University Press, 2016).

Chiriu, Andrea, 'Summer 1953, Bucharest: The Third World Youth Congress and the Fourth World Youth Festival. The Italian Concerns', *Revista Română de Studii Eurasiatice* 8, 1–2 (2012): 105–18.

Connelly, Matthew, *A Diplomatic Revolution: Algeria's Fight for Independence and the Origins of the Post-Cold War Era* (New York: Oxford University Press, 2002).

Connelly, Matthew, 'Rethinking the Cold War and Decolonization: The Grand Strategy of the Algerian War for Independence', *International Journal of Middle East Studies* 33, 2 (2001): 221–45.

Deréky, Pál, 'Zoff bei den Wiener Weltfestspielen der Jugend und Studenten 1959 – Ungarische Exilstudenten als Apologeten des Volksaufstandes, *Wiener elektronische Beiträge des Instituts für Finno-Ugristik* (2007): 1–14, <http://www.univie.ac.at/webfu/texte/derekyoe.pdf> (last accessed 2 March 2020).

Drareni, M, 'Trente S.M.A. Ont Participé au Festival de Bucarest', *La Voix des Jeunes* (September 1953).

Drew, Allison, *We Are No Longer in France: Communists in Colonial Algeria* (Manchester: Manchester University Press, 2014).

[52] Cf. Peacock, 'The Perils of Building Cold War Consensus'; Predescu, 'Le Festival Mondial de la Jeunesse'.

Gauthé, Jean-Jacques, 'Le Scout est Loyal envers son Pays . . . Mouvements Scouts et Nationalismes en Europe et aux Colonies (1909–1962)', in Gérard Cholvy (ed.), *Le Scoutisme: un Mouvement d'Éducation au XXe siècle. Dimensions Internationales* (Montpellier: Université Paul Valéry, 2002): 219–47.

Goebel, Michael, *Anti-Imperial Metropolis: Interwar Paris and the Seeds of Third World Nationalism* (New York: Cambridge University Press, 2015).

Haase, Wolf, '"Wir kämpfen für ein neues Leben!" Ein Gang durch die Ausstellung der kolonialen Länder in Berlin', *Junge Welt* (16 August 1951).

Hautmann, Hans, 'Die Weltjugendfestspiele 1959 in Wien', *Mitteilungen der Alfred Klahr Gesellschaft* 3 (1999), <http://klahrgesellschaft.at/Mitteilungen/Hautmann_3_99.html> (last accessed 2 March 2020).

'Isani, 'Umar, 'Al-'alam al-jaza'iri wa al-kashshafa al-islamiyya al-jaza'iriyya marra ukhra [Again, on the flag and the Algerian Muslim scouts], in *al-Kashshafa al-islamiyya al-jaza'iriyya: dirasat wa-buhuth al-nadwa al-wataniyya al-ula hawla tarikh al-kashshafa al-islamiyya al-jaza'iriyya* (Algiers: al-Markaz al-watani li al-dirasat wa al-buhuth fi al-haraka al-wataniyya wa thawrat awwal nufambir 1954, 1999): 137–42.

Kaddache, Mahfoud, 'Historique des Scouts Musulmans Algériens', in Ali Aroua and Mohamed Tayeb Illoul (eds), *Le Groupe Emir Khaled de Belcourt. Un Maillon des Scouts Musulmans Algériens 1946–1962* (Algiers: Dahlab, 1991): 71–5.

El-Kechaï, Mohamed, *60 Années de Lutte ou la Longue Marche d'un Chef Scout Musulman Volontaire du Croissant Rouge* (Tizi-Ouzou: n.p., 1996).

El-Kechaï, Mohamed, 'En Route pour Prague avec l'Union Démocratique de la Jeunesse (1947)', in Chikh Bouamrane and Mohamed Djidjelli (eds), *Scouts Musulmans Algériens (1935–1955)* (Algiers: Dar El Oumma, 2010): 287–8.

Koivunen, Pia, '"A Dream Come True:" Finns Visiting the Lands of Socialism at the World Youth Festivals in the 1940s and 1950s', *Twentieth Century Communism* 4 (2012): 133–58.

Koivunen, Pia, 'Friends, "Potential Friends", and Enemies: Reimagining Soviet Relations to the First, Second, and Third Worlds at the Moscow 1957 Youth Festival', in Patryk Babiracki and Austin Jersild (eds), *Socialist Internationalism in the Cold War: Exploring the Second World* (London and New York: Palgrave Macmillan, 2016): 219–48.

Kotek, Joël, *Students and the Cold War*, trans. Ralph Blumenau (Basingstoke, London and New York: Macmillan/St Martin's Press, 1996).

Kotek, Joël, 'Youth Organizations as a Battlefield in the Cold War', *Intelligence and National Security* 18, 2 (2003): 168–91.

Krais, Jakob, 'Youth and Sports in Algeria's Diplomatic Struggle for International Recognition (1957–1962)', *The Maghreb Review* 42, 3 (2017): 227–53.

Krekola, Joni, and Simo Mikkonen, 'Backlash of the Free World: The US Presence at the World Youth Festival in Helsinki, 1962', *Scandinavian Journal of History* 36, 2 (2011): 230–55.

Lagha, Omar, 'Junge Algerier helfen uns Aufbauen. Ein Freundschaftsbekenntnis der Algerischen Pfadfinder', *Neues Deutschland* (10 August 1951).

Lagha, Omar, 'Lagha Omar an die Deutsche Jugend', *Junge Welt* (12 August 1951).

Le Foll-Luciani, Pierre-Jean, 'Algérianisation et Radicalisation: les Étudiants Communistes de l'Université d'Alger (1946–1956)', *Cahiers d'histoire. Revue d'histoire critique* 126 (2015): 97–117.

Le Foll-Luciani, Pierre-Jean, *Les Juifs Algériens dans la Lutte Anticoloniale. Trajectoires Dissidentes (1934–1965)* (Rennes: PUR, 2015).

Lemke, Michael, 'Die "Gegenspiele". Weltjugendfestival und FDJ-Deutschlandtreffen in der Systemkonkurrenz 1950–1954', in Heiner Timmermann (ed.), *Die DDR in Europa – zwischen Isolation und Öffnung*. Dokumente und Schriften der Europäischen Akademie Otzenhausen (Münster: Lit Verlag, 2005): 452–505.

Marangé, Céline, 'André Ferrat et la Création du Parti Communiste Algérien (1931–1936)', *Histoire@Politique* 29, 2 (2016): 190–219.

Nait-Challal, Michel, *Dribbleurs de l'Indépendance. L'Incroyable Histoire de l'Equipe de Football du FLN Algérien* (Paris: Éditions Prolongations, 2008).

Peacock, Margaret, 'The Perils of Building Cold War Consensus at the 1957 Moscow World Festival of Youth and Students', *Cold War History* 12, 3 (2012): 515–35.

Piccini, Jon, '"There is no Solidarity, Peace or Friendship with Dictatorship:" Australians at the World Festival of Youth and Students, 1957–1968', *History Australia* 9, 3 (2012): 178–98.

Predescu, Magda, 'Le Festival Mondial de la Jeunesse et des Étudiants, Moment d'Échanges Inattendus et Mal Contrôlés', *Studia Politica: Romanian Political Science Review* 17, 1 (2017): 131–55.

Ruhl, Andreas, *Stalin-Kult und Rotes Woodstock. Die Weltjugendfestspiele 1951 und 1973 in Ostberlin*. Wissenschaftliche Beiträge aus dem Tectum Verlag. Reihe Geschichtswissenschaft (Marburg: Tectum Verlag, 2009).

Rutter, Nick, 'The Western Wall: The Iron Curtain Recast in Midsummer 1951', in Patryk Babiracki and Kenyon Zimmer (eds), *Cold War Crossings: International Travel and Exchange across the Soviet Bloc, 1940s–1960s* (College Station, TX: Texas AM University Press, 2014): 78–106.

Stora, Benjamin, *Histoire de l'Algérie Coloniale (1830–1954)* (Paris: La Découverte, 1991).

Stora, Benjamin, *Histoire de la Guerre d'Algérie (1954–1962)* (Paris: La Découverte, 2004).

Stora, Benjamin, *Le Nationalisme Algérien avant 1954* (Paris: CNRS, 2010).

Sutton, Christopher, 'Britain, Empire, and the Origins of the Cold War Youth Race', *Contemporary British History* 30, 2 (2016): 224–41.

Watanabe, Shoko, 'Organizational Changes in the Algerian National Movement as Seen through the Muslim Boy Scouts in the 1930s and 1940s: The Struggle for Influence between the Association of Ulama and the PPA-MTLD', *Journal of Sophia Asian Studies* 30 (2012): 41–69.

7

TRAVELLING THEORIST: MEHDI BEN BARKA AND MOROCCO FROM ANTI-COLONIAL NATIONALISM TO THE TRICONTINENTAL

Nate George

Introduction

It is hard to imagine language more alarming to European and American imperialists and their allies than the terms Mehdi Ben Barka used to describe the conference he was organising. In May 1965, the Afro-Asian People's Solidarity Organisation elected the exiled Moroccan dissident to chair the preparatory committee for the upcoming 'First Conference of Solidarity of the Peoples of Africa, Asia, and Latin America'. Better known simply as 'the Tricontinental', the conference was the first that was set to bring Latin America into the framework of Afro-Asian anti-colonial summitry. In conversation with the Havana press on 30 September 1965, Ben Barka pinpointed the forces that converged to make the 1960s a moment pregnant with global revolutionary possibilities:

> [The Tricontinental] is historic because of its composition, because the two great contemporary currents of the World Revolution will be represented in this Conference: the current which started with the October Revolution in the Soviet Union, and which is the current of socialist revolution, and the parallel current of the revolution for national liberation . . .

> This Conference is also historic because it takes place in Cuba; because the Cuban Revolution is in effect the concretisation of the union of these two historic currents of the World Revolution; because Cuba has known her revolution for national liberation and is now accomplishing her socialist revolution; therefore, it was the best choice for the celebration of this meeting.[1]

Less than one month after making this link between the traditions of socialist and anti-colonial revolutions, Ben Barka was abducted from the streets of Paris, never to be seen again. His disappearance sparked an international scandal, leading to a highly publicised trial and a break in diplomatic relations between France and Morocco.[2] While the question of who was behind the 'Ben Barka Affair' has been an international mystery leading to intense speculation for decades, a recent confession by an Israeli Mossad agent involved in his assassination has shed light on many uncertainties. On 29 October 1965, French police kidnapped Ben Barka off the streets of Paris, Moroccan intelligence officers tortured him to death, and agents of Mossad doused his body with acid and buried him in a forest on the outskirts of Paris.[3]

Despite his grisly fate, Ben Barka's vision for the Tricontinental was briefly realised during the first two weeks of January 1966, when 512 delegates from 83 states or movements, 64 observers, 77 guests and 129 members of the foreign press convened in Havana for the last major international conference of the Third World project during its peak years of struggle against Euro-American imperialism and colonialism.[4] Designing a framework and bringing

I thank Eskandar Sadeghi-Boroujerdi, Nathan Citino, Ussama Makdisi and Derek Ide for their insightful comments.

[1] This quotation is an edited composite of two translations (one in English, one in Spanish) of a speech given in French, of which no record was found. Executive Secretariat of OSPAAAL, 'First Solidarity Conference', 4; Ben Barka, 'Estrategia Global'.

[2] Ben Barka's assassination inspired numerous articles, books and films. CIA involvement has been alleged but not proven. See for example Guérin, *Les Assassins*.

[3] See the interview with Mossad agent Rafi Eitan on the Israeli TV programme *Uvda*, 1 December 2014, <http://www.mako.co.il/tv-ilana_dayan/2015-75230c07c760a410/Article-92ac6ecd0960a41006.htm> (last accessed 14 May 2019) (I thank Leena Dallasheh for her translation from Hebrew); and Bergman and Nakdimon, 'Ghosts of Saint-Germain Forest'.

[4] Senate Committee on the Judiciary, 'Tricontinental Conference', 47. See also Faligot, *Tricontinentale*.

together this universe of peoples and organisations was no easy task. Among the many efforts involved, the labour and thought of Mehdi Ben Barka stand out as a key link in executing the tricontinental idea.

Yet Ben Barka's role is hardly recognised outside of a niche francophone literature, read mostly in France and Morocco. By emphasising the transformative role of political practice upon the development of his thought over several distinct conjunctures, this chapter seeks to recover the key contribution of Ben Barka – along with other the Arab militants, movements and states – in building the tricontinental coalition and framework for action, a contribution that is still too often elided or dimly understood. Secondly, the political evolution of Ben Barka illustrates well the historical trajectory of global anti-colonialism and its transformation, from national independence movements that drew upon liberal political traditions, into national liberation revolutions operating in a dense internationalist and socialist framework, the framework of tricontinentalism.[5] Central to both of these themes is Ben Barka's role in defining the concept of neocolonialism, institutionalising it within tricontinentalist milieux and organising revolutionary opposition. Thirdly, it also recovers the dialectical relationship between revolution and counterrevolution, absent in many accounts of the radical left, and how the relationships between these antithetical forces shaped one another.

The Education of Mehdi Ben Barka

As much as anyone, the Ben Barka family was well-schooled in the harsh reality of underdevelopment. Mehdi Ben Barka was born in Sidi Fettah, a popular quarter of Rabat, in 1920, his home being shared by the families of his maternal uncle and paternal aunt. The three families had neither running water nor electricity.[6] Ben Barka's father Ahmed was a *faqih* and a secretary for a successful Tangiers merchant trading in sugar, tea and olives. His mother Fattouma worked as a seamstress in her home, alongside raising her seven children. Ben Barka's intelligence was noted from a young age and, after he had attended a neighbourhood Qur'an school, nationalists in Rabat paid for his education in elite French colonial schools, viewing the young boy

[5] See Young, *Postcolonialism*.

[6] For biographical details, this chapter relies on Daoud and Monjib, *Ben Barka*.

as full of promise. At fourteen, he joined his first political organisation, the Moroccan Action Committee (MAC), whose literature he read, copied and distributed.

Ben Barka's famed international travels and multinational organising work began with his higher education. The outbreak of the Second World War in September 1939 prevented Ben Barka from pursuing his studies in metropolitan France. Instead, he enrolled in the University of Algiers. Wartime colonial Algiers exposed Ben Barka to an intriguing network of international militants in a period marked by the struggle against fascism and colonialism. Upon arrival, he entered a student political milieu that included French *pied noirs*, Algerians, Tunisians and Moroccans. Ben Barka consorted with members of the radical populist Algerian People's Party (PPA), led by Messali Hadj, as well as Habib Bourguiba's Neo-Destour Party.[7] This budding Maghribi student activist group was rounded out by a few anti-colonial *colons*, such as Albert-Paul Lentin, future journalist and attendee at the Havana Tricontinental.

Amid this crowd, Ben Barka became the vice-president of the influential Association of North African Muslim Students, which was founded in 1927 and from which graduated numerous leading Maghribi nationalists.[8] From Algiers, Ben Barka organised conferences on Moroccan and international topics while he reconstituted cells of the Moroccan National Party, which like the PPA had suffered following a wave of protests and French repression in 1937. After earning his *licence* in mathematics in 1942, Ben Barka returned to Morocco. While setting up nationalist cells, he taught maths in several schools. These included the Collège Imperial, where one of his students was the fourteen-year-old crown prince Moulay Hassan, who, as king, probably ordered Ben Barka's assassination in 1965.

Independence: 'A Form in Need of Content'

Ben Barka was the youngest signatory of the Independence Manifesto of 11 January 1944, the document that publicly announced the appearance of the Independence Party (*hizb al-istiqlal*, hereafter, Istiqlal). Istiqlal's primary

[7] On Messali Hadj and the emergence of the PPA see McDougall, *History of Algeria*, 166–78.
[8] Ageron, 'L'Association', 28.

objective was to eject the French and restore deposed sultan Mohammed ben Youssef to the throne of an independent, constitutional monarchy.[9] This bold declaration earned him his first prison sentence. His political activity as one of the leading organisers of Istiqlal caused him to spend years in colonial prison and internal exile.

The alliance of Istiqlal with the monarchy, which enjoyed popular legitimacy due to its symbolism as a locally rooted sovereign in opposition to the French colonial administration, would prove to be both its road to power and its fatal mistake.[10] Istiqlal's ties to the figure of the king only increased after he was exiled by the French to colonial Madagascar and replaced by a puppet monarch in 1953.[11] Restoring the 'legitimate' sovereign then proved to be the most effective rallying cry, and Istiqlal exploited it fully. As chairman of Istiqlal's Executive Committee, Ben Barka played a key role in the nationalist underground between the end of the Second World War in 1945 and official Moroccan independence in 1956. His contributions included organising cells, training cadres, editing the party journal, establishing and maintaining relations with the newly organised armed resistance movement centred in the Rif, and negotiating the treaty for independence at Aix-Les-Bains in September 1955.[12]

The internal struggle over the structure of political power began immediately after independence in March 1956, inaugurating a contest between the palace and Istiqlal.[13] When the newly crowned King Mohammad V created a powerless National Consultative Assembly, it overwhelmingly elected

[9] For the full text of the Istiqlal manifesto, see Halstead, *Rebirth*, 281–5.

[10] For the turn of the nationalists towards the sultan, which was consolidated in 1934, see Halstead, *Rebirth*, 203–5; Joffé, 'Moroccan'. Unlike the Khedive in Egypt or the Beylicate in Tunisia, Morocco's ʿAlawite dynasty was not ethnically distinct from its subjects. And unlike the Hashemite kingdoms of Jordan and Iraq, founded in the 1920s with British assistance, the Moroccan dynasty possessed some three hundred years of local history. See Hudson, *Arab Politics*, 221; Joffe, 'Morocco'.

[11] The disposition of the sultan incensed Maghribi nationalists beyond Morocco. The second anniversary of the sultan's removal was the occasion for an FLN-led mass uprising in northern Algeria in August 1955. McDougall, *History of Algeria*, 200–2.

[12] Ashford, *Political Change*, 61; Daoud and Monjib, *Ben Barka*, 93–153.

[13] See Pennell, *Morocco*, 163–70.

Ben Barka as its president. In this position, Ben Barka became intimately familiar with the problems facing the newly independent country and the options available to redress them. While the early 1950s saw an economic boom, development stagnated after independence. European investment disappeared, the richest agricultural lands continued to be owned by a small concentration of French settlers and Moroccan landlords withheld their own capital from productive investment.[14] In the realm of security, the same French-trained men who policed the nationalist movement now worked for the king, while French and American military bases remained.

In his new-found position as statesman, Ben Barka began travelling internationally, studying different models of development. He met with Nasser, Bourguiba, Ho Chi Minh and Mao Tse-Tung, and even visited the Tennessee Valley Authority.[15] He returned inspired, and began a crusade for economic and social development in Morocco, initially sponsored by the king. Like many mid-century modernisers, Ben Barka developed a passion for infrastructure. But he combined public works with mass participation, viewing development as a process for national mobilisation. In the summer of 1957, he linked the two by founding a public works corps that constructed the 'Road to Unity', the first road joining the former areas of the colonial protectorates, the French north and the Spanish south. But by the final meeting of the assembly in April 1959, he had reached the limit of reformism in a monarchical system committed to economic liberalism.

Neither the king nor the much of leadership of Istiqlal had any desire to enact the radical changes Ben Barka deemed necessary and saw under way in Egypt, Vietnam, or China: land reform, mass literacy campaigns, the modernisation of infrastructure, nationalisation of industry and the expulsion of foreign military bases. The limitations of the Istiqlal coalition of king, party and old social classes (the *makhzen*) became unbearable, as did the establishment's continued reliance on France. This experience led Ben Barka to later conclude that 'independence by itself is nothing more than a form in need of content'.[16]

[14] Amin, *Maghreb*, 164–80.

[15] Evins, 'Distinguished World Visitors'.

[16] Ben Barka, 'Africa after Independence', 166.

From Nationalism to Tricontinentalism: The UNFP

After attempts to hold together the fracturing Istiqlal movement proved futile, Ben Barka joined with the left opposition to create a new party, the National Union of Popular Forces (UNFP). These forces included Mohammed 'Fqih' al-Basri, a leader of armed struggle against the French in the early 1950s; Istiqlal veterans Abdallah Ibrahim, Abderrahim Bouabid and Abderrahmane Youssoufi; Mahjoub Bin Siddiq, leader of the Moroccan Labour Union (UMT); the National Union of Moroccan Students; and a number of Istiqlal cadres, including the future intellectual giant Mohammed Abed al-Jabri, who edited the UNFP newspaper.[17] The new formation essentially split Istiqlal supporters along the lines of class and generation, with the established bourgeois – in both the material and ideological sense – and older elements staying within the Istiqlal.[18] At its foundational meeting in a Casablanca cinema in September 1959, the UNFP unveiled its programme. Domestically, it called for 'real democracy' under a constitutional monarchy, land reform, full employment, industrial planning, nationalisation of key economic sectors and a modern education system.[19] Foreign affairs were equally stressed. The party called for the evacuation of the remaining US and French military bases, pledged support for the Algerian people and all others waging liberation struggles, called for a 'unified Maghreb built on Arab brotherhood and African solidarity', and supported diplomatic non-alignment and 'the consolidation of international peace'. With the founding of the UNFP, Ben Barka had entered a fully tricontinental agenda.

At first, the monarchy welcomed the brewing split in Istiqlal, which it encouraged in December 1958 by naming the leftist Abdallah Ibrahim as prime minister and allowing him to form a government – sans Ben Barka.[20] After weakening Istiqlal, Mohammed V launched his first wave of repression

[17] Aksikas, *Arab Modernities*, 62–3.

[18] For a detailed analysis of the causes and consequences of the split – if somewhat marred by an Orientalist framework – see Waterbury, *Commander*, 169–232.

[19] For the full programme see National Union of Popular Forces, 'Charter', 77-9.

[20] Prime Minister Ibrahim and Minister of National Economy Bouabid even drew up a practical Five Year Plan for industrialisation covering the years 1960–4. It was never implemented. Amin, *Maghreb*, 180–7.

against the UNFP. The king finally dismissed the government in May 1960, taking it over himself. Ben Barka fled to Paris in February 1960, where he organised much of the Moroccan opposition from his apartment.

Afro-Asian Horizons

In April 1960, Ben Barka was elected to join the Executive Committee of the Afro-Asian People's Solidarity Organisation (AAPSO) at its meeting in Conakry, Guinea. Ben Barka became known for his great capacity to organise, the clarity of his interventions and his ability to reconcile opposing viewpoints. His political location was agreeable to many agendas. On the one hand, anti-colonial conservatives could not question his status as a veteran of the Moroccan national movement who had chaired the National Consultative Assembly; neither could he be seen as an 'agent' of any particular radical regime. On the other, revolutionaries understood he had been cast into exile by a monarch intent on maintaining ties with the colonial powers. He espoused a socialism acceptable to nationalists and a nationalism acceptable to Marxists. In the age of the Sino–Soviet split, both communist powers could only look upon him favourably because his framework was clearly socialist, yet he did not represent a declared Marxist-Leninist party aligned with either side. He linked two regionalisms by advocating African causes to Arabs, and Arab causes to Africans. As his Algerian comrade Mohamed Harbi recounted, 'the international conjuncture was in favour of Mehdi Ben Barka'.[21] His extensive travels in Afro-Asian lands both widened his horizons and made him a practical and subjective link in the relations of solidarity. His profile and that of the UNFP – which was now accepted as the legitimate representative of Morocco in these forums – rose steeply.

In September 1961, Nasser called on Ben Barka's organisational skills to mediate between Egypt and Syria upon the dissolution of the United Arab Republic. Nasser would tap Ben Barka again to negotiate the prospective but ill-fated unity between Nasser and the new Syrian and Iraqi Baʿath governments in June 1963.[22] Though unable to bridge the gap, his selection as favoured mediator between Arab nationalist governments reveals the level of

[21] Harbi, 'Ben Barka et Les Nationalistes Arabes', 139.

[22] Daoud and Monjib, *Ben Barka*, 288.

regional respect he obtained. His proximity to Nasser would only increase. Representing both the UNFP and AAPSO, he attended the inaugural conference of the Nasser-inspired Non-Aligned Movement in Belgrade in 1961, taking a keen interest in Yugoslavia's path of development.

Defining Neocolonialism

Intellectually and functionally, Ben Barka played a major role in defining the theory of neocolonialism. While often credited to Ghanian president Kwame Nkrumah, who published a book outlining the theory in 1965, the term was institutionalised in the Afro-Asian lexicon at the third and final All-African Peoples Conference (AAPC) held in Cairo in March 1961.[23] Ben Barka formed and presided over the committee on neocolonialism and the United Nations.[24] This committee established one of the earliest working definitions of the term, which was strongly influenced by the unfolding crisis in the Congo. The resolution defined neocolonialism most simply as 'the survival of the colonial system in spite of formal recognition of political independence'.[25] The means, it stressed, were often indirect and came in the guise of unequal trade, technical, military and economic agreements, or even under UN auspices. Its goal was 'the balkanisation of newly-independent States' and 'systematic division' of the anti-colonial coalition. The 'perpetrators' were identified as 'such countries as the USA, Federal Germany, Israel, Britain, Belgium, Holland, South Africa and France'. The colonial powers, the resolution warned (and the January assassination of Patrice Lumumba in the Congo exposed this), would escalate into open intervention if indirect subversion did not work. Ben Barka's skilful chairmanship of the committee was able to resolve differences among the conservative and revolutionary African states in order to produce this unity.[26] As if to illustrate their theory, one month later the CIA sent an army of Cuban counterrevolutionary exiles to overthrow the island's revolutionary government in the failed Bay of Pigs invasion.

[23] On the AAPC, see Wallerstein, *Africa*, 33–5, 38–9, 51–3.

[24] Central Intelligence Agency, 'All Africa Peoples Conference in 1961'.

[25] All-African Peoples Conference, 'Statement on Neocolonialism'.

[26] Daoud and Monjib, *Ben Barka*, 259–60; Wallerstein, *Africa*, 52–3.

The concept of neocolonialism was the prerequisite for linking Latin America to the Afro-Asian anti-colonial framework. But it was also significantly shaped by Ben Barka's engagement with Latin American history. Later, at the Third Conference of AAPSO held in Moshi, Tanganyika in February 1963, he argued that precedents for the neocolonial order could be found in two examples: British inter-war imperialism, and Latin America under US hegemony. British colonial authorities granted formal independence to Egypt in 1922 and Iraq in 1932 to promote what Lord Curzon called 'an Arab façade' to mask their own decisive political leverage.[27] But Ben Barka argued that what was once an 'infrequent' phenomenon was now 'converted into a clear, systematically-applied policy' in the neocolonial era.[28] As he saw it, political decolonisation became the favoured strategy for the imperial powers following the reconfiguration of Western capitalist structures around US interests after the Second World War. The American-led reconstruction of Western Europe made it 'inevitable that [Europe] should similarly adopt US modes of relations with the New World, in other words, that it create its own "Latin America"'.[29] He called for increased attention to the 'problem of power'. Was independence earned by victory over the coloniser or in collaboration with him? Was state control vested in hereditary interests or a popular national liberation movement? 'The time when independence was something progressive has passed', he concluded. 'Today only the political and economic content of that independence has progressive meaning.'[30] At Moshi, Ben Barka was elected secretary of co-ordination and a member of the Executive Committee devoted to enlarging AAPSO to include Latin America.[31]

The 'Revolutionary Option'

Armed with his extensive international experience and stature, over the winter of 1961–2 Ben Barka prepared a wide-ranging assessment of the course of the Moroccan national movement for the UNFP's second party congress.

[27] British Foreign Secretary Lord Curzon sought to create an 'Arab façade ruled and administered under British guidance and controlled by a native Mohammedan and, as far as possible, by an Arab staff'. Eastern Committee Fifth Minutes, 24 April 1918, CAB 27/24. Cited in Stivers, *Supremacy*, 28–9.

[28] Ben Barka, 'Present Problems', 152.

[29] Ibid., 153.

[30] Ibid.

[31] Daoud and Monjib, *Ben Barka*, 284.

He discussed his report, complete with a proscriptive plan of action, in his Geneva apartment with Mohamed Harbi of the FLN and Abdallah Laroui, one of Morocco's leading intellectuals.[32] Report in hand, he returned to Morocco in May 1962 to attend the party conference. Ben Barka's country was now under the austere reign of his former student, Hassan II, after the latter's father died unexpectedly during surgery. Entitled 'Revolutionary Option in Morocco', it was published only posthumously alongside other writings by Maspéro in Paris, Dar al-Taliʿa in Beirut and OSPAAAL in Havana.[33] It remains one of his most significant written works.

For Ben Barka, internationalist consciousness was not merely a slogan or a distant ideal, but a fundamental prerequisite for social transformation. Tellingly, 'Revolutionary Option' did not open with an analysis of the internal conditions favourable to revolution, but with a position on the international setting: 'The most important phenomenon is without any doubt the accelerated development of the liberation of the colonised peoples. Our horizons, as the party of a recently liberated country, have broadened considerably.'[34] Between 1958 and 1962 most of Africa achieved political independence from European masters, with the glaring exceptions of the Portuguese colonies and apartheid South Africa, where liberation movements were quickly gathering steam. To Ben Barka, this new-found independence was 'unquestionably of capital importance . . . because it already introduces a sure change in the international strategic and political balance'.[35] For Moroccans, he argued, no revolution was more important than Algeria's, which at the time of his writing was on the verge of total victory. However, noting the momentum generated by the victories of anti-colonial struggles did not mean that he believed the forward march of the revolution was unstoppable. Ben Barka contextualised the achievement of independence by warning of the immediate challenge neocolonial interests and instruments posed to the newly liberated states.

In order to combat the alliance of the monarchy, the landowners and the elements of the bourgeoisie dependent upon French capital and markets, Ben Barka proposed a counter-alliance of the working class, the peasantry, the

[32] Harbi, 'L'Option Révolutionnaire', 53.

[33] Bin Baraka, *Al-ikhtiyar al-thawri*; Ben Barka, *Political Thought*.

[34] Ben Barka, 'Revolutionary Option in Morocco', 27.

[35] Ibid., 28.

intellectuals and the progressive bourgeoisie, united in a revolutionary party under a clearly delineated programme. The UNFP must become the 'instrument' of their aims, and this relied on careful cultivation of cadres and cells at the party's base. 'The daily fulfilment of the most humble tasks by the militants', he clarified, is 'the best school for cadres, the best training for a spirit of fight and sacrifice for the cause of the people.'[36] In keeping with this spirit of grass-roots organisation, he called for the creation of specific mass organisations catering for the diverse needs of Moroccans. He particularly called for a women's organisation and for ensuring the continued politicisation of trade unions.[37] A clear declaration of war on the Moroccan power structure, 'Revolutionary Option' was an ambitious and audacious plan of action. However, the expansive international references were unfamiliar to some other members of the leadership, who were focused on more straightforward internal politics.[38] The report itself was shelved, though during the conference Ben Barka advanced many of its theses, which were enthusiastically received.

The Counterrevolutionary Road

While the UNFP did not officially choose the 'revolutionary option', the increasingly radical posture of the party was noticed by interested observers, most notably the palace. The UNFP's clamouring for the promulgation of a constitution was met with a counter-proposal from King Hassan, who announced his own constitution enshrining his vast powers in November 1962. The day after the UNFP called for a boycott of the referendum, unknown assailants rammed Ben Barka's car off the road. He survived this first attempt on his life with only a neck injury. Istiqlal lent its support to the constitution and the UNFP's boycott failed. The first parliamentary elections followed in spring 1963. The king's royalist party, recently formed to combat Istiqlal and the UNFP, the Front for the Defence of Constitutional Institutions, won a plurality of seats, yet their share was matched by those of the divided Istiqlal and the UNFP.[39] Ben Barka himself scored an overwhelming victory in his Casablanca district. This pretence of

[36] Ibid., 71.

[37] Ibid., 72–4.

[38] Daoud and Monjib, *Ben Barka*, 275.

[39] See Schaar, 'King'.

democracy did not last long. In mid-July, King Hassan launched a campaign against the UNFP. Hundreds of party members and a number of top cadres were arrested, jailed, sometimes tried.[40] On 26 July the government announced that the UNFP was plotting to overthrow the monarchy. As Ben Barka was meeting with Nasser in Cairo, police ransacked his apartment. In the process they carted away the archive he had amassed during his time in Istiqlal and the UNFP in two trucks.[41] Accused of receiving weapons and funding from Algeria, Ben Barka was charged with undermining state security and the attempted assassination of the king. The king severed all communication with Algeria. In March 1964, Ben Barka was sentenced to death in absentia, the second death sentence he would receive in a span of four months. He would never return to Morocco.

The dilemmas of decolonisation, as well as Ben Barka's internationalist evolution, were perhaps most starkly revealed after the Moroccan army invaded Algeria in late September 1963. A nervous King Hassan, worried about the consolidation of a revolutionary regime on his western border – one that aided the UNFP and commanded their respect – seized several border towns inside Algeria with the intention of expanding his frontiers. Meanwhile, Algerian president Ahmad Ben Bella was in the midst of putting down an armed rebellion of ex-FLN supporters in the Kabylia region, an uprising he suspected King Hassan of supporting.[42] Speaking on the airwaves of Cairo's *Voice of the Arabs* on 16 October, Ben Barka issued a statement strongly denouncing Morocco's 'grave treason, not only to the dynamic Algerian Revolution, but, in general, to all Arab revolutions in favour of liberty, socialism and unity, and to the world national liberation movement in its entirety'.[43] He called instead for Moroccans to '[paralyse] the criminal hands that have appropriated power and that are armed, financed and led by the imperialists'.[44] Internationally, he asked 'the popular masses of Africa and

[40] American journalist John Cooley was present at the UNFP headquarters in Casablanca during a mass arrest. 'Morocco Arrests'.

[41] Daoud and Monjib, *Ben Barka*, 289.

[42] Gleijeses, *Conflicting Missions*, 39.

[43] Ben Barka, 'Appeal', 183.

[44] Ibid., 185.

Asia' to apply pressure for peaceful negotiations under the auspices of the Organisation of African Unity. Rather than provoking revolutionary sentiment in Morocco, the statement backfired and evoked wide hostility. The king did not hesitate to denounce the 'traitors'. By contrast, the Istiqlal leader Allal el-Fassi was the leading champion of 'Greater Morocco' expansionism, while the Party of Liberation and Socialism, the successor to the Moroccan Communist Party, also supported the king's position in the war.[45]

On 22 October the stakes escalated considerably when, at Ben Bella's request, hundreds of Cuban troops, tanks and artillery landed in Oran to train and fight alongside the Algerians.[46] Egypt sent men and heavy weapons shortly thereafter, while the Soviets supplied MiG fighter jets.[47] When the better equipped King Hassan appealed to the USA for arms, Washington's deliveries were more limited. The Kennedy administration was wary of intensifying the already spiralling Cold War polarisation. Instead Hassan summoned the head of Mossad, Meir Amit, to Marrakech. Amit provided Hassan with weapons, surveillance equipment and advanced training – as well as intelligence on Ben Barka and the Moroccan opposition in Cairo and Algiers.[48] Meanwhile, neither the Arab League nor the Organisation of African Unity were persuaded by the king, who was clearly viewed as the aggressor setting a dangerous precedent for war over colonial borders. Faced with his isolation from tricontinentalist powers, and assured of only lukewarm support from Washington, King Hassan backed off. An anti-imperialist alliance had defeated an important counterrevolutionary challenge.

However, Mossad's support for Hassan was richly rewarded by significantly – albeit still covertly – upgrading the two countries' relations. Mossad was allowed the ability to establish a permanent station in Rabat, Israel began selling Morocco used French tanks, and Moroccan General Mohammed Oufkir travelled to Israel for security training in 1964.[49] On 9 November, a military court convicted Ben Barka of 'high treason' and sentenced him to

[45] Reyner, 'Morocco's International Boundaries'; Daoud and Monjib, *Ben Barka*, 303.

[46] Gleijeses, *Conflicting*, 45.

[47] Byrne, *Mecca*, 218–19.

[48] Segev and Shumacher, 'Israel–Morocco', 52–3.

[49] Alpher, *Periphery*, 26.

death. Ben Barka, who had done so much to organise the Moroccan nationalist movement and to rally support around the monarchy, now called for its abolition, and vocally sided with his socialist neighbour. The nationalist had transcended his nation.

Travelling Theorist

Condemned to death and exile, Ben Barka spent a great deal of time in Cairo and Algiers, where he became something of an advisor to presidents Ben Bella and Nasser.[50] 'In a way, he was like my second Minister of Foreign Affairs', Ben Bella recalled years later. 'In fact, he was my real Minister of Foreign Affairs.'[51] Travelling on an Algerian passport, Ben Barka used the two revolutionary capitals as hubs for different purposes. In Cairo, the site of the permanent secretariat of AAPSO, Ben Barka could throw himself into his international organising on the state level. Nasser put him into action on the Congo file, where both Egypt and Algeria were heavily invested, tasking him with supporting the successors of Lumumba in the Congo, the Simbas.[52] In Algiers, he mixed with the emerging vanguard of global revolutionary forces then gravitating towards the nascent republic: Che Guevara, Frantz Fanon, Henri Curiel, militants from the African National Congress and the Portuguese colonies, and a host of radical students, exiles, journalists, interlopers.[53] From Algiers, he envisioned creating a school to train cadres and a research centre and journal devoted to the issues of national liberation, a prototype for Havana's *Tricontinental.*

During this second exile, Ben Barka reflected more seriously on the limitations of decolonisation. He clarified his views on the content of independence in an unpublished article written in December 1963. The tasks were ideological as well as material. 'We must from the start give the word *development* the emotional content that the word *independence* has had', he insisted. 'It is necessary that the mystique of the latter replace that of the other, or more

[50] For an example of a report written by Ben Barka for Ben Bella, see Youssoufi, 'Rapport', 141–9.

[51] Bitton, *Ben Barka*, 66:03.

[52] Daoud and Monjib, *Ben Barka*, 306.

[53] On internationalist Algeria see Simon, *Algérie*; Byrne, *Mecca*; Mokhtefi, *Algiers*.

exactly, it is necessary to show that the profound truth, hidden up to now, but essential to independence, is development.'[54] Ben Barka emphatically opposed a simply quantitative approach. The extent of development could not be understood by measuring per capita income, foreign investment, tourist infrastructure, educational enrolment or the delusions of success within a monocultural economy. Instead, Ben Barka offered another focus: '*The objective basis of development is none other than the productivity of human labour in a given society.*'[55] Only an effective mobilisation of labour could solve the problem of capital accumulation facing most newly independent states.[56] This mobilisation could occur only if 'the masses' were organised and educated, and if the state were the democratic representative of working-class interests and not imperial capital and its local compradors.[57] This formula is what Ben Barka refers to as 'the content of socialism', and represents what he learned from the development of the People's Republic of China, the Soviet Union, Cuba, Ghana, Algeria and Egypt after 1961.[58]

Endings: 1965

The last months of Ben Barka's life were packed with important developments that punctuated the end of the Bandung decade. In March 1965, thousands of US troops landed in South Vietnam to shore up the faltering anti-communist regime, marking a dramatic escalation of the struggle for power in southeast Asia. On the last day of April, US Marines also landed in the capital of the Dominican Republic to counter the advance of revolutionary forces. In May, AAPSO met in Winneba, Ghana. In Ben Barka's estimation, the consolidation of the strength of a homogeneous bloc of national liberation governments was able to finally overcome the tensions produced by the Sino–Soviet split in order to re-centre discussions around the struggle against colonialism.[59] He

[54] Emphasis in original. Ben Barka, 'Africa', 163.

[55] Emphasis in original. Ben Barka, 'Africa', 164.

[56] At the time of this writing, he was revisiting the works of Marx and Rosa Luxemburg, whose influence can be seen by this emphasis on the problem of capital accumulation. Daoud and Monjib, *Ben Barka*, 309.

[57] Ben Barka, 'Africa', 170.

[58] Ibid., 166–71.

[59] Youssoufi, 'Rapport'.

urged the delegates not to succumb to either defeatism or maximalism when he argued that 'the struggle against imperialism is a long fight which must be pursued even under conditions of peaceful coexistence'.[60] His revolutionary realism helped to bridge tensions between the diverse states (PRC–USSR, India–Pakistan, Malaysia–Indonesia) and movements (in southern Africa, for instance). After delegates elected him to lead the preparatory committee for the Tricontinental, Ben Barka worked hard to ensure both Moscow and Beijing would both attend, travelling to both communist capitals to personally ensure their participation.

The forward motion did not last long. Following Morocco's largest urban demonstrations and strikes in March 1965 – which the army only suppressed by killing hundreds – King Hassan declared a state of emergency, shut down parliament, and dismissed the prime minister on 7 June. The pretences of democratic governance in the country had ended. Soon after, on 19 June, Ben Barka's key ally and outspoken tricontinentalist leader, Algerian president Ahmad Ben Bella, was overthrown in a military coup. Algeria's new leaders, a more conservative wing of the FLN, promptly cancelled the Second Summit of Afro-Asian Heads of State, the direct sequel of the famous Bandung conference, slated to be held in Algiers just days later.[61] On 30 September, events began leading to the overthrow of Indonesian president Sukarno and the slaughter of communists and their suspected supporters, destroying another pillar of the Third World project. Ben Barka's assassination in October must be seen as part of this global counterrevolutionary offensive.

Conclusion

The Tricontinental was held in Havana as scheduled in January 1966. It met only once. While Nasser called for the second conference to be held in Cairo in 1968, on the occasion of the tenth anniversary of AAPSO's first meeting, Israel's crushing victory over Egypt, Syria and Jordan in June 1967 resulted in the conference's cancellation.[62] As Ben Barka had warned, the Zionist state played an important role in suppressing Third World aspirations, and not just those of the Arabs.

[60] Quoted in Wallerstein, *Africa*, 96.

[61] Byrne, *Mecca*, 230–1; McDougall, *History of Algeria*, 249–53.

[62] Organization of American States, *Report*, 93.

This chapter has traced the evolution of Mehdi Ben Barka from his humble origins to his role as a leading organiser for Morocco's national independence and his move into the vanguard of tricontinental struggle. Neither simply a politician nor an intellectual, his most distinctive contribution was his understanding of the powerful interactions between the local, national, regional and international political scales, and the necessity of co-ordination at all levels. His education in colonial Algiers exposed him to an international milieu of political organising that was at once nationalist, regionalist, internationalist and leftist. As a main organiser of the Istiqlal underground during the struggle for independence, he was instrumental in formulating the demand for the return of the monarch as the principal objective of the anti-colonial movement. But he soon realised that deeper social transformation was necessary to achieve a sovereign, democratic and just society. His reflections on these problems made him a spearhead in defining and institutionalising neocolonialism as a concept in the global anti-colonial political arsenal. In sum, Ben Barka was pivotal in building a workable tricontinentalism that – for a brief yet crucial period – co-ordinated many of the anti-colonial forces of Africa, Asia and Latin America.

Bibliography

Ageron, Charles-Robert, 'L'Association des Étudiants Musulmans Nord-Africains en France durant l'Entre-Deux-Guerres: Contribution à l'Étude des Nationalismes Maghrébins', *Revue Française d'Histoire d'Outre-Mer* 70, 258–9 (1983): 25–56.

Aksikas, Jaafar, *Arab Modernities: Islamism, Nationalism, and Liberalism in the Post-Colonial Arab World* (New York: Peter Lang, 2009).

All-African Peoples Conference, 'All-African Peoples' Conference Statement on Neocolonialism', 31 March 1961, <https://www.pambazuka.org/global-south/africa-all-african-peoples-conference-statement-neocolonialism> (last accessed 14 May 2019).

Alpher, Yossi, *Periphery: Israel's Search for Middle East Allies* (Lanham, MD: Rowman & Littlefield, 2015).

Amin, Samir, *The Maghreb in the Modern World: Algeria, Tunisia, Morocco*, trans. Michael Perl (Harmondsworth: Penguin, 1970).

Ashford, Douglas E., *Political Change in Morocco* (Princeton: Princeton University Press, 1961).

Baraka, al-Mahdi Bin, *Al-ikhtiyar al-thawri fi al-maghrib* [The revolutionary option in Morocco] (Beirut: Dar al-Tali'a, 1966).

Barka, Mehdi Ben, 'Africa After Independence', in *The Political Thought of Ben Barka* (Havana: Tricontinental, 1968): 159–71.

Barka, Mehdi Ben, 'Appeal Made on Occassion of the Algerian–Moroccan Conflict', in *The Political Thought of Ben Barka* (Havana: Tricontinental, 1968): 183–6.

Barka, Mehdi Ben, 'Estrategia Global a Escala Tricontinental', in Ulises Estrada and Luis Suárez (eds), *Rebelión Tricontinental: Las Voces de Los Condenados de La Tierra de África, Asia y América Latina* (Melbourne: Ocean Press in association with Ediciones Tricontinental, 2006): 15–22.

Barka, Mehdi Ben, 'Present Problems of National Revolution in Africa and Asia', in *The Political Thought of Ben Barka* (Havana: Tricontinental, 1968): 149–57.

Barka, Mehdi Ben, 'Revolutionary Option in Morocco', in *The Political Thought of Ben Barka* (Havana: Tricontinental, 1968): 13–76.

Barka, Mehdi Ben, *The Political Thought of Ben Barka* (Havana: Tricontinental, 1968).

Bergman, Ronen and Shlomo Nakdimon, 'The Ghosts of Saint-Germain Forest', *Ynet*, 23 March 2015, <http://www.ynetnews.com/articles/0,7340,L-4639608,00.html> (last accessed 14 May 2019).

Bitton, Simone (ed.), *Ben Barka: The Moroccan Equation* (New York: Icarus Films, 2003).

Byrne, Jeffrey James, *Mecca of Revolution: Algeria, Decolonization, and the Third World Order* (Oxford: Oxford University Press, 2016).

Central Intelligence Agency, 'The All Africa Peoples Conference in 1961', 1 November 1961, <https://www.cia.gov/library/readingroom/docs/CIA-RDP78-00915R001300320009-3.pdf> (last accessed 14 May 2019).

Daoud, Zakya and Maâti Monjib, *Ben Barka: Une Vie, Une Mort* (Paris: Éditions Michalon, 2000).

Evins, Joe L., 'Distinguished World Visitors Beat Path to TVA', *Congressional Record* (28 July 1958): 15,349.

Executive Secretariat of OSPAAAL, 'First Solidarity Conference of the Peoples of Africa, Asia and Latin America' (Havana: OSPAAAL, 1966).

Faligot, Roger, *Tricontinentale: Quand Che Guevara, Ben Barka, Cabral, Castro et Hô Chi Minh Préparaient La Révolution Mondiale (1964–1968)* (Paris: La Découverte, 2013).

Gleijeses, Piero, *Conflicting Missions: Havana, Washington, and Africa, 1959–1976* (Chapel Hill: University of North Carolina Press, 2002).

Guérin, Daniel, *Les Assassins de Ben Barka: Dix Ans d'Enquête* (Paris: G. Authier, 1975).

Halstead, John P., *Rebirth of a Nation: The Origins and Rise of Moroccan Nationalism, 1912–1944* (Cambridge: Harvard University Press, 1967).

Harbi, Mohamed, 'Ben Barka et Les Nationalistes Arabes', in René Gallissot and Jacques Kergoat (eds), *Mehdi Ben Barka: De l'Indépendance Marocaine à La Tricontinentale* (Paris: Karthala, 1997): 133–9.

Harbi, Mohamed, 'L'Option Révolutionnaire de Ben Barka', in *Ben Barka Vingt Ans Après: Les Droits de l'Homme Au Maroc* (Paris: Arcantère, 1986): 47–54.

Hudson, Michael C., *Arab Politics: The Search for Legitimacy* (New Haven: Yale University Press, 1977).

Joffé, E. G. H., 'The Moroccan Nationalist Movement: Istiqlal, the Sultan, and the Country', *The Journal of African History* 26, 4 (1985): 289–307.

Joffe, George, 'Morocco: Monarchy, Legitimacy and Succession', *Third World Quarterly* 10, 1 (1988): 201–28.

McDougall, James, *A History of Algeria* (Cambridge: Cambridge University Press, 2017).

Mokhtefi, Elaine, *Algiers, Third World Capital: Freedom Fighters, Revolutionaries, Black Panthers* (London: Verso, 2018).

'Morocco Arrests 130 Leaders of Party Opposed to the King', *New York Times* (18 July 1963).

National Union of Popular Forces, 'The Charter of the UNFP', *The Political Thought of Ben Barka* (Havana: Tricontinental, 1968): 77–9.

Pennell, C. R., *Morocco: From Empire to Independence* (Oxford: Oneworld, 2003).

Reyner, Anthony S., 'Morocco's International Boundaries: A Factual Background', *Journal of Modern African Studies* 1, 3 (1963): 313–26.

Schaar, Stuart, 'King Hassan's Alternatives', *Africa Report* 8, 8 (1963): 7–12.

Segev, Samuel, and Yvette Shumacher, 'Israel–Morocco Relations from Hassan II to Muhammad VI', *Israel Journal of Foreign Affairs* 2, 3 (2008): 49–60.

Senate Committee on the Judiciary, 'The Tricontinental Conference of African, Asian, and Latin American Peoples' (Washington: Government Printing Office, 1966).

Simon, Catherine, *Algérie, Les Années Pieds-Rouges: Des Rêves de l'Indépendance Au Désenchantement (1962–1969)* (Paris: La Découverte, 2011).

Stivers, William, *Supremacy and Oil: Iraq, Turkey, and the Anglo-American World Order, 1918–1930* (Ithaca: Cornell University Press, 1982).

Wallerstein, Immanuel, *Africa: The Politics of Independence and Unity* (Lincoln: University of Nebraska Press, 2005).

Waterbury, John, *The Commander of the Faithful: The Moroccan Political Elite – A Study in Segmented Politics* (New York: Columbia University Press, 1970).

Young, Robert J. C., *Postcolonialism: An Historical Introduction* (Malden: Blackwell, 2001).

Youssoufi, Abderrahmane, 'Rapport Rédigé par Mehdi Ben Barka à l'Intention du Président de la République d'Algerie (10 Juin 1965)', in René Gallissot and Jacques Kergoat (eds), *Mehdi Ben Barka: De l'indépendance Marocaine à La Tricontinentale* (Paris: Karthala, 1997): 141–9.

8

MARXISM OR LEFT-WING NATIONALISM? THE NEW LEFT IN EGYPT IN THE 1970s

Gennaro Gervasio

Introduction

The recent fiftieth anniversary of the Six Day War of June 1967 has reopened academic and public debate on the causes and consequences of the Arab defeat (*al-naksa*).[1] The defeat marks a profound break in the contemporary history of the Middle East and North Africa,[2] with its political and social consequences still felt today. The most immediate consequence of the defeat, at the ideological level, was the beginning of the decline of 'socialist' and 'progressive' Arab nationalism, and the unravelling of Egyptian president Gamal 'Abd al-Nasir (Nasser) as its undisputed leader and hero. Many consider the *naksa* as simply the beginning of a reactionary politics, embodied by the rebirth of political Islam. This, however, obscures an important part of the political and intellectual history of the Arab world in the twentieth century.[3] While the *naksa* pushed many intellectuals and militants towards alternative Islamist politics, it also helped liberate others from the weight

[1] See for example Zekri, 'The Arabs' Groundhog Day', <https://en.qantara.de/content/egyptian-historian-khaled-fahmy-on-the-six-day-war-the-arabs-groundhog-day> (last accessed 1 November 2018). For a reading, from an Egyptian perspective, see Mansur (ed.), *Fi tashrih al-hazima*.

[2] Laroui, *The Crisis*.

[3] Haugbølle, 'The New Arab Left', 498–9; Hanssen and Weiss (eds), *Arabic Thought*.

of the charisma of the defeated leader, driving them towards more radical theories and political action, and thus laying the foundations of and strengthening the Arab New Left (*al-yasar al-jadid*). While the historical imprint of New Left was fleeting, a study of its rise and fall provides a glimpse into an alternative political vision after the 1967 war, and undermines the narrative of the inevitability of the rise of political Islam.

While the history of the theory and political practice of the Arab Left has mostly been a niche topic in the academy,[4] the analysis of the Arab New Left has seen increased attention in very recent times. Studies, however, have mainly focused on Lebanon and Syria,[5] and have almost entirely ignored Egypt.[6] This chapter therefore aims to describe and analyse the birth and development of the New Left in Egypt. It shows that the New Left formed both in reaction to the hegemony of the regime in political life and as a critique of the substantial and problematic support of the Old Left (or 'official Left', *al-yasar al-rasmi*) for the state under Nasser.[7] In particular, on the basis of official documents, both published and underground press, and personal interviews with some of the militants, this chapter examines the experience of the 'Far Left', embodied by *al-tanzim al-shuyu'i al-misri* (The Egyptian Communist Organisation, TshM),[8] founded in 1969, which became the Egyptian Communist Workers' Party (ECWP, *hizb al-'ummal al-shuyu'i al-misri*) in 1975.

[4] Among the few exceptions are: Laqueur, *Communism and Nationalism*; Agwani, *Communism*; Rodinson, *Marxisme*; Ismael, *The Arab Left*; Jabar (ed.), *Post-Marxism*; Ismael, *The Communist Movement*. In Arabic: Murqus, *Tarikh*; al-Turkmani, *Al-Ahzab*.

[5] For example Bardawil, *When All This Revolution Melts into Air* and 'Dreams'; Haugbølle and Singh, 'New Approaches to Arab Left Histories'; Sing, 'Arab Self-Criticism'; Frangie, 'Historicism'; Guirguis, 'Vietnam'. On the Arab Left and the 'Arab Uprisings' of 2010–11, see Kalfat, *Mapping of the Arab Left*.

[6] On the history of the Egyptian Left: al-'Alim (ed.), *Sab'un*; Beinin and Lockman, *Workers*; Botman, *The Rise*; Ismael and El-Sa'id, *The Communist*; Labib, *Shuyu'iyyun*; Gervasio, *Al-haraka*.

[7] The adjective 'official' (*rasmi*) has been used polemically, during interviews, both by some Marxists who had adopted a critical stance towards the Old Guard's decision to fold the parties to join the institutions and by some of the former members of *al-Tali'a*'s editorial board, with self-criticism. In this essay, I will use the term 'New Left' to describe the new radical communist groups formed in the early 1970s, and 'Official Left' or 'Old Left' to describe those who in 1965 agreed to dissolve their parties and be absorbed into the state apparatus.

[8] Former militants of this group use the acronym 'TshM' extensively.

The decision to focus on the TshM/ECWP is justified by various factors, among which is access to a larger number of publications than those of the other underground parties. But the main reason remains that, compared to the other two large Marxist groups, the TshM/ECWP can more legitimately be considered part of the new Arab Left due to significant elements of rupture with the previous communist waves. Some militants and scholars are reluctant to extend the label 'New Left' to all underground communist groups born in the 1970s,[9] given the apparent continuity between the second and third movements. These continuities lie in theoretical production, in political practice and, above all, in the presence of some leaders of the 'old guard' – including members of the editorial staff of *al-Tali'a* – in the circles which would later become the re-established Egyptian Communist Party (ECP, *al-hizb al-shuyu'i al-misri*) and the Egyptian Communist Party 'January 8' (ECP, *al-hizb al-shuyu'i al-misri '8 yanayr'*).[10]

The Egyptian Left between Nasser and Sadat

If it is undeniable that a new radical leftist current originated in the Arab Levant in the long 1960s,[11] it is equally true that Egypt, epicentre of the crisis, did not remain immune to this wave of political and cultural fervour.[12] The first glimpses of this were evident in popular Egyptian reaction to Nasser's resignation. When Egyptians took to the streets after Nasser's resignation, they not only asked him to remain in place and face the consequences of the defeat, but, significantly, expressed an unwillingness to be completely marginalised in the decision-making process. Those protests helped open up

[9] Fathi, 'Tarikh'.

[10] The Trotskyite League (*'usbat al-trustskiyyin*) is the only group of the 'Third Wave' of the Egyptian Communist Movement without any link with the older Marxist generation, and by far the smallest one.

[11] Haugbølle, 'The New Arab Left', 499–500.

[12] *Self-Critique after the Defeat*, a book published by the then-young Syrian philosopher Sadiq Jalal al-'Azm in Beirut in 1968, is considered by many Egyptian Marxists to be one of the founding texts of the post-*naksa* Arab 'New Left'. In the book, al-'Azm criticised 'pseudo-revolutionary' Arab regimes, and engaged in self-criticism for supporting them. He called on young Arab revolutionaries to radicalise the Left, and to look at the examples of Cuba, China and Vietnam, and the Palestinian Resistance. See al-'Azm, *Al-naqd*, and Kalfat, author's interview, on the book's impact on the birth of the Egyptian New Left.

political space for critique and resistance, providing the conditions in which new political alternatives were beginning to be imagined. The years from 1968 up until the war of October 1973 saw various sectors of the population, previously neutralised by the regime,[13] occupying increasing spaces of political action. The protest movements during this time began from places of traditional nationalist and progressive activism – the factories and universities. It was within these spaces that the New Left would find many supporters.

In 1968, student protests threatened to spread throughout the country and signalled the first major instance of anti-government sentiment in decades. The protests had a long-lasting impact and opened up a space for more independent political action. An analysis of the protests is beyond the objectives of this chapter, but it is important to point out that even when the demonstrations evolved into a real anti-government uprising, such as in Alexandria in November 1968,[14] no political alternative to the regime was put forward, nor did there exist any independent force capable of channelling the request for political participation. The limited scope of the movement can be explained with two reasons. The first is that the regime had monopolised all political life, and the second is that popular demands remained mostly – even if not exclusively – limited to the patriotic request for people's involvement in operations at the front. Yet the protest movement of 1968–9 contained the seeds of the resumption of political activism in the early 1970s, and it is also undeniable that only Nasser's death in September 1970 opened a space for independent political action. In this respect, while Nasser had never been the direct target of student and popular anger, his successor Anwar al-Sadat (Sadat), who had consolidated his hold on power with the 'Corrective Revolution' (*thawrat al-tashih*) in May 1971,[15] was the main target of the rage and sarcasm of the early generation of 1970s militants. These militants saw him as the symbol of indecision (*taraddud*) and defeatism (*istislamiyya*).

The student movement of 1971 and 1973[16] was also significant in the rebirth of independent political action in Egypt, especially for the Left. Most

[13] Kandil, *Soldiers*, Ch. 1.

[14] Hussein, *Class conflict*, 322–6.

[15] On Sadat's Egypt, see for example Beattie, *Egypt*.

[16] Gervasio, *Al-haraka*, 252–66, and Gervasio, 'An Egyptian 1968?'. On the history of the Egyptian student movement see Abdalla, *The Student*. On the 1960s–1970s generation, see 'Abdallah and Baha' al-Din Sha'ban, *Al-haraka*; Salamuni, *Al-Jil*.

students who began their political militancy in universities in the 1970s belonged to the broad Left,[17] their political formation having been under state socialism. Yet this new generation (*al-jil al-jadid*) also looked towards global Third World resistance movements for inspiration. The Palestinian *fida'i* (fighter), the Vietnamese Viet Cong and Ernesto Che Guevara all became mythologised by Egyptian leftist students. Perhaps the most appropriate definition for this student Left is 'spontaneous Left' (*yasar tilqa'i*),[18] precisely because of the ease with which they were attracted by radical socialist and Marxist ideas. However, like much of the emerging 'Third Communist Movement', this new wave of activists placed emphasis on the national or patriotic question (*al-qadiyya al-wataniyya*) to the detriment of the social question (*al-qadiyya al-ijtima'iyya*), just like the previous generation, from which it paradoxically claimed to distance itself. Young Egyptian militants entered the Left, in the words of the 1970s student leader Ahmad Baha' al-Din Sha'ban, through the 'door of Nationalism'.[19] This is understandable, given the Israeli occupation of Sinai, but the emphasis placed almost solely on the national and pan-Arab question proved a barrier, in the long run, to the spread of Marxist thought among the population. Former student activists dominated the New Left, which meant the near-total hegemony of intellectuals in the movement, to the detriment of workers and peasants.

While the development of the New Left occurred in the universities, Marxist circles (*halaqat*) already existed since the late 1960s. Therefore, before looking briefly at the relationship between university activism and Marxist organisations,[20] it is necessary to deal with the genesis of the latter.

The roots of the New Left can be located towards the end of the 'second communist movement' (*al-haraka al-thaniya*), before the 1967 defeat.[21] The

[17] Shukri, *Egypt*, 93.

[18] As suggested by al-'Amrusi, interview with author.

[19] Baha' al-Din Sha'ban, interview with author.

[20] The most accurate – and dramatic – testimony to this relation is Salih, *Al-mubtasirun*, based on the notebooks of the author, herself a militant in both the student and the communist movement, within TshM/ECWP. On her experience, see Hammad, 'Arwa Salih'.

[21] Researchers and former militants usually divide the history of Egyptian communism into three *movements* (*harakat*): the first from the outset (1920s) until the early 1930s; the second from the late 1930s until the parties' self-dissolution in 1965; and the third from the early 1970s up until today.

two major clandestine Marxist organisations that survived the police repression of the late 1950s were the Egyptian Communist Party (ECP) and *Haditu* (*al-haraka al-dimuqratiyya li al-taharrur al-watani*, Democratic Movement of National Liberation). Both organisations decided to fold at the beginning of 1965[22] and join the 'only socialist current', personified by the regime's Arab Socialist Union (ASU). While many Marxists entered the ASU 'in a personal capacity', and found work in the monthly state-sponsored magazine *al-Tali'a* ('The Vanguard'),[23] others were not so lucky, suffering permanent exclusion from jobs in the state-run cultural and media sectors. In 1965, these marginalised militants, together with those opposed to the decision to dissolve the parties, formed a new organisation, *wahdat al-shuyu'yyin* (Unity of Communists). In addition to some older Marxist militants, such as the literary critic Ibrahim Fathi, the brightest intellectuals of the 1960s generation, including the writers Jamal al-Ghitani and Yahya al-Tahir 'Abdallah, the literary critic Sabri Hafiz and the journalist Salah 'Isa, joined *wahdat al-shuyu'yyin*.[24] The very foundations of this group, however, were fraught, as its members had decided to associate on the basis of a refusal to co-operate with the state instead of on a coherent platform.

Wahdat al-shuyu'yyin had a short life. In October 1966, it came under attack during Nasser's last great anti-Marxist purge; its militants were jailed, accused of belonging to an 'underground pro-Chinese group'.[25] Even those who had agreed to be absorbed into the state apparatus were not spared. Some of the leaders of the 'official Left', including the editor of *al-Tali'a*, Lutfi al-Khuli were jailed.

In was in this straitened political context that the 1967 defeat occurred, the student and labour movements began to organise, and former militants sought underground spaces to meet and discuss their ideas. In was in this late 1960s period that Marxist study circles (*halaqat*) began to form. It would be a stretch to consider these small groups of intellectuals, isolated and without any platform or political activity, as substantial political organisations. Their obsession with secrecy, justified no doubt by the efficiency of the regime's

[22] The self-dissolution documents are reproduced in al-'Alim, *Sab'un*, 398–400.

[23] On the birth of *al-Tali'a*, see Ginat, *Lutfi*; Yahya, 'Ab'ad', 9–11.

[24] 'Isa, al-Ghitani, Fathi: interviews with author.

[25] Ibid.

repressive apparatus, made communication between the various groups virtually impossible. The groups often ignored each other's existence.[26] Nonetheless, these *halaqat* were central to the birth of the 'Third Movement' (*al-haraka al-thalitha*) of the Egyptian communists that began in the 1970s. The Egyptian Communist Workers' Party (ECWP), formed in 1975, was one of the movement's most significant products.

The ECWP: The Trajectory of a New Left Party

The genesis of the *halaqa* from which the ECWP originated is particularly interesting because it also has a literary facet. The roots of the ECWP are undoubtedly to be found in the brief experience of *wahdat al-shuyu'iyyin*, and in particular in its inspirer, Ibrahim Fathi. His ideas, after he had left prison with other alleged Maoists on the eve of the 1967 war, were further radicalised by the *naksa*. After the defeat, he devoted himself, with some of his companions, to two parallel projects. On the one hand, in an attempt to free writers from state-monopoly and sponsorship, Fathi proposed cultivating a new generation, an Egyptian literary avant-garde. On the other, he tried to form a communist organisation on a new basis and with new energies.[27] Through the independent literary magazine *Galery 68*[28] and other, mostly literary, work in the association *kuttab al-ghad* (Writers of Tomorrow), Fathi drew young intellectuals into the Marxist circle *Khamis wa al-Baqri*.[29] It was from *Khamis wa al-Baqri* that *al-tanzim al-shuyu'i al-misri* (the Egyptian Communist Organisation, known by the Arabic contraction TshM) was born in December 1969. At the time of its foundation, TshM could, therefore, already count on an internal organisational structure and on some political analyses, mainly written by Fathi. TshM was established by a very small number of intellectuals, including the sociologist Hasanayn Kishk, the economist Salah al-'Amrusi and the writers Khalil Kalfat and Zayn al-'Abidin Fu'ad. The organisation expanded quickly, mainly due to the influx of new supporters recruited on university campuses in the early 1970s.

[26] Kishk, interview with author.

[27] Fathi, interview with author.

[28] On *Galery 68*, see Kendall, 'The Theoretical Roots'.

[29] These are the names of the leaders of the first workers' uprising after July 1952 in Kafr al-Dawwar, who were sentenced to death by the Free Officers.

It is important to underline here the most characteristic positions of the TshM, which explains its primacy in Egyptian universities and the intellectual milieu in the first half of the 1970s. The members of this group, hastily described by Ismael and El-Sa'id as 'young extremists without political experience',[30] were in fact the authors of an attempt to break an older tradition of Egyptian Marxism.

The establishment of the TshM was founded on a refusal to 'dress the Nasserite regime with revolutionary clothes', and a denunciation of former communist militants, like Michel Kamil, an eminent member of *al-Tali'a*'s editorial board, who had accepted co-optation with the regime in exchange for little or nothing.[31] Indeed, Michel Kamil's attempt to re-establish an independent communist organisation without any serious self-criticism of the deal with Nasser in 1965 appeared to the young militants as 'right-wing deviationism' without any revolutionary prospect.[32]

The most obvious break with the official Left was the rejection of its vision of the Nasserist regime, an issue that would be the subject of reflection and debate, both within the group and with the other organisations of the New Left.[33] In clear contrast to the experiences of the 1950s and 1960s, the TshM denied any progressive character to the Nasserite regime, considering it the expression of the 'bureaucratic bourgeoisie', destined to return sooner or later to an alliance with the forces of world imperialism and the pre-revolutionary bourgeoisie at home. In the earliest available political documents, written in the aftermath of the June defeat, 'a resolution of the contradiction between (local) power and imperialism' was foreshadowed, with the return of Egypt to the Western camp and the simultaneous rise of the reactionary forces of old and new capitalism.[34] It is important to underline the peculiarity of this reading made by TshM, since it allowed the group to develop a convincing

[30] Ismael and El-Sa'id, *The Communist*, 131.

[31] Fathi, interview with author.

[32] Author's interviews with TshM's founders, especially al-'Amrusi and Kishk.

[33] The most elaborate argument on this fundamental issue is to be found in Salih, 'Al-burjwaziyya al-biruqratiyya'.

[34] 'Ali, 'Kayfa tahall'. This short undated text opens a (partial) collection of documents produced by TshM/ECWP from the outset until 1976, published in Beirut in 1979.

analysis of the regime's evolution under Sadat, recognising it as a 'natural continuation of the path begun by its predecessor'.[35] In the 1970s, the ECP echoed the Official Left by invoking 'the defence of the Nasserite conquests' (*al-makasib al-nasiriyya*).[36]

Despite formulating one of the most radical theories around the role of the state, the TshM faced major challenges, in terms of internal organisation, propaganda strategies and the social origin of the militants. First of all, despite the claim to be the true party of the Egyptian working class, the organisation was mainly made up of urban intellectuals 'with a limited presence in factories and only symbolic one in rural areas'.[37] While the TshM merged in 1971 with a Marxist group of workers active in Alexandria, all the leaders (the 'Central Committee') and the overwhelming majority of members were still from petty- and middle-bourgeois urban backgrounds. This helps to explain the choice to work on producing theoretical texts and disseminating revolutionary propaganda among the educated classes, to the detriment of direct action within the working and peasant classes.

The TshM experienced its greatest success among university students, starting in 1972–3. The members, many of whom were of university age or a little older, were able to penetrate the campus successfully, circulating *kuttab al-ghad*, and disseminating a fresh political radicalism that attracted many students disappointed by Nasserism's unfulfilled promises. Students had been bitterly disillusioned by official leftist rhetoric, and the TshM presented itself as a real break (*inqita'*) with the 'collaborationist' tradition of 1960s Egyptian communism.[38]

As already mentioned, the starting point of the TshM founders' analysis, entrusted to the pen of Ibrahim Fathi, was not only condemnation of the communist parties' decision in 1965 to disband, but above all the rejection of the old left's appraisal of the Nasser regime.[39] Influenced by the Stalinist

[35] Author's interviews with TshM's founders.

[36] T. Th. Shakir (pseudonym of Michel Kamil and other ECP 're-founders'), *Qadaya*.

[37] Kishk, interview with author.

[38] Ibid.

[39] 'Ali, 'Tab'iyyat al-sulta'; the first document written by Fathi after the establishment of TshM addresses the class nature of the Nasserist regime.

theory of revolutionary phases, various communist parties had, in different ways and times, recognised a character of 'national and democratic revolution' in the Nasser regime. Their minor complaint was its authoritarian drift. By contrast, the TshM saw Nasserism as irredeemable, a 'demagogic system' that had immobilised the masses. Unlike other communist parties, the TshM also criticised the USSR in its 'Stalinist deformation'. The TshM were heavily influenced by recent Maoist thought. It is not a coincidence that the TshM was formed after the IX Congress of the Chinese Communist Party (1969) in which Mao described the Soviet regime as socialist imperialist. While the TshM never expressed such a radical criticism of the Soviets, it is clear that it was very open to Maoist influences and, to a lesser extent, those from the European and Third World Left.[40] This position was due to Fathi's predominantly internationalist view (*ru'ya umamiyya*), which was a rarity – with the exception of the small Trotskyists' League – within Egyptian Marxism, with its mainly nationalist and pan-Arabist approach that had facilitated its partial co-optation by the Nasser system.[41]

The TshM/ECWP was certainly the 'oldest' formation of the Third movement, and it began printing its bulletin *al-Intifad* (The Uprising) from 1972, in conjunction with the student movement. Despite what was said about Fathi's early theoretical publications, *al-Intifad* gave significant attention to the national question, launching the Maoist slogan of 'a popular war for the liberation of the occupied Arab Territories'. In fact, a look at the writings of TshM members between 1970 and the 1973 War shows a focus on the 'Middle Eastern question',[42] together with theoretical elaborations on the nature and social composition of the system in power.

These early 1970s writings wrongly predicted that the Sadat regime would never launch an attack against Israel, because its class nature prioritised 'the return of Egypt to the imperialist camp', of which Israel was the stronghold in the Middle East.[43] This position, which denied any legitimacy to a government incapable of retaking by force what had been occupied in the war, was

[40] Kalfat, interview with author.

[41] Shukrallah, interview with author.

[42] See for example Salih, 'Hawla mudd'.

[43] Salih, 'Didd mafahim'.

another reason for the party's success among students. Instead, the Egyptian 'victory' in the October 1973 War, albeit limited, and especially the major propaganda that lionised the 'Hero of the Crossing' (*batal al-'ubur*), seemed to contradict the group's forecasts.

However, before analysing the reaction of the *tanzim* to Sadat's great political-diplomatic victory, it must be remembered that at that time the party's leadership was in jail. The dynamics that led to the arrests is important in understanding the ECWP's future political and programmatic line. The leadership soon realised the risk of remaining a closed club of urban intellectuals. Therefore, at the end of 1971, while the TshM expanded into universities, a group of workers active in Alexandria entered the organisation, representing the working class, until then almost completely absent. The State Security Forces managed to infiltrate this cell, and one of the militants confessed under torture the names of the Central Committee members, who were promptly arrested.[44]

This event is of fundamental importance above all because the hardship of prison life marked Ibrahim Fathi in particular, driving him towards the margins of the group, with notable consequences for the political line in the second part of the 1970s. Moreover, the betrayal by one of the workers and the ease with which the police had infiltrated the cell further strengthened the organisation's emphasis on secrecy, to the detriment of internal democracy and proselytism among the working classes.

As for the October war, the TshM's leadership reacted to what seemed a clear defeat of their expectations. Khalil Kalfat warned that 'all that glitters is not gold': despite the bombastic propaganda by the state media, which had 'infected' also *al-Tali'a* and the 'reformists' of the future ECP. For him the war had been nothing but a limited initiative in order to bring the country back 'into the orbit of US imperialism'.[45] If this position was 'revolutionary', according to TshM's press, and effectively anticipated future political developments, nonetheless it was a mistake to have bet on the regime's inability to fight. In particular, the belief that the regime was, due to the predominance

[44] Kishk, al-'Amrusi, Shukrallah: interviews with author.

[45] Salih, 'Laysa'.

of old and new reactionary forces, incapable of and not interested in military action was the result of an analysis that was too mechanical and that did not take into account, among other things, Sadat's personality and ambitions.

The TshM's belief that the new regime was following a defeatist line with respect to the conflict with Israel, in continuity with the steps taken by Nasser since 1967, proved to be correct. In any case, from 1973 onwards the analysis of developments on the Arab–Israeli front, together with marked attention to international political issues, constituted the backbone of the TshM's vast production.[46]

The wave of strikes in early 1975, due to the very first social effects of *Infitah* – the policy of economic 'opening' launched in 1974 which imposed privatisation and cuts to subsidies for basic necessities – culminated in March in the occupation of factories at Mahalla al-Kubra. This presented new challenges for the radical left. TshM played a role, although not on the front line, in the demonstrations in Helwan and Alexandria, where it was the only organised Marxist group among the workers. The worsening economic conditions, the new wave of the student movement and Sadat's diplomatic rapprochement with Israel seemed to offer, in the eyes of some young militants, the most suitable conditions for penetrating the masses, aiming at direct action and contemplating – at least in theory – people's armed struggle for liberation.[47]

Following the announcement of the Egyptian Communist Party's re-establishment in May 1975, the TshM in September proclaimed its transformation into the Egyptian Communist Workers' Party. At the same time, the Central Committee published a detailed report explaining why 'communist education of the masses through the dissemination of the party press' was a higher priority than direct action.[48] From the theoretical point of view, relying on the Maoist approach, the leadership believed it was premature to start revolutionary action without first educating the people. The experience of hard prison, however, had given rise to some mistrust towards workers and a certain fear that the increase in party militants could encourage more infiltration and, consequently, new arrests. Obviously, the CC did not declare itself

[46] For example Salih, 'Al-taswiyya'.

[47] Zahran and Shukrallah: interviews with author.

[48] ECWP, 'Taqrir 9/5', 1–20.

against the recruitment of new militants inside the factories; however, instead of 'proletarianising the students' (*ta'mil al-talaba*), as the younger militants wanted, it held that it was necessary to 'acculturate the workers' (*tathqif al-'ummal*), to make them the 'conscious vanguard' of the next socialist revolution.[49] Moreover, to justify the preference given to activity in the universities, the party leadership stated that students, once graduated and absorbed into the production system, would play the role of 'transmission belt' (*halaqa wasita*) between workers and the party. The ECWP leadership, firmly controlled by Kalfat, saw the party as a vanguard of revolutionary intellectuals. They believed that they needed to spread class consciousness with publications that presented a correct vision of the local and international situation, and awaken the consciousness of the subaltern classes and of the petty bourgeoisie marginalised by the Sadat regime, which would in turn pave the way for the socialist revolution.[50]

Since its foundation in September 1975, the ECWP has published four monthly or bi-weekly (underground) publications. Two of them, the 'old' *al-Intifad*, begun in 1972, and the 'new' *al-shuyu'i al-misri* (The Egyptian Communist) in September 1975, were intended for public distribution. As for the others, reserved for internal circulation, *al-Amn* (Security) was dedicated to security issues, while *al-sira'* (The Conflict) contained debate among the militants on theoretical and organisational issues. Considering that even at times of maximum expansion the ECWP did not reach 300 full-time members,[51] one can appreciate the volume and level of intellectual debate within this group. *Al-shuyu'i al-misri* was even considered by the militants of the other radical groups, with the exception of the 'old guard' of the ECP, the avant-garde publication hub of the entire Egyptian Marxist movement. In this sense, *al-Shuyu'i al-misri* could be considered the '*al-Tali'a* of the radical left' because of its special attention to national liberation and communist movements worldwide, and for its Arabic translation of texts produced by the international Marxist movement. Moreover, like the magazine of the

49 ECWP, 'Editorial', *al-sira'*, 11 (30 September 1975): 1ff.

50 Ibid.

51 Some former members reported 'around 500 active members', but the majority of those interviewed confirmed 'between two and three hundred members', which I believe is a more likely figure.

Official Left, the mouthpiece of the ECWP also at times published avant-garde poetry and other literature.

While the party's publication strategy gave it a certain advantage on campuses, this would prove fickle in the face of an Islamist expansion in the universities. However, the Left's unstable position in student politics in the second part of the 1970s was not only dependent on state-sponsored Islamist expansion. The Left's preference for the 'national question', reinforced by its denunciation of Sadat's 'betrayal' of the Arab cause, and, significantly, its misreading of social tensions within Egyptian society, contributed to its inability to present itself as a viable alternative to both the regime and political Islam.

While dissatisfaction among some members towards the party's political line had been contained before, it exploded at the end of 1976, when a significant number of militants choose to leave the ECWP.[52] Internal debate was focused on ways of intensifying party action among the working masses (*al-'amal al-jamahiri*), and when the regime announced the first free 'open' elections since 1952, scheduled for the autumn of 1976, many saw this as an opportunity. A 'dissident group' within the ECWP – which described itself as *takattul* ('bloc') – favoured presenting party members as independent candidates in poorer areas during the elections. They did not think they would actually be elected to Parliament, but believed the very process of campaigning would serve to develop a more effective mode of propaganda.[53] Faced with rejection by the majority of the ECWP's CC, who adhered to the 'refusal of any recognition of the regime in power', most of the *takattul* decided to leave. From the interviews I collected, it is clear that the number of militants in disagreement with the official line was higher than those who actually abandoned the ECWP. Many preferred to remain, in the name of democratic centralism, fuelling internal debate in the pages of *al-Sira'*.[54]

The exit of members more open to political action undoubtedly weakened the ECWP just when, paradoxically, the regime was giving it the biggest

[52] ECWP, 'Qirar', 1–20.

[53] Zahran, one of the *takattul*'s leaders: interview with author.

[54] Al-'Amrusi, interview with author. An in-depth account of the internal debate is offered by S. Kamil, *Khilafatuna* (unpublished, undated manuscript, 431 pp.).

publicity possible by accusing it of being behind the January 1977 popular uprising. The state published the name of the party and of some arrested members in newspapers and periodicals in Egypt and throughout the Arab world,[55] although the communist movement as a whole played a marginal role in the riots. The revolt, a reaction to cuts to state subsidies on basic necessities, ended, despite the bloody repression of the army, only when the regime reversed its policy. The ECWP, like all the other groups of the radical left, failed to exploit social tension and the regime's growing crisis of legitimacy to increase the number of its militants with direct action. Instead it continued to insist on disseminating its 'revolutionary press'.

The party's publications between 1977 and the death of Sadat in October 1981[56] continued to focus on the 'national question', especially after the president's trip to Jerusalem.[57] No doubt the arguments were insightful and nuanced, but on an operational level even the most radical fraction of the Third Movement failed to go beyond denouncing the 'national betrayal' (*al-khiyana al-wataniyya*). What is striking from a retrospective reading of the party press is an almost total inability to offer the public a reason to mobilise beyond opposition to the 'betrayal' and 'normalisation'. Furthermore, one should highlight the worrying absence of the Left's analytical reflection on the rise of political Islam, beyond a comparison between Egypt and Iran after the triumph of Khomeini in 1979.[58]

Nonetheless, Sadat's obsession with the 'communist threat', equal only to his short-sightedness towards the much more real rise of political Islam, once again made the radical left the main target of state repression. ECWP members were jailed in 1980[59] and then, to a lesser extent, in September 1981, with one of the largest waves of arrests in the modern history of the country.

[55] 84 citizens were arrested on the charge of being ECWP members, although the list also included ECP, *8 yanayr* members. See 'Abd al-Raziq, *Misr*, p. 124.

[56] Ismael and El-Sa'id (in *The Communist*, p. 147) wrongly maintain that after January 1977 the ECWP was reduced to 'sparse circles' and that it ceased its publications, whereas I have found issues of *al-shuyu'i al-misri* until 1981, and of *al-Intifad* until ECWP's merging with *8 yanayr* in 1989.

[57] ECWP, *Mawqif*, 30 November 1977; ECWP, *Bayan*, December 1977.

[58] 'Bayan', *al-shuyi'i al-misri*, 43 (March 1979): 6–10.

[59] *Ma al-'amal?*, 30 (February 1981): 1.

Conclusion

Recent studies have relaunched debate about the history of the 'New Arab Left', before and after the *naksa*. This attention has so far translated into some historical reconstructions, mostly focusing on the Arab East, and almost entirely ignoring Egypt. This chapter helps to fill this gap, by looking at key debates and at the political practice of the 'New Left' in Egypt after 1967.

By the second half of the 1960s, a younger generation of intellectuals and activists, gathered mainly in the TshM/ECWP group, attempted to break with the Old Left that had been co-opted by the Nasser regime in the 1960s. The theories they produced and their new radical positions signalled the third wave of communism in Egypt. The ECWP represents the oldest, the most 'extreme' and, arguably, the most important group, in terms of intellectual influence, within this third wave. The impact of this group, focusing as it did mainly on producing publications, on Egyptian cultural life far surpassed its performance as an underground opposition political party. Members of this group produced novels, poetry, literary criticism, journalism and figurative arts. Its members included the literary critic Ibrahim Fathi, the writers Mahmud al-Wardani, Khalil Kalfat, Arwa Salih and Yahya al-Tahir 'Abdallah, the poets Zayn al-'Abidin Fu'ad and Khalid Juwayli, the journalists Hani Shukrallah and Farid Zahran, and others.

Despite its intellectual prowess and courage, the TshM/ECWP had lines of continuity with the old Left, especially its unbalanced attention to national and regional issues to the detriment of both internal social issues and its relationship with the Egyptian working class. A focus on a publication strategy and an inability to take action at opportune times also weakened the party. These limitations, despite the good intentions stated in the aftermath of the *naksa*, are fundamental to understanding the gradual isolation of the Left within Egyptian society in the 1980s and 1990s, paradoxically as most parts of the population started to suffer from the effects of the neoliberal economic reforms adopted by all governments since Sadat.

Note. I wish to thank Ifdal Elsaket, Andrea Teti and Laure Guirguis for their thoughtful comments.

Bibliography

'Abdalla [*sic*], Ahmad, *The Student Movement and National Politics in Egypt 1923–1973* (London: Saqi, 1985).

'Abdallah, Ahmad and Ahmad Baha' al-Din Sha'ban, *al-haraka al-tullabiya al-haditha fi misr: tajrubat rub' al-qarn* [The modern student movement in Egypt: a quarter-century experience] (Cairo: Markaz al-Jil, 1993).

'Abd al-Raziq, Husayn, *Misr fi 18 wa 19 yanayr* [Egypt on 18 and 19 January] (Cairo: Dar Shuhdi, 3rd edn, 1985).

Agwani, M. S., *Communism in the Arab East* (London: Asia Publishing House, 1969).

'Ali, Mustafa Mursi [pseudonym of Ibrahim Fathi], 'Kayfa tahall sultat al-burjwaziyya tanaqudataha ma'a al-imbiryaliyya!' [How does the bourgeois power solve its contradictions with Imperialism!], in Hizb al-'Ummal al-Shuyu'i al-Misri (ECWP), *Masar al-khiyana. Min al-hazima ila al-mubadara* [The path of betrayal: from the defeat to the [peace] initiative] (Beirut: Dar al-Katib, 1979): 3–4.

'Ali, Mustafa Mursi [pseudonym of Ibrahim Fathi], 'Tab'iyyat al-sulta al-burjwaziyya fi misr' [The bourgeois nature of power in Egypt], 1970, repr. with an introduction by Salih M. Salih [pseudonym of Khalil Kalfat], *al-Tariq* occasional papers 4 (July 1981): 5–27.

Al-'Alim, Muhammad Amin (ed.), *Sab'un aman 'ala al-haraka al-shuyu'iyya al-misriyya. Ru'ya tahliliyya-naqdiyya* [Seventy years of the Egyptian communist movement. A critical-analytical view] (Cairo: Qadayya fikriyya, 1992).

Al-'Azm, Sadiq J., *Al-naqd al-dhati ba'd al-hazima* [Self-criticism after the defeat] (Beirut: Dar al-Tali'a, 1968).

Al-Turkmani, 'Abdallah, *Al-ahzab al-shuyu'iyya fi al-mashriq al-'arabi* [The communist parties in the Arab East] (Beirut: Markaz al-An, 2002).

Bardawil, Fadi, 'Dreams of a Dual Birth: Socialist Lebanon's World and Ours', *Boundary 2* 43, 3 (2016): 313–35.

Bardawil, Fadi, *When All This Revolution Melts into Air: The disenchantment of Levantine Marxist Intellectuals*, unpublished PhD thesis (New York: Columbia University, 2010).

Beattie, Kirk J., *Egypt during the Sadat Years* (London and New York: Palgrave Macmillan, 2000).

Beinin, Joel and Lockman, Zachary, *Workers on the Nile: Nationalism, Communism, Islam and the Egyptian Working Class* (Princeton: Princeton University Press, 1987).

Botman, Selma, *The Rise of Egyptian Communism 1939–1970* (Syracuse: Syracuse University Press, 1988).

Di Capua, Yoav, 'The Slow Revolution: May 1968 in the Arab World', *American Historical Review* 123, 3 (2018): 733–8.

Fathi, Ibrahim, 'Tarikh in'izal al-yasar al-misri wa-inqisamihi' [History of the isolation of the Egyptian Left and its fragmentation], *al-Hiwar al-mutamadin* (19 May 2013), <http://www.ahewar.org/debat/s.asp?aid=354964> (last accessed 20 November 2018).

Frangie, Samer, 'Historicism, Socialism and Liberalism after the Defeat: On the Political Thought of Yasin al-Hafiz', *Modern Intellectual History* 12, 2 (2015): 325–52.

Gervasio, Gennaro, *Al-haraka al-markisiyya fi misr, 1967–81* [The Marxist movement in Egypt, 1967–81] (Cairo: al-Markaz al-qawmi li-l-tarjama, 2010).

Gervasio, Gennaro, 'Il Socialismo senza Socialisti di Nasser' [Nasser's Socialism without Socialists], *Storia del pensiero politico* VII, 1 (2018): 23–42.

Gervasio, Gennaro, 'An Egyptian 1968? The Student Movement and the (Re)Birth of a Radical Left in Egypt', paper presented at *'We all Wanna Change the World': The Revolutionary Sixties in the Mediterranean and the Middle East* workshop, Berlin, Centre Marc Bloch, 11–12 October 2018.

Ginat, Rami, *Egypt's Incomplete Revolution: Lutfi al-Khuli and Nasser's Socialism in the 1960s* (London: Frank Cass, 1997).

Guirguis, Laure, 'La Référence au Vietnam et l'Émergence des Gauches Radicales au Liban, 1962–1976', *Monde(s). Histoire, Espaces, Relations* 14, 2 (2018): 223–42.

Hammad, Hana, 'Arwa Salih's The Premature. Gender in the History of the Egyptian Left', *Arab Studies Journal* 24, 1 (2016): 118–42.

Hanssen, J. and Max Weiss (eds), *Arabic Thought against the Authoritarian Age* (Cambridge: Cambridge University Press, 2018).

Haugbølle, Sune, 'The New Arab Left and 1967', *British Journal of Middle Eastern Studies* 44, 4 (2017): 497–512.

Haugbølle, S. and Manfred Sing, 'New Approaches to Arab Left Histories', *Arab Studies Journal* 24, 1 (2016): 90–7.

Hussein, Mahmoud, *Class Conflict in Egypt 1945–1970* (New York: Monthly Review Press, 1973).

Hizb al-shuyu'i al-misri (ECP), *Barnamaj al-hizb* [The party programme] (Cairo: 1980).

Hizb al-'ummal al-shuyu'i al-misri – al-lajna al-markaziyya (ECWP – Central Committee), 'Taqrir 9/5' (9/5 Report), *al-sira'* 4 (May 1975): 1–20.

Hizb al-'ummal al-shuyu'i al-misri, 'Editorial', *al-sira'* 11 (30 September 1975): 1–5.

Hizb al-'ummal al-shuyu'i al-misri (ECWP), *Qirar min al-lajna al-markaziyya bi-shan nashat al-takattul* [CC decision on the splinter action] (15 October 1976): 1–20.

Hizb al-ʿummal al-shuyuʿi al-misri (ECWP), *Mawqif hizb al-ʿummal al-shuyuʿi al-misri min khatwat al-sadat al-khiyaniyya* [ECWP's position on Sadat's step towards the betrayal] (30 November 1977).

Hizb al-ʿummal al-shuyuʿi al-misri (ECWP), *Mawqif hizb al-ʿummal al-shuyuʿi al-misri min qimmat al-ismaʿiliyya* [ECWP's position on the ismailiyya summit] (December 1977).

Hizb al-ʿummal al-shuyuʿi al-misri (ECWP), 'Bayan min hizb al-ʿummal al-shuyuʿi al-misri hawla suqut nizam al-shah' [ECWP statement on the fall of the Shah regime], *al-shuyuʿi al-misri* 43 (March 1979): 6–10.

ʿIsa, Salah, *Muthaqqafun wa-ʿaskar* [Intellectuals and military] (Cairo: Madbuli, 1986).

Ismael, Tareq Y., *The Arab Left* (Syracuse: Syracuse University Press, 1976).

Ismael, Tareq Y., *The Communist Movement in the Arab World* (Abingdon: Routledge, 2005).

Ismael, Tareq Y. and Rifaat El-Saʿid, *The Communist Movement in Egypt 1919–1988* (Syracuse: Syracuse University Press, 1990).

Jabar, Faleh A. (ed.), *Post-Marxism in the Middle East* (London: Saqi, 1997).

Kalfat, Khalil (ed.), *Mapping of the Arab Left* (Tunis: Rosa Luxembourg Stiftung – North Africa Office, 2014).

Kamil, Samir, *Khilafatuna: didd al-inhiraf al-biruqrati al-inʿizali al-tasfawi* [Our disagreements: against bureaucratic, isolationist and capitulationist deviation], unpublished manuscript, n d.

Kandil, Hazem, *Soldiers, Spies, and Statesmen: Egypt's Road to Revolt* (London: Verso, 2012).

Kendall, Elisabeth, 'The Theoretical Roots of the Literary *Avant-garde* in 1960s Egypt', *Edebiyat: Journal of M.E. Literatures* 14, 1–2 (2003): 39–56.

Labib, Fakhri, *Al-shuyuʿiyyun wa ʿAbd al-Nasir* [The communists and Nasser] (Cairo: Markaz al-Buhuth al-ʿArabiyya, 1992).

Laqueur, Walter, *Communism and Nationalism in the Middle East* (London: Routledge & Kegan Paul, 1956).

Laroui, Abdallah, *The Crisis of the Arab Intellectual: Traditionalism or Historicism?* (Berkeley: University of California Press, 1976).

Mansur, Khalid (ed.), *Fi tashrih al-hazima. Harb Yunyu baʿd 50 ʿam* [Explaining the defeat. The June War 50 years later] (Cairo: al-Maraya, 2017).

Murqus, Ilyas, *Tarikh al-ahzab al-shuyuʿiyya fi al-watan al-ʿarabi* [A history of the communist parties in the Arab nation] (Beirut: Dar al-Taliʿa, 1964).

Nasser, Gamal Abdel, 'Bayan al-raʾis jamal ʿabd al-nasir ila al-shaʿb wa al-umma bi iʿlan al-tanahhi ʿan riʾasat al-jumhuriyya min mabna al-idhaʿa wa al-tilifizyun' [Statement by President Jamal 'Abd Al-Nasir to the people and the nation about his resignation from the Presidency of the Republic from the TV and Radio Headquarters] (9 June 1967), *Bibliotheca Alexandrina*, <http://nasser.bibalex.org/Speeches/browser.aspx?SID=1221&lang=ar> (last accessed 18 February 2018).

Rodinson, Maxime, *Marxisme et Monde musulman* (Paris: Seuil, 1972).

Salamuni, Hisham, *Al-jil alladhi wajaha 'abd al-nasir wa al-sadat* [The generation that opposed Nasser and Sadat] (Cairo: Dar Qaba, 1999).

Salih, Arwa, *Al-mubtasirun* (Cairo: Dar al-Nahr, 1996); trans. into English by Samah Selim, *The Stillborn* (London and New York: Seagull Press, 2018).

Salih, Salih M. [pseudonym of Khalil Kalfat], 'Al-burjwaziyya al-biruqratiyya: bayna al-fahm al- markisi wa shu'hudhat al-mutamarkisyyin. Munazara mu'jiza ma'a al-rafiq t. th. shakir wa akharin' [The bureaucratic bourgeoisie: between the Marxist understanding and the juggleries of the pseudo-Marxists. A short debate with comrade T. Th. Shakir and others] (1975), repr. in *al-Tariq* occasional papers, 5 (August 1981).

Salih, Salih M. [pseudonym of Khalil Kalfat], 'Hawla mud fatrat waqf itlaq al-nar' [On the ceasefire's extension]. In ECWP, *Masar al-khiyana*: 11–19.

Salih, Salih M. [pseudonym of Khalil Kalfat], 'Hawla qadiyyat al-istiqlal wal-nidal al-mu'addi lil-imbiryaliyya [On the question of independence and anti-imperialist struggle]. In ECWP, *Masar al-khiyana*: 20–8.

Salih, Salih M. [pseudonym of Khalil Kalfat], 'Laysa kull ma yalma' dhahaban' [All that glitters is not gold], ECWP, *Masar al-khiyana*, 55–77.

Salih, Salih M. [pseudonym of Khalil Kalfat], 'Al-taswiyya al-istislamiyya: muqaddimat wa-nata'ij' [The defeatist settlement: premises and results], ECWP, *Masar al-khiyana*: 78–89.

Shakir, T. Th. [pseudonym of Michel Kamil and others], *Qadaya al-taharrur al-watani wa al-thawra al-ishtirakiyya* [Issues on national liberation and the socialist revolution] (Beirut: Dar al-Farabi, 1974).

Shukrallah, Hani, 'Political Crisis and Political Conflict in Post-1967 Egypt', in Owen, Roger and Charles Tripp (eds), *Egypt Under Mubarak* (Abingdon: Routledge, 1989): 53–101.

Shukri, Ghali, *Egypt, Portrait of a President, 1971–1981: The Counter-Revolution in Egypt* (London: Zed Press, 1981).

Sing, Manfred, 'Arab Self-Criticism after 1967 Revisited: The Normative Turn in Marxist Thought and its Heuristic Fallacies', *Arab Studies Journal* 25, 2 (2017): 144–90.

Yahya, Karim, 'Ab'ad siyasiyyah fi tajrubat "al-Tali'a"' [The political dimension in the experience of al-Tali'a], *al-Tali'a*, special commemorative issue (2000): 9–22.

Zekri, Sonja, 'The Arabs' Groundhog Day. Egyptian historian Khaled Fahmy on the Six-Day War', *Qantara.de* (23 June 2017), <https://en.qantara.de/content/egyptian-historian-khaled-fahmy-on-the-six-day-war-the-arabs-groundhog-day> (last accessed 1 November 2018).

Interviews

Jamal al-Ghitani (d. 2015), writer, ECP former member (Cairo 17 April 2001).

Ahmad Baha' Sha'ban, former leader of the 1970s student movement. Currently General Secretary of the Egyptian Socialist Party (Cairo, 12 May 2001).

Hani Shukrallah (d. 2019), journalist, former TshM/ECWP member (Cairo, 30 December 2002).

Salah al-'Amrusi (d. 2015), economist, TshM/ECWP co-founder (Cairo 31 May 2001).

Farid Zahran, journalist and researcher, former ECWP member (Cairo, 14 May 2001).

Hasanayn Kishk (d. 2019), sociologist, TshM/ECWP co-founder (Cairo, 2 June 2001).

Salah 'Isa (d. 2017), journalist and researcher, former member of *Wahdat al-shuyu'iyyin* (Cairo, 23 May 2001).

Ibrahim Fathi (d. 2019), literary critic, TshM co-founder and theorist (Cairo, 30 May 2001).

Khalil Kalfat (d. 2015), writer and translator, TshM/ECWP co-founder and main theorist (22 January 2003).

9

NON-ZIONISTS, ANTI-ZIONISTS, REVOLUTIONARIES: PALESTINIAN APPRAISALS OF THE ISRAELI LEFT, 1967–73

Maha Nassar

Introduction

On 4 June 1967, a 991-page special issue of *Les Temps Modernes* hit newsstands and bookshops. The volume, dedicated to the Arab–Israeli conflict, consisted of essays written by Palestinian, Arab and Israeli writers that were addressed primarily to the French and European left. Aware of growing tensions between Arabs and Israelis (but unaware that war was about to break out) the journal's editor, the philosopher Jean-Paul Sartre, promised in his introduction that he would treat the topic with 'neutrality'. Essays were divided into an 'Arab' camp and an 'Israeli' camp; they were written by leading political figures and intellectuals of their time and were clearly intended to sway European leftists to their respective framing of the conflict.[1]

As the historian Yoav Di-Capua has recently shown, the Arabs were at a clear disadvantage. Only a few days before the special issue appeared, Sartre, along with sixty-seven other prominent French intellectuals, signed a public statement in support of the Jewish state.[2] For a variety of structural and

[1] Di-Capua, *No Exit*, 239–42.

[2] Ibid.

cultural reasons, the European left (with a few exceptions[3]) leaned heavily towards the Israeli perspective, especially regarding Israel's legitimacy. Most thinkers on the European left saw Israel's establishment as redeeming the horrors of the Holocaust, a trauma that was still fresh in their minds. For them, the necessity of having a state for the Jewish people outweighed whatever wrongs the Palestinians suffered as a result of Israel's establishment. As a result, the Arab–Israeli conflict needed to be solved in a way that would retain the legitimacy of the Jewish state.

For Palestinian and other Arab intellectuals, Israel was an illegitimate settler-colonial entity that was established against the wishes of the indigenous population. They believed that the ethnic cleansing of the Palestinian people in 1948 and the ongoing colonisation of their land should be opposed by the European left in the same manner that it opposed other settler-colonial regimes throughout the world. To them, the European left's refusal to do so smacked of hypocrisy and ignorance. Moreover, while they saw how anti-Semitism in Europe culminated in the horrors of the Holocaust, they did not believe that establishing an ethno-national Jewish state was the proper solution. The Lebanese intellectual Gebran Majdalany, a member of the pro-Iraqi Baath Party in Lebanon, summed up the divide well in his contribution to *Les Temps Modernes*:

> There are two ways of thinking about the Palestinian problem. The first is based on a *fait accompli*, so to speak, of the state of Israel, and to seek a solution by accepting it. The second, 'less realistic' way is to reject a priori this *fait accompli*. Most European socialists have opted for the first way . . . We claim that the creation of Israel is an inhumane and anti-socialist decision that leads to a reinforcement of anti-Semitism and creates new, more serious and more costly problems than the ones it was supposed to solve.[4]

The fault lines Majdalany highlighted in his essay became more deeply entrenched in the immediate aftermath of the 1967 June War. On the one hand, while Europeans called on Israel to withdraw from the Arab lands

[3] Perhaps the most prominent exception is the French leftist writer Maxime Rodinson, whose essay 'Israel: fait colonial?' in the *Les Temps Modernes* special issue laid the groundwork for a European leftist critique of Israel as a settler-colonial regime.

[4] Majdalany, 'Israel et les socialistes arabes', 281–2.

occupied during the June War, their belief in its fundamental legitimacy meant they refused to question the Zionist underpinnings or settler-colonial imperatives of the state itself. For them, the resolution of the Arab–Israeli conflict was through diplomacy. On the other hand, for many Arab intellectuals on the left – including the Palestinians – Israel's land grab during the war confirmed that Israel was a settler-colonial entity akin to other settler-colonial regimes around the world. They maintained that, faced with such an implacable enemy, the only solution was revolutionary armed struggle.

In light of this formula, following the war the Palestine Liberation Organisation (PLO) launched a 'global offensive' that linked their struggle with those of other anti-colonial movements around the world.[5] One aim of this push was to convince European intellectuals of the Arab/Palestinian framing of their struggle as an anti-colonial liberation movement against a settler-colonial regime. Another aim was to push back against the Israeli media campaign that sought to present the Palestinians and Arab states as belligerently seeking to annihilate the Jewish people.[6] But to do so, Palestinian intellectuals recognised that they needed to understand more fully internal Israeli political dynamics, especially during a period of growing internal dissension within the state. One of the key venues in which intellectuals, scholars and political activists discussed internal Israeli developments was the PLO's Research Center in Beirut (PLO-RC). The PLO-RC's major Arabic publications, including *al-Yawmiyyat al-Filastiniyya* (Palestinian Diary) and *Shu'un Filastiniyya* (Palestine Affairs), as well as numerous academic books and other printed works, provided a venue for Palestinian and Arab writers to exchange ideas and share scholarly information about all matters relating to Palestine. The PLO-RC employed dedicated researchers and attracted a broad spectrum of intellectuals and writers, including Ghassan Kanafani and Mahmoud Darwish, who published analytical and research pieces there.

In this chapter I compare and contrast how Palestinian intellectuals and researchers appraised three Israeli leftist entities who were especially prominent between 1967 and 1973: the communist, non-Zionist Rakah Party, the Trotskyist anti-Zionist Matzpen group and the Maoist revolutionary

[5] Chamberlin, *Global Offensive*.

[6] For more on the Israeli media campaign to delegitimise Palestinian claims, see Shemesh, 'Did Shuqayri?'.

organisation the Red Front. The activities of these groups inside Israel, coupled with their growing engagement with leftist intellectuals in Europe and the Arab world, gave Palestinians in exile an opportunity to engage with the ideas of Israeli non-Zionist and anti-Zionist leftists more directly than before. In doing so they opened up new political and intellectual spaces in which Palestinians could critique the relationship between Zionism and colonialism within a global leftist context. While these groups were marginal in the Israeli Jewish political sphere, they had a long-term impact on how Palestinians positioned themselves within global leftist formations. Thus, far from being an insignificant episode in intellectual history, I argue that Palestinians' engagement with the non-Zionist, anti-Zionist and revolutionary Israeli Left had a much longer afterlife than scholars have hitherto acknowledged.

Historical Background

For nearly three decades after Israel's foundation, the Israeli political landscape was dominated by socialist Zionism. With its roots in pre-1948 Labour Zionism, the centre-left Mapai party held control of the Israeli political leadership throughout the 1950s and 1960s. It was occasionally challenged from the left by Mapam, a Marxist-Zionist party, although Mapam also joined Mapai-led coalitions following the 1959 and 1965 Knesset elections. Despite various ideological differences between them, both parties shared a belief that Zionism and socialism were fundamentally compatible with each other and that Zionism was at its root an anti-imperialist liberation movement.[7]

Challenging this belief in the compatibility of Zionism and socialism was the pro-Soviet communist Maki party. Maki's composition of Ashkenazi Jews, Mizrahi Jews and Palestinian citizens of Israel, along with its support from the Soviet Union, allowed it some ability to manoeuvre within the Israeli political scene despite falling outside the Zionist ideological consensus. Throughout the 1950s Maki challenged a wide range of Israeli domestic and foreign policies from an internationalist and anti-imperialist perspective, albeit while insisting on the legitimacy of the state itself.[8] During the 1960s, a younger generation

[7] Beinin, *Was the Red Flag*.

[8] For more on Maki's attitude towards the state of Israel, see Robinson, *Citizen Strangers* and Nassar, *Brothers Apart*.

of activists who were influenced by the rise of revolutionary Arab nationalism challenged the internationalist basis of the party, leading to a split between the Jewish and Arab members in 1965. The Jewish-dominated party retained the name 'Maki' and gradually moved back into the Zionist fold. The new party, which was dominated by Palestinian citizens of Israel, adopted the name 'Rakah' and took an increasingly pro-Palestinian stance, moving it further outside the Zionist political consensus.[9] Thus Rakah was the only Israeli political party to oppose the 1967 War both before and after 5 June 1967, and it was one of the most vociferous critics of the Israeli occupation of Arab lands.

Some Palestinian intellectuals and political organisers in exile followed these developments in Israel closely. They understood that the Palestinian struggle for freedom needed to be fought on the ideological as well as the political and military levels. The few studies written by Palestinian academics in the 1950s highlight the lack of systematic information that was available to them, and the study of Israel in general was done in a scattered rather than a collective or systematic manner. With the establishment of the Institute for Palestine Studies in 1963 and the PLO-RC two years later, Beirut became a research hub for a more systematic Arab study of the Palestinian–Israeli conflict, and specifically of Israeli affairs. Both institutions published numerous studies on various aspects of Israel's social and economic underpinnings as well as its political landscape. Since they had no direct access to the state itself, their entries relied on press reports and other published materials.

Seeking to systematise knowledge production in a way that would be of use to Arab researchers, the PLO-RC soon began publishing a detailed compendium of daily events relating to the Arab–Israeli conflict. Entitled *al-Yawmiyyat al-Filastiniyya*, according to its inaugural essay written by Fayez Sayigh, its goal was to 'facilitate the efforts [of students and researchers] to obtain news of the developments related to the cause in its chronological sequence, day by day'.[10] Drawn from 'some sixty newspapers and journals published in seven Arab countries, the USA, Britain, France, West Germany, People's Republic of China, Soviet Union and Occupied Palestine', each volume covered a six-month period and ran to several

[9] Nassar, *Brothers Apart*, 137.

[10] Sayigh, *Al-Yawmiyyat al-Filastiniyya* (1965): 1, 5.

hundred pages.[11] The volumes included news items relating to military developments and guerrilla activities, Arab political developments, Israeli and Arab relations with countries around the world, Zionist and anti-Zionist organisations, particularly in the West, and news about the conditions of Jews in various countries around the world that could have a bearing on Zionist and Israeli efforts to increase Jewish immigration.

The 1967 War brought a renewed sense of urgency to these efforts. But the affiliates of the PLO-RC were also acutely aware that there continued to be a strong Arab and Palestinian repulsion against any activity that could be interpreted as lending Israel legitimacy in the Arab world. Therefore, the PLO-RC editors had a great deal of trepidation when they decided to translate into Arabic the essays from *Les Temps Modernes* written by Jewish Israelis and publish them in a volume entitled *From Contemporary Zionist Thought*. In the preface, PLO-RC director Anis Sayigh wrote that he and his colleagues were hesitant to publish 'an entire book that does not contain anything except articles by the enemy' since it could be seen as furthering Zionist propaganda in the Arab world. But ultimately they decided that it was necessary to do so because 'the twenty-two articles that make up this book express the most recent, the clearest and the most honest [examples] of what the enemy has published from its thought [that is] directed at the western mindset, especially the leftist mindset in the West. And it is this mindset that Arabs will encounter in their media efforts before any other.'[12] Sayigh's explanation of why they published the essays highlights the awareness Palestinian intellectuals had that their struggle for liberation needed to be waged in European leftist intellectual circles just as much as on the battlefields.

But rather than only convey Zionist views, the PLO-RC was also eager to highlight views within Israel that went against the hegemonic Zionist positions. To that end, they began paying growing attention to Rakah, Matzpen and, eventually, the Red Front.

Rakah

Both the Rakah Party and the PLO-RC were established in 1965, but the latter seems to have been unaware of the former, likely because the PLO-RC did

[11] Ibid.

[12] Sayigh, *Min al-fikr*, 5–7.

not have access to the party's publications.[13] That lack of awareness continued into the immediate aftermath of the June War, which may help explain why Anis Sayigh did not distinguish between Rakah's non-Zionist positions and the other Israeli views in his introduction to the PLO-RC's book on modern Zionist thought.

Rakah's unique policy positions started to become more familiar to Palestinians in exile over the course of 1968. *Al-Yawmiyyat* reported that the Soviet Union recognised Rakah as the only legitimate Israeli Communist Party because of its clear opposition to the June War; as a result, Rakah was the only party from Israel that the Soviet Union invited to the quadrennial World Youth Festival, which was held that August in Sofia, Bulgaria. The international gathering of leftists from around the world included members of a joint Palestinian–Jordanian delegation, many of whom were able to meet with Rakah delegates for the first time. These included the famed poets Mahmoud Darwish and Samih al-Qasim (both of whom were Rakah members) as well as party operatives who could more clearly articulate their positions on a range of issues.[14]

Those meetings sparked greater PLO-RC interest in the Rakah members and their activities. That interest also came at a time when Palestinian citizens of Israel voted for Rakah in growing numbers (especially in the 1969 elections) and when they were being apprehended by the Israeli security services on charges of joining Palestinian resistance groups.[15] *Al-Yawmiyyat* reported increasingly on the arrests and detentions of these activists, placing reports of their arrests alongside those of Palestinian guerrilla activity. In doing so, they discursively connected Rakah members to the Palestinian struggle for liberation.

Al-Yawmiyyat also reported on Rakah's position on the broader conflict, especially its insistence that UN Security Council Resolution 242 was the only basis for resolving the Arab–Israeli dispute. Several entries in *al-Yawmiyyat* quoted Rakah leader Meir Vilner vehemently criticising the Israeli government for its ongoing occupation of Arab lands in violation of Resolution 242.

[13] The initial list of Israeli news sources included thirteen Israeli newspapers, but did not include Rakah's Arabic newspaper *al-Ittihad* or its Hebrew counterpart *Zo Haderech*. See Fayiz Sayigh's introduction in *Al-Yawmiyyat al-Filastiniyya* 1, n. p.

[14] Nassar, *Brothers Apart*, 163–70.

[15] Qahwaji, 'Al-ʿarab fi isra'il', 105.

On the first anniversary of the June War, Vilner wrote an editorial in *al-Ittihad* in which he insisted that 'Israel must fundamentally change its official policy towards working on implementing the Security Council Resolution of 22 November 1967 because there is no alternative to withdrawal'.[16] *Al-Yawmiyyat* regularly covered Rakah's frequent demands that Israel withdraw from the occupied territories.[17]

Likewise, *al-Yawmiyyat* also reported more regularly on the statements Rakah leaders made condemning Israeli military actions against its neighbours. These included Rakah's official statements against Israel's raid against Lebanon in February 1972 and its strikes against Lebanon and Syria in September of that year. *Al-Yawmiyyat* quoted from Rakah's press statement that described the air strikes as 'a crime against peace and security', and cited an editorial in *al-Ittihad* describing the strikes as 'a manifestation of the worsening crisis and the futility of Israel's official policy'.[18] Rakah delivered an even harsher rebuke a few months later: in December the party's Central Committee issued a statement stating that the strikes, 'which are done in the name of fighting terrorism, constitute clear military terrorism in an attempt to defeat the Palestinian Arab people's struggle for their just rights'.[19]

While these entries in *al-Yawmiyyat* are listed without commentary, the growing frequency of Rakah's statements in these volumes suggests that PLO-RC researchers had a greater interest in and greater access to Rakah's political statements than before. They also reflect Rakah's own positioning of itself as a voice of fairness and justice in calling for Palestinian rights from within the Israeli body politic. Nonetheless, while Rakah vehemently opposed Israeli policies on the domestic and foreign fronts, the party rarely connected its vociferous criticism of Israeli state actions to a larger criticism of Zionism itself. Moreover, Rakah was operating mainly in the Israeli domestic sphere. Although party members occasionally participated in international forums like the World Youth Festival, the Rakah leaders were not as interested in directly appealing to the global left by positioning the Palestinian cause

[16] *Al-Yawmiyyat al-Filastiniyya* 7 (1968): 350.

[17] See for example *Al-Yawmiyyat al-Filastiniyya* 14 (1971): 140, 465 and 671.

[18] *Al-Yawmiyyat al-Filastiniyya* 16 (1972): 223 and 319.

[19] *Al-Yawmiyyat al-Filastiniyya* 16 (1972): 465.

within the context of anti-colonial liberation struggles. Therefore, while their activities were reported on as noteworthy instances of dissent, they did not garner much interest or excitement from Palestinian intellectuals abroad.

This was in contrast to Matzpen, which offered a more vociferous critique of Zionism and was more interested in appealing to the global left. The rise of Matzpen also came at a time when the PLO-RC started to move beyond recording events into analysing them. As a result, Matzpen intellectuals, especially those based abroad, could serve as a guide to the Israeli political landscape.

Matzpen

In 1961, a group of Trotskyists broke off from the communist Maki party to form the Israeli Socialist Organisation. The small group soon came to be known by the name of its journal, *Matzpen* (Compass). The journal offered many of the same criticisms of Israeli policies that the communists levelled against the state, and Matzpen members often campaigned on behalf of the communists during Israeli elections. But unlike Rakah, the group was independent from Soviet dictates, allowing its members greater latitude in thinking about the relationship between socialism, communism, Zionism and revolution.

To be sure, Matzpen was a marginal group in the Israeli political landscape with never more than a few dozen members at a time. But it was keen on raising awareness about its radical critique of Zionism, especially after the 1967 War. Matzpen members staged various protests in Tel Aviv, Jerusalem and elsewhere against the occupation and war, but unlike with other such protests, the group's slogans more clearly condemned Zionism as the underlying ideology of the state.[20] At first Matzpen was largely ignored in the Israeli and international press, which resulted in little coverage of the group in *al-Yawmiyyat*.

That started to change in June 1970 when several Matzpen young persons embarked on a speaking tour in the USA and Europe, where they were hosted by various leftist student and youth groups. Matzpen co-founders Akiva Orr, Haim Hanegbi and Moshe Machover further articulated their group's

[20] Fiedler, 'Israel in Revolution'.

position in an essay that appeared in the January–February 1971 issue of *New Left Review*. In it, the authors laid out the class basis of Israeli society and the ways in which Zionist state structures, like the Histadrut, actually worked against the proletariat. The essay also gave an overview of the political landscape in Israel, summarising the positions of the Zionist and non-Zionist lefts in Israel. While the former included groups like Mapam and its more recent offshoot Siach, the latter group included Rakah and Matzpen.[21]

With several Matzpen leaders living in the UK at the time, their more radical critique of Zionism reached a greater number of Palestinian activists and intellectuals, especially those who were travelling to or living in Europe. London-based Palestinian activists Wassim Abdallah and Ghada Karmi, for example, met frequently with Matzpen leaders at local social and political events.[22] Members of Matzpen also sought to establish connections with Palestinians in Jordan while Palestinian activists, particularly those affiliated with the Democratic Front for the Liberation of Palestine, likewise sought to learn more about the organisation.[23]

This interest in connecting to one another in turn led to greater coverage of Matzpen in Arab leftist and nationalist press outlets, including *al-Hadaf*, *al-Hurriyya* and *Dirasat 'Arabiyya*.[24] At the same time, the PLO-RC expanded its operations to include more regular analysis of its events, rather than just recording them. In April 1971 the centre launched a monthly academic journal entitled *Shu'un Filastiniyya* (Palestinian Affairs) that featured articles on various aspects of the Israeli–Palestinian conflict written by Palestinian intellectuals as well as researchers affiliated with the PLO-RC.

The second issue featured a lengthy interview that PLO-RC researcher Layla Salim al-Qadi conducted with an unnamed Matzpen leader in London as part of her research for a book she was writing about the group. In it, the leader discussed the group's ideological evolution since its foundation in 1963, including its shift away from the positions of Rakah. He argued that Rakah's insistence on UN Security Council Resolution 242 as a basis for the

[21] Hanegbi et al., 'The Class Nature', 76–98.

[22] Torbinder, 'Matzpen'.

[23] Ibid.

[24] Al-Qadi, *Al-munazzama al-ishtirakiyya*, 25.

resolution of the Arab–Israeli conflict revealed the party's limited political horizon. To him, focusing only on the territories captured by Israel in 1967 would leave in place the Zionist structures of the state that went back to 1948. Matzpen, in contrast, called for the dismantling of the Zionist institutions of the state. According to the leader, the real difference between the two groups' political visions was 'between a revolutionary solution and a non-revolutionary solution'.[25]

With armed struggle so central to the Palestinian liberation movement at this time, and with Palestinians discussing among themselves the place of Jews in a future secular democratic state, much of the interview between al-Qadi and the Matzpen leader dealt with the group's views around these two issues. The Matzpen leader endorsed armed struggle as a means of achieving liberation, since 'revolutionary violence is legitimate in the face of a repressive regime'. At the same time, he questioned whether attacks against civilians could achieve its goals and win the 'war of nerves' in the current political climate.[26] He also criticised Fatah for refusing to recognise that 'the Israeli people constitute a national group and not just a religious community', and emphasised that Israelis needed to have a say in their future.[27] Thus, he distinguished between different uses of violence: 'The use of violence as a means to defeat Zionism is legitimate and fully justified, but its use as a means to impose any solution, even if it is the correct solution, on the Israeli people after the defeat of Zionism is certainly not justified.'[28] Thus while Matzen's views aligned somewhat with those of the PLO leadership, they diverged in places.

Three months after the interview ran, al-Qadi's full study was published by the PLO-RC, featuring an introduction by the well-known Palestinian leftist writer and critic Ghassan Kanafani. He wrote that the appearance of Matzpen was significant since it came at a time when Mapam and other groups on the Zionist left had 'sunk into the mire of racism, imperialism and regression', while Rakah 'overdoes the righteousness' of its position:

[25] Al-Qadi, 'Muqabala maᶜa masᵓul', 93.

[26] Ibid., 99–100.

[27] Ibid., 102.

[28] Ibid., 103.

'accepting the Israeli entity [while] fighting for the fall of the ruling class from the inside'.[29] For Kanafani, Matzpen's significance was twofold: first, it was the only political group in Israel that fundamentally questioned the Zionist ideology that underpinned the Jewish state; and second, through the Trotskyist media networks in Europe it was able to influence leftist European student groups after the 1967 War.[30] Since Matzpen's criticism of Israel as a settler-colonial state aligned with the Arab leftist analysis of the conflict, its views lent additional weight to Arab and Palestinian leftist positions at a time when many European leftists supported Israel and viewed the Arab stance with disdain.

But Kanafani also warned against overestimating Matzpen's importance or revolutionary potential. He noted that Matzpen was a small group with never more than a few dozen members, and it was unlikely to unilaterally overturn Zionist hegemonic structures. More importantly, Kanafani argued, there were fundamental contradictions in Matzpen's position regarding its assessment of Zionism and its position on the role of revolutionary violence to overturn settler-colonial rule. Matzpen leaders' overemphasis on class analysis, according to Kanafani, led them to underestimate the role of specifically Zionist colonialism in their analysis, which meant they could not account for 'how the Israeli working class benefits from the Israeli colonial reality'. Moreover, by equating 'Zionist regression and Arab regression', they ignored the fact that one type of regression was grounded in colonialism while the other was grounded in anti-colonial liberation.[31]

This led Kanafani to his sharpest criticism of Matzpen, namely its view that while violence was justified to overturn Zionism, it was not justified to impose a particular political order on Israelis after the defeat of Zionism. According to Kanafani, 'These two beliefs are contradictory, and the reality is that the one negates the other' because they assume that the violence that would be needed to defeat Zionism would somehow be able to leave in place the political structures of the state.[32] Citing Matzpen's own writings on how

[29] Kanafani, 'Muqaddima', 7–8.

[30] Ibid., 8–9.

[31] Ibid., 14–16.

[32] Ibid., 16–17.

deeply Zionism was entwined in both the colonisation of Palestinian land and the structures of the Israeli state, Kanafani wrote: 'after all this it remains possible in Matzpen's analysis to not only remove the Zionist character [of the state] violently without tearing up this nationalist country but also to keep the political order standing.'[33] For Kanafani, the revolution to defeat the Zionist state of Israel necessitated overturning all the political institutions of the state, since they were by definition enmeshed in the state's colonial infrastructure. Matzpen's inability (or unwillingness) to fully embrace the Palestinian cause as a liberation struggle – rather than as a conflict between two nationalist movements – meant, to Kanafani, that it could not be relied upon to be part of the revolutionary movement. Soon some members of Matzpen would come to the same conclusion.

Revolutionary Communist Alliance – Red Front

In September 1972 several members of Matzpen split off from the group and formed the Revolutionary Communist Alliance – Red Front. They described themselves as 'a group of Arab and Jewish socialists who have dedicated themselves to joint struggle for the workers of the two peoples'. While their goals sounded nearly identical to those of Matzpen, they argued that they needed to start a new group because they had been let down by Matzpen's leaders 'who regard Marxism as an ancient theory'. They were also fed up with 'pacifists' and 'radical youths' who were drawn to Matzpen primarily to express their opposition to war and their affiliation with the New Left.[34] Most significantly, they rejected Matzpen's refusal to undertake revolutionary action to follow up on its anti-colonial, anti-Zionist beliefs.

Three months later, on 7 December 1972, the Israeli police announced the discovery of a '*fida'i* cell' inside Israel called the Red Front. Twenty people were arrested on charges of belonging to this group: eighteen Palestinian citizens of Israel living in Galilee and two Jewish Israelis. According to a police spokesman, they were planning attacks in the north and centre of the country and to spy on behalf of Syria, where they had allegedly received military training. In an interview on Radio Israel, Amir Be'eri, one of the top generals

[33] Ibid., 17–18.

[34] 'Split in Matzpen', 148.

in the northern section of the Israeli police, said that unlike previously apprehended groups, this cell had a larger number of members that included for the first time Jewish youth.[35] *Al-Yawmiyyat* reported on the arrest of additional people over the following week, along with the heavy Israeli news coverage of the group.

As the accused awaited trial, the poet Mahmoud Darwish, who had grown up inside the Green Line but by this time worked in the PLO's Beirut offices, wrote an essay in *Shu'un Filastiniyya* on the Israeli reaction to the Red Front. Darwish was keenly aware of how Israeli leaders capitalised on the public's anxieties about the Arab–Israeli conflict to increase repression against critics at home,[36] and he saw the same thing happening in the case of the Red Front. He wrote:

> The Israeli authorities are taking advantage of this issue to turn all dissidents into spies in the view of Israeli public opinion, whether those dissidents were arrested on charges of [belonging to] an underground organisation and have yet to be tried, or whether they are dissidents outside of this realm. Arab and leftist forces in Israel oppose the dangerous campaign of pillorying and incitement . . . The nightmare of 'security' will once again sully Israeli life. Repression of the left will become 'a security necessity' and escalation of the oppression of the Arabs will remain as 'a security necessity'. But the question of Israel's legitimacy has erupted – within Israeli consciousness itself.[37]

Darwish saw the emergence of the Red Front – and the Israeli reaction to it – as a significant turn in the evolution of revolutionary thinking and action within Israel. Moreover, the fact that the Red Front contained both Palestinian and Jewish Israelis challenged the Israeli political consensus that positioned Zionism and anti-Zionism along a strict Jewish–Arab axis.

Darwish's claim that the Red Front phenomenon was a significant turning point in Israeli politics held sway in the PLO-RC. Once the trial commenced a month later, the PLO-RC followed it closely, paying particular attention to how the leaders of the Red Front understood their actions and their goals.

[35] *Al-Yawmiyyat al-Filastiniyya* 16 (1972): 459.

[36] Nassar, *Brothers Apart*, 174–7.

[37] Darwish, 'Isra'iliyyat', 226.

Shu'un Filastiniyya published the depositions of the Red Front's Palestinian leader, Daud Turki, and its highest-ranking Jewish member, Ehud (Udi) Adiv. While both vehemently denied the most serious accusation – giving sensitive information to members of the Syrian intelligence – they did not shy away from their revolutionary views that encompassed not just Israel, but the Arab world as well. Turki stated clearly that he was inspired by revolutionary leaders like Che Guevara and Mao Ze Dong in order to bring about a socialist revolution, not only in Israel, but in the Arab world as well. Yet he was realistic about his group's abilities, saying: 'I do not mean tomorrow or the day after tomorrow . . . we twenty or a hundred persons cannot try to topple a government or overthrow a regime.' At the same time, he was unapologetic about the necessity of revolutionary action: 'We can only change or topple this government by force. I readily admit this.'[38]

In his testimony, Adiv explained why Rakah and Matzpen were unsatisfactory places as a political home. Rakah's focus on having Israel accept and implement UN Security Council resolution 242 'shows an absolute lack of understanding or a conscious disregard of the nature of the Zionist movement' as a colonial regime that dated back much further than 1967.[39] As for Matzpen's ideologues, 'they have a sound theory, or ideology; what they lack is the chapter entitled "what is to be done" to reach the multi-national socialist Middle East they talk of'. Moreover, Matzpen's insistence that a solution cannot be imposed by force, according to Adiv, 'leads to nothing but talk'.[40]

Adiv argued that a solution could only come by turning the Arab–Jewish conflict into one of class struggle. 'This can only be done if the Jews will prove to the Arabs, who have been fighting Zionism for dozens of years, that they [the Jews] are on their side, that they are prepared to sacrifice everything they have, to be subjected to the same "treatment" and to share everything with them. Without this no Arab will have confidence that the sincerest Jewish revolutionary is really revolutionary.'[41] As a result of his full embrace

[38] Their testimony was translated into English and published by the *Journal of Palestine Studies*. See 'The Red Front Trial', 144–6.

[39] Ibid., 149.

[40] Ibid.

[41] Ibid., 150.

of the Palestinian struggle, Adiv was sentenced, along with Turki, to seventeen years in prison – the longest sentences handed down to any of the Red Front members.[42]

The Red Front trial garnered significant attention from the PLO-RC, in large part because the group's leaders had met with Habib Qahwaji while in Damascus. Qahwaji was a Palestinian citizen of Israel and co-founder of the Arab nationalist Ard movement. He was arrested in the wake of the 1967 war; after his release, he took up residence in Damascus, where he also was a member of the PLO-RC. Qahwaji's knowledge and support of the group gave them added weight in the Palestinian arena.

Moreover, for many Palestinians, the fact that Adiv in particular was willing to sacrifice his own freedom by standing by his convictions during the trial demonstrated more clearly than before that there were Jewish Israelis who supported their call for revolutionary action to bring about a single democratic state in all of historic Palestine. In his 1974 speech to the United Nations, PLO Chairman Yasser Arafat saluted Adiv: 'As he stood in an Israeli military court, the Jewish revolutionary, Ehud Adiv, said: "I am no terrorist; I believe that a democratic State should exist on this land." Adiv now languishes in a Zionist prison among his co-believers. To him and his colleagues I send my heartfelt good wishes.'[43] In a further sign of how the Red Front group was brought into the Palestinian revolutionary fold, the PFLP-GC included Adiv and Turki in its list of prisoners to be released as part of a prisoner exchange agreement with Israel in 1985 (which they were).

Ultimately, the revolutionary stance of the short-lived Red Front animated Palestinian thought more than the stances of either Rakah or Matzpen, as reflected in the publications of the PLO-RC. Despite Rakah's strong opposition to Israeli aggressive actions taken during and after the 1967 war, its focus on operating within the Israeli domestic sphere and its refusal to question the settler colonial nature of the state prior to 1967 led Palestinians to see it as straying only modestly from the Zionist consensus. And while Matzpen's anti-Zionism and its support for revolutionary action led the group to establish ties with some Palestinian activists in Europe and with members

[42] *Al-Yawmiyyat al-Filastiniyya* 17 (1973): 263.

[43] United Nations General Assembly, article no. 70.

of the DFLP, the group's unwillingness to countenance revolutionary action to install a new social order in Palestine led other intellectuals like Kanafani to see its positions as inherently contradictory. In contrast, the Red Front's unabashed support for revolutionary action, and especially its inclusion of Jewish members as equals, highlighted to Palestinians the necessity of not falling into the trap of framing the Palestine cause as an ethno-national struggle between Arabs and Jews. While the PLO eventually abandoned its call for revolutionary action and embraced the two-state framework, Palestinian intellectuals and activists have continued to draw on the liberatory calls of the non-Zionist and anti-Zionist Israeli Left to push back against Israel's framing of the Palestine issue as one of conflict and to emphasise Palestinians' struggle for freedom and equality.

Bibliography

Al-Qadi, Layla Salim, *Al-munazzama al-ishtirakiyya al-isra'iliyya – matsbin* [The Israeli socialist organisation – Matzpen] (Beirut: Munazzamat al-Tahrir al-Filastiniyya – Markaz al-Abhath, 1971).

Al-Qadi, Layla Salim, 'Muqabala ma^ca mas'ul fi'l-munazzama al-ishtirakiyya al-isra'iliyya – Matsbin' [An interview with a leader of the Israeli socialist organisation – Matzpen], *Shu'un Filastiniyya* 2 (May 1971).

Beinin, Joel, *Was the Red Flag Flying There?* (London: I.B. Tauris, 1990).

Chamberlin, Paul Thomas, *The Global Offensive: The United States, the Palestine Liberation Organization, and the Making of the Post-Cold War Order* (Oxford: Oxford University Press, 2012).

Darwish, Mahmud, 'Isra'iliyyat: al-jabha al-hamra' [Israeli affairs: the Red Front], *Shu'un Filastiniyya* 17 (January 1973): 225–6.

Di-Capua, Yoav, *No Exit: Existentialism, Jean-Paul Sartre and Decolonization* (Chicago: University of Chicago Press, 2018).

Fiedler, Lutz, 'Israel in Revolution – Matzpen, the Palestine Conflict, and the Hebrew Nation', *Israel Studies* 22, 3 (2017): 153–76.

Hanegbi, Haim, Moshe Machover and Akiva Orr, 'The Class Nature of Israeli Society', *New Left Review* (January–February 1971). Repr. in Machover, *Israelis and Palestinians: Conflict and Resolution* (Chicago: Haymarket Books, 2012): 76–98.

Kanafani, Ghassan, 'Muqaddima' [Introduction], in al-Qadi, Layla Salim, *Al-munazzama al-ishtirakiyya al-isra'iliyya – matsbin* [The Israeli socialist organisation – Matzpen] (Beirut: Munazzamat al-Tahrir al-Filastiniyya – Markaz al-Abhath, 1971).

Majdalany, Gebran, 'Israel et les Socialistes Arabes', *Les Temps Modernes* 253 (July 1967): 281–94.

Nassar, Maha, *Brothers Apart: Palestinian Citizens of Israel and the Arab World* (Stanford: Stanford University Press, 2017).

Qahwaji, Habib, 'Al-ʿarab fi isra'il baʿd ʿudwan 1967' [The Arabs in Israel after the 1967 aggression], *Shuʾun Filastiniyya* 4 (September 1971): 100–25.

'The Red Front Trial: The Depositions of Daud Turki and Ehud Adiv', *Journal of Palestine Studies* 2, 4 (Summer 1973): 144–50.

Robinson, Shira N., *Citizen Strangers: Palestinians and the Birth of Israel's Liberal Settler State* (Stanford: Stanford University Press, 2013).

Sayigh, Anis, *Min al-fikr al-sahyuni al-muʿasir* [From contemporary Zionist thought] (Beirut: Munazzamat al-Tahrir al-Filastiniyya – Markaz al-Abhath, 1968): 5–7.

Sayigh, Fayiz (ed.), *Al-yawmiyyat al-filastiniyya* [Palestinian diary] (Beirut: Munazzamat al-Tahrir al-Filastiniyya – Markaz al-Abhath, 1965).

Shemesh, Moshe, 'Did Shuqayri Call for "Throwing the Jews into the Sea"?' *Israel Studies* 8, 2 (2003): 70–81.

'Split in Matzpen', *Journal of Palestine Studies* 2, 3 (Spring 1973): 148–50.

Torbinder, Eran, 'Matzpen: Anti-Zionists in Israel' (documentary, 2003), <https://www.youtube.com/watch?v=hfcFno2pqJg> (last accessed 2 March 2020).

United Nations General Assembly, Twenty-Ninth Session. A/PV.2282 and Corr. 1, 13 November 1974, <https://unispal.un.org/DPA/DPR/unispal.nsf/0/A238EC7A3E13EED18525624A007697EC> (last accessed 2 March 2020).

10

'DISMOUNT THE HORSE TO PICK SOME ROSES': MILITANT ENQUIRY IN LEBANESE NEW LEFT EXPERIMENTS, 1968–73

Laure Guirguis

> Philosophy does not begin in an experience of wonder, as ancient tradition contends, but rather, I think, with the indeterminate but palpable sense that something desired has not been fulfilled, that a fantastic effort has failed.[1]

Introduction

What may best characterise worldwide revolutionary dynamics in the 1960s and 1970s lies in the junction between challenging a political and economic order and contesting social and cultural norms. A history of the New Left in the Arab East could be written through this lens and examine its numerous attempts to overthrow interlocking systems of power and oppression: to bridge the gap between workers, peasants and students, to rethink the connection between social struggles and national emancipation, and to experience new forms of organisation, of leadership, of social life and of gender relationships. From this perspective, this chapter traces the reframing of the Maoist notion of militant enquiry through the experiments of the

[1] Critchley, *Infinitely Demanding*, 3.

OCAL in-the-making, with a special focus on the trajectory of the sociologist Waddah Charara.

Born in Lebanon's southern city of Bint Jbeil in 1942, into a Shi'ite milieu that was undergoing profound societal, economic and ideational changes,[2] Charara co-founded Socialist Lebanon (SL, 1964–71) and shortly afterwards the Organisation of Communist Action in Lebanon (OCAL, 1971), whose creation resulted from the merger between Socialist Lebanon (SL), the Organisation of the Lebanese Socialists (OLS, 1969–71) and, to a lesser extent, the Union of the Lebanese Communists (1968–71) that split from the Lebanese Communist Party.[3] The most significant New Left group in Lebanon, the OCAL constituted a crucible of ideas, which proved decisive in the formative years of individuals who would become leading figures on the academic and artistic stage. After he cut short his activities just prior the outbreak of the Lebanese wars (1975), Charara devoted his time to writing on diverse topics, ranging from Arab poetry and neighbourhood sociality in Lebanon to Arab political and social issues, and up to the rise of Hizbullah.[4] Three questionings, though, drove his intellectual path: thinking the diversity of power and solidarity relationships, the dynamics of violence, and the structuration of the state.

In keeping with Werner and Zimmermann's programmatic lesson on 'entangled histories', the reflection starts with the assumption that the transnational, the local and the global do not consist in pre-existing scales of reference, and it interrogates their constitutive interactions.[5] The present study is aimed at deciphering how militant circulations and processes of the re-signification of representations and know-how have transformed all elements under consideration, beginning with the milieux of action, up to the militants themselves, and their way of framing problems, defining actions to be taken and locating themselves in this breadth of local/global

[2] Abisaab, *The Shi'ites of Lebanon.*

[3] Bardawil, *When All This Revolution Melts into Air*; Beydoun, 'Liban Socialiste'; Favier, *Logiques de l'Engagement*; Guirguis, 'Vietnam'; Taqi al-Din, *Al-yasar al-lubnani.*

[4] Waddah Charara has published, among other writings, *Al-salam al-ahli al-barid: lubnan al-mujtama'*; *Dawla hizbullah.*

[5] Werner and Zimmermann, 'Penser l'Histoire Croisée', 7–36.

interconnectedness. Adopting a constructivist and dynamic approach, I combine the analysis of the main paths of transmission of the notion of militant enquiry with the study of the intertwining of theorisation processes and bodily involvement in various milieux. By doing so, I give emphasis to the constant interplay between reading and translating, experiments on the ground and theorisation.

This piece draws on face-to-face and online interviews with former militants carried out between 2016 and 2019. It brings into conversation militant theoretical writings and memoirs, as well as the main publications released by the organisations under consideration: texts written by Mohsen Ibrahim, the leader of the Organisation of the Lebanese Socialists (OLS, 1969–71); the roneographed periodical *Lubnan al-Ishtiraki* (*Socialist Lebanon*, 1966–71) published by the eponymous group, whose members became leading cadres in the Organisation of Communist Action in Lebanon (OCAL, 1971) and in the editorial committee of *al-Hurriyya*; and the weekly journal *al-Hurriyya*, the mouthpiece of the Lebanese branch of the Arab Nationalist Movement (ANM), and then of the OCAL and the Popular Democratic Front for the Liberation of Palestine (PDFLP, 1969), another offspring of the ANM. Militant testimonies and writings belong to different periods, beginning with the period under study and continuing up until now. Depending on the issue under consideration, I may therefore use these diverse oral and written materials as sources, as documents or as academic references; confront militant political or theoretical assessments with militant actions; or highlight the intertwining of militant past and present voices and their current critical re-interpretation of former stances.

Militant Enquiry: Paths of Translation

The notion of militant enquiry goes back to Mao Ze Dong, who stated, for instance: 'Dismount the horse to pick some roses' or 'Without enquiry, no right to speak'.[6] In sum, revolutionaries must listen to the people whom they presume to serve and carry out enquiries on their current living conditions. Worker centrality, knowledge as opposition and the partiality of the point of

[6] Mao Ze Dong, *Contre l'idolâtrie du livre* (1930).

view thereafter constituted axial notions in the Italian *operaist* conception of militant enquiry. The notion subsequently encompassed an array of heterogeneous practices, which were implemented by leftist organisations in 1960s and 1970s Italy, and were eventually transposed to France beginning with 1967 and to Lebanon, among other sites. Tracing the various legacies of the *operaismo* – as represented by the *Quaderni rossi* and Classe Operaia – to the post-1968 extra-parliamentary groups of the *Nuova Sinistra*, such as Lotta Continua, would go far beyond the scope of this chapter.[7] In this first section, I restrict myself to identifying the main channels of transmission of the notion, namely militant circulations and publications.

Charara evokes, with a certain emotion, his political baptism one day in January 1953 when all pupils rushed out of school and, braving the driving rain, marched in support of the Algerian struggle, chanting, 'No to colonization! Long live to the Algerian revolution!'[8] At the age of fourteen, he became a member of the Baath Party that was gaining momentum in the second generation of the educated elite and in his family. After the political awakening in his family circle and at school, he received an extensive militant and theoretical training in France. He obtained a Master's degree in sociology from the University of Lyon,[9] where he read the essential Marxist and Maoist texts and discovered new trends in left-wing literature, from Althusser to *Socialisme et Barbarie*. He affiliated with the *réseau Jeanson* in support of the Algerian liberation struggle and with the Union of Communist Students (UEC), which had taken a critical stance towards the French Communist Party, especially with regard to the party's reluctance to take sides with the Algerian cause.[10] Upon his return to Lebanon in 1962, the encounter with Fawwaz Trabulsi (Lebanon, b. 1941) was decisive in the creation of SL. Initially trained at the Anglophone American University in Beirut (AUB), which, in the late 1950s and early 1960s was the hotbed of Arab Nationalist activism,[11] Trabulsi

[7] See Bobbio, *Storia*; Vigna, 'Les Luttes'.

[8] Charara, interview with author, Beirut, 4 March 2018.

[9] Charara, *Transformations* was his Master's dissertation.

[10] On the UEC, see Varin, 'Les Étudiants Communistes'; Quashie-Vauclin, 'La Jeunesse Dure Longtemps'.

[11] Anderson, *The American University of Beirut*; Rabah, *A Campus at War*; Kazziha, *Revolutionary Transformation*.

thereafter settled in Manchester and London, where he moved in the New Left milieu and established contact with several Arab and, especially, Yemeni militant networks.[12] Like most militants of the New Left worldwide, they regularly read *Le Monde*, *Les Temps Modernes* and the books released by the French left-wing publishing house Maspéro. In particular, *Les Temps Modernes* was key in the genesis of Socialist Lebanon and, therefore, of the Organisation of the Communist Action in Lebanon.

Charara and Trabulsi intended to create a journal which, similarly to *Les Temps Modernes*, would contribute to the debates arising from the important texts of the day, such as *The Wretched of the Earth* by Frantz Fanon. They discussed the idea with Bachir al-Da'uq, who had founded in Beirut the publishing house Dar al-Tali'a and the journal *Dirasat 'Arabiyya*, which became key forums for the diffusion of leftist and secular ideas in the region. Dar al-Tali'a published numerous 'committed translations',[13] ranging from *Egypt: Military Society*, by the Egyptian Marxist historian Anwar Abdel-Malek and *Class Struggles in Egypt* by Mahmoud Hussein, to Trabulsi's first translation, *The Revolution Betrayed* by Leon Trotsky.[14] Under the auspices of the Institute for Palestinian Studies in Beirut, whose director Mahmud Sueid was a founding member of Socialist Lebanon, Ahmad Beydoun, Waddah Charara and Fawwaz Trabulsi also translated into Arabic the special issue of *Les Temps Modernes* devoted to the Arab–Israeli conflict.[15]

In 1968, Maspéro, *Les Cahiers de Mai* and *Les Temps Modernes* began regularly reporting on Militant Enquiry and, more generally, on worker initiatives in France and in Italy.[16] Charara closely followed the emergence of the Italian New Left, especially Lotta Continua, and the actions undertaken in the French suburbs by the Proletarian Left. He personally knew Mahmoud Hussein, the pen name of Bahgat al-Nadi and Adeel Rifaat, born Eddy Levy,

[12] Trabulsi, *Sura al-fatat*.

[13] Trabulsi, interview with author, Beirut, 10 December 2016.

[14] Abdel-Malek, *Égypte*; Hussein, *La Lutte des Classes*.

[15] *Les Temps Modernes. Le Conflit Israélo-arabe* 253 bis (1 July 1967). On the history of this special issue and of the Sartrean journey in the Middle East aimed at winning the French Left to the Palestinian cause, see Nassar, in this volume; Di Capua, *No Exit*; Guirguis, 'The Arab New Left and May '68'.

[16] Panzieri, *Conception Socialiste*.

whose brother Benny Levy became a leader of the Proletarian Left. Although personal and political divergences prevented Charara and Hussein from working together long-term, they had nevertheless exchanged ideas and co-operated in a few instances, when Charara translated into Arabic *Class Struggles in Egypt* or, a couple of years later, when Mahmoud Hussein co-ordinated a special issue of the journal *al-Massira* on the Egyptian Student Movement, to which Charara contributed a piece.[17] By contrast, no direct relations were established between SL/the OCAL and Lotta Continua or other groups of the *Nuova Sinistra*. However, *al-Hurriyya* devoted numerous articles to Italian militant experiments and leftist politics, publishing, for instance, a report in 1970 on Luciana Castellina's article 'Rapport sur la Fiat', initially released in *Les Temps Modernes*, and extensive translations of *Il Manifesto*'s stance on revolution on a global scale.[18] Indeed, *al-Hurriyya* not only covered world and Arab politics, revolutionary struggles and protest movements worldwide, but it circulated translated texts written by prominent revolutionary and Marxist figures, ranging from Che Guevara and Amilcar Cabral to Paul Sweezy, Maxim Rodinson and Fred Halliday. Yet, theories and know-how travel only through the creative mediation of experiments in context, and I now turn the gaze towards the challenges that Lebanese militants intended to meet when they resorted to the militant enquiry.

Action Committees and Militant Enquiry: The Impossible Linkage between Lebanese Social Demands and the Palestinian National Struggle

In 1964, opposition to the renewal of Fouad Chehab (b. Lebanon 1902, r. 1958–64)'s term of office as President constituted the founding gesture of SL. Born into a noble Maronite family of the Kesrwan, commander of the Lebanese Armed Forces Fouad Chehab was appointed President with the backing of both the USA and the majority of Muslim constituencies, to succeed Camille Chamoun (Lebanon, 1900–87, r. 1952–8) in the aftermath of the 1958 insurrection.[19] Directing attention towards state-building, he

[17] Guirguis, 'The Arab New Left and May '68'; *al-Massira, La Révolte.*

[18] Respectively: Castellina, 'Rapport'; *al-Hurriyya* 501 (1970); 561, 562, 563, 564 (1971).

[19] Trabulsi, *A History*, 133–7; Schayegh, 1958.

introduced an ambitious reform agenda. Certainly, SL militants acknowledged that the reforms had provided some successful results regarding regional development, the establishment of a National Social Security Fund, or a law school in the Lebanese University that broke the effective monopoly on teaching law hitherto held by the Jesuit University. However, the Chehabist state-building process resulted in a significant strengthening of the executive that henceforth exercised a tight control over electoral processes, trade activities and trade unions.[20] SL denounced the rule of security agencies and the ensuing obstacles to the development of trade unions and social mobilisations, as well as the tight grip that Egyptian Intelligence maintained on Lebanese administrative, police and political staff.[21] In doing so, SL was also criticising the political line of the Front of progressive forces, parties and personalities in-the-making headed by the Druze leader of the Socialist Progressive Party, Kamal Jumblatt (Lebanon, 1917–77), which brought support to Chehab.[22]

The refusal of Chehabism was grounded in a critical analysis of the economic policy of the regime. From the late 1930s up to the early 1960s, the Lebanese economy became dominated by the tertiary sector, while Chamoun's rule enhanced the unbridled development of the banking system. Muslim and Christian oligarchies firmly opposed Chehab's attempts to rationalise the banking sector, which ultimately favoured the new cliques linked to Chehabism benefiting from speculation.[23] SL denounced the singular stance of the Lebanese ruling elites whose domination relied on 'the imperialist pillage of the Arab region', whereas Lebanon stood 'on the margin of the Arab region in regard to political problems threatening to destabilise its rulers'.[24] Correlatively, SL pointed out the contradictions of the so-called Arab progressive regimes: by calling for national independence and by precisely 'restricting the battle to this sole aspect', they managed to 'survive the June 1967 defeat and

[20] Trabulsi, *A History*, 138–55.

[21] Socialist Lebanon, *Al-'amal al-ishtiraki*; Charara, 'Bidayyat', and interview with author, 27 April 2018.

[22] For a later assessment of the political achievements and failures of the Front, see *Lubnan al-Ishtiraki* 9 (1968). On Jumblatt, see al-Khazen, 'Kamal Jumblatt'.

[23] *Lubnan al-Ishtiraki* 1 (1966); *al-Hurriyya* 490 (1969).

[24] Charara, 'Al-muqawamatan', part 1.

even to secure a popular base', but they remained economically dependent on 'international imperialism, first and foremost on the USA, and bound to it by fear of the rise of efficient socialist forces' that would threaten their political and economic powers.[25]

The accelerated changes occurring in 1968 and 1969 and the new centrality of the Palestine question in Lebanon led SL to believe in the imminent revolution. Beginning with 1968, strikes broke out within all sectors, fuelling a massive rush to militant groups. Meanwhile, the Karameh battle (March 1968) fostered the rise of the Fatah to power positions in the Palestinian Liberation Organisation (PLO, 1964), which it had joined in the aftermath of the June War, and provided a new, heroic representation of the Palestinian fighter, the *fida'i*. SL militants observed in several instances, from Tripoli to the Beqaa and through Beirut, that the sympathy expressed towards the Palestinian cause seemed to be deep and massive enough to give reason to hope for overwhelming the multifarious divisions and allegiances within Lebanese society, which had until then impeded the development of trade unionism and social mobilisations. Henceforth, two months after the Karameh battle, SL diagnosed a qualitative change in Palestinian action that placed it 'for the first time, among the revolutionary national liberation movements'.[26] SL interpreted this change and its echoes in Lebanese society as a challenge to Nasser's apparent wait-and-see policy and to the duplicity of Arab so-called progressive regimes, but also as a response to Arab regimes preventing the rise of trade unionism.[27]

However, the increasing presence of Palestinians in southern Lebanon and in several camps throughout the country led to Israeli attacks in the South and up to Beirut. The unprecedented Israeli raid on a non-military target, Beirut international airport, on 28 December 1968, in response to the *fida'i* attack on an Israeli airliner in Athens airport two days earlier, triggered the crisis over Lebanon's sovereignty and its role in defining a regional strategy. As guerrilla infiltrations into southern Lebanon continued, they enhanced both confrontations between Palestinians and the Lebanese army and demonstrations in support of the *fida'i* actions. As the fighting escalated in numerous areas, on

[25] *Lubnan al-Ishtiraki* 14 (1968).

[26] *Lubnan al-Ishtiraki* 11 (1968); also see Sayigh, 'Turning Defeat' and Guirguis, 'Vietnam'.

[27] Charara, 'Al-muqawamatan', part 1; Ibrahim, *Limadha*, 138–42.

23 April 1969 the Lebanese army brutally repressed demonstrations denouncing the 'reactionary policies of the Lebanese government towards the *fida'i* action' and calling for 'the opening of southern borders for guerrilla operations against Israel'.[28] A turning point in several respects, 23 April brought 'the issue of PLO armed presence into the open'.[29] The ensuing negotiations, between Yasser Arafat, the Lebanese army commander General Emile Boustani and Gamal Abdel Nasser, led to an unusual compromise, the Cairo Agreement, which acknowledged the right of Palestinians to control their refugee camps in Lebanon and to launch attacks against Israel from southern Lebanon:[30]

> In analysing the Israeli–Lebanese–Palestinian confrontations, I was betting that the ability of the Lebanese government to defend the national territory was at stake in this battle and that, naturally, it would not be able to meet this challenge. Following a very formal logic rather than an empirically-grounded argument, I was therefore anticipating the collapse of the regime and pretending that we should replace it.[31]

This overreaching aim, and the militant texts' frequently assertive tone, should not lead us to dismiss the disorientation of the militants, or the group's experimental stance, at a time of precipitate change, for the upsurge in strikes and social dissent highlighted the discrepancy between the key role SL theoretically attributed to workers and the predominantly student base of the organisation. This unprecedented configuration also revealed the gap between 'the routine of propaganda work and the call for solidarity with Palestinians', which, 'in order to be efficient, would have required an intense, popular, pan-Lebanese, mobilisation'.[32] How to draw on the sympathy expressed towards the Palestinian resistance in order to foster the formation of a revolutionary organisation that would effectively link the Palestinian struggle to social demands, and co-ordinate the Palestinian and Lebanese resistances? 'We did not have the slightest answer to these questions', Charara would state today.[33]

[28] *Al-Nahar*, 22 April 1969.

[29] Al-Khazen, *The Breakdown*, 142.

[30] Ibid., 140–74.

[31] Charara, 29 May 2018.

[32] Charara, 12 May 2018.

[33] Ibid.

Catalysed by the 23 April momentum, the marriage of convenience between SL and the OLS also stemmed from the two groups both admitting their limits. Benefiting from a broad militant base, the leaders of the OLS had, up to 1969, not raised concerns about defining a theoretically-grounded political line. They needed SL's analytical skills to fill their weekly journal, *al-Hurriyya*. For its part, SL consisted in a tiny group of intellectuals in-the-making who needed to renew the group's militant basis, and *al-Hurriyya* would precisely provide them with a media platform with which to address a broader audience. Hence, SL and the OLS agreed on a framework that would allow for experimenting with new forms of action while providing a period for reflection, of a sort, at a time of disruption and uncertainty. This framework can be summed up in two phrases: 'Action Committees', and 'Enquiry'. It was aimed at channelling militant energy in a loose organisational framework supposedly independent from the existing organisations. From April 1969 until the announcement of the creation of the OCAL in July 1971, the merger between the OLS and SL concretised through editorial work at the weekly *al-Hurriyya* and through this formula aimed at co-ordinating different fields of struggle: The Palestinian resistance, worker demands in various sectors, student and teacher movements.

A few militants were sent to Jordan to get an idea about the mood on the ground and to investigate Palestinian organisations' modes of action. The text that acted as a call for the formation of Action Committees, 'The two Resistances: The Palestinian and the Lebanese', drew on these enquiries discussed at length among militants and on analysis of the increased tensions between the camps and their environment, as well as between the Palestinians and the Lebanese authorities, in order to outline a proposal for regulating the relationships between the two resistances.[34] Notwithstanding the solidarity with the Palestinians, the influx of refugees and *feda'iyin* had led to diverse kinds of exactions, especially in the South. As early as the end of 1968, inhabitants of border villages, in Bint Jbeil, in Cheeba or in Kfar Hamam, wrote petitions or held protests in response to Palestinian behaviour, although they carried out these actions discreetly due to the aura surrounding the Palestinian resistance.[35] Thus, in this prospective framework, Charara advocated the formation of a Lebanese–Palestinian

[34] Charara, 'Al-muqawamatan', part 1 and 2.

[35] Beydoun, 9 May 2017; Charara, 12 June 2018. Franjieh, 'How Revolutionary'.

opposition front that would grant autonomy to both parties, while giving to the Lebanese organisations the authority to frame the policy of solidarity towards Palestine. For their part, the Palestinians would refrain from exacerbating Lebanese tensions and restrict themselves to preserving their territorial integrity, without opening hostilities against Israel. Palestinian organisations would have contributed to Lebanese organisations benefiting from the sympathy expressed towards the Palestinians. Conversely, this would have 'anchored the Palestinian resistance in local, social, and class struggles, allowing it to not remain prisoner of student or Muslim walls, which would have scuppered the project'.[36] Militants started visiting the camps and talking with local leaders of the Fatah and PDFLP, as well as with the *feda'iyin*, showing their solidarity with the Palestinians. They organised fundraising and collected identity papers for the Palestinians, or helped with constructing shelters in southern Lebanon.[37]

Spread across several schools, universities and workplaces, militants invited newcomers to gather, to discuss a text or to establish offices devoted to formulating slogans and publishing leaflets. In factories, they helped to organise meetings and clarify workers' demands. They offered to publish reports and to act as an arbiter. 'From the workers in melting and textile factories or in tobacco companies, to the teachers in technical colleges, through the mobilisations against the overhaul of the labour law, we were called up from all sides. We met delegations, discussed with people, produced leaflets: it became a real industry', remembers Charara.[38] Militants conducted enquiries in schools and factories in Beirut and throughout the country, which they regularly published in *al-Hurriyya*.[39] These enquiries led to stimulating interactions. Not only were they discussed within militant circles, but they had a mobilising effect: 'It was striking to verify *in situ* how our discussions with pupils, students, or workers could bear immediate effects on triggering a mobilisation, be it in the short or in the long term.'[40]

[36] Charara, 4 July 2018.

[37] Charara, 27 April 2018; Beydoun, 9 May 2017.

[38] Charara, 27 April 2018.

[39] On the student movement, see *al-Hurriyya* 500, 501, 502 (1970); on the strike of tobacco planters in Ghazieh, see *al-Hurriyya* 532–3 (1970); on the peasant revolt in the Akkar, see *al-Hurriyya* 540 (1970).

[40] Charara, 27 April 2018.

Despite these promising experiments, SL militants experienced some disappointments. The suggestions formulated by SL regarding the reform of the educational system were not heard,[41] and the proposed framework of co-ordination between the two resistances met with limited support. Then, Black September (1970) cast doubt on the confidence placed in the ability of the Palestinian resistance to play the role of 'detonator' of the Lebanese and Arab contradictions and prompted the leadership to place more emphasis on the worker axis. Facing several challenges, the OCAL failed to efficiently organise and, a fortiori, to create mechanisms of reproduction. A thorough assessment of the respective weight of the numerous obstacles that impeded leftist efforts could be discussed at length and would be beyond the scope of the present essay. In short, Trabulsi, Charara and Beydoun nowadays broadly agree on the following hindering factors. Action Committees developed, albeit enthusiastically, all over the map, at the expense of a debate about defining political norms and the role of the organisation. This brought to the forefront, for instance, the issues of militant professionalisation and of the workerisation of the movement, which would have required them to develop an activity for the long term and to bring activism into Christian neighbourhoods where most of the factories were located. Furthermore, internecine wars between individuals or groups inside the OCAL, among leftist groups and in the pro-Palestinian camp prevented the creation of a wider left-wing coalition. Finally, according to Charara:

> The accelerated transfer of the Palestinian resistance from Jordan to Lebanon after Black September was the prevalent factor. In the headlong rush to the war, whose challenges and consequences far exceeded not only our small organisation's political capacities but that of the whole pro-Palestinian camp, street and social mobilisations would have constituted a negligible force. As for the Palestinians, their recent disproportionate weight on the national stage created the illusion of power, whereas they became fragmented pawns and bargaining chips in the hands of police-regimes. And there, to me, what happened then was at complete odds with my thoughts, my wishes, my desires. There was a deep gulf between the initial project and, some ten years later, this intricate knot of contradictions and conflicts. I was not prepared for this, and I did not have a taste for this.[42]

[41] *Lubnan al-Ishtiraki* 9 (1968); Socialist Lebanon, *Al-'amal al-ishtiraki*, 121–53.

[42] Charara, 4 July 2018.

Militant Enquiry in the Beirut Poverty Belt and the Changing Notion of Revolution

Charara resigned from the OCAL Political Bureau (autumn 1971) and received a PhD in Arab and Islamic Studies at Paris-4 Sorbonne University (1971–2). Upon his return to Lebanon in the summer of 1972, he and a few comrades settled in the southern Beirut neighbourhood of Tariq al-Jadida to assess the prospects for some form of militancy to succeed in this milieu. During the 1960s, the rising commercial-financial elite managed to control the sale of fertilisers, the cost of production and distribution and the prices of the product as well as the terms for loans. This provoked not only the impoverishment of share-croppers and small producers, but also the decline of the up-to-then powerful families of big landowners.[43] Palestinian refugees and destitute persons pushed out of rural areas by economic necessity swelled the population in Beirut's southern and eastern environs. In Tariq al-Jadida, this (then) mainly Shi'ite shanty town surrounded by Palestinian camps, the Ministry of the Interior was harassing inhabitants to end settlement construction that was considered illegal. The ministry itself and its henchmen, however, operated outside of a legal framework. Militants helped co-ordinate garbage collection and street cleaning. Relaying the inhabitants' demands, they wrote petitions, organised meetings and encountered the local representative persons. Personal disagreements and political divergences regarding the OCAL's goals and modes of action surfaced anew, leading to Charara, Beydoun and a few dozen militants being expelled from the OCAL in the spring of 1973.[44] Headed by Mohsen Ibrahim and Fawwaz Trabulsi, the OCAL entered the front of progressive forces, parties and personalities under the leadership of Kamal Jumblatt, and descended into war, whereas Charara settled in the impoverished neighbourhood of eastern Nabaa.

Charara was no exception. He found himself in this microcosm at the junction between the evolving landscape of militancy in Christian milieux and the increased involvement of Shi'ite organisations in social action, marked by the emergence of Musa Sadr's Movement of the Dispossessed and Amal.[45] He

[43] Trabulsi, *A History*.

[44] Charara, *Al-majmu'a*. See also the communiqué published by the Political Bureau of the OCAL in *al-Hurriyya* 628 (1973).

[45] Abisaab, 'Sayyid Musa al-Sadr'; Mervin, 'Les Yeux de Moussa Sadr'.

regularly met with Makram Quzah, an admirer of Hilarion Capucci (Syria, 1922–2017),[46] and with a former Trappist turned worker-priest belonging to the Prado community (some twenty members of the Prado community were living together in the eastern neighbourhood of Beirut in the early 1970s). His path crossed with a Shia Sayyid who became a fervent supporter of Khomeini after walking out of the Baath Party, and with an 'agent' of the Hizbullah-in-the-making who had taken part in the tobacco planters' protest movement in 1973. He frequently encountered Grégoire Haddad, Archeparch of the Melkite Greek Catholic Archeparchy of Beirut and Jbeil, the 'Red Bishop of Beirut', who had founded the Social Movement in 1960. Benefiting from the support of then-President Fouad Chehab, Haddad had worked with the public authorities in the framework of a development policy and thereafter increasingly relied on ad-hoc co-operation with different organisations and personalities to remedy state inability or refusal to cope with social issues. Beginning with 1962, he co-operated with Musa Sadr in both social action and Christian–Muslim dialogue.

At different stages in their militant life, several individuals gravitated towards this neighbourhood, from militants of the Fatah Student Brigade and former members of the OCAL up to Christian students.[47] In addition to Christians who individually affiliated with Palestinian and left-wing organisations but had henceforth severed ties with their community, some Christian students and several priests had adopted a critical stance towards the Lebanese ruling elites, the Churches' official positions and the prevailing Christian right-wing political party, the Kataeb.[48] Lebanese Christian radicalisation around Third-Worldist and social or, even, socialist claims occurred through various channels, from student circulations to the impact of the Second Vatican Council and renewal movements in Orthodox Churches, right up to Christian transnational networks which engaged in social action (as epitomised by Latin American Liberation Theology) and

[46] Capucci, Archbishop of Caesarea in the Melkite Greek Catholic Church and Patriarcal Vicaire of Jerusalem, is known for his support for the Palestinian cause.

[47] Dot-Pouillard, 'Les Maos'; Sing, 'Brothers in Arms'.

[48] See in particular the pamphlet 'The Church We Want, the Church We Refuse', in *Notre Eglise*.

which supported national emancipation struggles – for example, French Christian leftists (their mouthpiece, *Témoignage Chrétien*).[49]

Charara drew inspiration from French and Italian writings and experiments. By taking a radical anti-party stance, the post-1968 experiments of the *Nuova Sinistra* marked, in a way, a rupture with the *operaismo* and the Italian political context of the late 1950s and 1960s.[50] Most militants of Lotta Continua, however, stemmed from the *operaismo*.[51] In short, by transposing *operaist* understanding of the militant enquiry in post-1968 Italy, Lotta Continua introduced two major shifts. Firstly, challenging the centrality of the production site, it advocated widening of the fields of intervention: students were asked to live workers' lives, and workers to expand the scope of the struggle from the factory to daily living environments.[52] This is precisely what happened during the contentious Fiat episode in Turin: the demands ultimately included the living conditions of workers, most of whom were day-to-day labourers from impoverished southern families.[53] Secondly, the practice of the enquiry henceforth required a total involvement of the body in the sites of struggle. This conception of the struggle in numerous sites of power and conflict led to a redefining 'revolution', which, from a critical juncture marked by the seizure of power, became a process or, even, a multiplicity of processes.

Similarly, Charara moved from a Leninist conception of the revolution led by a vanguard party (*c.* 1968–70) towards an intricate understanding of power plays in various sites of the social fabric, which implies conceiving of 'revolution' as the conjunction of several conflicts (*c.* 1972–3). From a militant perspective building on the Maoist notion of 'mass line' that captured revolutionary imaginations worldwide at that time, this meant foregrounding 'the masses' own struggles and making them master their own movements through practice', wrote Charara and Beydoun in their 1973 critical assessment of the OCAL's organisational and political lines.[54]

[49] Tarek Mitri and Boutros Labaki, interviews with author, Beirut, 24 September 2019; Favier, *Logiques*, Ch. 4; *Les Travaux et les Jours* (April–June 1970).

[50] Vigna, 'Les Luttes'.

[51] Bobbio, *Storia*.

[52] Vigna, 'Les Luttes'.

[53] Castellina, 'Rapport'; *al-Hurriyya* 501 (1970).

[54] Charara, *Al-majmu'a*.

In Nabaa, Charara and a few comrades attempted, in early spring 1973, to mobilise inhabitants around a municipal demand regarding pipe overflows that had occurred during the winter. Stories were circulating about a pregnant woman swept away by the flood who had had to give birth before term. They printed leaflets, organised meetings and launched an intensive campaign of door-to-door visits. They visited a thousand homes and often embarked on lengthy discussions with inhabitants on various topics. Having realised that Musa Sadr, Sayyid Muhammad Husayn Fadlallah and the Supreme Shiʿa Council had started occupying the field of social action in the area, they invited them to join efforts towards this initiative. They received different sorts of feedback. The informal representative of Musa Sadr initially did not understand what Charara and his comrades wanted from him. Charara therefore explained that they would appreciate him expressing his sympathy for their endeavour. The man exclaimed: 'but I find you very sympathetic. You want me to kiss you?' As for the local representative of the Supreme Shiʿa Council, he started laughing, saying: 'Ah! You are inviting the brother to dance with the sister, this is quite exciting.' Turning to Fadlallah, he remained stiff, frozen; he listened to their exposé and, after a deathly hush, he reacted saying that he would never co-operate with non-Islamist individuals. The very day of the scheduled demonstration, no one came, or almost no one apart from militants and sympathisers.[55]

Far from being an isolated occurrence, this story appears highly significant regarding the challenges that Shi'ite involvement in social action, and in particular Sadr's *haraka al-mahrumin* (movement of the dispossessed), posed to the Lebanese Left. Quoting Frangie, Hanssen rightly notes that 'the assassination of Husayn Muruwwa in 1987 marked the end of the Lebanese Communist Party as a militant project of liberation and the starting point of its replacement by the Islamic resistance'.[56] The rise of Islamic trends competing with leftist claims for social justice, though, had started even before the outbreak of the war.[57] As for Charara, he would at that time dismiss the possibility of multifarious social struggles in various sites

[55] Charara, 12 June 2018.

[56] Hanssen, in this volume, referring to Frangie, in this volume.

[57] Abisaab, 'Sayyid Musa al-Sadr'; on the genesis of Hizbullah, see Charara, *Dawla hizbullah*.

coalescing and triggering a revolutionary situation, let alone the collapse of the regime.[58]

Conclusion: From Revolution to Social Sciences, and Beyond

The ultimate failure in Nabaa marked the end of Charara's militant trajectory, although he remained living in the area until the outbreak of the war. During a period plagued by the progressive loss of perspective, the militant enquiry in Nabaa nevertheless turned out to be a decisive experience in several respects. There, militant enquiry incrementally gave way to sociological enquiry. The 'poverty belt' fraught with social tensions and criss-crossed by competing political forces undoubtedly constituted a privileged site in which to scrutinise how different kinds of solidarity ties were forged and transformed; to examine the reframing of local/regional power roles and relations; and to decipher contradictory signs in daily behaviours, from manifestations of trans-class, -sect or -clan solidarity to the crystallisation of antagonisms that indicated the country's slide into violence in the interweaving of collective and individual dynamics.

Thereafter a matrix of lived memories, images and meanings, Nabaa has nurtured the questionings that drove Charara's intellectual path. Understanding the slide to war pushed him to experience the limits of sociological analysis, and to experiment with new paths in thinking and writing about this issue. In turning the gaze towards sliding-to-war Nabaa, he also engages in conversation with younger generations, and attempts to provide a satisfactory answer to his second daughter asking: 'How could we trust our parents' memories?'[59]

Bibliography

Abdel-Malek, Anouar, *Égypte: Société Militaire* (Paris: Seuil, 1962).

Abisaab, Rula Jurdi, 'Sayyid Musa al-Sadr, the Lebanese State, and the Left', *Journal of Shi'a Islamic Studies* 8, 2 (2015): 131–58.

Abisaab, Rula Jurdi and Malek Abisaab, *The Shi'ites of Lebanon: Modernism, Communism, and Hizbullah's Islamists* (Syracuse: Syracuse University Press, 2017).

[58] Charara, *Hurub*.

[59] Charara, 4 July 2018.

Al-Khazen, Farid, *The Breakdown of the State in Lebanon, 1967–1976* (Cambridge: Harvard University Press, 2000).

Al-Khazen, Farid, 'Kamal Jumblatt, the Uncrowned Druze Prince of the Left', *Middle Eastern Studies* 24, 2 (1988): 178–205.

Al-Massira, La Révolte des Étudiants Égyptiens (Paris: Éditions Maspéro, 1972).

Anderson, Betty, *The American University of Beirut: Arab Nationalism and Liberal Education* (Austin: University of Texas Press, 2011).

Bardawil, Fadi A., *When All This Revolution Melts into Air: The Disenchantment of Levantine Marxist Intellectuals*, PhD dissertation (New York: Columbia University mimeo, 2010).

Bardawil, Fadi A., 'Dreams of a Dual Birth: Socialist Lebanon's World and Ours', *Boundary 2*, 3 (2016): 313–35.

Beydoun, Ahmad, 'Liban Socialiste. Conditions d'Émergence et Cheminement d'un Groupe de Jeunes Militants "Gauchistes" dans le Liban des Années 1960', unpublished paper presented at the conference *Arab Generations*, Collège de France, Paris, June 2012.

Bobbio, Luigi, *Storia di Lotta Continua* (Milan: Feltrinelli, 1979).

Castellina, Luciana, 'Rapport sur la Fiat', *Les Temps Modernes* 279 (1969).

Charara, Waddah, *Transformations d'une Manifestation Religieuse dans un Village du Liban-Sud* (Beirut: Centre de Recherches de l'Institut des Sciences Sociales de l'Université Libanaise, 1968).

Charara, Waddah, 'Al-muqawamatan: al-filastiniyya wa al-lubnaniyya' [The two resistances: the Palestinian and the Lebanese], part 1, *Lubnan al-Ishtiraki* 16 (1969), and part 2, *Lubnan al-Ishtiraki* 17 (1970).

Charara, Waddah, *Al-majmu'a al-mustaqilla ('an al-munazzama al-'amal al-shuyu'i)* [The independent group of the OCAL] (Beirut: n.p., 1973).

Charara, Waddah, 'Bidayyat al-nidal al-musallah' [The beginning of the armed struggle], *Dirasat 'Arabiyya* 11, 3 (1975), and then published in *Hurub*, 13–46.

Charara, Waddah, *Hurub al-istitba'* [Wars of subjection] (Beirut: Dar al-Tali'a, 1979).

Charara, Waddah, *Al-salam al-ahli al-barid: lubnan al-mujtama' wa al-dawla, 1964–1967* [The cold civil peace: Lebanon, state and society] (Tripoli: Ma'had al-inama al-'arabi, 1980).

Charara, Waddah, *Dawla hizbullah: lubnan mujtama'an islamiyyan* [Hizbullah state: Lebanon as an Islamic society] (Beirut: Dar al-Nahar, 1996).

Critchley, Simon, *Infinitely Demanding: Ethics of Commitment, Politics of Resistance* (London: Verso, 2007).

Della Porta, Donatella, *Social Movements in Times of Austerity: Bringing Capitalism Back into Protest Analysis* (Cambridge: Polity Press, 2015).

Di-Capua, Yoav, *No Exit: Existentialism, Jean-Paul Sartre and Decolonization* (Chicago: University of Chicago Press, 2018).

Dot-Pouillard, Nicolas, 'De Pékin à Téhéran, en Regardant vers Jérusalem. La Singulière Conversion à l'Islamisme des "Maos du Fatah"', *Cahiers de l'Institut Religioscope* 2.

Favier, Agnès, *Logiques de l'Engagement et Modes de Contestation au Liban: Genèse et Éclatement d'une Génération de Militants Intellectuels (1958–1975)*, PhD dissertation (Paris: Aix-Marseille 3 University, 2004).

Franjieh, Samir, 'How Revolutionary Is the Palestinian Resistance? A Marxist Interpretation', *Journal of Palestine Studies* 2 (1972): 52–60.

Guirguis, Laure, 'Vietnam and the Rise of a Radical Left in Lebanon, 1962–1976', *Monde(s). Histoire, Espaces, Relations* 14, 2 (2018): 225–44.

Guirguis, Laure, 'May '68 and the Arab New Left: Transnational Entanglements at a Time of Disruption', *Critical Historical Studies* (submitted).

Hajjat, Abdellali, 'Les Comités Palestine (1970–2). Aux Origines du Soutien à la Cause Palestinienne en France', *Revue d'Études Palestiniennes* (Paris: Les Éditions de Minuit, 2006): 74–92.

Hussein, Mahmoud, *La Lutte des Classes en Égypte* (Paris: Maspéro, 1969).

Ibrahim, Mohsen, *Limadha? Munazzama al-ishtirakiyyin al-lubnaniyyin. Haraka al-qawmiyyin al-'arab min al-fashiyya ila al-nasiriyya. Naqd wa tahlil* [The organisation of the Lebanese socialists, why? The Arab nationalist movement from fascism to nasserism. Critique and analysis] (Beirut: Dar al-Tali'a, 1970).

Kazziha, Walid, *Revolutionary Transformation in the Arab World: Habash and his Comrades from Nationalism to Marxism* (London: Charles Knight, 1975).

Mao Ze Dong, *Contre l'idolâtrie du livre* (n.p., 1930).

Mervin, Sabrina, 'Les Yeux de Moussa Sadr', in Catherine Mayeur-Jaouen (ed.), *Saints et Héros du Moyen-Orient Contemporain* (Paris: Maisonneuve et Larose, 2002): 285–300.

Nolan, Mary, 'Where Was the Economy in the Global Sixties?' in Chen Jian, Martin Klimke, Masha Kirasirova, Mary Nolan, Marilyn Young and Joanna Waley-Cohen (eds), *The Routledge Handbook of the Global Sixties Between Protest and Nation-Building* (Oxford: Routledge, 2018).

Notre Église en Question (Beirut: Éditions de L'Orient, 1969).

Panzieri, Raniero, 'Conception Socialiste de l'Enquête Ouvrière', *Quaderni Rossi. Luttes Ouvrières et Capitalisme d'Aujourd'hui* (Paris: Maspéro, 1968).

Quashie-Vauclin, Guillaume, 'La Jeunesse Dure Longtemps. Quarante ans d'Historiographie des Organisations de Jeunesse Communistes Françaises', *Cahiers d'Histoire. Revue d'Histoire Critique* 116–17 (2011): 195–227.

Rabah, Makram, *A Campus at War: Student Politics at the American University of Beirut 1967–1975* (Beirut: Dar Nelson, 2009).

Sayigh, Yezid, 'Turning Defeat into Opportunity: The Palestinian Guerrillas after the June 1967 War', *Middle East Journal* 2 (1992): 244–65.

Schayegh, Cyrus, '1958 Reconsidered: State Formation and the Cold War in the Early Postcolonial Arab Middle East', *International Journal of Middle East Studies* 45, 3 (2013): 421–43.

Sieffert, Denis, 'L'Extrême-Gauche Française et la Question Palestinienne', *Matériaux pour l'Histoire de notre Temps* 4, 96 (2009): 59–62.

Sing Manfred, 'Brothers in Arms: How Palestinian Maoists Turned Jihadists', *Die Welt des Islams* 1 (2011): 1–44.

Socialist Lebanon, *Al-'amal al-ishtiraki wa tanaquddat al- wad' al-lubnani* [Socialist action and the contradictions of the Lebanese situation] (Beirut: Dar al-Tali'a, 1969).

Takriti, Abdel Razzaq, *Monsoon Revolution. Republicans, Sultans, and Empires in Oman, 1965–1976* (Oxford: Oxford University Press, 2013).

Taqi al-Din, Sulayman, *Al-yasar al-lubnani wa tajriba al-harb* [The Lebanese left and the experience of war] (Beirut: Dar al-Farabi, 2013).

Trabulsi, Fawwaz, *A History of Modern Lebanon* (London: Pluto Press, 2007).

Trabulsi, Fawwaz, *Surat al-fata bi al-ahmar: ayyam fi al-silm wa al-harb* [Portrait of a young man in red: days in peace and war] (Beirut: Dar Riad el-Rayyes, 1997).

Varin, Jacques, 'Les Étudiants Communistes, des Origines à la Veille de Mai 1968', *Matériaux pour l'Histoire de Notre Temps* 74 (2004): 37–49.

Vigna, Xavier, 'Les Luttes d'Usines dans les Années 68: Le Cas Français à la Lumière du Cas Italien', *Histoire & Sociétés. Revue Européenne d'Histoire Sociale* 10 (2004): 48–64.

Werner, Michael and Bénédicte Zimmermann, 'Penser l'Histoire Croisée: Entre Empirie et Réflexivité', *Annales. Histoire, Sciences Sociales* 1 (2003): 7–36.

11

THE 'CHE GUEVARA OF THE MIDDLE EAST': REMEMBERING KHALID AHMAD ZAKI'S REVOLUTIONARY STRUGGLE IN IRAQ'S SOUTHERN MARSHES

Philipp Winkler

Introduction

The story of Khalid Ahmad Zaki and his guerrilla war in southern Iraq (the Intifada, as it will be referred to hereinafter) 'barely rates a footnote in the numerous books on Iraq',[1] as Tariq Ali correctly notes, and, as Salaam Yousif laments, 'the history of the Marshes guerrilla campaign still awaits documentation'.[2] Outside the Arab context, this episode seems to remain almost completely unknown. So far as I know, Vijay Prashad is the first to include it in a study with global scope, putting it in the context of other failed Maoist rebellions against official communist party lines in his book *The Darker Nations*.[3] However, this chapter focuses on those left-wing activists to whom Zaki's story did matter, who were fascinated and enthralled by his endeavour, and in whose memory he still has a special place. Two films

[1] Ali, *Bush in Babylon*, 100.

[2] Yousif, 'Le Déclin de l'Intelligentsia', 67–8.

[3] Prashad, *The Darker Nations*, 161.

have been made about Zaki,[4] booklets have been published and ceremonies held in order to commemorate him, and he is featured in a great number of poems, novels and personal accounts produced by Arab, especially Iraqi, writers. Entering into a conversation with Traverso, this chapter explores the changing meanings commemorating Zaki has had for Arab left-wing trends under different historical conditions: while remembering the past was initially a mobilising and instigating force for his comrades, it later turned into a disillusioned, wistful melancholia.

Zaki's Life and the Intifada

Many details of Zaki's life are still unclear, and accounts vary or even contradict each other greatly with regard to numbers, dates and details. Due to its limited scope, its focus on the commemoration of Zaki and the fact that important documents were not (or are not yet) accessible to me, this chapter relates only a basic trajectory of his life as far as is necessary for understanding my argument. A thorough study that collects and evaluates all the dispersed sources on Zaki and the Intifada and extracts from them a detailed and exact account of the life of this extraordinary person remains a huge desideratum. Nevertheless, it is possible to set out something approaching a biographical outline.

Khalid Ahmad Zaki was born in Baghdad in 1935. He finished elementary school in Ramadi Province in 1948 and secondary school in Kut Province in 1954. His father was an irrigation engineer who frequently had to travel to the different provinces of Iraq, and Khalid often accompanied him.[5] Therefore he was able to visit many parts of the country, and during these visits met the poor inhabitants of the countryside and was deeply moved by

[4] The first is *Fata al-ʿiraq. Khalid Ahmad Zaki*, directed by Subhi Khazʿali and Qahtan Habib al-Mallak, a fifteen-minute film to commemorate Zaki, including interviews with his brother Ghazi and his friend Qahtan Habib al-Mallak. The other, 'Jifara al-ʿIraq', directed by the Iraqi filmmaker Tawfiq al-Tamimi, is a thoroughly researched 46-minute documentary based on hitherto unknown documents and testimonies. At the time of writing it is at the post-production stage and is scheduled to be released soon by the Iraqi media company Asiacell (information from personal correspondence with Tawfiq al-Tamimi, May, June and October 2018). I would also like to thank Tawfiq al-Tamimi for providing me with information and scans of documents pertaining to Zaki.

[5] Zaki, 'Khalid Ahmad Zaki', 1.

their dire circumstances. The desire to change their situation eventually made him join the Iraqi Communist Party (ICP).[6] In the second half of the 1950s, he went to London as a student. He soon got involved in the Iraqi Students Society in the UK, serving as its head for some time in the early 1960s.[7] The society had strong connections with other Arab and Iraqi students in Britain and all over Europe, and it organised frequent activities such as outings, demonstrations and festivals. It was heavily politicised and dominated by communist and other left-wing students.[8]

Zaki also took part in numerous other political activities. In early 1963, in the wake of the anti-communist terror campaign that followed the Baath coup in February 1963, he came to work with Bertrand Russell.[9] By that time, the famous philosopher had become a political activist, and a number of organisations and ardent young people had gathered around him and organised conferences, protests and publications on different topics, ranging from campaigns against nuclear armament up to support for the Vietcong or communist Cuba.[10] Among the most active members of Russell's group were Ralph Schoenman and Christopher Farley, who worked closely together with Zaki. After joining this circle, Zaki focused on supporting the prisoners in Iraq's jails during the 1963 period of Baath rule. Zaki's co-operation with Russell continued after the collapse of the Baath later that year, as oppression continued under the ʿArif regime.[11]

But Iraq was certainly not the only topic he took an interest in, for Zaki, as Qahtan al-Mallak describes him, was 'Iraqi in his core and international in his thinking'.[12] In a pamphlet published after his death, an 'Iranian Student' relates how, in 1965, Zaki supported a group of Iranians in a hunger strike for prisoners of the Shah's regime and praises the 'internationalist insight and sentiment of Khalid', who, as a 'true son of the oppressed Third

[6] Ibid.

[7] Al-Mallak, *Shadharat min tarikh jamʿiyyat* 197.

[8] 'Awraq Anis Ajiba', especially 13–14.

[9] Farley, 'On Khalid', 4, and Zaki, 'Khalid Ahmad Zaki', 2.

[10] On the political activism of Russell, see Monk, *Bertrand Russell*, 454–79.

[11] Ismael, *Rise and Fall*, 127–8.

[12] Al-Mallak, 'Kalima', 7.

World . . . considered all oppressed people as his own'.[13] Zaki also paid close attention to the war in Vietnam and was especially fascinated by the story of Che Guevara's rebellion in Cuba. He subscribed to the belief that popular guerrilla movements in Third World countries represented the right path of socialist resistance to imperialism and capitalism, and formed the avant-garde of the world revolution. Tariq Ali, remembering how he had protested in Lahore in 1961 after the news of the Congolese president Patrice Lumumba's death broke, was happy to find someone 'equally obsessed with the fate of the Congo'[14] in Zaki, whom he met in the 1960s in London. In January 1965, Zaki and Schoenman wrote an article on the situation in the Congo.[15] Reviewing the history of the country since the nineteenth century as an especially brutal example of Western racism, colonialism and imperialism, they analyse the events since the country's independence in 1960, focusing on the war of the Lumumbist guerrilla movement in eastern Congo and debunking Western propaganda about the conflict. The article praises the 'heroism' of the poorly armed rebels in the face of 'phosphorus bombs, rockets, modern aircraft and full-scale invasion'[16] by the old and new colonialists from Belgium and the USA. Many times, the situation is portrayed as a second Vietnam.[17] Interestingly, the same topic also inflamed the heart of Che Guevara, who a few months later, in spring 1965, secretly travelled to the Congo to support the struggle there.[18] Yet, while Zaki was concerned with numerous political causes all around the world, to use the words of Farley his 'heart . . . was elsewhere: he was planning his return home'.[19]

The Rift within the ICP and the Armed Struggle in the Marshes

Being exhausted and weakened by years of persecution and oppression, the leaders of the ICP adopted the so-called August Line in August 1964. Under

[13] Iranian Student, 'Khalid's Internationalism', 3.

[14] Ali, *Bush in Babylon*, 90.

[15] Schoenman et al., 'Death and Pillage in the Congo'.

[16] Ibid., 43.

[17] Ibid., 32–3, 35.

[18] Monk, *Bertrand Russell*, 465.

[19] Farley, 'On Khalid', 4.

Soviet influence, they opted for co-operation with the 'revolutionary democratic' ʿArif regime, which they attested was pursuing a non-capitalist path to development, claiming that the regime was carrying out some objectively revolutionary politics and thus should be supported by the party. Revolutionary opposition to it was denounced as an objectively wrong and adventurist strategy.[20] However, a strong opposition movement against the August Line soon emerged within the party. In the years after 1964, culminating in 1967, this lead to factionalism, inner strife and even internal coups and counter-coups, bringing about a hopelessly confusing situation within the ICP. Several factions brought up the idea of an armed uprising against the government, not only as a different strategy regarding the question of how to conquer political power, but also as a way out of the excessive factionalism and inner turmoil that had marred the party, and to re-unite the movement behind a new goal.[21]

Yet, this was mainly envisioned in the form of a military coup by communist-influenced elements within the army. Zaki, one of those who had strongly opposed the August Line from the very beginning, returned to Iraq in late 1966, secretly entering the country in disguise,[22] and vigorously immersed himself in these debates. In an internal note, he harshly criticised the idea of a military coup. While also advocating the use of force, applying what he had learned from other examples of armed struggle in the Third World, he stated that the army in a capitalist state is by nature always a reactionary factor and thus cannot be used as an instrument for revolutionary action. Instead, a long, protracted armed people's struggle in the shape of a popular guerilla war is the only viable way to a victory of the communist cause.[23] However, this position did not prevail in the ICP infighting of 1967, so eventually Zaki decided to start his planned guerilla war with his own small group of supporters.

As the setting for the uprising, they chose Iraq's southern marshes. These were not easily accessible by the forces of the central government, being a

[20] Franzén, *Red Star*, 142–61; Ismael, *Rise and Fall*, 118–25; Batatu, Old Social Classes, 1,035–40.

[21] Franzén, *Red Star*, 161–8, especially 164–5.

[22] As with many details of his life, the dates given for his return to Iraq differ, but most sources mention late 1966.

[23] Excerpts are quoted and paraphrased in Mahmud, *Al-siraʿ*, 106–8.

complex system of moving islands and waterways that are hard to surveil and move about in. Moreover, their inhabitants, the so-called Maʿdan, Shi'ite Arabs, were among the poorest segments of Iraqi society and the revolutionaries expected them to join their efforts. It seemed to be the perfect place for the revolution. The group wanted to start its activities with small strikes against the army, hoping that the poor peasant masses would join and support them, thereby enabling the rebellion to grow and eventually spread over the whole of Iraq. The revolution had to start not in the big cities of Iraq, but, Zaki was convinced, in the remote countryside, following the examples of Che Guevara and others who he read and admired.[24]

After an initial successful action against a police station, they lost their way in the quagmire, and the expected mass support of the peasants failed to materialise. Eventually, the group was attacked by the Iraqi army with helicopters and amphibious vehicles, and on 3 June the final confrontation took place. In the end, Zaki and two of his comrades died; the others were taken prisoner and later pardoned.[25] A few weeks after these events, the Baath took power again, and this time it would last.

Left-Wing Melancholia: Looking Forward

According to Enzo Traverso, left-wing melancholia 'does not mean a retreat into a closed universe of suffering and remembering; it is rather a constellation of emotions and feelings that envelop a historical transition, the only way in which the search for new ideas and projects can coexist with the sorrow and mourning for a lost realm of revolutionary experiences'.[26] Traverso traces this melancholia through left-wing accounts (by Karl Marx, Rosa Luxemburg and others) of numerous great defeats in different epochs, from the failed revolution of 1848 in France and the Paris Commune of 1871, the Berlin Spartacus Revolt of 1919 and the Nazis' rule of terror, to the post-Second World War defeats of Guevara in Bolivia

[24] Ismael, *Rise and Fall*, 153–4; Franzén, *Red Star*, 180–1.

[25] Accounts of the events are given in: Franzén, *Red Star*, 179–81; Batatu, *Old Social Classes*, 1098; Ismael, Rise and Fall, 149–54; Ali, Bush in Babylon, 91–3; 'Intifadat al-ahwar al-musallaha fi al-ʿIraq'; and Yousif, 'Le Déclin de l'intelligentsia', 67–9.

[26] Traverso, *Left-wing Melancholia*, xiv.

and Allende in Chile.[27] It is not just, he explains, a form of mourning and remembering, but also encourages further, renewed action, the defeats being received as mere setbacks and episodes on a road that will eventually lead to victory of the just cause. Those who were crushed by the forces of oppression turn not only into objects of mourning for the vanquished survivors, but also into even more reasons to revolt, for justice must be done to 'redeem' their otherwise futile deaths, a point famously already made by Walter Benjamin in his *Theses on the Philosophy of History.*[28]

The immediate reactions to Zaki's defeat fit well into this scheme. Already in August 1968, after news of his death had arrived, his friends held a commemorative meeting in London,[29] and about a year later they published a brochure to commemorate him entitled *The Death of an Iraqi Revolutionary.* It portrayed Zaki as a second Che Guevara: Guevara's statement 'a revolutionary is the one who makes revolution' is emblazoned on its cover; the first article, after an account of Zaki's struggle and death, gives a lengthy quotation from Fidel Castro's statement after Guevara's death, asserting that it also applies perfectly to Zaki.[30] The iconographic picture of the dead Che presented on a bier by Bolivian soldiers, which itself has many historical antecedents,[31] is closely mirrored in a picture of the dead Zaki presented by the Iraqi army that is shown on the cover of the brochure.[32] This picture is prominently featured in almost every publication commemorating Zaki.[33]

Furthermore, the setting of the Intifada also lent itself very much to that comparison: since the early Islamic period, the black slave rebellion of the Zanj and the uprising of the Qaramita in the ninth and tenth centuries

[27] Ibid., 32–8.

[28] Benjamin, 'Theses on the Philosophy of History', 254, 255 and 260.

[29] Monk, *Bertrand Russell*, 544.

[30] The Front of Iraqi Revolutionaries, 'Editorial', 2.

[31] Traverso, *Left-wing Melancholia*, 39–41.

[32] The *Death of an Iraqi Revolutionary* (front cover).

[33] It is also shown on the cover of al-Mallak, Al-shahid, and on page 5 this book features a poem referring to the photograph and the resting, smiling expression on the dead revolutionary's face, with the picture as the background to the poem. Tariq Ali also shows it at the end of his paragraph on Zaki: see Ali, *Bush in Babylon*, 100.

created the myth of the Marshes as a centre for revolutionary activity.[34] Like the forests of the Congo or the hills of eastern Cuba, they had always been a place that the rulers of the country found hard to control. The abject poverty of their inhabitants further enhanced this image. Farley accordingly stresses how Zaki was greeted with 'renewed hope' by the 'miserable, exploited peasantry' inhabiting this 'region of malaria and intense heat'.[35]

Just as with Guevara's death at the time, this commemoration of Zaki's death served the specific function for his friends and comrades inside and outside Iraq of spurring further fighting, thus giving the tragic story an optimistic spin: the spilled blood of revolutionaries like Zaki will 'give life to the seeds of liberation and will turn that country into a volcano spelling destruction on the oppressors',[36] the authors say, expressing their conviction that those oppressors 'will one day have to face justice of the revolution',[37] for when 'one Khalid goes, there are other Khalids and there will be a great many to come'.[38] Farley is sure that Zaki's memory will live on 'long after the overthrow of the despicable and corrupt regimes against which he pitted his life',[39] an overthrow that still seemed inevitable to him. Schoenman, in his message to a commemorative meeting, enthusiastically states: 'He was leaving for Iraq . . . going to the battle for which our lives were a preparation – the revolutionary struggle in which our deaths would be a moment in the suffering of millions.'[40] These lines place Zaki's death in the field in a defiant, hopeful context, a milestone in a battle comprising suffering and loss, but eventually leading to victory. To give an example from inside Iraq, Haifa Zangana in her non-fictional account of her political activities, *City of Widows*, remembers how, as a communist guerrilla in northern Iraq in the early 1970s, she 'had been influenced by [Zaki's] revolutionary ideas and life, which restored hope in the future of the struggle against the military Baath regime and the pro-Soviet Communist Party. Khalid for many of us had the aura of Che Guevara.'[41]

[34] Abdullah, *A Short History of Iraq*, 42.

[35] Farley, 'On Khalid', 4.

[36] The Front of Iraqi Revolutionaries, 'Editorial. A Year after Khalid (Balance Sheet)', 2.

[37] Ibid., 3.

[38] Ibid., 3.

[39] Farley, 'On Khalid', 4.

[40] Quoted in Monk, *Bertrand Russell*, 471.

[41] Zangana, *City of Widows*, 65.

Thus, Zaki was immediately portrayed as a second Guevara, a heroic fighter for the oppressed peoples of the Third World, defying Soviet patronising and party conformism in favour of guerrilla war, who gave his own life to follow that course.

Left-Wing Melancholia: Looking Backward

However, as Traverso explains, there is also a different kind of left-wing melancholia. Especially after 1989/1990, he says, communists and leftists in general mainly focused on remembering past glory and hopes without really having something to look for in the future. After the downfall of 'real existing socialism' erased any utopias, this 'culture of mourning does not work anymore. The loss appears irreparable; it cannot be mourned and sublimed in the living flow of a political movement.'[42] There is thus a second version of left-wing melancholia, one that does not point to a possible alternative within reach, in circumstances where it is '*precisely the lack of a new spirit* and vision that annihilates any attempt to distance oneself from the lost object and to overcome the loss'.[43] This version is a stubborn clinging to a cause lost long ago because the only alternative – in the face of the absence of any emancipatory movement – would be to accept the dim present. It thus represents 'the obstinate refusal of any compromise with domination'[44] instead of a hopeful look into the future.

Turning to the later commemorations and depictions of Zaki, we find exactly this second kind of melancholia; a melancholia not focused on the future, not portraying him as a tragically failed pioneer in whose footsteps victory will arrive, but rather viewing his actions as a heroic effort that was, despite its nobility, bound to fail. This can be grasped already from the very words used to describe it: Yousif, writing in 2007, calls Zaki and his comrades 'romantic and idealist', their Intifada a 'complete debacle'.[45] Prashad speaks of a 'quixotic insurgency',[46] while Tariq Ali calls it a 'self-inflicted'[47] and 'awful tragedy'[48]

[42] Traverso, *Left-wing Melancholia*, 48.

[43] Ibid., 45, emphasis mine.

[44] Ibid.

[45] Yousif, 'Le Déclin de l'Intelligentsia', 68.

[46] Prashad, *The Darker Nations*, 161.

[47] Ali, *Bush in Babylon*, 89.

[48] Ibid., 100.

and frankly acknowledges its total insignificance within the greater picture of history.[49] Qahtan al-Mallak says that Zaki and Guevara were 'the last two exemplary fighters in our Third World that sacrificed their lives for the principles and values they believed in'.[50] So, it was clear to him by then that nobody actually took up their cause and successfully completed it, as was still expected by those writing about him immediately after his death. Haifa Zangana, who, as mentioned above, was encouraged by Zaki's example in the early 1970s, again features his story in her fictionalised account of her life of defeats and imprisonment, *Dreaming of Baghdad*, written in exile. But he now is introduced with a notably different tone: the protagonist, while in a secret training camp in northern Iraq, is visited by 'Umm Khalid', who, despite being only 45, appears as a sick, aged and confused old woman, broken by grief over the loss of her son.[51] The protagonist is led to think: 'O mothers of a country that has long known naught but fear and oppression, how quickly old age descends upon your bodies and minds!'[52] Hence, while remembering Zaki might, in the years directly after his death, have served as an incentive for further action, looking back some decades later he appears as a symbol of tragic defeat.

A Delusive Co-operation and Its Discontents: The Demise of the Arab Communist Parties

While the above-quoted references to Zaki often meet the criteria of what Traverso analysed as typical post-Soviet melancholia, prevalent globally in the period after 1989/1990, there are some notable differences pertaining to specific aspects of the Iraqi/Arab situation or, in a wider picture, the Third World in general, which put Zaki's example in a special context which I am going to expound. For, as Traverso notices, the timelines of memory in the twentieth century differ between different regions; for example, between the First and the Third World.[53] He frames a period from 1959 to 1975 in which armed struggle in the Third World seemed to be a promising endeavour for some on the Left, and in this context we must place Zaki's Intifada.

49 Ibid.

50 Al-Mallak, 'Kalima', 7, emphasis mine.

51 Zangana, *Dreaming of Baghdad*, 61–5.

52 Ibid., 64.

53 Traverso, *Left-wing Melancholia*, 12–14.

Contrasting this revolutionary trend, the communist parties in Arab states like Iraq, Syria, Egypt and Algeria, all self-proclaimed forerunners of 'socialist' politics in the Arab world, had during this period accepted the status of junior partners of regimes labelling themselves socialist and progressive, partnerships supported, or rather urged, by the Soviet Union for mainly strategic reasons. This resulted in situations where they found themselves between co-operation with and persecution by the authorities, often at the same time. Eventually, these alliances led to a steep decline in the Communists' power in those countries, as they were caught up between facing persecution, betraying their ideals, being reduced to meaningless fig-leaves of the ruling regimes, and facing the accompanying steady decline of their support and popularity among the people.[54] Hence they had their moments, or rather periods, of disaster, defeat and decline much earlier than the ultimate downfall of communism in 1989/1990 on a global scale. Zaki, in his turn, was part of a radical trend present in all these parties, inspired by the Cuban and Vietnamese revolutions to refuse this tactic prescribed by Moscow and to start armed struggle instead.

After his death and the takeover of the Baath, the Iraqi authorities cracked down brutally on the remaining cells of the revolutionary faction, eventually capturing ʿAziz al-Hajj, the leader of the ICP Central Command, who changed sides, publicly renounced communism and revealed his former comrades to the authorities.[55] Thus the revolutionary current of the ICP basically ended; small groups continuing the fight against the Baath in the Kurdish areas remained marginal.[56] The official wing of the ICP eventually even joined the Baath in a 'National Progressive Front' in 1973, until the latter felt strong enough to dispose of the Communists and crack down on them in 1978 and 1979.[57] What followed was Saddam Hussain's unrestrained reign of terror, lasting until 2003 when it was ended – not by the people's uprising, but by an invasion of the USA, perceived by the Arab Left as yet another disaster, which has led to occupation, civil war, sectarianism and chaos.

[54] Jabar, 'The Arab Communist Parties in Search of an Identity', 93–6, especially 95.

[55] Kelidar, 'Aziz al-Haj: A Communist Radical', 186–7; and Yousif, 'Le Déclin de l'Intelligentsia',69–70.

[56] Franzén, *Red Star*, 181–2.

[57] Ibid., 206–21, 238–43.

With hindsight, it is clear that the end of any hope for a Communist victory was already determined by the early 1970s with the crushing of the resistance against co-operation with the regime. As mentioned above, this constellation was not unique to Iraq, but its main features were also found in many other Arab countries. Prashad even extends it to other parts of the Third World, comparing the cases of the Indonesian, Sudanese and Iraqi Communist parties, the 'three largest communist parties . . . in Asia, Africa, and the Arab lands'[58] respectively, which all faced a similar fate.[59] In this light, Zaki's uprising in Iraq can be read as a desperate last-ditch effort to defy these fatal tactics representing the traditional Soviet-advocated view, and start a revolution against the forces of oppression instead of trying to co-operate with them. The takeover of the Baath within weeks after Zaki's death, which turned into a nightmare lasting for decades, seemed to bring home this point even more.

This timely coincidence between the last attempt of the communists to avoid being sidelined and the final and lasting ascent to power of their enemies makes the events seem especially dramatic and symbolic. They thus offer themselves as a focal point of Arab left-wing melancholia far beyond the borders of Iraq, as the arguably most famous of the many artistic references to Zaki's story,[60] Haidar Haidar's *Walima li sha'b al-bahr* (first published in 1983), shows: Haidar is himself a Syrian, the novel is set in Algeria, its protagonists are Iraqis, and it became most famous after its republication in Egypt caused a major controversy in 2000.[61] It tells the story of two Iraqi communists who supported Zaki's revolutionary movement and then left Iraq to avoid persecution, now working as teachers in Algeria. But they soon find out that even this 'promised land' of Arab revolution is far from being the socialist paradise they imagined, but a land of poverty, ignorance, exploitation, authoritarian religion and oppressive traditions, all overseen by a new

[58] Prashad, *The Darker Nations*, 158.

[59] Ibid., 158–64.

[60] A list of further references in poetry, art and writing is given in Yousif, 'Le Déclin de l'Intelligentsia', 68–9.

[61] For a summary of these events in Egypt and the contents of the novel, see Hafez, 'The Novel, Politics and Islam', Gabriel, 'Islamist Protest' and al-Ahnaf, 'L'affaire Haydar Haydar'.

ruling class of military men who have hijacked an already less than half-hearted socialist revolution, while the subservient communists are oppressed or exiled. Against this harsh and sobering present, the Marshes Intifada is evoked as the positive but irretrievably lost counter-image in numerous flashbacks and discussions of the characters.

Conclusion

Immediately after his death, Khalid Ahmad Zaki began to be remembered by his friends and comrades as a Middle Eastern Che Guevara; his story lent itself easily to that comparison, as he was perceived as another heroic anti-imperialist fighter who died trying to instigate revolution among peasant masses in the Third World. Yet, the specific Arab context of his activities gave this picture a peculiar spin: he functioned as a symbol of resistance to the overwhelming trend of collaboration with 'progressive' regimes that proved to be so disastrous for the Arab Left.

While remembering his defeat in the era directly after his death served to spur and instigate further action aimed at achieving the ends he died for, which at the time still seemed a real possibility for his comrades, later commemorations have had a rather resigned, mournful and depressed tone, remembering his goals as a dream that never became true.[62]

Note. While there is no place to thank the many people who helped me researching the issues treated in this chapter, I would like to express my gratitude to the late Faleh A. Jabar, who provided me with invaluable information, contacts and suggestions, especially in the early phase of my research on this topic. His brilliant contributions to the field of Iraqi studies will be sorely missed.

Bibliography

Abdullah, Thabit A. J., *A Short History of Iraq* (Harlow: Longman, 2011).

Ali, Tariq, *Bush in Babylon. The Recolonisation of Iraq* (London: Verso, 2004).

Al-Mallak, Qahtan Habib, 'Kalima', in Qahtan Habib al-Mallak (ed.), *Al-shahid khalid ahmad zaki. Batal intifadat al-ahwar – haziran 1968* [The martyr Khalid Ahmad Zaki, hero of the guerrilla in the marshes – June 1968] (Baghdad: Dar al-Mallak li al-Funun wa al-Adab wa al-Nashr, n.d.): 7.

[62] Haydar, *Walima*, 16, 21 and 133–40.

Al-Mallak, Qahtan Habib, *Shadharat min tarikh jam'iyyat al-talaba al-'iraqiyyin fi al-mamlaka al-muttahida* [Fragments from the history of the Iraqi student society in the UK] (Baghdad: Dar al-Mallak li al-Funun wa al-Adab wa al-Nashr, 2013).

'Awraq anis ajiba', in *Shadharat min tarikh jam'iyyat al-talaba al-'iraqiyyin fi al-mamlaka al-muttahida* [Fragments from the history of the Iraqi students society in the UK] (Baghdad: Dar al-Mallak li al-Funun wa al-Adab wa al-Nashr, 2013).

Batatu, Hanna, *The Old Social Classes and the Revolutionary Movements of Iraq. A Study of Iraq's Old Landed and Commercial Classes and of its Communists, Ba'thists, and Free Officers* (London: Saqi Books, 2004).

Benjamin, Walter, 'Theses on the Philosophy of History', in Walter Benjamin, *Illuminations* (New York: Schocken, 2007): 253–64.

Farley, Christ, 'On Khalid', *The Death of an Iraqi Revolutionary. Khalid A. Zaki. A Martyr of Armed Struggle in the Countryside of Southern Iraq* (London: n.p., 1969).

Franzén, Johan, *Red Star over Iraq. Iraqi Communism before Saddam* (New York: Columbia University Press, 2011).

Gabriel, Judith, 'Islamist Protest over Novel Ignites Political Turmoil', *al Jadid. A Review & Record of Arab Culture and Arts* 6, 31 (Spring 2000): 4.

Ghanim, Mauqif Khalaf, *Naziha al-dulaymi wa-dawruha fi al-haraka al-wataniyya wa al-siyasiyya al-'iraqiyya* [Naziha al-Dulaymi, her role in the national and political movement in Iraq] (Baghdad: Dar ar-Ruwad al-Muzdahira, 2014).

Hafez, Sabry, 'The Novel, Politics and Islam. Haydar Haydar's *Banquet for Seaweed*', *New Left Review* 5 (September/October 2000): 117–41.

Haydar, Haydar, *Walima li a'shab al-bahr (nashid al-mawt)* [Banquet for seaweeds: song of death] (Beirut: Dar Amwaj, 2000).

'Intifadat al-ahwar al-musallaha fi al-'iraq' [Guerrilla in Iraqi's marshes] in Qahtan Habib al-Mallak (ed.), *Al-shahid khalid ahmad zaki. Batal intifadat al-ahwar – haziran 1968* [The martyr Khalid Ahmad Zaki, hero of the guerrilla in the marshes – June 1968] (Baghdad: Dar al-Mallak li al-Funun wa al-Adab wa al-Nashr, n.d.): 14–22.

Iranian Student, 'Khalid's Internationalism', *The Death of an Iraqi Revolutionary. Khalid A. Zaki. A Martyr of Armed Struggle in the Countryside of Southern Iraq* (London: n.p., 1969): 3.

Ismael, Tareq Y., *The Rise and Fall of the Communist Party of Iraq* (Cambridge: Cambridge University Press, 2008).

Jabar, Faleh A., 'The Arab Communist Parties in Search of an Identity', in Faleh A. Jabar (ed.), *Post-Marxism and the Middle East* (London: Saqi Books, 1997): 91–107.

Kelidar, Abbas, 'Aziz al-Haj, A Communist Radical', in Abbas Kelidar (ed.), *Integration of Modern Iraq* (New York: St Martin's Press, 1979): 183–92.

Khaz'ali, Subhi, and Qahtan Habib al-Mallak, *Fata al-'iraq. Khalid ahmad zaki* [Khalid Ahmad Zaki, an Iraqi hero], film (Baghdad: Dar al-Mallak li al-Funun wa al-Adab wa al-Nashr, n.d.).

Mahmud, Najm, *Al-sira' fi al-hizb al-shuyu'i al-'iraqi wa-qadayat al-khilaf fi al-haraka al-shuyu'iyya al-'alamiyya* [The conflict within the Iraqi communist party and the rupture in the international communist movement] (Paris: n.p., 1980).

Monk, Ray, *Bertrand Russell. The Ghost of Madness 1921–1970* (London: Vintage, 2001).

Prashad, Vijay, *The Darker Nations. A People's History of the Third World* (New York: The New Press, 2008).

Sa'id, 'Ali Karim, *Al-'iraq. Al-birriyya al-musallaha. Harakat hasan sari' wa-qitar al-mawt 1963 min tarikh al-iraq al-siyasi al-mu'asir madrasat al-'urafa'* [Iraq. The armed beret. The movement of Hasan Sari and the train of death 1963: from the modern history of Iraq] (Beirut: al-Furat li al-Nashr wa al-Tawzi', 2002).

Schmidinger, Thomas, *ArbeiterInnenbewegung im Sudan. Geschichte und Analyse der ArbeiterInnenbewegung des Sudan im Vergleich mit den ArbeiterInnenbewegungen Ägyptens, Syriens, des Südjemen und des Iraq* (Frankfurt am Main: Peter Lang, 2004).

Schoenman, Ralph and Khalid Zaki, 'Death and Pillage in the Congo', *Africa and the World* 4 (January 1965): 21–47.

The Front of Iraqi Revolutionaries in Britain (Founding Committee), 'Editorial. A Year after Khalid (Balance Sheet)', *The Death of an Iraqi Revolutionary. Khalid A. Zaki. A Martyr of Armed Struggle in the Countryside of Southern Iraq* (London: n.p., 1969): 1–3.

Traverso, Enzo, *Left-wing Melancholia. Marxism, History, and Memory* (New York: Columbia University Press, 2016).

Yousif, Salaam, 'Le Déclin de l'Intelligentsia de Gauche en Irak', *Revue des Mondes Musulmans et de la Méditerranée. L'Irak en Perspective* 117–18 (2007): 51–79.

Zaki, Ghazi Ahmad, 'Khalid ahmad zaki', in Qahtan Habib al-Mallak (ed.), *Al-shahid khalid ahmad zaki. Batal intifadat al-ahwar – Haziran 1968*, mulhaq, 1–6 (Baghdad: Dar al-Mallak li al-Funun wa al-Adab wa al-Nashr, n.d.)

Zangana, Haifa, *City of Widows. An Iraqi Woman's Account of War and Resistance* (New York: Seven Stories Press, 2007).

Zangana, Haifa, *Dreaming of Baghdad* (New York: Feminist Press at the City University of New York, 2009).

12

CRISIS AND CRITIQUE: THE TRANSFORMATION OF THE ARAB RADICAL TRADITION BETWEEN THE 1960s AND THE 1980s[1]

Jens Hanssen

Introduction

In this chapter, I revisit two moments of crisis and critique in twentieth-century Arab intellectual history: a public debate between Arab leftists and nationalists in Cairo in 1961, and the emergence of Arab Marxists' scholarship on Materialism and Arabic-Islamic philosophy ten years later. Both moments are embedded in their global and regional contexts, but are articulated by two sets of intellectuals. The first pits Muhammad Hasanayn Haykal (1923–2016) against Clovis Maksoud (1926–2016) over the relationship between the organic intellectual and the state. Haykal's *Crisis of the Intellectuals* (1961) was an attempt by Nasser's 'court intellectual' to goad a reluctant leftist vanguard into his president's project of Egyptian state building.[2] Haykal summoned Arab intellectuals to Cairo for a three-month-long conference in 1961, the result of which was a compromise of sorts: Nasser's adoption of Arab Socialism as state doctrine in the Egyptian

[1] This chapter is part of research funded by my Insight Grant (435–2014–1616) of the Social Sciences and Humanities Council of Canada.

[2] Maqsud, *Azma al-yasar al-'arabi*; Haykal, *Azmat al-muthaqqafin*.

National Charter of 1962.[3] The second moment focuses on the Arab Left's historical-philosophical turn launched by the late Tayyib Tizini (1929–2019) around 1970. Other interlocutors and subsequent commentaries, concluding with Husayn Muruwwa's *Materialist Tendencies in Arabic–Islamic Philosophy* (1978), complement my discussion. I contend that my preliminary findings historicise our knowledge of the complexities of the Arab Left and teach us to step out of our particular academic moments when practising cultural critique in response to today's crises.

Most immediately, the 'puzzle' I am interested in is the twin concepts of 'crisis' and 'critique'. The modern Middle East has been saturated with crisis talk, so much so that a new crop of economic historians are developing methodologies in order to avoid the reification of the crisis paradigm.[4] And yet, we have no idea about the genealogy of the term '*al-azma*', etymologically or discursively.[5] The *nahda* texts are often replete with self-criticism and immanent critique which animated both religious reform and literary revival discourses.[6] But they do not invoke an intellectual 'crisis', or define crisis in political terms.[7] The term '*al-azma*' seems to emerge in the 1950s, when rare books such as Ishaq al-Husayni's *The Crisis of Arabic Thought* began to appear in Arabic. Certainly, imperialism and colonial rule have generated ample (self-) criticism since the early *nahda*.[8] But colonial rule, and particularly the 'carrot' of independence built into the Mandate system after the First World War, obstructed the movement from criticism to crisis awareness. As Reinhart Koselleck reminds us, in the cases of eighteenth-century France and Germany, 'while the progressive bourgeoisie provoked a political decision through its

[3] Abdel-Malek, 'The Crisis of the Intellectuals', Ch. 5 in his *Egypt: Military Society*, 189–221; Ginat, *Egypt's Incomplete Revolution: Lutfi al-Khuli and Nasser's Socialism in the 1960s*, 15: 'socially, the "Decrees of July 1961" constituted the most significant step taken by Nasser since he assumed power'.

[4] Jakes, *Egypt's Occupation.*

[5] The 'Suez Crisis' of 1956 was a crisis for the British empire. Nasser's nationalisation of the Suez Canal was his great triumph.

[6] Sachs, 'Futures of Literature'.

[7] Butrus al-Bustani's *Muhit al-muhit* (1870: 8) defines '*al-azma*' in general terms as 'stricture and adversity'.

[8] Hanssen and Safieddine, *The Clarion of Syria: A Patriot's Call against the Civil War of 1860.*

rash criticism and rigorous morality, [its liberal] philosophy of history served to paper over . . . crisis awareness'.[9]

In the Arab world, competing crises of consciousness emerged in the 1950s and found creative expression in Beirut where the 'militant liberalism' of Yusuf al-Khal's modernist Lebanonist journal *Shi'r* challenged the pan-Arabist and Sartrean existentialist *al-Adab* of Suhail Idris.[10] Each group accused the other of cultural isolationism. While the latter espoused Third World internationalism and enlisted literature to struggle against social inequality and neo-colonial dependency, the former professed cosmopolitanism and worried about the standardisation and depersonalisation of life at the hands of Arab tradition and communism. At a landmark conference on Arabic Literature in Rome in late 1961 organised by the CIA-funded Congress for Cultural Freedom (CCF), the *Shi'r* group's crisis-critique argued against Arab authenticity discourses and valorised poetic autonomy in such anti-nationalist terms that even the American organisers had second thoughts about *Shi'r*'s Cold War efficacy.[11] But Arab leftists, too, struggled among themselves finding a role between Arab nationalism and international communism and the place of the past in the present crisis. It was Clovis Maksoud's influential *The Crisis of the Arab Left* (1960) which may have articulated programmatically the structural challenges for the Arab Left after independence for the first time. To this protracted immanent critique we now turn.

The Global Context of Decolonisation

Anti-colonial struggle had raised revolutionary consciousness globally; it was incited and sustained by the Vietnamese victory at Dien Bien Phu in 1954, the Bandung conference in 1955, the Algerian Revolution of 1954–62 and the Cuban Revolution of 1959. In the Mashriq, the unification of Syria and Egypt, the Lebanese Left's uprising against President Chamoun and the Iraqi Revolution marked 1958 as the year of revolution.[12] Decolonisation raised

[9] Reinhard Kosellek, *Critique and Crisis: Enlightenment and the Pathogenesis of Modern Society*, 137.

[10] Creswell, *City of Beginnings: Poetic Modernism in Beirut*; Di-Capua, *No Exit.*

[11] Creswell, *City of Beginnings*, 31–50.

[12] Louis and Owen, *The Revolutionary Year: The Middle East in 1958.*

awareness that the neo-colonial and racist order of things, whether in Israel, Congo, Vietnam, Angola or South Africa, could only be maintained by military force and physical, economic, legal and discursive violence. The question that dominated anti-colonial forces ever since was how to react to this violence, with what kind of counter-violence to resist, and how to bring about a future unbeholden to Western forms of economic and cultural imperialism.

On the one hand, it was a time of Third World optimism. The global non-Alignment Movement was in full swing and Nasser's Cairo became one of its epicentres. The first Afro-Asian Women's Congress was held in the Egyptian capital in January 1961, and the Third Meeting of the All-African Peoples' Conference convened only a fortnight after the Arab intellectuals' meeting ended.[13] On the other hand, the United Arab Republic between Egypt and Syria unravelled acrimoniously, and Nasser launched his ill-fated campaign in North Yemen which arguably began to tilt the Arab Cold War between revolutionary republics and reactionary monarchies in the latter's favour.[14] The Arab region was also a central stage of the global Cold War, where ailing imperial powers and aspiring superpowers competed with each other for political, economic and cultural influence by sponsoring coups, ordering assassinations, offering military aid and investing in cultural diplomacy – here COMINTERN, there CCF.[15]

Recognition of the synchronicity of anti-colonial resistance worldwide led to a sense of empowerment. But, if it turned out that the change the anti-colonial movements fought for was not the change we got, it was not for lack of anticipation or overly optimistic 'romantic vindicationism', as David Scott has recently suggested in respect of the Caribbean case.[16] Amilcar Cabral, agronomist and leader of the Guinea-Bissauian armed struggle against Portuguese colonialism, offered a Fanonian counterpoint to the task of the anti-colonial intellectual. Cabral presented both a vindication of the use of counter-violence and a warning that armed struggle without self-reflection and careful analytical

[13] *The First Afro-Asian Women's Conference, Cairo, 14–21. January 1961*; Wallerstein, *Africa: Politics of Unity*, 1967; Hauser, *No One Can Stop the Rain*; Cooper, *Africa since 1940*.

[14] Kerr, *The Arab Cold War*; Orkaby, *Beyond the Arab Cold War*.

[15] Westad, *The Global Cold War*; Prashad, *Darker Nations* and *Poorer Nations*.

[16] Scott, *Conscripts of Modernity*, 55, 79–84.

calibration was counterproductive. To his question 'What kind of Weapon is Theory?' he answered that 'we are not going to succeed in eliminating imperialism by shouting or slinging insults [but by] taking up arms'. He declared that no revolution will succeed without a revolutionary theory. Cabral's speech at the First Solidarity Conference of the Peoples of Africa, Asia and Latin America in Havanna in 1966 went to the heart of the anti-colonial struggle and the unity of theory and practice. What strikes me as remarkable, and is really quite surprising given that Cabral spoke in Castro's Cuba, is that Cabral insisted that 'national liberation and social revolution are *not* exportable commodities'. In other words, a blind internationalism was doomed without an ideological framework that could account for the 'varied experiences' of past struggles.[17]

The theories produced by Fanon, Cabral, Nasser and many others on the anti-colonial frontlines inspired Black liberation in the USA and the New Left in Europe, particularly in the wake of Nasser's victory at Suez in 1956.[18] Street demonstrations and student protests combined to politicise the university and challenge the production of Eurocentric knowledge.[19] This theory-and-praxis movement culminated in the summer of 1968, as students in Paris, Berlin, San Fransisco and Montreal rose up.[20] But, as François Cusset and others have observed, after this remarkable moment had revolutionised the curriculum and institutionalised Black studies and Women's studies, for example, global critique underwent a profound shift in terms of both content and location. Street and campus politics drifted apart as French poststructuralism captured American universities and became anathema for mass politics and the question of liberation.[21]

While the Arab defeat in June 1967 may have marked the end of Arab decolonisation as a military and Panarab-party project, the Palestinian revolution and its *fida'i* discourse began to capture the imagination of the '68 generation globally.[22] But amid the clamour of militant commitment to

[17] Cabral, *Unity and Struggle*, 119–37.

[18] Katsiaficas, *The Global Imagination of 1968*; Ross, *Fast Cars, Clean Bodies*; Kelly, *Freedom Dreams*; Slobodian, *Foreign Front.*

[19] Felsch, *Der lange Sommer der Theorie.*

[20] Austin, *Moving Against the System.*

[21] Cusset, *French Theory*; Lionnet and Shih, *The Creolization of Theory.*

[22] Lubin, *Geographies of Liberation*; Feldman, *A Shadow over Palestine.*

Palestine, Marxism-Leninism and Maoism, which even infected the hitherto anti-Communist *l'art pour l'art* poet Adonis, critical Arab voices questioned the young generation's revolutionary readiness and offered immanent critiques of the sustainability of *fida'*-ism itself.[23] While some Arab leftist dropouts directed their criticism at themselves and embraced Islamist identity, others turned towards 'deep theory' in an attempt to place their project of liberation on more solid intellectual foundations. Many debated critical theory, from Hegel to Marcuse; others turned to Arabic-Islamic history of philosophy (from Ibn Rushd to Ibn Khaldun), and discovered Hannah Arendt, Michel Foucault and – inspired by Marx's early texts – historical materialism.[24] At around the same time as the dreams of a socialist future turned into the sectarian nightmare of the Lebanese civil war, in Western academia anti-colonial theory turned into postcolonial studies, a transition that Edward Said both launched with his foundational book *Orientalism* in 1978 and lamented subsequently for its depoliticising, identitarian effects.[25] That same year, Husayn Muruwwa published his 'project of a lifetime' and Arab Marxism's theoretical *summa*, *Materialist Tendencies in Arabic-Islamic Philosophy*, in war-torn Beirut. This monumental study was arguably the most sophisticated and last Marxist attempt to blend the medieval Arabic-Islamic heritage ('*al-turath*') with dialectical Materialism before Muhammad 'Abid al-Jabiri gave *al-turath* an Islamic and Foucauldian frame in his multi-tome *Arab Reason* project in the 1980s and 1990s.[26]

Maksoud: *The Crisis of the Arab Left*, 1960

Clovis Maksoud and Muhammad Hasanayn Haykal each published their seminal books in the space of one year. Both addressed the same issue: the crisis of the leftist Arab intellectual. Both came out of the same anti-colonial problem-space. And yet they offered very different answers to the problem

[23] Al-'Azm, *Self-criticism after the Defeat*; Murqus, *The Spontaneity of Theory in Guerilla Practice.*

[24] Bardawil, 'The Inward Turn and Its Vicissitudes'; Hanssen, 'Hannah Arendt in Arab Political Culture'.

[25] Adel Iskander and Hakem Rustem (eds), *Edward Said: A Legacy of Emancipation and Representation* (California University Press, 2010); Abu-Manneh, *After Said.*

[26] Al-Jabiri, *Arab-Islamic Philosophy*; *The Formation of Arab Reason.*

of how the Arab world could overcome the residues of Western imperialism and develop on its own terms. Maksoud's *The Crisis of the Arab Left* (1960) identified a twofold crisis: bourgeois national liberation achieves a feeling of political liberty without real social equality, while economistic socialism only achieves a feeling of collective sovereignty at the expense of real political liberty. As an Arab whose first name – Clovis – Nasser once ridiculed as the epitome of French Catholic imperialism, Maksoud grappled with majoritarian rule.[27] To prevent Arab nationalism from turning totalitarian, the leftist vanguard, whose 'will to achieve progressive goals was not matched by its theoretical and organisational skills', must replace idealism, identity and isolationism with 'substantive socialism' and on this basis it must act in the service of the people and not the other way round.[28]

Published a year before the Cairo conference, *The Crisis of the Arab Left* served as the Arab socialists' 'position paper'. Maksoud was born in Oklahoma and educated in Lebanon, where he graduated from the American University of Beirut (AUB) in the year of the *nakba*. Like so many of this cohort of AUB students, he joined radical parties. He became a leading theorist for Kamal Jumblat's Progressive Socialist Party.[29] While Jumblat's socialist humanism was still manifest in Maksoud's *Crisis of the Arab Left*, after Nasser's victory at Suez he had begun to shift his theoretical work to the Baath Party where he operated in the later mould of independent radical leftists like Elias Murqus (1929–91) and Yasin al-Hafiz (1930–78).[30] Maksoud had a long and distinguished career as Arab League ambassador to India from 1961 to 1966 and to the USA and UN in the 1980s, before he famously and publicly resigned from his post after the Iraqi invasion of Kuwait in 1990.[31]

In *The Crisis of the Arab Left*, Maksoud laid out his critique. The Arab Left is both real and rooted in the Middle East,[32] has increasingly popular appeal over the 'racist, religious, tribal and fascist' Right, and has become

[27] Maqsud, *Azma al-yasar al-'arabi*, 113–21.

[28] Ibid., 53.

[29] Richani, *Dilemmas of Democracy and Political Parties in Sectarian Societies*, 41.

[30] On Jumblat's political philosophy, see Hanssen (2014a).

[31] Maqsud, *Min zawaya al-dhakira*.

[32] Maqsud, *Azma al-yasar al-'arabi*, 26–7.

'an effective political force since the Palestine War . . . because the defeat showed up the Arab leadership's incapacity and bankruptcy'. But it had not yet been able to control, or even influence, political events since 1948.[33] Leftists, especially vanguardist intellectuals, need to recognise that they have to operate at grass-roots level to attract the masses, not least since the army has captured the state in Egypt and Iraq.[34]

Maksoud defined the Left ecumenically as 'all sectors striving towards the inclusion of the masses in politics, and for the minimisation of class differences'. This broad aim requires firm commitment to 'the practical-theoretical connection', for material conditions determined thought, and progress was the 'true expression of life'.[35] Despite his call for 'substantial socialism', Maksoud's analysis remained locked in leftist battles of positions. The Arab Left ought to reject communism, represented by arguably the best-organised parties with the largest memberships in the region, as a 'capitalist plot' and demand an anti-Stalinist stance. The Arab Left needed to organise in its own progressive parties if it was to overcome vanguardist isolation and translate its theoretically superior analysis into meaningful political and socio-economic change.

In Syria, 'a progressive class rose from within the ranks of the military' during a period of democratic rule since the ouster of Col. Adib al-Shishakli in 1954. In Egypt the situation was different. After the Free Officers' coup of 1952 the military encouraged 'the rise of a technocratic class'.[36] Because of this 'intellectual openness', progressives from around the Arab world aligned themselves with the Egyptian regime, especially after the Bandung conference.[37] The dilemma here was that the Egyptian military-technocratic complex rebelled against the political system as a whole instead of democratising it, which, according to Maksoud, remains the task of the intellectuals.[38]

[33] Ibid., 6–8, 31–4.

[34] Ibid., 53–60.

[35] Ibid., 11.

[36] Ibid., 34–5.

[37] Ibid., 63–6.

[38] Ibid., 43–51.

The Cairo Conference: The Intellectual and the Postcolonial State in 1961

The Cairo gathering of young leftist theoreticians and an older, nationalist generation of Egyptian littérateurs from March to July 1961 was, in the words of one participant, 'the greatest controversy launched by the government since 1952'.[39] It is unclear who participated in Haykal's event and how often the participants physically met. Anouar Abdel-Malek, whose account this section treats as a main source, had left Egypt for France in 1959, for example. In fact, much of the debate seems to have occurred on the pages of *al-Ahram*, *Ruz el-Yusuf* and *al-Masa'*. At the height of the Arab Cold War and the Algerian Revolution, it pitted Nasserist nationalists, independent Marxists, Arab socialists, liberal intellectuals and conservative secular literateurs against each other in such a way that Haykal could fashion himself as agenda-setter and mediator. Possibly in recognition of the quality of his *The Crisis of the Arab Left*, the director of the Arab Socialist Association (ASA), the Free Officer Kamal Rif'at, invited Maksoud into this socialist 'think tank' and to participate in the deliberations in Cairo. The ASA provided a space for heated internal debates about what kind of socialism best suited Egypt, and what role the intellectuals played in the young Arab revolutionary republics at a time when Nasser's regime kept communists and independent Marxists in jail. Lutfi al-Khuli, himself a recently released Egyptian Marxist lawyer and *al-Ahram* opinion page editor, was also a regular fixture in the ASA.[40] Other recently released Egyptian leftists whom Haykal added to *al-Ahram*'s editorial board also participated in the Cairo gathering, as did Jubran Majdalani from Lebanon, Khayr al-Din Hasib from Iraq, and the FLN cadre Muhammad Harbi.[41]

In addition to al-Khuli's *al-Ahram* group and the members of the ASA circle, participants included Egyptian academics like Murad Wahba, Magdi Wahba, 'Abd al-Malik 'Awda and Louis 'Awad, professor of English literature at Cairo University and eminent historian of the Egyptian *nahda*,

[39] Abdel-Malek, *Egypt: Military Society*, 190.

[40] Ginat, *Egypt's Incomplete Revolution*, 49–69.

[41] Ibid., 55–7.

right-wing Nasserists like the chairman of the National Educational Committee, Major Salah Dessouki, the ageing *nahdawi* 'Abbas Mahmud 'Aqqad, the Darwin translator Isma'il Mazher, the pro-American positivist, Zaki Naguib Mahmud,[42] and the popular historian of Egypt, Husayn Fawzi.

At the heart of the debate was the relationship between the military rulers and the Marxists. The Egyptian Left had refused to be recruited into the state apparatus without prior resolution of the problem of the relations between the Revolutionary Command Council and themselves, many of whom had spent extended periods in prison. Nasser had famously poured scorn on Egyptian academics in his *The Philosophy of Revolution*, as 'sycophants and self-absorbed miracle performers who have no clue about making themselves useful to society'.[43] But without these very intellectuals, so Haykal baited his colleagues, neither renewal nor mobilisation was possible.

Lutfi al-Khuli started the public deliberations on 12 March with a series of articles in *al-Ahram* on 'The Crisis of the Arab Intellectuals'. He identified three overlapping intellectual crises: stifled creativity, lack of historical depth and a decline in critical method.[44] Dr 'Abd al-Malik 'Awda offered a practical explanation for what he considered were the three main factors contributing to the intellectual crisis since 1945: isolation, withdrawal into self and diffusion.[45] The Cairo University Professor Magdi Wahba registered a sixfold 'crisis in confidence' among Egyptian intellectuals, including: the non-participation

[42] On Naguib, see von Kügelen, *Philosophie, Wissenschaft, und Religion*, 108–12. See also Binder, 'Hermeneutics of Authenticity', in his *Islamic Liberalism: a Critique of Development Ideologies*, 299–314.

[43] After a visit to a university, Nasser stood up and said, 'Every one of us is able in his own way to perform a miracle. His primary duty is to bend every effort to his work. And if you, as university professors, were to think of your students' welfare, and consider them as you should . . . you would be in a position to provide us with the fundamental strength to build up our motherland.' Gamal Abdul-Nasser, *Egypt's Liberation*; *The Philosophy of the Revolution*, 37.

[44] Largely because of a 'gap between their aspirations and the moral and material depression of Egyptian society'. He argued that 'Arab society today needs intellectuals who can impart light to people's eyes and inculcate [their people with] the nation's traditional values and information about human achievements in order to expand their horizons'. Ginat, *Egypt's Incomplete Revolution*, 57.

[45] Abdel-Malek, *Egypt: Military Society*, 192.

of the intellectuals in the army's action of July 1952; the feeling of frustration; withdrawal into self ('the intellectuals return to their cultural barracks'); the poverty of the Egyptian intellectuals, a fact that 'compels them to appear as propagandists for the government instead of being its critics'; and, finally, 'the overabundance of civilisation that was a result of the imitation of foreign models to such a point that the Wafdists, the Moslem Brotherhood or the Communists alike could not provide a revolutionary theory or philosophy of society'. He concluded that, on the one hand, the 'intellectual feels that Gamal Abdel Nasser is basically right'. At the same time, Wahba asserted, intellectuals are naturally inclined towards critique: 'this internal contradiction in the very heart of the Arab intellectual's personality tears him apart inside and makes him an unproductive being.'[46]

'Aqqad, in turn, complained that modern Arab intellectuals had become too focused on rights, forgetting their duties to the nation.[47] Mazher added that 'the intellectuals had wandered away from spiritual values'.[48] And Zaki Naguib Mahmud opined that the meeting had been 'called too soon, before maturity's arrival, which could bring only disappointment'.[49] One Dr Khafif claimed that Egyptian intellectuals had been void of any meaningful revolutionary input until 1961. Louis 'Awad disagreed: 'This revolution existed in its entirety before 1952; otherwise it would have been impossible for it to occur.'[50] Generations of secular intellectuals, not the military, he and others argued, had made Arab independence conceivable in the first place.

Muhammad Hasanayn Haykal: *The Crisis of the Intellectuals*

Haykal's book *The Crisis of the Intellectuals* was published after the Cairo conference and consisted of seven chapters that he had previously published as articles in the Egyptian press in response to the debates during the Cairo gathering.[51]

[46] Ibid., 195.

[47] 'The modern intellectual always thinks of what he calls his rights, of what he believes them to be, and very seldom of his obligations.' Abdel-Malek, *Egypt: Military Society*, 192.

[48] Abdel-Malek, *Egypt: Military Society*, 192.

[49] Ibid., 192.

[50] Ibid., *Egypt: Military Society*, 195.

[51] Unfortunately, the book does not reference the time of publication of each article. I was therefore unable to reconstruct the chronology of the debate.

Haykal had graduated in journalism from the American University of Cairo and cut his teeth as a war correspondent, first in the Second World War and then in the War for Palestine three years later. It was there that he met the thirty-year-old Colonel Gamal Abd al-Nasir and struck up a lifelong friendship with him. Nasser's occasional speechwriter and political adviser, Haykal became editor-in-chief of *al-Ahram* in the wake of the Suez triumph. He continued to play an important role in Egyptian and Arab affairs even though he did not get on with Sadat and criticised Mubarak severely in the 2000s.

In *The Crisis of the Intellectuals'* first chapter, Haykal asks: 'Is there a crisis? Where did it begin? And how did it unfold?' The problem, as he saw it, was intellectual fragmentation during the United Arab Republic, and he explains that his motivation for hosting the conference was to merge the revolutionary driving forces – the vanguard consisting of 'the army and the masses' – with the intellectual class 'who had the opportunity to learn from them in order to extend and sustain the revolution'.[52] In a sustained response to Murad Wahba's cultural autopsy, Haykal claimed that there were only 'three crises between the revolutionary vanguard of experience' and the overly 'pessimistic intellectuals . . . with [all their] knowledge' and historical consciousness: the intellectuals' demand for the army's return to barracks after 1952; the return to parliamentary life and political parties after 1954; and their general preference for 'elected deputies [lit., men of trust] over experts and technocrats'.[53] And a crisis there was. In subsequent articles/chapters Haykal opined that those who claimed that there was none failed to accept that the fact that the military had to enter politics was evidence for it. It was the army that responded to the calls of the masses, and if it was the only social force to implement social democracy, then intellectuals had a problem.[54]

Nasser had famously claimed in his *The Philosophy of Liberation* that a role was waiting to be filled for him and the Free Officers. Haykal recognised that the new leadership needed the intellectuals to 'direct' them in this 'role play'. But for him, intellectuals first had to live down their history of collusion with the British and the monarchy before 1952. Even though he

[52] Haykal, *Azma al-muthaqqafin*, 11–13.

[53] Ibid., 52.

[54] Ibid., 39.

granted that intellectuals participated in the July revolution too, the stigma of nefarious foreign influence hung over them on the pages of *The Crisis of the Intellectuals*. If they called for a return to parliamentary life, this reeked of a return to the party system so discredited under British rule. The genius of the revolutionary forces was that they confronted the political system *tout court* and effected auspicious change that intellectuals only theorised.[55] And yet, a closer look at Haykal's defence of the military path to development reveals both his embrace of modernisation theory and his deep suspicion of both leftists, whom he cursed as communists throughout the book, and liberals. Haykal effectively rejected Clovis Maksoud's project of the Arab Left's socialism that 'guarantees individual liberty to participate in the social',[56] or Jumblat's 'socialist humanism', and instead championed single-party rule as the purveyor of national liberation and Arab identity at the cost of individual liberty.

Tayyib Tizini: The Arab Left 'materialises' Arabic-Islamic Philosophy

> The becoming-philosophy of the world is at the same time a becoming-world of philosophy, its realisation is its destruction.[57]

The book *Project for a New Perspective on Medieval Arabic Thought* by the then 33 year-old Syrian Philosopher Tayyib Tizini may not have aged well.[58] Nevertheless, its originality and impact cannot be over-estimated within the post-'67 intellectual effervescence. Possibly the first book-length interpretation of Aristotelian influence on Abbasid-Andalusian philosophy by an Arab Marxist, Tizini's study offered the kind of analytical substance that Maksoud had demanded in 1960. Submitting the work as a doctoral dissertation to the University of (East-) Berlin, Tizini drew on his supervisor Hermann Ley's

[55] Ibid., 64.

[56] Maqsud, *Azma al-yasar al-'arabi*, 173–4.

[57] Karl Marx's dissertation *Differenz der Demokritischen und Epikureischen Naturphilosophie*, cited in Henri Lefebvre, *Dialectical Materialism*, 17.

[58] Tizini, *Mashru' ru'ya jadida li al-fikr al-'arabi fi al-'asr al-wasit*; von Kügelgen, *Averroës und die Arabische Moderne*, 237–60.

Studie zur Geschichte des Materialismus (1957) and on Ernst Bloch's *Avicenna und die Aristotelische Linke* (1952).[59] For these German Marxists, Arabic-Islamic philosophy along an Ibn Sina–Ibn Tufayl–Ibn Rushd–Giordano Bruno–Karl Marx '*isnād*' served as a materialist foil to provincialise the Western history of philosophy and to challenge Stalin's mechanistic doctrines that had discredited Materialism and Marxism alike. Bloch even claimed that, without Avicenna and the Aristotelian Left, 'Marx would not have been able to stand on its feet the Hegelian world-idea so naturally'.[60] Tizini's materialist *turath* project, by contrast, aimed to launch an Arab cultural revolution. He argued that historical materialist conditions particular to the emergence of Islam animated competing physical, metaphysical and practical approaches to creation, causation and change, culminating in Mut'tazilite rationalism, and al-Kindi's and al-Farabi's harmonisation of Greek philosophy and Islamic creed.[61] Like Bloch, Tizini credits Ibn Sina with overcoming the Aristotelian dualism of form and matter, God and world. After Ibn Sina it became conceivable to think of the self-generative power of the natural world.[62] Modern Materialism which emerged out of natural philosophy in the early eighteenth century as an approach to understanding the constitution of the world of things and the relationship of humans to nature was indebted to the Avicennan tradition.[63]

Immediately after its publication, Tizini's Arabic book generated a lively debate in Arab intellectual circles, including Islamic thinkers like the influential Egyptian scholar of Islam, Muhammad 'Imara (b. 1931), and the Moroccan philosopher of Islamic history and self-professed Foucauldian, Muhammad 'Abid al-Jabiri (1936–2010), who popularised the concept of

[59] Ernst Bloch, *Avicenna and the Aristotelian Left*.

[60] Bloch, *Principle of Hope*, 208.

[61] Tizini, *Materialieauffassung*, 29–68.

[62] Ibid., 69–79.

[63] Lefebvre, *Dialectical Materialism*. Materialism's disreputableness is as old as the term itself, and the word 'materialist' continues to be used to charge capitalists and Marxists alike with greed, lust, atheism and immorality. See A. Schmidt, *Die Geschichte des Materialismus*, 53: 'While Bruno still speaks of Epicurians in his *Von der Ursache, dem Prinzip und dem Einen*, the term "*Materialismus*" is first used in the correspondence between Samuel Clarke and G. W. Leibniz in 1717.'

al-turath al-islami in the West. 'Imara published his book *Materialism and Idealism in Ibn Rushd's Philosophy* a year before Tizini's s study appeared in Arabic, and articulated the idea that 'Ibn Rushd did not just anticipate, but superseded, materialism by combining it with religious ideas'.[64] al-Jabiri, who had cut his political teeth under the guidance of the trade union leader Mahdi Ben Barka, taught Tizini's materialism book as a core text in his high-school classes before he turned against Marxism as one of three forms of reality-averse (*salafi*) thought in his *Critique of Arab Reason*, a multi-tome study that has dominated modern Islamic thought since the 1980s.[65]

Materialism continued to offer Arab leftists a viable analytical tool-kit for dissecting and overcoming the cultural crisis of the Arab world into the 1980s. In 1980, the Syrian dissident theoretician of the reconciliation between Marxism and Arab nationalism, Elias Murqus, published a translation of Bloch's early 1960s Tübingen lectures, and Zaynab Khudhayri wrote her important doctoral thesis *Ibn Rushd's Influence on Medieval Philosophy* with a serious materialist and secularist bend and a nod to Tizini and Bloch.[66] But arguably the most comprehensive and sophisticated account of the materialist tradition of Arabic-Islamic philosophy was Husayn Muruwwa's *Materialist Tendencies in Arabic-Islamic Philosophy*.[67] Born in 1910, Muruwwa was destined for clerical greatness. But while studying in the Shi'ite seminaries of Najaf, he discovered for himself *nahdawi* writers and, through them, Marxism and, later, social realism. After stints in Baghdad and Moscow, he returned to Lebanon in 1949 and joined the Communist Party in 1954. Following his participation in the Second Conference for Asian and African Writers in Cairo in 1962, Muruwwa dedicated himself to systematising the dialectical relationships between: theory and praxis; culture and politics; global anti-imperialism and local, Lebanese class struggle; and Arabic-Islamic *turath* and the materialist canon of European philosophy.[68]

[64] Kügelgen, *Averroës und die Arabische Moderne*, 201.

[65] Kügelgen, *Averroës und die Arabische Moderne*, 226, 262, 268. The other two *salafi* tendencies, according to al-Jabiri, are al-Afghani's and Abduh's reformist Islam and the liberal Orientalism of Western scholars.

[66] Khudhayri, *Athar Ibn Rushd fi falsafa al-'usur al-wusta*.

[67] Husayn Muruwwah, *Naza'at al-maddiyya fi al-falsafa al-'arabiyya al-islamiyya*.

[68] Di-Capua, 'Homeward Bound'; Younes, 'A Tale of Two Communists'. See also Frangie, this volume.

In *Materialist Tendencies in Arabic-Islamic Philosophy* Muruwwa identified a crisis in Arab thought, a crisis he had first articulated in an article for *al-Thaqafa al-Wataniyya* on the occasion of the communist celebration of the 1,000th *hijri* anniversary of Ibn Sina's birth in 1952.[69] The remedy he prescribed in 1978 was a methodological critique.[70] At a time when 'Salafists attacked the relations between Aristotle's logical and philosophical heritage and prominent Islamic logicians and philosophers', Muruwwa contended that the Abbasi-Andalusian legacy for Arabic-Islamic philosophy and its place in the present struggle had not really been dealt with properly by Arab intellectuals and academics.[71] Either historians worked on isolated historical details or they produced grand commonplaces about the scientific genius of the Arabs.[72] Philosophers like 'Abd al-Rahman Badawi merely offered idealist and metaphysical theories and were devoid of historical dynamics and socio-economic contexts.[73] Tizini was the first to introduce a historical materialist methodology into study of the Arab past. But, reminiscent of Benjamin's anti-historicist dictum 'For every image of the past that is not recognised by the present as one of its own concerns threatens to disappear irretrievably', Muruwwa argued that what has been missing, even in Tizini's trail-blazing work, was a theory of the present – an investigation of the stakes philosophy has in today's liberatory and revolutionary needs.[74]

Conclusion

As Samer Frangie argues in this volume, the assassination of Husayn Muruwwa in 1987 marked the end of the Lebanese Communist Party as a militant project of liberation, and the starting point of its replacement by the Islamic resistance. Within the narrative of this chapter, his assassination also marked the end of the Arab Left's development of a dialectical

[69] Di-Capua, 'Homeward Bound', 49.

[70] Muruwwa, *Naza'at al-maddiyya*, 23–32.

[71] Ibid., 18–19.

[72] Representative of this popular approach was the Lebanese historian 'Umar Farrukh's *'Abkariyya al-'arab fi al-'ilm wa al-falsafa* (1945), published as *The Arab Genius in Science and Philosophy* by the American Council of Learned Societies, Washington, 1954.

[73] Muruwwa, *Naza'at al-maddiyya*, 18, fn. 1.

[74] Muruwwa singles out Mahdi 'Amil's work as the exception that proves the rule. Muruwwa, *Naza'at al-maddiyya*, 7. See Walter Benjamin's fifth thesis on *The Concept of History*.

alternative to identitarian conceptions of Arab and Islamic histories that Muruwwa saw spreading in the 1970s. The probing of Arab materialism that Tayyib Tizini had begun in the aftermath of the 1967 defeat was not the only alternative to emerge in the 1970s. The Arab Left rose in the 1960s in part to overcome retreats into the spiritual, personalist and individual domains, against what many conceived as academic leftovers from colonial-era quietism: formal logic, textualism, mysticism and gnosis.[75]

If Clovis Maksoud had hoped that socialist humanism would provide the substance and content of a new philosophy of praxis, the Cairo conference of 1961 turned out to be merely a staking out of positions between Marxism and Arab nationalism. To the extent that the Marxists resisted being co-opted into the Nasserist project, it came at the expense of political marginalisation. After Sartrean existentialism fell out of favour in Egypt because of Sartre's 'betrayal of Palestine' in 1967, a new, more radical leftist student movement emerged in the 1970s.

The engagement with German philosophy in general and Marxist materialism in particular was another way in which the Arab Left responded to 1967. During the brutal 1980s in which the Lebanese civil war and the Iran–Iraq war decimated critical thinkers left, right and centre, the Arab Left was no closer to transforming its analytical superiority into political power than it had been when Maksoud called for it in 1960. But if the Arab Left's progressive idea that the right critique will necessarily overcome any crisis seems overly optimistic, universalist and future-oriented in hindsight, today's practice of critique would have come across as defeatist, particularist and conservative to the anti-colonial thinkers of the past.

Bibliography

Abdel-Malek, Anouar [1962], *Egypt: Military Society* (New York: Vintage, 1968).

Abdul-Nasser, Gamal, *Egypt's Liberation; The Philosophy of the Revolution*, introd. Dorothy Thompson (Washington: Public Affairs Press, 1956).

Abu-Manneh, Bashir (ed.), *After Said: Postcolonial Literary Studies in the 21st Century* (Oxford: Oxford University Press, 2018).

[75] Abdallah Laroui, *The Crisis of the Arab Intellectual; Traditionalism or Historicism?*, 3–5.

Austin, David, *Moving Against the System: The Black Writers Congress 1968 and the Making of Global Consciousness* (London: Pluto Press, 2018).

Al-'Azm, Sadek J., *Self-Criticism After the Defeat* (London: Saqi Books, 2011).

Al-Bustani, Butrus, *Kitab Muhit al-muhit* [The circumference of the ocean] (Beirut: 1870).

Al-Husayni, Ishaq, *The Crisis of Arabic Thought* (Beirut: Dar Beirut li al-Taba'a wa al-Nashr, 1954).

Al-Jabiri, Mohammed Abed, *Arab-Islamic Philosophy; a Contemporary Critique*, trans. from the French by A. Abbassi (Austin: University of Texas Press, 1999).

Al-Jabiri, Mohammad Abed, *The Formation of Arab Reason: Text, Tradition and the Construction of Modernity in the Arab World* (London: I. B. Tauris, 2011).

Bardawil, Fadi, 'The Inward Turn and Its Vicissitudes: Culture, Society, and Politics in Post-1967 Arab Leftist Critiques', in M. Bouziane, C. Harders and A. Hoffmann (eds), *Local Politics and Contemporary Transformations in the Arab World: Governance Beyond the Center* (New York: Palgrave Macmillan, 2013): 91–109.

Bardawil, Fadi, *When All This Revolution Melts into Air: The Disenchantment of Levantine Marxist Intellectuals*, PhD dissertation (New York: Columbia University mimeo, 2010).

Binder, Leo, *Islamic Liberalism: A Critique of Development Ideologies* (Chicago: University of Chicago Press, 1988).

Bloch, Ernst, *Avicenna and the Aristotelian Left*, trans. L. Goldman and P. Thompson (New York: Columbia University Press, 2018).

Bloch, Ernst, *The Principle of Hope*, Vol. 1 (Cambridge, MA: MIT Press, 1995).

Brouwers, Michaelle L., *Political Ideology in the Arab World: Accommodation and Transformation* (Cambridge: Cambridge University Press, 2009).

Cabral, Amilcar, *Unity and Struggle* (New York: Monthly Review Press, 1979).

Cooper, Fred, *Africa since 1940* (Cambridge: Cambridge University Press, 2002).

Creswell, Robin, *City of Beginnings: Poetic Modernism in Beirut* (Princeton: Princeton University Press, 2019).

Cusset, François, *French Theory: How Foucault, Derrida, Deleuze, & Co. Transformed the Intellectual Life of the United States* (Minneapolis: University of Minnesota Press, 2008).

Di-Capua, Yoav, 'Homeward Bound: Husayn Muruwwa's Integrative Quest for Authenticity', *Journal of Arabic Literature* 44 (2013): 21–52.

Di-Capua, Yoav, *No Exit: Arab Existentialism, Jean-Paul Sartre & Decolonization* (Chicago: Chicago University Press, 2018).

Felsch, Philipp, *Der lange Sommer der Theorie: Geschichte einer Revolte* (Frankfurt am Main: Fischer, 2016).

Farrukh, 'Umar, *'Abkariyya al-'arab fi al-'ilm wa al-falsafa* (Beirut: al-Maktaba al-'Ilmiyya, 1945). Trans. as *The Arab Genius in Science and Philosophy* (Washington: American Council of Learned Societies, 1954).

Feldman, Keith, *A Shadow over Palestine: The Imperial Life of Race in America* (Minneapolis: University of Minnesota Press, 2015).

Frangie, Samer, 'On the Broken Conversation between Postcolonialism and Intellectuals in the Periphery', *Studies in Social and Political Thought* 19 (2011): 41–54.

Frangie, Samer, 'Theorizing from the Periphery: The Intellectual Project of Mahdi Amil', *IJMES* 44 (2012): 465–82.

Ginat, Rami, *Egypt's Incomplete Revolution: Lutfi al-Khuli and Nasser's Socialism in the 1960s* (Portland: Frank Cass, 1997).

Hanssen, Jens (2014a) 'Between Minorities and the Masses: Kamal Jumblat (1917–1977)', at *Structures of Personalized Power in the Modern Middle East*, conference held at UCLA in honour of Roger Owen, May 2014, <http://www.international.ucla.edu/news/article.asp?parentid=126397> (last accessed 2 March 2020).

Hanssen, Jens (2014b) 'Translating Revolution: Hannah Arendt in Arab Political Culture' (Otto-Suhr Institut, Berlin), <www.HannahArendt.net> (last accessed 2 March 2020).

Hanssen, Jens and Hicham Safieddine, *The Clarion of Syria: A Patriot's Call against the Civil War of 1860* (Berkeley: University of California Press, 2019).

Hanssen, Jens and Max Weiss (eds), *Arabic Thought against the Authoritarian Age: Towards a History of the Present* (Cambridge: Cambridge University Press, 2018).

Hauser, George, *No One Can Stop the Rain: Glimpses of Africa's Liberation Struggle* (1989).

Haykal, Muhammad H., *Azmat al-muthaqqafin* [The crisis of the intellectuals] (Cairo: Dar al-Udaba', 1961).

Iskander, Adel and Hakem Rustem (eds), *Edward Said: A Legacy of Emancipation and Representation* (Berkeley: University of California Press, 2010).

Jakes, Aaron, *Egypt's Occupation: Colonial Economism and the Crises of Capitalism* (Stanford: Stanford University Press, 2020).

Katsiaficas, George, *The Global Imagination of 1968: Revolution and Counterrevolution* (Oakland, CA: PM Press, 2018).

Kelly, Robin, *Freedom Dreams: The Black Radical Imagination* (Boston: Beacon Press, 2002).

Kerr, Malcolm, *The Arab Cold War: Gamal 'Abd al-Nasir and His Rivals, 1958–1970* (Oxford: Oxford University Press, 1971).

Khudhayri, Zaynab, *Athar Ibn Rushd fi falsafa al-'usur al-wusta* [The influence of Ibn Rushd on medieval philosophy] (Cairo: Dar al-Thaqafa li al-Nashr wa al-Tawzi', 1983).

Kosellek, Reinhard [1959], *Critique and Crisis: Enlightenment and the Pathogenesis of Modern Society* (Cambridge, MA: MIT Press, 1988).

Kügelen, Anke von, *Philosophie, Wissenschaft, und Religion: Religionskritische Positionen um 1900* (Berlin: Klaus Schwartz Verlag, 2017).

Kügelen, Anke von, *Averroës und die Arabische Moderne: Ansätze zu einer Neubegründung des Rationalismus im Islam* (Leiden: Brill, 1994).

Laroui, Abdallah, *The Crisis of the Arab Intellectual; Traditionalism or Historicism?*, trans. D. Commell (Berkeley: University of California Press, 1976).

Lefebvre, Henri [1940], *Dialectical Materialism*, trans. J. Sturrock (London: Cape, 1970).

Lionnet, Françoise and Shu-mei Shih, *The Creolization of Theory* (Durham, NC: Duke University Press, 2011).

Louis, Roger and Roger Owen, *The Revolutionary Year: The Middle East in 1958* (London: I. B. Tauris, 2002).

Lubin, Alex, *Geographies of Liberation: The Making of an Afro-Arab Political Imaginary* (Durham, NC: University of North Carolina Press, 2014).

Maqsud, Klufis, *Azma al-yasar al-'arabi* [The crisis of the Arab Left] (Beirut: Dar al-'Ilm li al-Malayin, 1960).

Maqsud, Klufis, *Min zawaya al-dhakira: mahattat rihlah fi qitar al-'uruba* (Beirut: al-Dar al-'Arabiyya li al-'Ulum Nashirun, 2014).

Marx, Karl [1841], *Differenz der Demokritischen und Epikureischen Naturphilosophie*, in Karl Marx und Friedrich Engels, *Werke* 40 (Berlin: Dietz Verlag, 1968), 264–2.

Marx, Karl, *Theses on Feuerbach* (1845).

Murqus, Ilyas, *'Afawiyya al-nazariyya fi al-'amal al-fida'i* [The spontaneity of theory in guerrilla practice] (Beirut: Dar al-Haqiqa, 1970).

Muruwwah, Husayn, *Naza'at al-maddiyya fi al-falsafa al-'arabiyya al-islamiyya* [Materialist tendencies in Arabic-Islamic philosophy] (Beirut: Dar al-Farabi, 1979).

Orkaby, Asher, *Beyond the Arab Cold War: The International History of the Yemen Civil War, 1962–68* (Oxford: Oxford University Press, 2017).

Prashad, Vijay, *Darker Nations: A Popular History of the Third World* (New York: The New Press, 2007).

Prashad, Vijay, *Poorer Nations: A Possible History of the Global South*, foreword by Boutros Boutros-Ghali (London: Verso, 2013).

Richani, Nazih, *Dilemmas of Democracy and Political Parties in Sectarian Societies: The Case of the Progressive Socialist Party of Lebanon 1949–1996* (New York: St Martin's Press, 1998).

Ross, Kristin, *Fast Cars, Clean Bodies: Decolonization and the Reordering of French Culture* (Cambridge, MA: MIT Press, 1995).

Sachs, Jeffrey, 'Futures of Literature: *Inhitat, Adab, Naqd*', *Diacritics* 37, 4 (2007): 32–43, 45–55.

Schmidt, Alfred, *Die Geschichte des Materialismus*, ed. K.-J. Grün and O. Hein (Leipzig: Salier Verlag, 2017).

Scott, David, *Conscripts of Modernity: The Tragedy of Enlightenment* (Durham, NC: Duke University Press, 2004).

Slobodian, Quinn, *Foreign Front: Third World Politics in Sixties West Germany* (Durham, NC: Duke University Press, 2012).

The First Afro-Asian Women's Conference, Cairo, 14–21 January, 1961 (Cairo: Amalgamated Press of Egypt, 1961).

Tizini, Tayyib, *Mashru' ru'ya jadida li al-fikr al-'arabi fi al-'asr al-wasit* [A new perspective on Arabic thought in the Middle Ages] (Damascus: Dar Dimashq, 1972).

Wallerstein, Immanuel, *Africa: Politics of Unity: An Analysis of a Contemporary Social Movement* (New York: Random House, 1967).

Westad, Odd Arne, *The Global Cold War* (Cambridge: Cambridge University Press, 2007).

Younes, Miriam, 'A Tale of Two Communists: The Revolutionary Project of the Lebanese Husayn Muruwwa and Mahdi 'Amil', *Arab Studies Journal* 24 (2016): 98–116.

13

THE AFTERLIVES OF HUSAYN MURUWWA: THE KILLING OF AN INTELLECTUAL, 1987

Samer Frangie

Introduction

On Wednesday 18 February 1987, amid raging street battles tearing apart West Beirut, the left-leaning Lebanese daily *al-Safir* headlined its front page as follows:

> *A War of Position Between Amal and the Progressives and Communists in its Second Day: 30 Killed and 120 Wounded*
> *A New Political and Security Map for West Beirut*
> *Kanaan Personally Supervises the Ceasefire and an Invitation to Jumblat and the Leaders of the Parties to visit Damascus Today.*[1]

The civil war was entering one of its darkest moments, with the conflict between former allies spiralling out of control.[2] The head of the Syrian

[1] *Al-Safir* (18 February 1987).

[2] Against the background of the sieges of the Palestinian camps, the Iranian–Syrian negotiations regarding Lebanon and the growing hold of the Syrian regime over the 'Lebanese dossier', the Shi'ite militia of Amal and the Druze militia of the Progressive Socialist Party allied with the Lebanese Communist Party (LCP) fought an all-out war over the control of the Muslim neighbourhoods of Beirut, or what was known as 'West Beirut'.

intelligence in Lebanon, Ghazi Kanaan, was in charge of asserting the Syrian regime's control over the unfolding events of the Lebanese civil war. The battles of February 1987, which ended with the entry of the Syrian army into West Beirut, were to become a crucial step in the establishment of the *Pax Syriana*, the regional and domestic arrangement that ended the civil war and established the parameters of the post-war settlement that followed.

Under the main headline was a short piece entitled 'The Assassination of Husayn Muruwwa' and signed 'al-Safir'. The piece broke the news of the assassination of the Lebanese intellectual and member of the Central Committee of the Lebanese Communist Party (LCP), Husayn Muruwwa (1910–87). The murder was attributed to the 'civil war' that had been raging since 1975, a war of which the latest episode was covered in the headline above. Muruwwa, an intellectual and writer, and a symbol of tolerance and openness, was killed by unnamed attackers, 'without memory', who ignored the achievements of their victim, according to the unsigned eulogy.[3] An absurd and violent war had led ignorant assassins to their tolerant victim – this was the story on the morning of Wednesday 18 February 1987.

The political headline and the eulogy coexisted uneasily on the front page of the leftist daily, and called for some clarification of their possible connections. The 'official' interpretation was provided on the same page by the owner and chief editor of *al-Safir*, Talal Salman, for whom the assassination was the result of the absurd violence raging in Beirut, a violence that could only stop with the intervention of Damascus.[4] The assassination was depoliticised: Muruwwa was killed because of his tolerance, his assassins were unnamed barbarians, the murder was not a targeted action but the result of an absurd and senseless violence. The pacification of Beirut was not simply a military process, but also a discursive one. The victims of the allies of the Syrian regime had to be de-politicised, left in a political limbo where unnamed killers assassinate cultural symbols.

[3] 'Ightiyal husayn muruwwah' (The assassination of Husayn Muruwwa), *al-Safir* (18 February 1987): 1.

[4] Talal Salman, 'Hatta yakun liqa dimashq salaman bayn al-mukhtalifin badal al-harb bayn mutahalifin' (Let the meeting of Damascus be a peace between enemies rather than a war between allies), *al-Safir* (18 February 1987): 1.

The year 1987 was pivotal, not only for the unfolding events of the Lebanese civil war, but, more importantly for this essay, for the Lebanese Left and its subsequent histories. Muruwwa was not assassinated solely because of his cultural credentials. He was the latest victim in a series of assassinations that targeted leftist intellectuals and militants, as part of a process to weaken the Lebanese Left and replace it with the emerging Islamic resistance. His killers were not unnamed militiamen, but were close to the emerging political force. In 1987, the processes unleashed by the sectarian civil wars on the one hand and the Iranian revolution on the other coalesced in the military defeat of the LCP and the transformation in the registers of resistance. The left ceased to be a political player, to become instead an object of memory, its end coinciding with that of the civil war. Muruwwa died as a citizen, an intellectual and a cultural symbol, not as a member of a political party.

The Afterlives of an Autobiography, 1985

A few years before the assassination, in 1985, the Lebanese poet and writer Abbas Baydoun (b. 1945) conducted a series of interviews with Muruwwa, published in *al-Safir* over six editions.[5] The interviews became Muruwwa's autobiography, published under the title *I Was Born As an Old Man (or a Cleric) and I Will Die As a Child* (*Wulidtu shaykhan wa amutu tiflan*, 1990). The title alluded to the main trope of the biographical narrative, namely a story of a transition from tradition to modernity, from religion to communism, from Najaf to Beirut, or from old age to youth. The autobiography became iconic in the manner it integrated the various ruptures of Muruwwa's life with a historical trajectory that culminated in Marxism, providing a biographical grounding to the teleological self-assurance of the Arab Left. Muruwwa's trajectory from a religious education, through *nahdawi* authors and into Marxism mirrored the self-history of the left as the last moment in a story that moves from the religious reformism of the nineteenth century through the *nahda* of the early twentieth century and into the various socialist and communist experiments of its second half.

[5] For more information on Husayn Muruwwa's life, see Browers, 'Between Najaf and Jabal 'Amil'; Di-Capua, 'Homeward Bound', 21–52; Gran, 'Islamic Marxism', 106–20; Naef, 'Shi'i-Shuyu'i'; Tamari, 'Reclaiming the Islamic Heritage', 121–9.

If the 1987 assassination was at the intersection of two processes, the unfolding civil war and the demise of the left, the 1985 autobiography straddled another transformation that started with the dark years of the eighties and culminated in the post-war period. This transformation saw the demise of the left as a theoretical and ideological system. The post-civil war coincided with another post-war, the global post-Cold War, and the subsequent turn to liberalism imposed a 'self-critical' take on the autobiographies of the left. The years that followed the end of the civil war witnessed the publications of numerous autobiographical accounts, spanning different literary genres, narrating the experiences of the 'generation of the sixties'.[6] Whether through interviews, autobiographies or autobiographical fictions, the lived history of the left became one of the vehicles through which questions of self-criticism, ideological reconversion, memory and the civil war circulated. The promised conversion *to* Marxism was replaced by a disillusioned conversion *from* Marxism to different forms of proto-liberal thought, one that was often phrased in confessional terms.[7]

In the changing political and ideological conjuncture, Muruwwa's biography became doubly out of tune: out of tune with the political sensibility of the Lebanese post-war, but out of tune also with the liberal mood of the early 1990s and the disillusionment with Marxism or Leftism. Muruwwa's recollections might have been one of the last autobiographies 'that demonstrate the mastery of different worlds by successfully forming one's own life between them and from them',[8] a resolution that was not available to the subsequent generations whose experience was one of crisis and disillusionment. It is this non-availability that forms the topic of this essay, the unravelling of the 'sense of an ending', to use Kermode's terms[9] on the afterlives of Muruwwa's biographical sketch. By tracing these afterlives, from Muruwwa's biographical

[6] For some examples of these works, see Baydoun, *Sa'at al-takhalli*; Beydoun, 'Adraktu hadhihi al-ayam', 249–70; al-Bizri, *Sanawat*; al-Daif, *Dear Mr. Kawabata*; Maalouf, *Les Désorientés*; Trabulsi, *Surat al-fata bi al-ahmar*.

[7] For some examples of this conversion, see Bardawil, *When All This Revolution Melts into Air*; Schumann, 'The "Failure"', 404–15.

[8] Philipp, 'The Autobiography', 602–3.

[9] Kermode, *The Sense of an Ending*.

interview to the Lebanese artist Rabih Mroué (b. 1967)'s redeployment of his image, through the revisiting of this moment by the Lebanese poet and writer Abbas Baydoun (b. 1945) in his autobiographical essays and the travelling of Muruwwa to Western academe as a Shi'ite intellectual, the essay maps the changing sensibilities that surround the memories of the Lebanese Left.

The present essay, as such, is not about Muruwwa's autobiography, or the biographies of the left in general. Rather, it is fundamentally about the travel of texts across changing political conjunctures and their interpretations against the shifting contours of the present. Far from simply being a trove of micro details with which to colour the macro histories of the left, biographical and autobiographical works can be read as representative of broader naratorial and affective dispositions, dispositions that are to be excavated and read often against thc grain of the present. More specifically, the afterlives of Muruwwa's text provide one of the ways through which we can understand what is at stake in the manifold ways we inhabit the 'futures past' that haunt our present.[10] Marxism without its teleological guarantees translated into biographies without resolution, leaving the act of conversion stranded without any sense of ending. It is this rupture in the tradition of the left that has marked our present and that Muruwwa's afterlives illustrate.

A Transnational Story of Conversions

I was Born As an Old Man (or a Cleric) and I Will Die As a Child (*Wulidtu shaykhan wa amutu tiflan*) traced the intellectual and political transformations of Husayn Muruwwa, across ideological traditions and geographical spaces. These transformations culminated in his final residence in Beirut, as a member of the LCP engaged in what he called *mashru' al-'umr*, the project of a lifetime, namely the reclaiming of the progressive and radical elements in the Arab Islamic heritage, or *turath*, through a dialectical and materialist reading of this tradition. This project coalesced in a massive study of *turath* entitled *al-naza'at al-maddiyya fi al-falsafa al-'arabiyya al-islamiyya*, or *Materialist Trends in Arab-Islamic Philosophy*, published in 1978. *Wulidtu shaykhan* provides a glimpse into Muruwwa's trajectory from Najaf to *al-naza'at al-maddiyya*, the story of a cleric in-the-making turned communist intellectual.

[10] Koselleck, *Futures Past.*

The biographical interviews start with Muruwwa's childhood as a cleric-in-the-making. Born in 1910 (or 1908), in the Shi'ite region of Jabal Amil in South Lebanon, Muruwwa was destined to follow in the footsteps of his father, sheikh Ali Muruwwa, a cleric who, like his predecessors, studied in Najaf. From an early age, Muruwwa's place in this long genealogy of religious scholars was settled, with his father subjecting him to a strict upbringing which, as he recalled, deprived him of the innocence of his childhood, hence the title of the autobiographical interviews. Muruwwa's future, like that of his ancestors, 'pointed eastward toward Iraq',[11] and despite the death of his father he would be sent to Najaf at the age of fourteen, via Beirut, Damascus and Baghdad. As he wrote in his autobiography, 'there were no signs on the road, but we used to guide ourselves through the signs left by those who preceded us'.[12] Najaf was still closer to Jabal Amil than Beirut, the new capital of the modern state of Lebanon.

It is in Najaf that the 'conversion' started, or as Muruwwa puts it in another essay, 'From Najaf, Marx Entered my Life'.[13] Next to the loosely structured religious training offered in Najaf, Muruwwa was exposed to a wide range of writings, most of which were disapproved of by his colleagues and teachers. From poetry to the canon of the *udaba* and the reformist writers of the *nahda*, the literary and political imagination of Muruwwa was transformed in ways which could not be restricted any more to the strict confines of the existing religious curriculum. The young student was not alone in expressing these doubts, as a movement of discontent with the ossified structures of Najaf was growing. This was partly the result of the activism of young reformist clerics from Jabal Amil, some of whom formed an association known as *al-shabiba al-ʿamiliyya al-najafiyya* (amili-najafi youth). Muruwwa published an essay in the Amili journal *al-ʾIrfan* in defence of some of their claims. Faced by the rejection and censure of most of his colleagues and teachers, Muruwwa, deeply distraught, left Najaf in 1928.

Over the next six years, Muruwwa moved between Damascus, Beirut and Baghdad. He enrolled at Damascus University, where he studied law

[11] Di-Capua, 'Homeward Bound', 26.

[12] Muruwwah, *Wulidtu shaykhan*, 30.

[13] Muruwwah, 'Min an-Najaf', 2–3.

and literature and began his career as a writer. But he would be persuaded to resume his religious education, and in 1934 he returned to Najaf and became a *mujtahid* in 1938, even though he knew by then than he would not continue a religious career. It is this decision that cemented the narrative of rupture that structured the biographical interviews. But the rupture would wait a few years before being cemented through sustained engagement with Marxism.

After Najaf, Muruwwa moved to Baghdad, where he taught, wrote and got involved in politics. It is there that he was exposed to Marxism, through texts such as the *Communist Manifesto*, *Capital* and Lenin's *The State and Revolution*. In the subsequent years, he deepened his interest in Marxist theoretical works and got closer to the communist camp in Iraq, even though he would not join the Iraqi Communist Party. The tipping point was the events of 1948 in Iraq, known as the *wathbah*, a series of clashes with the government caused by the popular reaction against the Anglo–Iraqi treaty and the harsh repression of communists. During the uprising of 1948, Muruwwa, as he recalled, was impressed by the discipline and integrity of the communists, which, in conjunction with the growing appeal of materialism, led him even closer to the communist camp. He was exiled from Iraq in 1949, following the publication of an article critical of the Iraqi prime minister Nuri as-Sa'id (1888–1958). Muruwwa returned to Lebanon and joined the Lebanese Communist Party in 1951. The conversion was complete. The *mujtahid* became a comrade.

As Di-Capua noted, Muruwwa's trajectory seems to support the thesis of a modernist conversion from Shi'ism to Marxism, one influenced by Taha Hussein's 'emancipatory narrative of conversion and rebirth'.[14] This thesis received further support in being a collective act of transformation, as Silvia Naef showed in her study of conversion to communism in the holy city of Najaf.[15] In other words, it was in the spirit of the times. Against this thesis of a rupture, Di-Capua stressed the integrative dimension of Muruwwa's intellectual project, bringing together various strands of thought in 'a relentless quest for cultural authenticity in times of modern rupture'.[16] Muruwwa's turn

[14] Di-Capua, 'Homeward Bound', 22.

[15] Naef, 'Shi'i-Shuyu'i'.

[16] Di-Capua, 'Homeward Bound', 24–5.

to *turath*, according to this reading, brought together the various intellectual influences of Muruwwa in the 'project of a lifetime'.

For the sake of this essay, it is less important to determine whether Muruwwa's dominant experience is one of rupture or of integration. Rather, what is important to note is that a sense of resolution was available to Muruwwa and his generation, a sense of resolution that recoded ruptures as diachronic stages rather than synchronic shifts. Marxism was still a promise of reconciliation, one that provided the grounds for a resolution of the various ruptures and their synthesis into a 'project of a lifetime'. The presence of such promise was not a question of individual choice or capacity. Rather, it was the result of an underlying ideological and theoretical problem-space, in which Marxism was still an answer, or *the* answer. The ruptures faced by the young *mujtahid* turned communist comrade could still be integrated into an overarching historical arc that pointed towards Marxism. The historical trajectory played out transnationally between Jabal Amil, Najaf, Damascus, Baghdad and Beirut, and a certain resonance existed between the individual, social and ideological levels of this historical transformation. In a way, this was the promise of communism, a promise of integration and totalisation.

Armed with this promise, Muruwwa became part of the Central Committee of the Lebanese Communist Party from 1965, even though his militant days were mostly cultural. He contributed to the journal of the party, *al-Tariq*, and then established *al-Thaqafa al-wataniyya* with Muhammed Dakrub (1929–2013) in 1951, under the editorial guidance of Farajallah al-Helu (1906–59). Muruwwa became a literary critic, campaigning for a Marxist-influenced cultural renewal, alongside his colleagues Raif Khuri (1913–67) and Umar Fakhuri (1895–1946). Alongside his literary interest, Muruwwa was engaged in a project of rereading and re-interpretation of the Islamic *turath*, a project that culminated with his magnum opus *al-naza'at al-maddiyya*. The interviews ended in 1985. Two years later, Muruwwa was assassinated.

Stunted Conversion

Muruwwa's story of a transnational conversion hid another conversion, one foregrounded by Abbas Baydoun in his short introduction to the biographical interviews. Baydoun located Muruwwa's trajectory and conversion against the experience of a generation of young clerics and literary figures whose political coming of age in the 1930s coincided with the solidification of the modern state of Lebanon. These young clerics were following in the footsteps of an early wave of reforms in Jabal Amil.[17] Yet these reforms could not reverse the process that saw the gradual dismantling of the world of the nineteenth-century *ulema* and its replacement with new cultural imaginaries, modes of subjectivities and political vocabularies. As Baydoun recalled in his interview with Fadi Bardawil, these young clerics, displaced by the structures of the emerging nation-state, were rendered 'provincial' or 'autochthonous' to the new capital city and its political, aesthetic, linguistic and cultural concerns.[18]

Baydoun's introductory essay starts with an enumeration of the sorry fate of some of the main representatives of this reformist moment, such as Musa al-Zayn Sharara (1902–86), Abd-el-Mutlib al-ʾAmin (1916–74) and Sadr al-Din Sharaf al-Din (1912–70), whose pioneering reformism led them to a state of social isolation or alienation in the emerging national field. Muruwwa – and this is what rendered him exceptional for Baydoun – 'survived' his generation and the transformations that brought it to its end. The rupture with Najaf was a collective process that could still be comprehended from inside the co-ordinates of the tradition of Jabal Amil. Yet looming on the horizon was a more difficult exile, to Beirut and through it to the institutions of modern Lebanon. This transition was the real experience of exile, Baydoun wrote, as opposed to the 'internal exile' to Najaf.[19] By stressing the national at the expense of the transnational aspect of the journey, Baydoun included in the story of Muruwwa a dimension that was often missed by the narratives around his ideological conversion. Yet, even with this change in focus, the left remained a promise, this time the promise of adaptation to the structures of the modern nation-state.

This was in 1985. In 1987, Husayn Muruwwa was assassinated, putting an end to the two conversions that formed the background of his autobiography.

[17] This generation followed in the footsteps of what Sabrina Mervin has called the 'Shi'ite reformism' or 'modernism' of Jabal ʿAmil in the late nineteenth and early twentieth century; see Mervin, *Un Réformisme Chiite*.

[18] Bardawil, *When All This Revolution Melts into Air*, 64–5.

[19] Muruwwah, *Wulidtu shaykhan*, 10.

In its wake, the autobiographies of leftist intellectuals took a more inward turn, reflecting the growing rift between the individual and political trajectories and the unravelling of the sense of ending provided by the embrace of communism. It is this new biographical sensibility that is expressed in the work of Abbas Baydoun, who, between 2011 and 2014, published four novels that can be termed autobiographical.[20] 'I write autobiography to say that I am not proud of it', Baydoun declared,[21] to capture his mode of life-writing that stressed the stagnation or stunted conversion of the generation after. The transnational gave way to a national perspective, and the sense of resolution was replaced by a sense of stagnation and disillusioned resignation.

In 'A Device for Removing Illusions' (*alat li-naz'i al-awham*) the last vignette of the first book, *Frankenstein's Mirrors* (*Maraya frankenshtayn*), Baydoun sketched an autobiographical essay that resonated with that of Muruwwa, albeit as its disillusioned successor.[22] In contrast with Muruwwa's transformational trajectory, Baydoun's essay stagnated, turned on itself, constantly reflecting on its own development, narrating the experience of a stunted growth, or a false conversion. Baydoun's trajectory started from the same rupture with a traditional environment as that of Muruwwa. But whereas the latter had to struggle against dominant traditional values, pushing against them in the name of a rising modern ideology, Baydoun found these traditions already waning, rendering the rupture, as he wrote, 'too easy'. The class of *ulema* that formed the background of Muruwwa's biography were already rendered irrelevant by the time Baydoun was growing up:

> this was the period when the *ulemas* took off their turbans, and some of them went as far as proving their beliefs through western studies of their religion and prophet. Those who were the most disciplined were those that suffered the most. Some of them went mad, others committed suicide, others killed their wives, while the rest roamed the streets. Some of them fell victim of a depression, only to be rescued from it by death . . .

20 Baydoun, *Maraya frankenshtayn*; *Album al-khisara*; *Sa'at al-takhalli*; *Al-shafiyyat*.

21 'Interview with Abbas Beydoun', *al-Khalij* (15 April 2013), <http://www.alkhaleej.ae/supplements/page/43356dc6-554c-4efd-b312-7b61cfd93cc3)> (last accessed 2 March 2020).

22 Baydoun, *Maraya frankenshtayn*, 137–53.

When Baydoun's generation 'bypassed them, they surrendered easily', he wrote; 'we left behind us things that did not show any resistance'.[23] This easy generational victory was the cause of Baydoun's stunted growth, leaving him and his generation under the impression that nothing existed outside of their ideological constructions. 'This experience led to our regression to a state of irresponsible childhood',[24] Baydoun wrote, setting the theme of the autobiographical essay as the journey of an irresponsible child amid the radical era of the 1960s and its ideological self-delusions. Childhood no longer had the connotations of a playful beginning, as it had with Muruwwa's transition from a sheikh to a child. Rather, it referred now to a state of stunted growth, to an individual biography that stagnated despite the political and ideological transformations that surrounded it, to the absence of both ruptures and resolution. From there on, the autobiographical essay flowed as a story of self-delusion that culminated in the Lebanese Left's support for the civil war and its 'revolutionary violence', a violence that cost Muruwwa his life.

Inheriting Muruwwa

What remained was an inexplicable feeling of nostalgia, Baydoun wrote towards the end of his essay: 'A nostalgia to no one or to nothing in particular, with the feeling growing stronger the more it lacked an object.'[25] Baydoun succumbed to this inexplicable feeling at the end of the essay, the way one succumbs to an 'old love'.[26] It was this connection to the past that was to be inherited by the Lebanese artist and playwright Rabih Mroué (b. 1967), the grandson of Husayn Muruwwa, a connection that formed one of the running threads of his work.[27] In one of his early performances, *Three Posters* (2000), written with the Lebanese writer Elias Khoury (b. 1948), Mroué started, from the videotaped testimony of a communist soon-to-be-martyr, Jamal

[23] Ibid., 140.

[24] Ibid., 141.

[25] Ibid., 148.

[26] Ibid., 153.

[27] Mroué was part of the LCP, albeit for a brief period. As Elias notes: 'Unlike that of the other artists who do not specifically subscribe to an ideological doctrine, Mroué's work is involved with working through his own biographical attachment to communist ideals after the elimination of the Left in Lebanon'; in Elias, *Surviving Images*.

al-Sati, to tackle the question of the history of the left and its memory. In one of the scenes, Mroué, playing himself, dedicated the show to the memory of the martyrs of the Lebanese National Resistance Front, of which Husayn Muruwwa was one.

Muruwwa was still a name in a list of martyrs, assassinated by the allies of the Syrian regime, an uncomfortable martyr in an ideological space that was dominated in 2000 by the same allies. In subsequent works, Mroué tackled the memory of the left, but he returned to Muruwwa in 2009, in a political conjuncture radically transformed by the rise to dominance of Hizbullah, the Shi'ite militia that inherited the left, despite participating in its destruction. In his lecture performance *The Inhabitants of Images* (2009), Mroué examined the changing political conjuncture through the transformation in the visual landscape of Lebanon. Against the regimented posters of the martyrs of Hizbullah, Mroué inserted the image of Husayn Muruwwa, as a commentary on the rise to power of the Shi'ite party, a commentary made through the register of absence. The image of Muruwwa is not hanging on a wall in the street, but left in private spaces, Mroué noted. This image, he concluded, 'would be our image today, an absent one. The absence of their party, of our party, of the role of the Left.' The private archives have become the repository of the ruins of the political left.

The trajectory that started with Baydoun, from the transnational to the national, continued with Mroué, this time, from the national to the private. It is in this context that Mroué turned to the idioms of the family, recoding Muruwwa explicitly as a grandfather. In 2014, Mroué, together with his brother Yasser (b. 1970), wrote *Riding on a Cloud*, a performance that chronicled the life of Yasser, wounded in the Lebanese civil war. On 17 February 1987, Yasser was wounded by a sniper as he was rushing home upon hearing the news of the assassination of his grandfather, Husayn Muruwwa. Yasser's injury, his grandfather's death and the end of the left as a political project intersected on this fateful day, foregrounding the question of the inheritance of a lost political ideology, or recoding the public defeat in private terms. As Yasser stated in the performance:

> I joined the Communist Party, just like all my brothers did. My grandfather was a communist. His children became communists like him. And his children's children became communist as well. Therefore, we are all communists

> by inheritance, except for my grandfather. Communism is in our blood, not in our mind. Strangely, when my grandfather died, we all stopped being communists.[28]

Despite stopping being communists, Yasser and Rabih remained descendants of the left, or inheritors, having to sift through its ruins for what might still be affirmed in the present. Yasser was shot by a sniper as he crossed a street in Beirut. The bullet hit his head and caused partial paralysis and aphasia, a disorder that caused impairments in speech and language modalities. The afterlives of the left are not a mediated memory, mediated through images, videotapes or texts, but rather a visceral and direct experience, one that is found in the shards of a bullet lodged in the brain of a brother. At the age of seventeen, Yasser, as he stated jokingly in the performance, had to return to kindergarten rather than go to university as planned. Husayn Muruwwa transitioned from old age to childhood; Abbas Baydoun remained stuck in childhood; Yasser had to return to childhood.

Converting to the Present

With Abbas Baydoun and Rabih Mroué, a certain intergenerational conversation reached its end, one that took Muruwwa from a transnational model of conversion to a private reminder of the defeat. From the reformists of the early twentieth century in Jabal Amil to the contemporary art scene of post-war Lebanon, the figure of Muruwwa accompanied the transformations in the leftist tradition. But his afterlives were not restricted to the various shatterings of this tradition in the work of Baydoun and Mroué. Muruwwa's transnational autobiography travelled beyond the scope of the Lebanese national field and was folded into another generational succession, which provided his trajectory with a different sense of ending. This generational lineage was that of Shi'ite Islamic thought, with Muruwwa being recoded from the last communist into one of its generations.

Spurred by the growing questioning of the foundational distinction between the secular and the religious in Arab thought and the increasing salience of the 'Muslim Question', the academic gaze turned to excavating

[28] Rabih Mroué, *Three Posters* (2000), theatre performance and video.

the traditions of the Islamic other. And it is in these traditions that Muruwwa reappeared as one of the intellectuals belonging, albeit differently, to the tradition of the left and that of Shi'ite political thought. In their study of the development of Shi'ite political thought in Lebanon, Rula Jurdi Abisaab and Malek Abisaab moved beyond the antagonism between the left and Shi'ite Islamic thought, to recode Marxism and communism as a stage in the formation of modern Shi'ite Islamism.[29] Muruwwa formed one of the moments in which the two traditions collided, a collision that was resolved in the subsequent development of modern Shi'ite Islamism. In a similar spirit of studying the imbrications of the 'secular' and the 'religious' in Arab political thought, Michaelle Browers located Husayn Muruwwa in the second generation of 'Shiʿi intellectuals', as she called them, a lineage which culminated with the generation of Hizbullah in Lebanon.[30]

What these biographies underscored, in addition to the need to question the secular/religious divide in the study of Arab thought, is the different sense of ending offered by political Islam, a sense of ending that recoded Muruwwa as a marginal figure in a tradition that has a present. Read against the various forms of 'left-wing melancholia'[31] deployed by the Lebanese successors of Muruwwa, these genealogies seemed to offer the communist intellectual a new lease of life, albeit as part of a different intellectual tradition, a tradition that had generations of intellectuals, rather than simply childhood, to depart from, be stuck in or return to.

The afterlives of Muruwwa are not about Muruwwa and his intellectual trajectory, but about the travel of texts across political conjunctures and the present moment from which such texts are read. The urgent question is less about the historical figure that is being *historicised* and more about the present of the *historicising* gaze, a present whose contours are yet to be determined. From what present are we *historicising* the left and for what stakes? Muruwwa's sense of resolution is out of sync with the sensibilities of the present. The tragic inheritance or the Islamist resolution seems exhausted by now, leaving the leftist tradition without a sense of ending. It is this sense of

[29] Abisaab, *The Shi'ites of Lebanon.*

[30] Browers, 'Between Najaf and Jabal ʿAmil', 6–9.

[31] Traverso, *Left-wing Melancholia.*

ending that is now needed, to avoid the permutations of childhood that have dominated the leftist narration of itself.

Bibliography

Abisaab, Rula Jurdi, and Malek Abisaab, *The Shi'ites of Lebanon: Modernism, Communism, and Hizbullah's Islamists* (Syracuse: Syracuse University Press, 2017).

Al-Bizri, Dalal, *Sanawat al-sa'adat al-thawriyya* [The years of revolutionary happiness] (Beirut: Dar al-Tanwir, 2016).

Al-Daif, Rashid, *Dear Mr. Kawabata*, trans. Paul Starkey (London: Quartet, 1999).

Bardawil, Fadi A, *When All This Revolution Melts into Air: The Disenchantment of Levantine Marxist Intellectuals*, PhD dissertation (New York: Columbia University mimeo, 2010).

Baydoun, Abbas, *Maraya frankenshtayn* [Frankenstein's Mirrors] (Beirut: Dar al-Saqi, 2011).

Baydoun, Abbas, *Album al-khisara* [The album of loss] (Beirut: Dar al-Saqi, 2012).

Baydoun, Abbas, *Sa'at al-takhalli* [The year when we succumbed] (Beirut: Dar al-Saqi, 2013).

Baydoun, Abbas, 'Interview with Abbas Beydoun', *al-Khalij* (15 April 2013).

Baydoun, Abbas, *Al-shafiyyat* (Beirut: Dar al-Saqi, 2014).

Beydoun, Ahmad, 'Adraktu hazihi al-ayam' [I realised these days], in *Ahmed Beydoun: 'Alam al-ma'ani wa al-mabani*, Ism 'Alam 5 (Beirut: Manshurat al-jami'a al-antuniyya, 2011): 249–70.

Browers, Michaelle L., 'Between Najaf and Jabal 'Amil: A Portrait of Three Generations of Shi'i Intellectuals', *TAARII Newsletter* (2009).

Di-Capua, Yoav, 'Homeward Bound: Husayn Muruwwah's Integrative Quest for Authenticity', *Journal of Arabic Literature* 44 (2013): 21–52.

Elias, Chad (Illinois: Northwestern University mimeo, 2011).

Gran, Peter, 'Islamic Marxism in Comparative History: The Case of Lebanon, Reflections on the Recent Book of Husayn Muruwah', in Barbara Stowasser Freyer (ed.), *The Islamic Impulse* (Washington: Georgetown University Press, 1987): 106–20.

Kermode, Frank, *The Sense of an Ending: Studies in the Theory of Fiction* (Oxford: Oxford University Press, 1967).

Koselleck, Reinhart, *Futures Past: On the Semantics of Historical Time* (New York: Columbia University Press, 2004).

Maalouf, Amin, *Les Désorientés* (Paris: Le Livre de Poche, 2014).

Mervin, Sabrina, *Un Réformisme Chiite: Ulémas et Lettrés du Ǧabal 'Amil (actuel Liban-Sud) de la Fin de l'Empire Ottoman à L'indépendance du Liban* (Paris, Beyrouth, Damas: Karthala, CERMOC, IFEAD, 2000).

Muruwwah, Husayn, 'Min al-najaf dakhala hayati marks [From Najaf Marx entered my life]', *Al-Tariq*, 1984.

Muruwwah, Husayn, *Wulidtu shaykhan wa amutu tiflan* [I was born as an old man (or a cleric) and I will die as a child] (Beirut: Dar al-Farabi, 1990).

Naef, Silvia, 'Shi'i-Shuyu'i: Or How to Become a Communist in a Holy City', in Rainer Brunner and Werner Ende (eds), *The Twelver Shia in Modern Times: Religious Culture and Political Culture* (Leiden: Brill, 2001).

Philipp, Thomas, 'The Autobiography in Modern Arab Literature and Culture', *Poetics Today* 14, 3 (1993): 573–604.

Ross, Kristin, *May 68 and its Afterlives* (Chicago: University of Chicago Press, 2002).

Schumann, Christoph, 'The "Failure" of Radical Nationalism and the "Silence" of Liberal Thought in the Arab World', *Comparative Studies of South Asia, Africa and the Middle East* 28, 3 (2008): 404–15.

Tamari, Steve, 'Reclaiming the Islamic Heritage: Marxism and Islam in the Thought of Husayn Muruwah', *Arab Studies Journal* 3, 1 (1995): 121–9.

Trabulsi, Fawwaz, *Surat al-fata bi al-ahmar: ayyam fi al-silm wa al-harb* [Portrait of a young man in red: days in peace and war] (Beirut: Dar Riad el-Rayyes, 1997).

Traverso, Enzo, *Left-wing Melancholia: Marxism, History, and Memory* (Columbia: Columbia University Press, 2017).

AFTERWORD. THE ARAB LEFT: FROM RUMBLING OCEAN TO REVOLUTIONARY GULF

Abdel Razzaq Takriti

To reflect on the historical period covered in this volume is to be struck by the paramount role that the Arab Left, broadly defined, played in shaping it. By 1970, the vast majority of Arab peoples lived in states that officially advocated anti-colonialism, regional unity and socialism.[1] The largest and most consequential political formations – the Communist parties, the Baath and the Movement of Arab Nationalists (MAN) – were openly revolutionary in orientation and had either originally been Marxists or had initiated a transition, with uneven results, to Marxism and other varieties of socialism. All of these formations were transnational, simultaneously operating in multiple Arab countries. Tendencies and currents splitting from them or arguing against them embraced a range of radical world views, drawing on Maoism, Trotskyism, the New Left and other schools of thought. The transistor radio ensured that most Arab households were exposed, through the broadcasts of *Sawt al-Arab* (Voice of the Arabs), to the political discourse of Nasserism. The settler-colonial zones of Algeria and Palestine gave rise to two of the most influential liberation struggles on the global stage, mobilising millions of people in these countries and far beyond. Cairo, Algiers, Beirut

[1] These included the most heavily populated Arab countries – Egypt, Sudan, Algeria, Iraq and Syria – as well as the less densely populated states of Libya and South Yemen.

became prominent revolutionary hubs on the global solidarity map, hosting movements and figures from across the world and affording them diplomatic, material and military support.

The left – understood in the chapters of this volume as encompassing movements and figures that were anti-colonial in orientation, non-aligned or pro-Eastern Bloc in Cold War allegiance, secular in approach, reformist or revolutionary in social outlook and economically redistributive, promoting agendas ranging from social democratic welfarism to outright communist seizure of the means of production – played a defining role in social struggles. It established women's organisations, promoted feminist thought, and pushed for personal status reforms – through the efforts of such figures as Naziha al-Dulaymi, a communist and the Arab world's first female Arab cabinet minister. The left also formed trade unions, mobilised workers and organised labour agitation; it launched student uprisings, and carried out agrarian resistance at the hands of resolute organisers like Shahinda Maqlad. Culturally, it had an enormous presence. Palestine's national poet, Mahmoud Darwish, cut his teeth in the communist movement; its celebrated novelist, Ghassan Kanafani, was the official spokesperson of the Popular Front for the Liberation of Palestine (PFLP); its influential feminist, Mai Sayigh, was an eminent figure on the left wing of Fateh; and the doyen of its historians, Bayan Nuwayhed al-Hout, was a former Baath cadre. The red flag was also flying high in other settings. The intellectual scene across the region was dominated by thinkers who had belonged to the left or were associated with it: Munif al-Razzaz, Samir Amin, George Tarabichi, Anouar Abdel-Malek, Sadiq Jalal al-Azm, Mahdi Amel and Abdallah Laroui, to mention just a few names out of many. The Arab literary canon as a whole was shaped by authors who had initiated their careers on the left or had inhabited its domains for their entire lives. Among hundreds of major writers, one thinks of Iraq's Bader Shakir al-Sayyab, Jordan's Ghaleb Halasa and Libya's Ibrahim al-Kouni, not to mention Egypt's Amal Dunqul. In the struggle for a secular society governed by social justice, leftist intellectuals battled the forces of sectarianism, the religious right and parochial local identities.

Despite this enormously rich legacy, aspects of which are illuminated in every part of this collection, the history of the Arab Left was literally shelved for several decades. Whereas the 1960s and 1970s witnessed the publication of instant classics such as Anouar Abdel-Malek's *Egypt: Military Society*, Hanna Batatu's *The Old Social Classes* and Fred Halliday's *Arabia Without Sultans*, subsequent decades saw a more limited output in the English language.[2] The reasons are well-known and are tediously rehearsed: the rise of religious movements, authoritarian retrenchment, Israeli military expansion, the recolonisation of key Arab states, the establishment of US hegemony over most regional governments, and the rapid spread of neoliberalism at the expense of socialist or social democratic projects. These phenomena were accompanied by the bureaucratisation of some leftist parties, the transformation of others from rebels against authority into repressive organs of the state, the ideological decline of communist currents in tandem with the collapse of the Soviet Union, and the major blows dealt against the Palestinian anti-colonial resistance structures. This is not to mention thc fall of the Arab regional security system. Whereas the 1950s and 1960s were synonymous with the quest for Arab unity and tricontinental cooperation, today's 'colonial present' is dominated by the descent into internal sectarian, ethnic and localised strife.[3] In this atmosphere, whatever traces left of the Arab Left were marked by a culture of defeat; hope was overtaken by melancholy and the celebrated progressive tradition of auto-critique seemed to give way to debilitating collective performances of self-flagellation.

Fortunately for current scholarship, the triumph of defeatism was not complete. Several participants in the events of the past chose to channel their energies into assiduous historical preservation rather than negative lamentation, sensing that their experiences were too consequential to be denied to future generations. One thinks here of Hani al-Hindi and Abdel Ilah al-Nasrawi's concerted effort at collecting and publishing selected documents of the Movement of Arab Nationalists, or of Karma Nabulsi's vision of pedagogically-oriented retrieval, analysis and online sharing of primary sources from the Palestinian revolution.[4] One also thinks of the remarkable literary

[2] Abdel-Malek, *Egypt: Military Society*; Batatu, *The Old Social Classes and the Revolutionary Movements of Iraq*; Halliday, Arabia Without Sultans.

[3] For the notion of the colonial present see Gregory, *The Colonial Present*. For an analysis of recent fragmentation see Bishara, *Fi al-mas'ala al-'arabiyya*.

[4] Al-Hindi and al-Nasrawi (eds), *Harakat al-qawmiyyin al-'arab*; Nabulsi and Takriti, The *Palestinian Revolution*, <http://learnpalestine.politics.ox.ac.uk> (last accessed 2 March 2020).

project of the Saudi novelist Abdel Rahman Munif. Splitting from the Baath after its Fifth National Conference in Homs, Syria in May 1962, he gradually retreated from party politics and turned instead into literature. His quintet *Cities of Salt* may have been underlain by the melancholic dictum prefacing its third volume: 'In times of defeat, and in the places of exile, merry is the talk of history, or the illusion of history.'[5] Yet, one of the most striking aspects of that novel is its obstinate spirit, its constant reminder on almost every page of the cruel absurdity of the status quo that the Arab Left had fought so hard to overturn. Against today's grinding actuality, and against all the histories it buried and the official narratives it propagated, the novel emerges as a massive project of historical excavation of Saudi history in particular and Gulf history in general, chronicling what had changed, what had remained, and what had been completely lost. The slow pace in which the experiences and struggles of ordinary oasis dwellers, urban workers and migrant labourers are recounted sharply contrasts with the galloping narrative in which the stories of grotesque palace excesses, petty intrigues and tragicomedies are told. The contrast in pacing arises out of substantive need rather than convenience, for it is the latter stories that tend to dominate perceptions of Saudi Arabia, and it is the former experiences that are regularly erased, and that accordingly require a serious pause and painstakingly detailed reconstruction. Given the fact that this collection has already engaged with a wide range of leftist trajectories in the Maghreb, Egypt, Bilad al-Sham and Iraq, it is only fitting to end it with some thoughts on the region from which Munif had originated and on which he had written so much: the Arabian Peninsula and its Gulf shore.

At first glance, the Arabian Peninsula seems to be far more important for understanding the demise of the Arab Left than its development. Save for Yemen, all of the region's major states continue to be governed by dynasties dating back to the eighteenth century. At a time when royal families were overthrown and socialist experiments were undertaken in most Arab countries east of Morocco, the Gulf emerged as a citadel of monarchism, unchecked tribal rule and unhinged consumerism; at a time when the majority of Arab countries sought to break away from the old British empire and its new US successor, the Gulf states continued to rotate in their orbit. Several of these states emerged

[5] Munif, *Mudun al-milh*. All translations in this chapter are mine.

as havens for social and religious conservatism, hosting Muslim Brotherhood exiles from Egypt, Syria and elsewhere. Under King Faisal, Saudi Arabia went even further. In addition to funding and exporting militant Salafism, it actively combatted the revolutionary transformation of the Arabian Peninsula, financially and militarily supported monarchist forces in Yemen and bogged down Nasser in a long-standing conflict that exhausted Egyptian forces in the run-up to the 1967 Six Day War. In short, much of the oil wealth of the Gulf was redirected into undermining progressive potentialities.

All of this is true, but what is equally true is that the Arabian Peninsula and the Gulf played a key role in anti-colonial resistance and gave rise to substantial leftist struggles. The region witnessed, in the rough terrain of North Yemen, the only war pitting republicans against monarchist factions in modern Arab history (1962–7), as well as three major armed struggles, in al-Jabal al-Akhdar in Oman (1957–9), South Yemen (1963–7) and Dhufar (1965–76). Given the fact that it was the last Arab region to witness British colonial withdrawal, it was home to vibrant movements demanding independence, from Bahrain's Hay'at al-Ittihad al-Watani to Saudi Arabia's Jabhat Tahrir Sharq al-Jazira. It was the birthplace of Fateh, which was the main Palestinian current in the late 1950s and early 1960s calling for the immediate launch of a revolution; it was an important recruitment and fundraising arena for the PFLP, the Democratic Front for the Liberation of Palestine (DFLP) and other formations; and it was a temporary home for leftist icons such as the legendary caricaturist Naji al-Ali. Mass popular protests in its streets, boycott campaigns in its shops and sabotage operations in its oilfields and RAF bases contributed to pan-Arab action against the 1956 Tripartite Aggression. Solidarity events in every one of its major cities helped raise substantial funds for the Algerian revolution. And the development of workers' consciousness in its oilfields led to major industrial strikes and uprisings.

This was enabled by popular movements that mobilised thousands of people. These, as an emerging literature is beginning to show, had their roots in the spread of the *nahda* and its ideas of political and social reform in the early twentieth century.[6] Merchant communities, especially in the more prosperous northern Gulf population centres of Kuwait and Bahrain, offered fertile

[6] The role of the *nahda* in Bahrain in particular is discussed in Alshehabi, *Contested Modernity*.

social ground for receiving and disseminating these ideas in their confrontation with the governing Anglo-Sheikhly order.[7] Throughout the 1920s and 1930s, they established associations, literary societies and schools, and they fought for elections and more representative government. This was not in isolation of broader transformations. Several notable civic leaders in Kuwait, to give one example, were active in transnational Arab nationalist formations such as the Clandestine Arab Movement (the Red Book Group) led by Professor Constantine Zureiq.[8] Although their reformist experiments were dealt major blows in the late 1930s, they laid the foundations for a more assertive radicalism in subsequent decades. Any serious reading of such works as the memoirs of the prominent Kuwaiti leader Dr Ahmad al-Khatib would reveal the extent to which 1950s Arab nationalists were influenced and supported – discreetly yet concretely – by an earlier generation of opposition figures who had come of age in the inter-war period.[9]

While recognising such intergenerational threads of continuity, the enormous changes that took place require even greater emphasis. From the late 1940s onwards, the Gulf experienced a profound process that was witnessed elsewhere in the Arab world: the rise of ideological parties and movements. Al-Khatib played an especially significant role in this process. Among the sons and daughters of the Gulf, he was the only founding member of a major secular political formation operating on a broad transnational Arab scale. With his American University of Beirut classmates George Habash, Wadie Haddad and Hamid al-Jbouri, he created the MAN, and was subsequently able to build it, over the course of the 1950s, as the leading political movement in Kuwait. That country's pre-eminence in that period as a regional centre of oil production and wealth attracted a huge number of Palestinians who had been ethnically cleansed during the 1948 *nakba*, substantially contributing to radical politics. Kuwait also attracted a great number of workers, students and visitors from Aden and the Protectorates, Dhufar, Oman,

[7] For the role of education in this process see al-Rashoud, *Modern Education and Arab Nationalism in Kuwait.*

[8] A detailed study of the 'Red Book Group' is provided in Juha, Al-haraka *'arabiyya al-siriyya.*

[9] Al-Khatib, *Al-kuwayt*; Takriti, 'Political Praxis in the Gulf', 86–112.

Trucial Oman and beyond. The MAN energetically recruited members from these countries in the late 1950s, and they eventually formed local branches that led struggles in their respective countries.

This coincided with the politicisation of hundreds of Gulf students. Many of them joined political movements outside of the region. Until the foundation of Riyadh University (later renamed King Saud University) in 1957, there was not a single university in the Arabian Peninsula. And until the establishment of Kuwait University in 1966, there was not a single university on the Gulf coast. Accordingly, students from the region attended higher education institutions in such cities as Cairo, Beirut, Baghdad and Damascus. They formed student associations in these capitals that were brimming with student action. A sense of the importance of these associations can be gained from many sources. For instance, Abdel Nabi al-Ikri – a future MAN leader who had started his studies in Beirut in 1961 – recalls that the 'Association of Bahraini Students was the earliest vista' through which he was able to 'view society, politics, and the world'. This student group 'reflected the diverse composition of Bahraini society . . . More importantly, it reflected the political dynamism and movements that were brewing under the surface', many of its members joining such groups as the MAN, the Baath and the National Liberation Front of Bahrain.[10]

Numerous students joined leftist political parties and movements at an earlier stage of their lives, recruited during their secondary school years by teachers from Palestine, Iraq, Syria and Lebanon. Due to its importance in shaping the political tendencies of the younger generation, teacher appointment emerged as a political battleground, a subject that deserves substantial future study.[11] The outcome of the education battles that were raging at the time very much depended on the interplay between British colonial authorities, local sheikhs and popular pressure. Consider the case of Qatar. Until 1956, education was shaped by the whims of the British Political Agent. In line with British

[10] Al-Ikri, *Zakirat al-watan wa al-manfa*, 27.

[11] Fortunately, some authors are beginning to tackle this question in different parts of the Arab world. For Egytian teachers in the Gulf see Tsourapas, 'Nasser's Educators and Agitators'. For a detailed study of Palestinian teachers in 1950s Jordan see Mezna Qato's fascinating doctoral dissertation on the subject *Education in Exile*.

policy, he consistently pushed for the recruitment of a-political or conservative teachers and tried as best he could to deport those with communist or Arab nationalist leanings. Under the watch of this colonial administrator, Qatari education was dominated by conservative educators connected to the Muslim Brotherhood. During the school year 1956–7, however, education was placed under the oversight of Sheikh Khalifa bin Hamad al-Thani. In the wake of the tripartite aggression against Egypt, and in an attempt to contain the massive popular political pressure emanating from that event, Sheikh Khalifa steered Qatari education in a different direction. He counterbalanced the influence of Muslim Brotherhood administrators and teachers mostly coming from Egypt by bringing nationalist educators from Syria. Abdallah Abdel Dayem, a Baathist, was hired as Director of the Education Department. The new teachers who worked under him included the Syrian Baathists Ahmad al-Khatib (not to be confused with the Kuwaiti leader) and Mahmoud al-Ayoubi, as well as the Palestinian-Libyan Mahmoud al-Mughrabi. All four were to have major future careers in nationalist politics. In Syria, al-Ayoubi eventually became a prime minister, Abdel Dayem a minister of education, and al-Khatib a member of the Presidential Council. As for al-Mughrabi, he played an important role as a Fateh leader in the early years of the Palestinian revolution before becoming the first Prime Minister of Libya after the overthrow of the monarchy in 1969.[12]

The individual trajectories of such leftist figures illustrate the importance of the Gulf as a space that incubated political leadership and network formation in the Arab world as a whole. Whereas the region is firmly associated with producing and hosting Islamic personages as well as exporting and re-exporting conservatism on a global scale, it was not solely, or even principally, viewed in those terms in the late 1950s. In 1957, amid the anti-colonial optimism that followed the failure of the tripartite aggression, the Syrian poet Suleiman al-Issa wrote one of the most famous lines of the era: 'From the rumbling ocean to the revolutionary Gulf, we heed your call Abdel Nasser!'[13] It was not incidental that al-Issa or his readers associated the Gulf

[12] Al-Kuwari, *Al-'awsaj.*

[13] This poem, 'Nashid li al-dawla al-'arabiyya', was very popular at the time and is still remembered by Gulf Arab nationalists such as al-Kuwari. See al-Kuwari, *Al-'awsaj.*

with revolution. Observers of the region at the time would have known of the solidarity mobilisations with Egypt, Algeria and Palestine that filled the streets of Kuwait, Doha, Sharjah and Dubai at the time, as well as mass-scale local struggles that took place in Oman, Bahrain and elsewhere.

In those years, to be sure, there was a tension between ruling families and British colonial power, and this tension sometimes rose to the level of contradiction. Although benefiting from imperial protection, the sheikhs were also limited by colonial control, experienced on a daily level through regular interference from Britain's men on the spot. Among sections of the younger sheikhly ranks there was also an almost inevitable attraction to the anti-colonial *zeitgeist* of the age that was not in small measure shaped by exposure to Egypt's *Sawt al-Arab* radio station as well as by constant frustration with the injustices unfolding in Algeria and Palestine. This might help to explain why Prince Talal bin Abdel Aziz and some of his Al Saud brothers – constituting the so-called Free Princes group – were inspired by Nasserism; why the former ruler of Sharjah, Sheikh Saqr al-Qassimi, tried to connect his emirate to Egypt as much as he could, losing his throne in the process; why the Baath was joined by someone like the current ruler of Sharjah, Sheikh Sultan bin Muhammad al-Qassimi; and why Sheikh Fahd al-Ahmad al-Jaber al-Sabah of Kuwait became a Palestinian *fida'i*, injured in action no fewer than three times.[14] Whereas several sheikhs were Arab nationalists, flirted with some leftist ideas and worked against colonial control in the Gulf and beyond, hardly any – as was to be expected – were communists.[15] Communism was also predictably unpopular among the ranks of merchants and professionals, social segments that were often classified in subsequent Marxist writings as part of the Gulf 'national bourgeoisie'. It did, however, find a foothold in the midst of a growing working class as well as some migrant populations.

[14] Talal bin Abdel Aziz spoke extensively of his relationship to Nasserism in his interviews with Aljazeera's 'Shahid 'ala al-'Asr'; as for Sheikh Sultan al-Qassimi, he recounts his experience with the Baath in his memoirs *Sard al-that*.

[15] The only exception with which this author is familiar is Muhammad Talib Al Bu Said, who was a member of Popular Front for the Liberation of Oman and the Occupied Arab Gulf (PFLOAG). He, however, did not belong to the ruling al-Sa'id branch of the Al Bu Sa'id family.

Prior to the development of the oil industry, the region did not have an industrial working class. This changed quickly after oil production commenced in Bahrain in 1932. The earliest industrial strikes in the region emanated from the oil fields, starting with the Bahrain Petroleum Company (BAPCO) workers' strike of 1938. Subsequent strikes sought to improve working conditions, but they also had an evident dimension of Arab solidarity to them. This was reflected in the fact that the largest Bahraini strike that took place in the two decades of the 1930s and 1940s was the 1947 BAPCO strike protesting against the United Nations' decision to partition Palestine. Strikes became an established repertoire of struggle in other countries as well, and they were present wherever oil was extracted. Kuwait, for instance, witnessed a massive strike in 1948, whereby six thousand workers laid down their tools for eleven days, despite a massive campaign of intimidation.[16] Similar strikes took place in Saudi Arabia and Qatar throughout the 1950s.

This working-class base was the main target of communist organising. The origins of communism in the area go back to 1946. On its meeting on 10 June of that year, the Tudeh Party of Iran decided to send some of its cadres to the Gulf to organise workers there, although it is not clear that this resulted in the immediate establishment of any local political formations.[17] After the 1953 coup against the Mossadegh government and the wave of repression that followed, several Iranian communist refugees arrived in Bahrain. These cadres, led by Hassan Nizam, contributed to spreading communist ideas, establishing the core cells of *Jabhat al-Tahrir al-Watani* (National Liberation Front, NLF) in February 1955. The influence of the Iraqi Communist Party (ICP) also contributed to the development of this nascent organisation. Several Bahrainis studying in Iraq were exposed to communism, and two Iraqi communist refugees fleeing the repression of the staunchly pro-British Nuri al- Sa'id government managed to enter Bahrain in the early 1950s, working as journalists on the *al-Khamila* newspaper before being deported to India by the British authorities.[18]

[16] Al-Mdairis, *Al-tawajuhat markisiyya al-kuwaytiyya*, 16.

[17] Ibid., 16.

[18] Al-Ikri, *Al-tanzimat al-yasariyya*, 22–3.

By 1962, the NLF issued its first political programme. Its first three points featured anti-colonial and democratic demands including independence from Britain, the 'liquidation of the British and American military bases of aggression and the withdrawal of foreign troops', and the replacement of the colonial administration with an elected constitutional government. Subsequent points focused on economic and social change, including the development of national industry, agricultural reform through 'the return of lands stolen from peasants and small landowners by the agents of colonialism'; the eradication of foreign monopolies; the defence of workers' rights and the creation of unions; raising the level of education; the provision of healthcare; establishing equality between women and men 'in all political, social, and economic rights', as well as achieving real equality between all citizens; joint struggle bringing together all the Arab movements fighting against colonialism; strengthening solidarity between Arab peoples and the Arab popular organisations of workers, students and intellectuals; and creating economic co-operation between Arab countries.[19]

This programme reflected two features of communist organising in this period. The first, as al-Ikri notes, was a greater focus on local reform as opposed to broader regional challenges. There was no specific reference to the anti-colonial questions of pan-Arabism, the unity of the Gulf Arab states, or Palestine, all of which were at the core of the visions of Arab nationalist formations competing with the communists'.[20] The liberation of Palestine, which was a popular demand in the region and a point highlighted by all nationalist forces, was merely implicit in the call for the liberation of all colonised Arab countries. As for the demands of Arab and Gulf unity, they were replaced by the call for co-operation between Arab states. These were recurring points of contention between the communist and nationalist wings of the left, not just in the Gulf but elsewhere in the region, causing enormous suspicion and friction between them. The stance of official Arab communist parties in support of the Soviet Union's adoption of the 1947 UN Partition Plan aggravated this tension. As Sune Haugbole notes in his chapter revisiting Khalid Bakdash's contradictory legacy in supporting this decision, this

[19] Ibid., 24–5.

[20] Ibid., 25.

policy generated an enormous backlash within the Arab communist movement. Yet, this was not enough to free communists in the Gulf from the stigma that earlier decisions of their comrades elsewhere in the Mashriq had visited upon them.

We may add another important note, which was that the programme of the NLF did not explicitly refer to socialism or communism, featuring demands that were overwhelmingly social democratic in character. This reflected the parameters of thought operating within the Gulf's public sphere at the time. In an atmosphere in which communism was officially criminalised and popularly derided, communist organisations, up to the early 1960s, initially chose to put forward reformist rather than revolutionary Marxist programmes. This was seen not just in Bahrain, but also in Saudi Arabia. The foundational event in the history of the labour movement in that country was the ARAMCO strike of 1953.[21] One of the most prominent leaders of the strike was Abdel Aziz Abu-Sneid, who was born to a Saudi father and an Iraqi mother and was exposed to communist ideas during his school years in Iraq. After returning to Saudi Arabia in the late 1940s, he met with Palestinian communists working for ARAMCO, including Muhammad Milhem Ayash. On the basis of his co-ordination with these figures a worker's committee was formed.[22] Out of the major strike the worker's committee had launched, the National Reform Front was established, morphing by 1958 into the National Liberation Front. The fact that this formation shared its name with the aforementioned group in Bahrain is not coincidental, for a number of Bahraini communists were active in establishing it. Just as state repression in Iran and Iraq led to the migration of communist cadres to Bahrain in the early 1950s, state repression in Bahrain led to the arrival of several Bahraini communist cadres in Saudi Arabia's eastern region in the late 1950s.[23] This shows the

[21] An important study authored by a political leader from that period discussing in depth the 1953 strike and its aftermath is al-Awami, *Al-haraka al-wataniyya sharq al-saudia*, 65–151. Although that strike was not the first one in the country (the earliest major labour mobilisation was the 1945 strike), it was much more organised and militant than previous strikes. English-language works that discuss the labour movement include Matthiesen, *The Other Saudis* and Vitalis, *America's Kingdom.*

[22] Al-Awami, *Al-haraka al-wataniyya sharq al-saudia*, fns 1, 74.

[23] Al-Ikri, 40.

degree to which the region was interconnected in that period, events in any one of its parts contributing to changes in others. In any case, the Saudi front operated within similar ideological parameters as its Bahraini sister, offering what could be described as an agenda for social democratic reform rather than communist revolution. The emergence of an actual Communist Party in Saudi Arabia had to wait until 1975.[24]

More explicit calls for socialism began to circulate in the Gulf and the Arabian Peninsula over the course of the 1960s. Several factors contributed to this. One of the most important was the shift in Nasserist economic policy and discourse, especially after the promulgation of the National Charter of May 1962. A major section of the charter, 'On the Inevitability of the Socialist Solution', announced: 'Socialism is the path to social freedom. Social freedom cannot be achieved except through affording equal opportunity for every citizen to acquire their just share of national wealth.'[25] The limits of Nasser's socialist vision – and its divergence from Marxist understandings of the term – are widely known, but what cannot be denied is that it had enormous implications for the legitimation of socialist discourse across the region, for all Arab political currents in the Mashriq were either in dialogue with Nasserism or were articulated against it, not least due to Nasser's unrivalled leadership in Arab politics and the dominance of the Egyptian media apparatuses in this period.

The Nasserist articulation of Arab socialism coincided with an increasing turn to the left on the part of the Baath and the Movement of Arab Nationalists. This was accompanied by more favourable assessments of the regional role of the Eastern Bloc. Although the stigma of the Soviet Union's enthusiastic support for the 1947 partition resolution and the creation of Israel continued to haunt the communist movement, growing Soviet support for Egypt and other Arab radical states allowed for a more positive impression of that country to develop. At the same time, the ideas of the 'New Left', explored in this volume by Gennaro Gervasio in his study of 1970s

[24] For recent scholarship on the Saudi left see Bsheer, 'A Counterrevolutionary State', 233–77; Matthiesen, 'Migration, Minorities, and Radical Networks', 473–504.

[25] 'Kalimat al-ra'is Gamal Abdel Nasser fi taqdim al-mithaq al-watani min jami'at al-qahira', 21 May 1962, <http://nasser.bibalex.org/Speeches/browser.aspx?SID=1015&lang=ar> (last accessed 29 May 2019).

Egypt, were beginning to make their appearance. Even more significantly, the Chinese, Cuban and Vietnamese experiences were beginning to attract greater attention, offering Third Worldist models of communist development and national liberation that played an important role in the rise of an Arab nationalist variant of Marxism, especially after the 1967 war. In the Arabian Peninsula and the Gulf, these new ideas and models were particularly influential in the two active sites of armed revolution that had emerged in the region in the same period: Dhufar in Oman, and Aden and the Protectorates in Yemen.

One of the noteworthy features of leftist politics in the Arabian Peninsula is that armed revolutions only took place in the southern part of the region. Although Saudi Arabia had a long history of opposition in its various regions, sometimes taking militant forms, it had a wealthy state that operated extensive patronage networks, promoted an effective conservative religious ideology, and possessed strong repressive apparatuses supported by the USA. And although Bahrain was a fertile ground – augmented by social cleavages, sectarian segmentation and access to radical ideas facilitated by higher levels of literacy – for opposition to Britain and the ruling family, the island's tiny size and its British-run security agencies ensured that events such as the popular intifada (uprising) of 1965 never developed into protracted armed struggles. Kuwait and Qatar were also geographically small, sharing with Bahrain a pancake-flat terrain unsuited to guerilla warfare, and they channelled their vast financial resources into absorbing popular pressure through generous welfare provisions. In the case of Kuwait, the long reformist reign of Sheikh Abdullah al-Salem al-Sabah (r.1950–65) offered enough democratic concessions, including a parliament and a constitution, to allow for the creation of a durable, if fragile, social contract. As for the Trucial States of Abu Dhabi, Dubai, Sharjah, Ras al-Khaimah, Ajman, Um al-Quwain and Fujairah, they were – despite their relative underdevelopment until the late 1960s – carefully watched by British authorities, especially after the establishment of the Trucial Oman Levies in 1951.[26]

[26] These troops were not only used for security operations, but sometimes even for the removal of rulers who proved too conservative or too radical for the effective perpetuation of the status quo. See Takriti, 'Colonial Coups', 878–909.

Yemen, in contrast, witnessed the only two revolutions in the Arabian Peninsula that managed to overthrow hereditary dynasties: the 1962 revolution in North Yemen, and the 1963 revolution in Aden and the Protectorates of South Arabia (South Yemen). The former took place against the Yemeni Imamate at the hands of the Free Officers led by Abdullah al-Sallal and directly supported by Nasserist Egypt, leading to the establishment of the Yemen Arab Republic. The latter was carried out by the National Liberation Front (NLF), which was led by cadres of the Movement of Arab Nationalists, as well as its political competitor the Front for the Liberation of Occupied South Yemen (FLOSY), which was sponsored by Egypt. After four years of armed operations, independence was secured, and the NLF emerged as the dominant force in the country, displacing FLOSY and eventually establishing the only Marxist state in the Arab world.[27]

Several structural conditions allowed for this revolutionary victory. Up to the mid-1960s, Aden was one of the most important ports in the world, and it accordingly gave birth to a mature and large labour movement that had developed an anti-colonial consciousness, spurred, to a considerable degree, by the presence of an exploitative class of foreign merchants. Political life in the economically underdeveloped territories surrounding this major city was enriched by a long history of global migration emanating from Hadramawt. Yemeni student and labour networks in Arab capitals like Cairo and Kuwait developed strong connections with the Baath, the MAN and the Egyptian authorities, producing a radical revolutionary leadership committed to the overthrow of colonialism as well as the fifteen local rulers protected by it. The dispersion and weakness of these rulers, and the endemic suspicion and infighting among them, undermined their ability to suppress serious radical challenges. Belated British colonial attempts to federate them and strengthen their coercive capacity through the 1959 Federation of Arab Emirates of the

[27] For the history of the development of the MAN in South Yemen see the chapter on the Yemeni branch in Barut, Muhammad Jamal, *Harakat al-qawmiyyin al-ʿarab*. For the PDRY period see Ismael and Ismael, *People's Democratic Republic of Yemen*; Halliday, *Revolution and Foreign Policy*; and Lackner, *P.D.R. Yemen*. An interesting study that examines social changes that were enacted by the revolutionary regime, especially from the prism of family laws and gender roles, is provided by Dahlgren, *Contesting Realities*.

South and the 1962 Federation of South Arabia added to their legitimation crisis, entrenching the popular rejection of local rulers as puppets of colonialism.[28] The geography of the Yemeni south also played a role: its rough, inaccessible and expansive topography – as well as the denser neighbourhoods of its main city Aden – allowed for both rural and urban warfare.

Geography and environment was also an enabling factor for armed struggle in the Omani province of Dhufar. Its highlands, covered by the mist of the monsoon for a good portion of the year, gave an excellent base for revolutionary guerillas fighting against the British-backed rulers of the al-Sa'id family. As in the Yemeni south, the leadership of the Dhufari struggle included many cadres of the MAN, adopting Marxism-Leninism following their Hamrin Conference of 1968.[29] These leaders were influenced by left-wing trends in the Palestinian revolution and gradually began to receive limited support from China and the USSR. Most crucially, their struggle benefited from the victory of the revolution in the Yemeni south. Women played an important role in this struggle. Indeed, this was the only arena in the Gulf in which female cadres bore arms. While some of the revolutionary women – like the sisters Laila and Buthaina Fakhro – came from Bahrain, the majority were rural fighters from Dhufar.[30]

By early 1976, the Dhufar revolution was defeated by an unrelenting military campaign that saw the deployment of the British SAS, the Iranian Imperial Army and the Jordanian military, not to mention generous financial backing from Saudi Arabia and Abu Dhabi. This signalled the demise of the last major leftist threat to the Gulf regional state system. Awash with cash after the post-1973 oil boom, the ruling regimes were richer than ever, and

[28] The MAN denounced the 1959 federation soon after its announcement in its booklet *Ittihad al-imarat al-muzayyaf mu'amara 'ala al-wihda al-'arabiyya* (1959).

[29] The new national charter that was drafted out of the Hamrin conference can be found in al-Jabha al-Shabiya Li Tahrir Oman, *Watha'iq al-nidal al watani*, 12.

[30] Several oral histories were conducted with female cadres from the Dhufar revolution. My own interviews were utilised in Takriti, *Monsoon Revolution*. Muna Jaboub also drew on oral histories with female cadres in her *Qiyadat al-mujtama'*. Despite the fact that they were written by male authors, memoirs also offer an important source base for exploring the social history of Dhufar, including that of women's participation in the revolution. See for example Muhanna, *Malh'amat al-khiyarat al-sa'ba*.

this accelerated one of the most rapid experiences of economic change in human history. A keen observer in the late 1970s would have noticed that Bedouin economic activity that had existed for millennia had all but disappeared, with very few nomadic population groups left living off the grazing of sheep or camels. Likewise, the old peasant economy was gone, in the absence of citizens tilling the soil and cultivating date palm groves with their own hands. Those living off the sea witnessed as many changes as those depending on the land. There were no longer any pearl divers, and the number of local shipping crews and fishermen massively shrank.

The erasure of the old economy coincided with local de-proletarianisation. Although many locals had become industrial workers in the oil fields of the 1940s and 1950s, they were no longer to be found in the lower ranks of that sector by the 1970s. In the richer and smaller Gulf states of Kuwait, Qatar and the UAE, the local working class had virtually disappeared and almost all menial and industrial jobs were taken over by foreign labour. As is well-known, citizenship in these states came with considerable economic privileges and access to a consumerist economy almost entirely supported by rent derived from resource extraction. The complete absence of citizenship rights or naturalisation prospects for foreign workers, combined with extremely high turnover, meant that the new working class brought from South Asia and elsewhere had no chance of effective long-term organising. Any agitation was subject to severe punishment and deportation.[31] Communism, socialism and other leftist world views could hardly survive, let alone flourish, in such a setting. This did not mean that all local Gulf citizens were affluent. Despite the persistence of stereotypes suggesting the ubiquity of obscene wealth, large swaths of Saudi Arabia, the largest country in the region by far, continued to be beset by poverty, underdevelopment and unemployment, offering an extreme example of uneven and combined development. Less oil-rich countries like Bahrain and Oman were also only able to secure an affluent lifestyle for some sections of the population. Nevertheless, local states had enough resources to ensure the loyalty of much of the population and the suppression of any radical alternatives. By the early 1980s, the left was grappling not only

[31] A detailed discussion of the dynamics of labour and citizenship in the contemporary Gulf is offered in Alshehabi, Hanieh and Khalaf (eds), *Transit States*.

with these structural realities but with regional and global transformations that enabled the rise of a conservative rather than a progressive tide.

The main themes that could be distilled from the experiences of the left in the Arabian Peninsula and the Gulf briefly surveyed above were shared in other parts of the Arab world. Indeed, any serious observer can hardly miss the interconnectedness of Arab political currents during the decades discussed in this volume. In the realm of regional solidarity, opposition to settler-colonialism and support for the grand revolutionary struggles in Algeria and Palestine took precedence, mobilising massive popular energies for many years. As has often been noted, Palestine had an immense influence on the trajectory of Arab communism as well as nationalism. Given its centrality in the Arab radical imagination, several chapters in this volume are dedicated to it or engage with it.

In her contribution, Orit Bashkin writes back Iraqi Jewish communists into the broader Arab Left tradition, illustrating that their Arab background not only culturally distinguished them from their Ashkenazi leftist counterparts, but also allowed them to politically connect with Palestinian Arabs, developing alongside with them a 'politics of empathy' that transgressed against the 'Arab' and 'Jewish' binary entrenched by ethno-sectarian Zionist visions. Hana Morgenstern's chapter views this process from the perspective of Palestinian writers, highlighting their joint effort, with Jewish Arab writers, in creating a literary vision rooted in Marxist anti-colonialism. Building on the research developed in her important book *Brothers Apart*,[32] Maha Nassar explores the ways in which the Palestine Liberation Organisation (PLO) Research Center approached and framed these debates taking place within the Israeli Left, illustrating the PLO leftist intellectuals' nuanced, and often sympathetic, approach to Mizrahi and Ashkenazi Israeli leftists, all the while highlighting the anti-colonial critique of their limits.

This critique was internationalist in its tone. Indeed, as in other regions, one of the main characteristics of the Arab Left – as is amply demonstrated in this volume – was its championing of revolutionary linkages across the world. In this light, the Arab Left should not be viewed as isolated from global anti-colonial tricontinental currents. By engaging the legacy of the

[32] Nassar, *Brothers Apart*.

Moroccan opposition leader Mehdi Ben Barka, Nate George highlights the role of Arab leftists in the construction of this tricontinental sphere. When it came to symbols and discourses, but also political and military strategies, that sphere played an enabling role in the Arab arena. One example out of many is to be found in the story of Khalid Ahmad Zaki. As Phillip Winkler shows here, Zaki emulated the Guevaran model in deciding to launch his communist armed uprising against the Iraqi state from the inaccessible margins of the southern marshes, earning, despite (or perhaps because of) his defeat and death, the symbolic title 'the Guevara of the Middle East'.

Internationalism, however, was not without its complications. Although issues such as Vietnam and South Africa enjoyed political consensus, some liberation struggles, particularly involving movements like the Sahrawi, generated debate and in some cases divergences. For instance, while the Sahrawi cause received support from Algeria and such Palestinian radical groups as the PFLP, it was approached, as Daniela Melfa shows, far less sympathetically by some sections of the Tunisian Left that associated it with separatism rather than anti-colonialism or anti-monarchism. If this illustrates anything, it is the need to disaggregate the Arab Left in light of its diverse stances and positions vis-à-vis various issues and struggles, all the while maintaining an appreciation of its rich commonalities and vibrant connections.

Among these commonalities, commitment to social and economic struggles was an unquestionably abiding concern. Although it does not feature prominently in this volume, the intersection between the left and feminist movements is a historical phenomenon that is worthy of far more serious study than has hitherto been attempted. The academic library is yet to include a comprehensive volume that focuses solely on this intersection on a pan-Arab scale. Likewise, and as Laure Guirguis suggests in her chapter, economic factors shaping leftist thought and practice require urgent highlighting and inquiry. After all, to speak of the left in a manner detaching it from economic struggles, erasing its heritage of countless strikes, unionisation drives and clashes with landlords, financiers and industrial capitalists, is to fundamentally distort its history.

In approaching these themes, it is essential to take into account the process described by Samer Frangie in his contribution on leftist afterlives, a process that saw the travel of leftist legacies from 'the transnational to the national' sphere and then 'from the national to the private'. Given the enormous weakening of the Arab Left since the end of the 1970s, a great deal of scholarly vigilance is required in reading posthumous melancholic reflections produced in an age of defeat. In particular, the current allure, often motivated by a latent or manifest orientalism, to reduce the history of the left to the history of its relationship to Islam and Islamism requires a great deal of resistance. As important as that relationship was, it should not be tackled on the basis of reading the past from the standpoint of the present, starting with the moment of seeming Islamist triumph and leftist despair backwards. There is also a pressing need to avoid equating the history of the left with the history of authoritarianism. This trend is evident, as Matthieu Rey's chapter suggests, in the case of the Baath, but it is also to be found extensively in the literature dealing with Nasser. Nasser surely played a central role in undermining the parliamentary process and in establishing the security state in Egypt; however, his policies could, and should, be viewed through prisms other than that of liberal democracy, including economic redistribution and social liberalism as well as national and global liberation.[33] These require nuanced treatment rather than mere reductionism. Last but not least, the discourse of 'crisis' that has become almost hegemonic in numerous leftist circles in the region is worthy of careful reconsideration. As Jens Hanssen argues in his piece, this discourse needs to be rigorously contextualised, for it appeared at a specific historical juncture, and was utilised by different leftist intellectuals towards varying political ends. This hints at the need for new intellectual histories of

[33] Nimer Sultany has recently offered an important critical reflection on this issue, arguing that, in much of the literature, 'Egypt's presidents Nasser and Sadat are both considered authoritarian . . . This uncritical labeling neutralises the difference between Nasser, the leftwing socialist leader who lifted millions from poverty, and Sadat, the rightwing leader who liberalised the economy, redistributed wealth upwards to the benefit of the upper classes, and sought to Islamise the constitutional order. It neutralises the difference between the former, who sought national sovereignty, including over the economy, and the latter, who plunged Egypt into political and economic dependency on the US. Finally, it erases the difference between a genuine republican leader and a mere populist or demagogue.' Sultany, 'Arab Constitutionalism', in Alvar Garcia and Frankenberg (eds), *Authoritarian Constitutionalism*.

the left, freed from a pathologically oriented analysis that begins with an era of misguided optimism and culminates with a never-ending stage of malaise.

At this very moment in time, we are approaching the anniversary of a decade of revolts, revolutions and intifadas, not just against undemocratic regimes but also against rapacious neoliberal capitalism and the neo-colonial geopolitics that contribute to sustaining these political and economic structures. Whereas the new generation of Arab radicals has demonstrated, time and again, its willingness to confront the political, social, economic and colonial questions, its engagement is unravelling in the absence of the organisational structures and tools that were possessed before. This is one of the key differences between past and present. Today, mass leftist parties and tight-knit clandestine groups have been replaced by loose networks, issue-based coalitions, social media spaces and monadic intellectual platforms. Although this was celebrated at the advent of the Arab Spring as a new form of horizontal politics, the limits of this form became glaringly clear as popular mobilisations were eventually caught between the Scylla of better-organised Islamic movements and the Charybdis of the security state. It is precisely at this historic juncture that the old histories of struggle acquire far more than antiquarian purchase, inviting urgent retrieval, from 'the rumbling ocean to the revolutionary gulf'.

Bibliography

Abdel-Malek, Anouar [1962], *Egypt: Military Society* (New York: Vintage, 1968).

Al-Awami, Sayid Ali al-Sayid Baqir, *Al-haraka al-wataniyya sharq al-saudia, 1953–1973, al-juz' al-awal* (Beirut: Riyad El-Rayyes, 2011): 93–123.

Al-Hindi, Hani, and Abdel Ilah al-Nasrawi (eds), *'Harakat al-qawmiyyin al-'arab: nashatuha wa tatawuruha 'abr watha'iqiha* [The movement of the Arab nationalists: its inception and development through the prism of its documents] (Beirut: Mu'sasat al-Abhath al-Arabiyyah, Vol. 1, 2002 and 2004).

Al-Ikri, Abdel Nabi, *Dhakirat al-Watan wa al-Manfa* [Memories of the homeland and exile] (Manama: Faradis li al-Nashr wa al-Tawzi', 2015).

Al-Ikri, Abdel Nabi, *Al-tanzimat al-yasariyya fi al-jazira wa al-khalij al-'arabi* [Leftist movements in the peninsula and the Arab gulf] (Beirut: Dar al-Kunuz al-Adabiya, 2003).

Al-jabha al-sha'biyya li tahrir oman, *Watha'iq al-nidal al-watani* [The documents of the national struggle] (Beirut: Dar al-Tali'a, 1974).

Al-Khatib, Ahmad, *Al-kuwayt, min al-imara ila al-dawla: zikrayat al-amal al-watani wa al-qawmi* (Casablanca: al-Markaz al-Thaqafi al- Arabi, 2007).

Al-Kuwari, Ali Khalifa, *Al-'awsaj: sira wa zikrayat* [The thistle: memoirs and memories] <http://dr-alkuwari.net/sites/akak/files/3.pdf> (last accessed 10 April 2019).

Al-Mdairis, Falah, *Al-tawajuhat al-markisiyya al-kuwaytiyya* [Kuwaiti Marxist trends] (Kuwait: Dar Qirtas, 2003).

Al-Rashoud, Talal, *Modern Education and Arab Nationalism in Kuwait, 1911–1961* (PhD thesis, SOAS, University of London, 2017).

Alshehabi, Omar, *Contested Modernity: Sectarianism, Nationalism, and Colonialism in Bahrain* (London: Oneworld, 2018).

Alshehabi, Omar, Adam Hanieh and Abdulhadi Khalaf (eds), *Transit States: Labour, Migration and Citizenship in the Gulf* (London: Pluto Press, 2014).

Barut, Muhammad Jamal, *Harakat al-qawmiyyin al-'arab: al-nash'a, al-tatawwur, al-mas'air* [The movement of the Arab nationalists: inception, development, and trajectories] (Damascus: al-Markaz al-'Arabi li al-Dirasat al-Istratijyya, 1997).

Batatu, Hanna, *The Old Social Classes and the Revolutionary Movements of Iraq. A Study of Iraq's Old Landed and Commercial Classes and of its Communists, Ba'thists, and Free Officers* (London: Saqi Books, 2004).

Bishara, Azmi, *Fi al-mas'ala al-'arabiyya* [On the Arab question] (Beirut: Markaz Dirasat al-Wihdah al-Arabiyyah, 2007).

Bsheer, Rosie, 'A Counterrevolutionary State: Popular Movements and the Making of Saudi Arabia', *Past & Present* 238, 1 (1 February 2018): 233–77.

Dahlgren, Susanne, *Contesting Realities: The Public Sphere and Morality in Southern Yemen* (New York: Syracuse University Press, 2010).

Gregory, Derek, *The Colonial Present: Afghanistan, Palestine, Iraq* (Oxford: Wiley-Blackwell, 2004).

Halliday, Fred, *Arabia Without Sultans* (London: Penguin, 1974).

Halliday, Fred, *Revolution and Foreign Policy: The Case of South Yemen, 1967–1987* (Cambridge: Cambridge University Press, 1990).

Ismael, Tareq Y. and Jacqueline S. Ismael, *People's Democratic Republic of Yemen: Politics, Economics, and Society* (London: St Martin's Press, 1992).

Jaboub, Muna, *Qiyadat al-mujtama' nahwa al-taghyir: al-tajruba al-tarbawiyya li thawrat dhufar, 1969–1992* [Leading society towards change: the educational experience of the Dhufar revolution, 1969–1992] (Beirut: Markaz Dirasat al-Wihdah al-Arabiyya, 2010).

Juha, Shafiq, *Al-haraka al-'arabiyya al-siriyya (jamaat al-kitab al-ahmar), 1935–1945* [The clandestine Arab movement (the red book group), 1935–1945] (Beirut: Furat, 2004).

Lackner, Helen, *P.D.R. Yemen: Outpost of Socialist Development in Arabia* (London: Ithaca Press, 1985).

Matthiesen, Toby, 'Migration, Minorities, and Radical Networks: Labor Movements and Opposition Groups in Saudi Arabia, 1950–1975', *International Review of Social History*, 59, 3 (2014): 473–504.

Matthiesen, Toby, *The Other Saudis: Shiism, Dissent, and Sectarianism* (Cambridge: Cambridge University Press, 2015).

Movement of Arab Nationalists, *Ittihad al-imarat al-muzayyaf mu'amara 'ala al-wihdah al-'arabiyya* [The fake union of emirates is a plot against Arab unity] (Movement of Arab Nationalists, 1959).

Muhanna, Kamel, *Malh'amat al-khiyarat al-sa'ba: min yamiyyat al-duktur kamel muhanna* [The epic of difficult choices: from the diaries of Doctor Kamel Muhanna] (Beirut: Dar al-Farabi, 2012).

Munif, Abdel Rahman, *Mudun al-milh: taqasim al-layl wa al-nahar* [Cities of Salt, vol. 3: Variations on night and day] (Beirut: al-Mu'asasa al-'Arabiyya li al-Dirasat wa al-Nashr, 1988).

Nabulsi, Karma and Abdel Razzaq Takriti, *The Palestinian Revolution* (Department of Politics and International Relations, University of Oxford, 2016), <http://learnpalestine.politics.ox.ac.uk> (last accessed 2 March 2020).

Nassar, Maha, *Brothers Apart: Palestinian Citizens of Israel and the Arab World* (Palo Alto: Stanford University Press, 2017).

Qato, Mezna, *Education in Exile: Palestinians and the Hashemite Regime, 1948–1967* (PhD thesis, University of Oxford, 2013).

Sheikh Sultan al-Qassimi, *Sard al-zat* [Narrating the self] (Cairo: Dar al-Shuruq, 2009).

Sultany, Nimer, 'Arab Constitutionalism and the Formation of Authoritarian Constitutionalism', in Alvar Garcia, Helena and Günter Frankenberg (eds), *Authoritarian Constitutionalism: Comparative Analysis and Critique* (Cheltenham: Edward Elgar, 2019).

Takriti, Abdel Razzaq, *Monsoon Revolution: Republicans, Sultans, and Empires in Oman, 1965–1976* (Oxford and New York: Oxford University Press, 2013).

Takriti, Abdel Razzaq, 'Political Praxis in the Gulf: Ahmad al-Khatib and the Movement of Arab Nationalists, 1948–1969', in Jens Hanssen and Max Weiss (eds), *Arabic Thought against the Authoritarian Age: Towards an Intellectual History of the Present* (Cambridge: Cambridge University Press, 2018).

Takriti, Abdel Razzaq, 'Colonial Coups and the War on Popular Sovereignty', *American Historical Review* 124, 3 (June 2019): 878–909.

Tsourapas, Gerasimos, 'Nasser's Educators and Agitators across *al-Watan al-'Arabi*: Tracing the Foreign Policy Importance of Egyptian Regional Migration, 1952–1967', *British Journal of Middle Eastern Studies*, 43, 3 (2016): 324–41.

Vitalis, Robert. *America's Kingdom: Mythmaking on the Saudi Oil Frontier* (Palo Alto: Stanford University Press, 2007).

INDEX

EU representative:
Easy Access System Europe
Mustamäe tee 50, 10621 Tallinn, Estonia
Gpsr.requests@easproject.com

www.ingramcontent.com/pod-product-compliance
Lightning Source LLC
Chambersburg PA
CBHW051953270326
41929CB00015B/2632
* 9 7 8 1 4 7 4 4 5 4 2 4 7 *